Y0-GUD-967

REFRAMING ALBRECHT DÜRER

Focusing on the ways his art and persona were valued and criticized by writers, collectors, and artists subsequent to his death, this book examines the reception of the works of Albrecht Dürer. Andrea Bubenik's analysis highlights the intensive and international interest in Dürer's art and personality, and his developing role as a paragon in art historiography, in conjunction with the proliferation of portraits after his likeness.

The author traces carefully how Dürer's paintings, prints, drawings and theoretical writings traveled widely, and were appropriated into new contexts and charged with different meanings. Drawing on inventories and correspondences and taking collecting practices into account, Bubenik establishes who owned what by Dürer in the 16th and 17th centuries, and characterizes the key locations where interest in Dürer peaked (especially the courts of Maximilian I in Munich, and Rudolf II in Prague). Bubenik treats the emergent artistic appropriations of Dürer-borrowings from or transformations of his originals-in conjunction with contemporary sources on art theory. The volume includes illustrations of numerous imitative works after Dürer.

As well as being the first book to fully address the early reception of the most important of German Renaissance artists, *Reframing Albrecht Dürer* shows how appropriation is a crucial concept for understanding artistic practice during the early modern period.

Andrea Bubenik is Lecturer in Art History at The University of Queensland, Australia.

The author and publisher gratefully acknowledge the support of the Australian Academy of the Humanities, and their award of a Publication Subsidy Grant to assist in the publication of this book.

VISUAL CULTURE IN EARLY MODERNITY

Series Editor: Allison Levy

A forum for the critical inquiry of the visual arts in the early modern world, *Visual Culture in Early Modernity* promotes new models of inquiry and new narratives of early modern art and its history. We welcome proposals for both monographs and essay collections which consider the cultural production and reception of images and objects. The range of topics covered in this series includes, but is not limited to, painting, sculpture and architecture as well as material objects, such as domestic furnishings, religious and/or ritual accessories, costume, scientific/medical apparata, erotica, ephemera and printed matter. We seek innovative investigations of Western and non-Western visual culture produced between 1400 and 1800.

Reframing Albrecht Dürer

The Appropriation of Art, 1528–1700

Andrea Bubenik

ASHGATE

© Andrea Bubenik 2013

All rights reserved. No part of this publication may be reproduced, stored in a retrieval system or transmitted in any form or by any means, electronic, mechanical, photocopying, recording or otherwise without the prior permission of the publisher.

Andrea Bubenik has asserted her right under the Copyright, Designs and Patents Act, 1988, to be identified as the author of this work.

Published by
Ashgate Publishing Limited
Wey Court East
Union Road
Farnham
Surrey, GU9 7PT
England

Ashgate Publishing Company
110 Cherry Street
Suite 3-1
Burlington
VT 05401-3818
USA

www.ashgate.com

British Library Cataloguing in Publication Data
Bubenik, Andrea.
Reframing Albrecht Dürer : the appropriation of art, 1528-1700. -- (Visual culture in early modernity)
1. Dürer, Albrecht, 1471-1528--Appreciation. 2. Dürer, Albrecht, 1471-1528--Influence. 3. Appropriation (Art)--Case studies. 4. Influence (Literary, artistic, etc.)
5. Imitation in art.
I. Title II. Series
759.3-dc23

ISBN: 978-1-4094-3847-2 (hbk)

Library of Congress Cataloging-in-Publication Data
Bubenik, Andrea, 1975-
Reframing Albrecht Dürer : the appropriation of art, 1528-1700 / by Andrea Bubenik.
pages cm -- (Visual culture in early modernity)
Includes bibliographical references and index.
ISBN 978-1-4094-3847-2 (hardcover) 1. Dürer, Albrecht, 1471-1528--Appreciation. 2. Appropriation (Art) I. Title.
N6888.D8B83 2013
740.92--dc23

2012025012

MIX
Paper from responsible sources
FSC® C018575

Printed and bound in Great Britain by the MPG Books Group, UK.

Contents

List of Illustrations

Appropriations of Dürer Prints

Appropriations of Dürer Drawings

55 Albrecht Dürer, *Lucretia*, 1508. Drawing, 422 × 226 mm. Vienna, Albertina. Photo © Albertina, Vienna

56 Anonymous after Albrecht Dürer, *Lucretia (bust)*, *c.*1580. Bronze medal, 52 mm diameter. London, Victoria and Albert Museum. Photo © Victoria and Albert Museum

57 Antonio Abondio after Albrecht Dürer, *Lucretia (bust)*, 1587. Cast bronze plaque, 93 × 72 mm. London, British Museum. Photo © Trustees of the British Museum

58 Johann Friedrich Leonart, *Head of a Woman (called Agnes Dürer)*, *c.*1670. Mezzotint, 99 × 66mm. London, British Museum. Photo © Trustees of the British Museum

59 Albrecht Dürer, *Virgin with Child*, 1512. Drawing, 418 × 288 mm. Vienna, Albertina. Photo © Albertina, Vienna

60 Daniel Fröschl after Albrecht Dürer, *Virgin with Child*, 1604–5. Watercolour on vellum, 430 × 320 mm. Vienna, Kunsthistorisches Museum. Photo © Kunsthistorisches Museum, Vienna

61 Albrecht Dürer, *Christ (Christ among the Doctors)*, *c.*1506. Brush drawing, 275 × 211 mm. Vienna, Albertina. Photo © Albertina, Vienna

62 Hans Hoffmann after Albrecht Dürer, *Christ (Christ among the Doctors)*, *c.*1580. Brush drawing, 261 × 205 mm. Budapest, Szepmuveszeti Museum. Photo © Museum of Fine Arts, Budapest

63 Aegedius Sadeler after Albrecht Dürer, *Christ (Christ among the Doctors)*, 1598. Engraving, 351 × 229 mm. London, British Museum. Photo © Trustees of the British Museum

64 Albrecht Dürer, *Angel (Feast of the Rosegarlands)*, 1506. Brush drawing, 270 × 208 mm. Vienna, Albertina. Photo © Albertina, Vienna

65 Hans Hoffmann after Albrecht Dürer, *Angel (Feast of the Rosegarlands)*, *c.*1580. Brush drawing, 249 × 228 mm. Budapest, Szepmuveszeti Museum. Photo © Museum of Fine Arts, Budapest

66 Aegedius Sadeler after Albrecht Dürer, *Angel (Feast of the Rosegarlands)*, 1598. Engraving, 358 × 227 mm. London, British Museum. Photo © Trustees of the British Museum

67 Albrecht Dürer, *Apostle with Cap (Heller Altar)*, 1508. Brush drawing, 317 × 212 mm. Vienna, Albertina. Photo © Albertina, Vienna

68 Aegedius Sadeler after Albrecht Dürer, *Apostle with Cap (Heller Altar)*, 1597. Engraving, 358 × 229 mm. London, British Museum. Photo © Trustees of the British Museum

69 Albrecht Dürer, *Madonna with the Multitude of Animals*, *c.*1503. Drawing, 319 × 241 mm. Vienna, Albertina. Photo © Albertina, Vienna

70 Jan Brueghel after Albrecht Dürer, *Madonna with the Multitude of Animals*, 1604. Oil on panel, 340 × 260 mm. Rome, Galleria Doria Pamphilij. Photo © ADP – Management Alinari Archives

71 Aegedius Sadeler after Albrecht Dürer, *Madonna with the Multitude of Animals*, after 1597. Copper engraving, 357 × 258 mm. Paris, Musée du Louvre. Photo © RMN Musée du Louvre – Renée-Gabriel Ojéda

72 Albrecht Dürer, *Hare*, 1502. Watercolour, 250 × 225 mm. Vienna, Albertina. Photo © Albertina, Vienna

73 Georg Hoefnagel, *Hare, Raurackl, Squirrel*, *c.*1575–80. Watercolour, 143 × 184 mm. Washington, National Gallery of Art. Photo © Washington, National Gallery of Art

74 Georg Hoefnagel, *Hare and Squirrels*, *c.* 1575–80. Watercolour, 143 × 184 mm. Berlin, Staatliche Museen zu Berlin. Photo © bpk – Kupferstichkabinett, SMB, Jörg P. Anders

Appropriations of Dürer Paintings

Plate 12 Anonymous, *Christ Among the Doctors*, seventeenth century. Oil on panel, 1230 × 1410 mm. Vienna, Kunsthistorisches Museum. Photo © Kunsthistorisches Museum, Vienna

Plate 13 Jobst Harrich, *Woman Taken In Adultery*, sixteenth century. Oil on copper, 730 × 840 mm. Paris, Musee du Louvre. Photo © RMN Musée du Louvre – René-Gabriel Ojéda

Acknowledgements

I started this book while at Queens's University in Kingston, Canada, and substantially revised it during my first years as a lecturer at the University of Queensland, Australia. Research was undertaken at institutions in the Czech Republic (Ustav Dějin Umění) and Germany (Zentralinstitut für Kunstgeschichte). As such, thanks are due to colleagues, friends, and institutions spanning three continents. I cannot help but think that this cultural exchange would have pleased the internationally minded Albrecht Dürer.

I wish to acknowledge the support of the Australian Academy of the Humanities, and their award of a subsidy to aid with publication costs: the inclusion of illustrations, some in colour, would have been impossible without their support. In Canada, sustained research was made possible thanks to a SSHRC Doctoral Fellowship, and for this financial support I thank the Social Sciences and Humanities Research Council of Canada. A Bader Fellowship made travel and research possible, and I am grateful for the support of the Dr Alfred Bader Fine Arts Association. Dr Bader's continued support of young scholars deserves emphatic recognition, as he has contributed immensely to a burgeoning of early modern scholarship in Canada. The publication of this book is but one outcome of many associated with his generosity.

Cathleen Hoeniger and Volker Manuth inspired my interest in Dürer studies, and their continued interest in my research is deeply appreciated. They have set for me examples of scholarly excellence, to which I continue to aspire. Sharon Gregory, David McTavish, and Sebastian Schütze read earlier versions of this book and offered helpful comments and suggestions. I am grateful for the thorough and critical commentary of the anonymous reader provided by Ashgate Publishing. The Publishing Manager at Ashgate, Erika Gaffney, was exceedingly patient and thoroughgoing in the process of bringing the book through its many stages of development. Sylva Dobalová and Lubomír Konečný were fundamental to making my research stay in Prague a productive and rewarding experience. Most emphatically, I thank Marcela and Vit Bubenik, Monica Bubenik, and Christopher Fox for their support and patience. For so many reasons, you all have my profound gratitude.

I especially wish to acknowledge two extraordinary individuals who contributed in so many ways to the beginnings of this book, but with whom I cannot share the joy of completing it. My aunt Jana Kouřilová-Sedlecká (1950–2009), whose love of Prague's art and architecture inspired me to become an art historian in the first place, and who inspired me even more during her long battle with cancer, during which she still found reasons to smile. My friend and fellow art historian Kateřina Dušková (1976–2003), who helped shape this project in its earliest stages through lively conversation and exchange of ideas, and whose tragic death came at such a young age. I dedicate this book to their memories.

Andrea Bubenik, Brisbane, 2012

Introduction – Reframing Dürer

The author of a new book on Albrecht Dürer will inevitably be faced with the question: why another study on Dürer? Easily one of the most written about of the Renaissance artists, Dürer is matched perhaps only by Leonardo da Vinci, Raphael and Michelangelo in terms of quantities of dedicated writings. In 1971, in the preface to his new book, published to coincide with the five-hundredth anniversary of Dürer's birth, the eminent Polish art historian Jan Białostocki described the current state of Dürer scholarship as follows:

> Fifty years ago it was stated in a new Dürer monograph that over the simple grave stone of the artist in the Nürnberg St. John cemetery scholarship had piled up an immense pyramid of books, pamphlets and articles. The recent five hundredth anniversary of the artist's death has increased considerably – if not in substance, at least in number and weight – this tremendous load of erudition, gossip and phantasy. It is therefore with great reluctance that an author starts to write a new book concerning Dürer.[1]

It is heartening that in spite (or perhaps because of) his 'great reluctance', Białostocki produced one of the most masterful and thought-provoking of the many publications to be associated with Dürer's name: *Dürer and His Critics 1500–1971: Chapters in the History of Ideas*. To evidence the 'immense pyramid of books, pamphlets and articles', Białostocki undoubtedly had at hand Mathias Mende's *Dürer Bibliographie*, a vital resource that contains annotations on more than 10,000 publications on Dürer.[2] As for the state of research today, some 40 years later, art historians know all too well that the 'pyramid' described by Bialostcoki has continued to grow unabated. In Jane Campbell Hutchison's *Albrecht Dürer: A Guide to Research* there are annotations for over 900 publications that have emerged between 1971 and 2000.[3]

Given this wealth of scholarship, it may seem absurd to propose that more remains to be said about Dürer. Yet this is precisely the claim with which I wish to preface this book. *Reframing Albrecht Dürer: The Appropriation of Art, 1528–1700* is a study of the reception of Dürer, and exists in part as a continuation of the ideas proposed by Białostocki proposed over a generation ago. To date, Białostocki's book is the only major publication that deals in a sustained manner with the topic of Dürer's reception; and since its publication in 1971, the ideas put forth have not been fully contended with. *Reframing Albrecht Dürer* seeks to overcome this perceived gap in scholarship. Białostocki's approach – a study of the history of ideas as manifest in the reception of Dürer – is largely the framework and inspiration for my own study. With his genuine scholarly approach, Białostocki opened up lines of research for the future, raising questions with great honesty and deliberation. If my own book can even begin to answer some of these questions, and perhaps raise a few more, it will have achieved its purpose.

While I share with Białostocki a focus on the historiography of the reception of Albrecht Dürer, I part company with him in three significant ways. First, I contend with a much shorter period of reception, 1528–1700, in part because I wish to investigate with greater precision and detail what I perceive to be (for reasons that will become apparent) one of the most crucial periods of Dürer's reception. Białostocki's book is bravely ambitious in addressing five centuries; my own study is more focused and contained. Secondly, while written responses to Dürer certainly feature prominently in my research, I am more concerned with artistic responses to Dürer: in other words, the ways in which his art was used and abused by artists subsequent to his death. While Białostocki does address artistic response, his discussion is all too brief, and a more sustained reflection is called for. Thirdly, the evidence gathered around Dürer's reception has led me to argue that the concept of appropriation can be used to characterize how some artists functioned in the sixteenth and seventeenth centuries. The perceived importance of appropriation is reflected by its inclusion in the subtitle of my book. While the term is usually reserved for modern art, for reasons that I hope to make clear it is a useful concept for the episodes of Dürer reception under scrutiny here.

In short, I believe that *Reframing Dürer* posits a fresh understanding of Dürer's reception, and includes a proposal for a new way to think about early modern reception. Taking as its starting point the immediate afterlife of Albrecht Dürer (1471–1528), it focuses on the artists, scientists and collectors who used, valued and criticized Dürer's art. During the period under scrutiny, 1528–1700, Dürer's pictures and theoretical ideas travelled widely and were incorporated into new contexts. The proliferation of portraits after his likeness is richly suggestive of an intensive and international interest in his art and personality (see Chapter 1). The inventories and correspondences of the period embody the emphatic interest in collecting Dürer at the most prominent of European courts, especially Munich and Prague (see Chapter 2). Most significantly, the numerous and varied artistic copies, imitations and emulations of Dürer's works and style, when treated in conjunction with seventeenth-century sources on art theory, demonstrate the significant functions that 'imitative works' after Dürer were charged with. Attitudes such as retrospection, competition and homage emerge as central to artistic practice, making appropriation in its various guises a valuable concept for understanding Dürer's reception (see Chapter 3).

Through all of this, not only does a thorough characterization of the sixteenth- and seventeenth-century reception of the most important German Renaissance artist emerge, but also an acknowledgement that one of the most noteworthy aspects of images is their potential to retain meaning long after creation and in diverse locations. In travel, images can gain potency, or become buried in obscurity. Inevitably, images evolve and experience many lives. As observers of the travels of images, an important task for today's art historian is to become attuned to a range of later contexts and the fresh evaluations that can emerge there. To this end, the year 1528 has been chosen as a starting point, the year of Dürer's death: implicit is the idea that images are not to be prioritized only during the era of their creation. Approaching the works of Dürer from this perspective is to place emphasis upon later audiences of his works. In charting influence and reception, much can be revealed about the movement and uses of images.[4] Which images endure? Who comes to possess them, make use of them, and why? These are important questions to be posed of Dürer's art, and represent an acknowledgement that the lives of images continue long after their original context has ceased to exist.

If there is another scholar to whom this book owes a debt, in terms of approach and method, it is Aby Warburg, who was long fascinated by the 'migration of images'.[5] The fluency implicit in the term migration makes it apt for characterizing reception. In migration, pictures are witnessed anew, adapted to different conditions, and experience a range of uses. In migration, pictures undergo histories of reception. As a witness of migration even the Dürer scholar, when faced with a pyramid of scholarship, realizes that new research remains to be done.

The Dürer-Renaissance: A Historiographic Debate

It will do well to be more precise as to why I have chosen to focus on the period of 1528–1700 for my own study of Dürer's reception. Given the enormous quantity of scholarship that surrounds Dürer (as has already been noted, articles, books, and exhibition catalogues focused on Dürer number in the thousands), it is rather surprising that no monograph dedicated to his reception during the early modern period has been published. Indeed, to date there are only two extended treatments on the reception of Dürer. In 1955, Heinz Lüdecke and Susanne Heiland published their *Dürer und die Nachwelt*, a pioneering work published under difficult circumstances in the former East Germany. Lüdecke and Heiland describe their study as 'a history of *the idea* of Dürer'.[6] Included are chapters on the writings of the German humanists, artists and theoreticians from Italy and the Netherlands, written perceptions about Dürer in the baroque, Enlightenment, Romantic and neoclassical periods, concluding with consideration of more contemporary authors such as Thomas Mann. Also included are 32 images, some of which were influenced by Dürer or made to commemorate him. The second extensive publication on

Dürer's reception has already been discussed, Jan Białostocki's *Dürer and his Critics 1500–1971, Chapters in the History of Ideas*.[7] Białostocki was Director of the Institute for Art History at the University of Warsaw, and he wrote *Dürer and his Critics* during an extended visit to the Institute for Advanced Study at Princeton University. As Białostocki himself points out, his book is similar in scope and intent to the Lüdecke and Heiland publication, but far more comprehensive. Additional topics include Dürer's image as a new Apelles, and Dürer and Raphael as twin cultural idols. Białostocki rightfully points out that the Lüdecke and Heiland publication was difficult to acquire in 1971 (and it continues to be so today), making his own work the most significant and accessible publication on Dürer's reception to date. Most recently, a short but highly useful essay by Jane Campbell Hutchison published in 2000 addresses the reception of Dürer over five centuries.[8]

These publications have two things in common: vast time frames of five centuries, and a focus on literary sources. I would argue that much is to be gained from my own narrowing of the time frame, and my expansion to include an extensive range of copies, imitations and emulations. Many of the images included here have received very little attention in previous scholarship. Most significantly, the period 1528–1700 has the added dimension of framing a peculiar episode in Dürer's afterlife, and indeed, a peculiar episode of artistic reception in general. It is not an exaggeration to say that no other artist experienced such an intense retrospective reaction in this period as Dürer. The relationships that developed between Dürer's art and his audiences – be they artists, collectors or critics – were emphatic, lively and in some instances, rather odd. It will do well to be more precise about this claim from the outset, by laying out the following question: what was peculiar about the reception of Dürer in the period 1528–1700?

While this book is in fact an extended response to this question, a brief examination of a historiographical problem will serve as a preliminary reply, as well as serving to situate my research within a scholarly debate that has yet to be resolved. In journal articles and exhibition catalogues, there is a term that has come to be used by a number of art historians when discussing this early period of Dürer's reception: the 'Dürer-Renaissance'. This term is used to qualify the intensive and even frenzied nature of the response to Dürer, usually characterized as culminating around 1600 and as having affected a number of artistic centres in central Europe, especially Munich and Prague. In a range of media, artists imitated and emulated Dürer in paintings and graphics, and also in media that Dürer himself never used: sculpture, medals, glazed earthenware plates and works in relief. No other Renaissance artist (with the possible exception of Raphael) was the subject of a comparably intensive retrospection. Of course, this is not to say that Dürer was the only artist whose work was imitated in the seventeenth century. Bernini imitated Michelangelo, Rubens imitated Titian, and Raphael was deemed *the* academic model in France and Italy. Yet the point bears repeating: no other artist experienced such an emphatic and pronounced reception in sixteenth and seventeenth centuries as Dürer. No other artist's *reception* has been characterized as a *renaissance*. The implications are broad: to speak of a 'renaissance' in conjunction with one artist is dramatic indeed. As will be shown in this book (especially in Chapter 3) the breadth of imitations of Dürer, the manner in which they were created, and the number of prominent artistic centres affected, is peculiar and noteworthy indeed.

As is so often the case with a point of historiography, the Dürer-Renaissance as a term denoting this particular phenomenon of reception, has both supporters and detractors. In what follows, a brief discussion of the historiography of this term will highlight its nuances and sometimes controversial nature.The term Dürer-Renaissance was first used by Hans Tietze and Erika Tietze-Conrat in the first of their three volume critical catalogue of Dürer's oeuvre, published in 1928. The Tietzes used the term in a peripheral comment, in a discussion focused on the reception of Dürer within his lifetime.[9] For the first prominent use of the term one must turn to Hans Kauffmann, one of the most significant German art historians to specialize in Northern Renaissance art.[10] Kauffmann's article 'Dürer in der Kunst und im Kunsturteil um 1600' deals with the influence of Dürer both in terms of written and artistic perceptions of his artistry. Kauffmann remarks on the Tietzes' use of the term Dürer-Renaissance, and suggests that a number of other terms are equally as fitting: 'Dürer revival' or 're-birth' are two of his suggestions.[11] In his conclusion, Kauffmann points out that around 1600 the reception of Dürer was not restricted to the German lands, nor was copying a phenomenon exclusively related to Dürer. He argues that there is little precedent for the number of copies that were made of Dürer and for the ways in which Dürer's works were received. An English text by an anonymous writer which includes the heading *Dürer Revived*, published in London in 1680, is mentioned by Kauffmann as affirmation that the Dürer-Renaissance was not restricted to Germany or the Netherlands.[12]

Since Kauffmann's seminal article, the term Dürer-Renaissance has been retained and gained some currency in publications until the present. Hans Georg Gmelin defines the Dürer-Renaissance as a phenomenon that began in 1580 and ended in 1630 in Germany and the Netherlands.[13] In an exhibition held in 1979, Gmelin brought together a number of copies of Dürer's self-portraits, discussed Hans Hoffmann as a copyist of Dürer, and considered the guises of imitation that are demonstrated in the print making of the period.[14] In two later publications, Gmelin examined the theme of the Dürer-Renaissance in even greater detail. He discussed the coloured graphics of the period as a phenomenon of the Dürer-Renaissance, arguing that the works of illuminators such as Georg Mack and Domenicus Rottenhammer had been traditionally undervalued and merited a thorough examination, given the quality of these hand-coloured prints.[15] Gmelin also identified pictorial and figural quotations from Dürer prints in paintings and sculpture – mostly sixteenth-century German – in the collections of the Hannover gallery.[16]

Other scholarly acknowledgements of The Dürer-Renaissance as a phenomenon include a more concerted focus on types of media used. An engaging treatment of imitations after Dürer's prints took place at an exhibition in Nuremberg in 1978 under the title *Vorbild Dürer*, and the exhibition showed the engravings and woodcuts by Dürer side by side with a vast array of sixteenth-century imitations.[17] As for imitations of paintings by Dürer, the most thorough examination of the phenomenon of the Dürer-Renaissance from this perspective remains the work of Gisela Goldberg, a scholar of the seventeenth-century court of Maximilian I, Archduke of Bavaria in Munich. In her excellent article 'Zur Ausprägung der Dürer-Renaissance in München', she includes aspects of collecting and art-making, as well as a list of Dürer copyists.[18] While Goldberg is at ease using the term Dürer-Renaissance, she suggests that the term 'retrospection' would be equally appropriate. In 1971, Goldberg was the curator of an exhibition at the Alte Pinakothek in Munich devoted exclusively to the topic of the Dürer-Renaissance, focusing on the holdings of the museum that can be considered as imitations and emulations of Dürer executed by artists at the Munich court.[19] In like fashion Karl Schütz discusses imitative works held in the Kunsthistorisches Museum in Vienna, in his *Albrecht Dürer im Kunsthistorischen Museum* published in 1994. The catalogue focuses on works stemming from Prague under the reign of Holy Roman Emperor Rudolf II, who was perhaps the most impassioned collector of Dürer to have ever lived.[20]

The term Dürer-Renaissance has been treated with hesitancy and criticism by some authors. Fritz Koreny points out that as a concept the Dürer Renaissance 'has rather been thrust upon criticism, and though the concepts of "revival" or "historicism" have been suggested as more appropriate, the meaning is precise enough'.[21] He cautions against overvaluing the 'Dürer movement' in light of the other achievements of artists and collectors, and suggests that the nature studies of the seventeenth century are one of the great achievements that emerged from the reception of Dürer.[22] As with the other commentators, Koreny defines the Dürer-Renaissance as a period of roughly 30 years, suggesting that its beginnings can be seen in Hans Hoffmann's nature studies in the 1570s. According to Koreny, after the Dürer-Renaissance peaked around 1600, it then slowly expired. By far the most concerted criticism of the term can be found in the catalogue for the 1981 exhibition in Frankfurt entitled *Dürers Verwandlung in der Skulptur zwischen Renaissance und Barock*, in which numerous sculptural treatments of Dürer motifs in the sixteenth and seventeenth centuries are discussed. Bernhard Decker, one of the exhibition curators, suggests that to use the term Dürer-Renaissance is to overstate the case, and that the imitations of Dürer can be historically situated, as can all imitative works. He qualifies the Dürer-Renaissance as a 'marginal problem' at best.[23]

I would argue that the visual evidence suggests otherwise: far from being a 'marginal problem', the Dürer-Renaissance in all its complexity remains an intriguing and unusual moment of reception that merits further investigation.

As suggested by David Freedberg, 'the study of copies and transformations remains one of the great tasks of the history of images'.[24] The Dürer-Renaissance opens up the floor to complex quotations and paraphrases, and the importance of considering later uses that works of art undergo. As demonstrated most recently in 2003 at the exhibition *Albrecht Dürer and his Legacy* held in London at the British Museum, there are numerous works in most major collections that have been associated with the Dürer-Renaissance, making the claim for marginality contentious.[25]

Other scholars have seen the need for further research into this peculiar case of early modern Dürer reception, without lingering on the semantics of the term Dürer-Renaissance. In a brilliant case study focused on the use of Dürer motifs by Hans Baldung and Lucas Cranach the Elder, Thomas DaCosta Kaufmann has discussed 'the hermeneutics' of reception manifest in later borrowings of Dürer, and his analysis raises significant issues of how to approach reception.[26] Eliška Fučiková, in her investigation of the use of Dürer at the court of Rudolf II in Prague, suggested that imitations and emulations are of particular interest for understanding the cultural climate of the seventeenth century.[27] Also significant is Dorothy Limouze's claim that the Dürer-Renaissance 'envinces a growing desire to record the cultural past that can be linked with the beginnings of art historical writing in northern Europe'.[28]

In short, there is a need for a fuller account of the Dürer-Renaissance, and this is in part what *Reframing Albrecht Dürer: The Appropriation of Art, 1528–1700* seeks to do. To begin, the first chapter is a preliminary consideration of how Dürer came to achieve the status of a paragon after his death. A consideration of 'writing and depicting Dürer', including early critical perceptions, the proliferation of his likeness, and especially the borrowings from his self-portraiture, will establish the foundations of the Dürer-Renaissance. Collecting is an essential aspect of this heightened reception, and underlies the investigations of Chapter 2. The inventories and correspondences of the period allow for an examination of collecting practices to establish precisely who owned works by Dürer, and the locations where interest in Dürer peaked. In what collections were works by Dürer to be found in the sixteenth and seventeenth centuries? Who had access, in particular, to his paintings, drawings and prints? Why was there such a wholesale removal of Dürer's altarpieces, which served crucial functions in their original locations, to Munich and Prague?

Answering these questions will aid toward an understanding of just why (and how) so many artists engaged in copying, imitating and emulating Dürer, the subject of Chapter 3. Imitation and emulation were an important part of humanist art practice, yet never before had such an intensive flurry of borrowing and paraphrasing in relation to one artist been experienced. Far from being seen as derivative, imitative works were respected by artists and patrons alike, with uses ranging from respectful homage, to playful intellectual games. As will be discussed in Chapter 3, works that incorporated motifs from Dürer were not necessarily thought of as lacking originality. Indeed, the modern day semantics surrounding the term 'original' hardly seem applicable. As Thomas DaCosta Kaufmann has suggested, these images attest to 'an era before originality replaced origin as a ground for artistic creation'.[29] The history of Dürer's reception must, therefore, include not only written perceptions of his artistry, but also an understanding of how artists received and incorporated his work into a framework very different from our own. Moreover, the concept of appropriation is useful for characterizing the diverse uses (and abuses) of Dürer, as will be developed in Chapter 3 and the concluding remarks.

I should like to make a brief note on the images that have been included here. Imitative works after Dürer are available for consultation (but rarely displayed) in most art collections in Europe: prints that have been transformed by colour, nature studies adapted as large-scale paintings, single panels paraphrased as triptychs, and so on. It will be well to note from the start that this will not be an exercise in connoisseurship or an attempt to solidify the body of work that can be ascribed to Dürer. While recognizing that problems of attribution are relevant to the issues at hand, the focus in what follows is upon works definitively known to be copies and emulations from the time of their creation. These images were not intended to deceive – they often include the monogram of the artist and/or an indication of Dürer as the source – and are characterized by transformations of Dürer's motifs in size, scale, or medium, which demonstrates an active interest of the artist in retrospection, competition and homage. It has not been possible to publish all the images that I encountered during my research; what I have included is just a selection of the more intriguing imitative works.

Through a consideration of the themes of writing and depicting Dürer, collecting and appropriating Dürer, a balanced and accurate portrayal of reception between 1528 and 1700 will be achieved. It is hoped that such a portrayal will be significant not only for an understanding of the peculiar episode of the Dürer-Reniassance, but also contribute to a broader understanding of modes of appropriation during the early modern period.

Notes

1 Jan Białostocki, *Dürer and His Critics 1500–1971: Chapters in the History of Ideas, Including a Collection of Texts* (Baden-Baden: Valentin Koerner, 1986): p. 11.

2 Mathias Mende, *Dürer-Bibliographie* (Wiesbaden: Harrassowitz, 1971). The exact number of entries: 10271.

3 Jane Campbell Hutchison, *Albrecht Dürer: A Guide to Research* (New York and London: Garland Publishing Inc., 2000). Hutchison points out that her bibliography is a supplement to Mende's *Dürer-Bibliographie*: she includes only the most basic items of pre-1971 literature, as well as the numerous publications from the 1971 Dürer Year celebrations that Mende was unable to include. The exact number of entries: 935.

4 For important studies on reception, see Wolfgang Kemp, *Der Anteil des Betrachters: Rezeptionsästhetische Studien zur Malerei des 19. Jahrhunderts* (Munich: Mäander, 1983); David Freedberg, *The Power of Images: Studies in the History and Theory of Response* (Chicago: University of Chicago Press, 1989); Martyn P. Thompson, 'Reception Theory and the Interpretation of Historical

Meaning', *History and Theory*, 32/3 (1993), pp. 248–272; Cathleen Hoeniger, 'The Reception of Correggio's *Loves of Jupiter*', in *Coming About: A Festschrift for John Shearman*, edited by Lars R. Jones and Louisa C. Matthew (Cambridge: Harvard University Art Museums, 2001): pp. 191–197.

5 Warburg applied the concept of exchange and migration not only in a geographical sense, but also in terms of epochs: images experience displacement both geographical and temporal, and understanding the effects of images in their new contexts was one of his major preoccupations. See Aby Warburg, *The Renewal of Pagan Antiquity: Contributions to the Cultural History of the European Renaissance*, introduction by Kurt W. Forster, translation by David Britt (Los Angeles: Getty Research Institute for the History of Art and the Humanities, 1999).

6 Heinz Lüdecke and Susanne Heiland, *Dürer und die Nachwelt* (Berlin: Rütten & Loening, 1955).

7 Jan Białostocki, *Dürer and His Critics*, 1986. *1500–1971: Chapters in the History of Ideas, Including a Collection of Texts* (Baden-Baden: Valentin Koerner, 1986).

8 Jane Campbell Hutchison, '"Ehrlich gehalten nah und feren": Five Centuries of Dürer Reception', in *Albrecht Dürer: A Guide to Research* (New York and London: Garland Publishing Inc., 2000): pp. 1–24.

9 Hans Tietze and Erika Tietze-Conrat, *Der junge Dürer* (Augsburg: B. Filser 1928), p. 260.

10 Hans Kauffmann, 'Dürer in der Kunst und Kunsturteil um 1600', *Anzeiger des Germanischen National-Museums (1940–1953)*, 1 (1954): pp. 18–60.

11 Kauffmann 1954, p. 53.

12 Kauffmann 1954, p. 55. The text Kauffmann refers to had as its original title *Book of Drawing, Limning, Washing and Colouring* (London 1660, 1666); however, the third edition was entitled *Dürer Revived*. See also Luigi Salerno, 'Seventeenth-Century English Literature on Painting', *Journal of the Warburg and Courtauld Institutes* 14 (1951): p. 248.

13 Hans Georg Gmelin, ed., *Dürerrenaissance um 1600*, (Hannover: Niedersächsische Landesgalerie Hannover, 1979): p. 1.

14 Gmelin 1979, pp. 1–10.

15 Hans Georg Gemlin, 'Illuminierte Druckgraphik um 1600: ein Phänomen der "Dürer-Renaissance"?', *Städel-Jahrbuch* 9 (1983): pp. 183–209.

16 Hans Georg Gmelin 'Vorbild und Rezeption: Motive aus Dürers Graphik in Kunstwerken der Niedersächsische Landesgalerie', *Weltkunst* 54/6 (1984): pp. 699–702.

17 *Vorbild Dürer: Kupferstiche und Holzschnitte Albrecht Dürers im Spiegel der europäischen Druckgraphik des 16. Jahrhunderts (Ausstellung des Germanischen Nationalmuseums Nürnberg, 8. Juli bis 10. September 1978)* (Munich: Prestel Verlag, 1978).

18 Gisela Goldberg, 'Zur Ausprägung der Dürer-Renaissance in München', *Münchner Jahrbuch der Bildender Kunst* 31(1980): pp. 129–175.

19 Gisela Goldberg, ed., *Dürer-Renaissance* (Munich: Alte Pinakothek, 1971).

20 Karl Schütz and Rotraud Bauer, eds, *Albrecht Dürer im Kunsthistorischen Museum* (Vienna: Kunsthistorisches Museum, 1994).

21 For Koreny's discussion of the 'Dürer Reniassance' see Fritz Koreny, ed., *Albrecht Dürer and the Animal and Plant Studies of the Renaissance*, translated by Pamela Marwood and Yehuda Shapiro (Boston: Brown, 1988): p. 16.

22 Koreny 1988, p. 16.

23 Bernhard Decker, 'Dürer-Nachahmungen und Kunstgeschichte – ein Problem am Rande? Dürer-Konstruktion eines Vorbildes, Gelingen, oder Mißlingen des Fortschritts', in *Dürers Verwandlung in der Skulptur zwischen Renaissance und Barock*, edited by Herbert Beck and Bernhard Decker (Frankfurt: Museum alter Plastik, 1981): pp. 385–489.

24 Freedberg 1989, p. 121.

25 Giulia Bartrum, ed., *Albrecht Dürer and his Legacy* (London: The British Museum Press, 2003).

26 Thomas DaCosta Kaufmann, 'Hermeneutics in the History of Art: Remarks on the Reception of Dürer in the Sixteenth and the Early Seventeenth Centuries', in *New Perspectives on the Art of Renaissance Nuremberg: Five Essays*, edited by Jeffrey Chipps Smith (Austin: Archer M. Huntington Gallery, 1985): pp. 23–39.

27 Eliška Fučíková, 'Umělci na dvoře Rudolfa II a jejich vztah k tvorbì Albrechta Dürera', *Umění* 20 (1972): pp. 146–66.

28 Dorothy Limouze, 'Aegedius Sadeler, Imperial Printmaker', *Bulletin of the Philadelphia Museum of Art* 85(362): pp. 2–24, at p. 7.

29 Kaufmann 1985, p. 24.

1

Writing and Depicting Dürer

In order to begin to characterize Dürer's reception in the early modern period, three lines of enquiry will be undertaken in this chapter. First, Dürer's reputation in early modern textual sources will be examined. Secondly, the proliferation of Dürer's likeness by means of commemorative portraiture, and thirdly, appropriations of his self-portraits, will highlight how artists depicting Dürer also contributed to his burgeoning posthumous reputation. Through writings and depictions, Dürer was firmly entrenched during the early modern period as a paragon. However, the speed and intensity with which this occurred is comparatively unique, as will be shown in the subsequent chapters on collecting and artistic appropriations.

From Autobiography to Art History

While it is beyond the scope of this chapter to include all written sixteenth- and seventeenth-century references to Dürer – I refer the reader here to Jan Bialostocki's *Dürer and His Critics*, which is focused more exclusively on written appreciations and criticisms of Dürer – it is vital to include those writers who would have been known to the collectors and artists of later chapters.[1] The humanists included here posited that a new tradition of art-making had been fostered by Dürer. His achievements as a printmaker, as well as his theoretical writings, are often used to characterize his artistic profile as distinct. He is often extolled as a Northern artist, who almost single-handedly transmitted Italian Renaissance ideals to his German counterparts. Writings about Dürer are indicative of the values promoted by the early humanist panegyrics in praise of local talent. To the modern reader, these statements can almost appear as a form of hagiography.

It will do well to preface this by saying something of writings *by* Dürer, which certainly contributed to his paragon status, and became collector's items in their own right. A number of writings from the hand of Dürer himself have been preserved: his own written records are amongst the most extensive of any Renaissance artist. Most astonishing and unprecedented is the so-called 'Family Chronicle', a formal history of Dürer's family which he compiled using the notes and documents of his father.[2] Written four years before his death, this is a highly conscientious summary of what Dürer knew to be a dying lineage, since he had no children of his own, or even any surviving nieces or nephews who were blood relatives. One can thus surmise that the 'Family Chronicle' was not written for dynastic reasons, or for the purpose of future genealogy, but because Dürer assumed that his life would be of interest to future generations given his international reputation.[3] At least three copies were made of the 'Family Chronicle', which is fortuitous given that the original has been lost. One copy was preserved by the Nuremberg goldsmith Hans Petzolt (1551–1633), who is known to have worked at the court of Rudolf II in Prague.[4] Joachim Sandrart would later publish it in 1675 in his *Teutsche Academie*.[5]

Apart from the 'Family Chronicle', Dürer also meticulously documented his own travels. Few Renaissance artists were as widely travelled as Dürer, and fewer still wrote so extensively about their experiences while in transit. As a young apprentice, Dürer undertook a journey that lasted four years (1490–94), with stops in Colmar and Basel, and likely Frankfurt and Cologne.[6] Later in his life he embarked on two seminal trips to Italy (1494 and 1505), and the letters that survive from his second trip are amongst the most important travel documents of the period.[7] As a mature artist Dürer traveled to the Netherlands (1520–1521), again keeping extensive records.[8] When he visited Brussels on this trip, Dürer expressed enthusiasm about a number of objects that had been sent to the Emperor Charles V from Mexico in the first documented exhibition of pre-Columbian art. Deeply appreciative of the range and quality of the objects that he saw, Dürer reflected that 'all the days of my life I have seen nothing that has gladdened my heart so much as these things, for I saw amongst them wonderful works of art, and I marveled at the subtle *ingenia* of men in foreign lands'.[9] Art was taking on an unprecedented mobility during the Renaissance, and the possibility for Dürer to marvel at objects from across the Atlantic is noteworthy indeed.[10]

Other writings by Dürer include his letters written to Jakob Heller in Frankfurt regarding the commission for the altarpiece for the Dominican church. Written in 1507 and 1509, these letters were preserved by Archduke Maximilian I of Bavaria (1573–1651), one of the major Dürer collectors of the period (who will be discussed in Chapter 2). The letters concern one of Dürer's most important commissions and are precious records of the technical procedures involved in the commission, as well as the relationship between the artist and patron. Dürer's diary of his trip to the Netherlands, one of the most important travel documents of its kind, was preserved by the Earl of Arundel (1585–1646), another major Dürer collector (who will also be discussed in Chapter 2). Other important writings by Dürer include his account of the death of his mother, and his description of an apocalyptic dream on a night in 1525, both of which were considered precious collector's items in the seventeenth century.

It is thanks to the careful preservation of Dürer's writings by avid collectors that anything is known of his history at all. Interest in Dürer was so heightened that even his letters and diaries were coveted items. It is a well-known fact that we are better provided with first-hand written evidence about Dürer than about any other non-Italian master of his, or any earlier time.[11] These writings were gathered together by Hans Rupprich in 1956, to form a hefty three-volume work that remains the definitive compilation of writings by and about Dürer. The first volume reproduces Dürer's published and unpublished writings, the second includes all the humanists who mention Dürer and or his work (in the original languages), and the third volume is a treatment of Dürer's theoretical publications.[12]

Moving on from Dürer's own writings, to writings *about* Dürer, we should note that his death in 1528 came very soon after the wholesale adoption of Protestantism in his native Nuremberg. Franz Fuhse, a nineteenth-century art historian, broadly suggested that an especially heightened interest in Dürer developed posthumously because the city was no longer marked by the uncertainty of pre-Reformation anxieties, because the Protestant faith had been formally accepted in Nuremberg in 1525. A calmer political climate certainly marked Nuremberg in the second half of the sixteenth century: the Peace of Nuremberg was signed in 1532, in 1555 the Peace of Augsburg would confirm the end of violence between Protestants and Catholics in Germany, and the University of Altdorf (just outside of Nuremberg) was founded in 1575. In short, Fuhse argues that the because the Protestant character of the city was secured historical interest in Dürer could develop unabated in the sixteenth century until the onset of the Thirty Years War in 1618.[13]

Yet caution must be exerted before drawing weighty conclusions about interest in Dürer based on religious positioning. While a number of Dürer's most enthusiastic supporters, such as Philipp Melanchthon and Christopher Scheurl, were avid supporters of Protestant reforms, Erasmus of Rotterdam, on the other hand, was a Catholic (albeit one who sympathized with the Protestants, in his particular branch of biblical humanism). The link of Dürer to the Protestant Reformation has been much discussed, especially in relation to the two panels depicting the so-called *Four Apostles*, or *Four Holy Men* (1526) as they are now more often referred to.[14] These paintings, which Dürer bequeathed to the Nuremberg Town Hall, have been interpreted as a summation of his Protestant beliefs and support for Luther's reformation. However, while issues of humanism and the Reformation are often juxtaposed, and much scholarship on Dürer often takes religion as a central tenet, the focus here is on documenting all forms of interest in Dürer. If one thing could be said, it is that his appeal seems to have been universal. His later collectors included both staunch Catholics (Maximilian I) and those who were more or less ambivalent on matters of religion (Rudolf II). For this reason, religious issues are best focused on elsewhere.[15]

The earliest writings on Dürer stem from Conrad Celtis, Erasmus of Rotterdam, Christopher Scheurl, Joachim Camerarius and Philipp

Melanchthon: all were friends of Dürer. Their accounts include oft-repeated phrases from the classical tradition, topoi, which in the writings of the sixteenth century were commonplace and extensively used as forms of expression. For example, in the sixteenth century it was commonplace for artists to be compared to Apelles, the Greek painter active in the fourth century who was reckoned to be the most praiseworthy and exceptional painter to have lived.[16] Indeed, the comparison is so frequent and persistent that, to use the phrase of Catherine Soussloff, 'the comparison of an artist to Apelles forms a *topos* within the genre that is both universal and specific in its signification'.[17] Around 1500 Dürer was already being referred to as 'another Apelles', then 'a new Apelles', and later the 'German Apelles'. To the modern reader, the designation of Apelles can appear almost as a cliché. However, as pointed out by Jan Białostocki,

> these literary *topoi*, or commonplaces, were used by humanist writers much as words were used; they served to express the content which the humanist wanted to put into words, and the fact that these ready figures of thought and speech inherited from the beloved classics were adopted does not mean that the first critics to praise Dürer in writing did not look at his works.[18]

It should also be acknowledged that not every artist was praised to the same extent as Dürer. The veneration of his artistry began early on, and reached unprecedented heights. Interest in Dürer only increased in the sixteenth century, and culminated in the seventeenth. In what follows, a chronological examination of key contemporary writings about Dürer will consolidate this point.

One of the earliest references to Dürer stems from Conrad Celtis (1459–1508), the most famed of the German Humanist scholars.[19] Born in Lower Franconia, Celtis studied in Cologne and Heidelberg, before receiving his doctoral degree in Nuremberg in 1487, when he was also named Poet Laureate by Frederick III. In addition to his extensive writings on poetry, Celtis was also influential for his teachings on world history. He made a career as a travelling scholar and delivered lectures throughout the German lands: in 1497 he was called to Vienna by Emperor Maximilian I, who granted him a title and a special teaching privilege. While preparing a book for publication, Celtis asked Dürer to design a woodcut representing *Philosophy*, and Dürer did so in 1502. In order to endear himself to Dürer, Celtis addressed to him three epigrams, in which he refers to the artist as 'a second Apelles'. In order to further illustrate Dürer's prowess as a painter, Celtis describes the ability of Dürer to depict reality so convincingly that upon completion of a self-portrait, Dürer's dog ran up to it and caressed it, thinking to be his master.[20] This is a prime example of the methods used by humanists to extol the virtues of their subjects, namely, the use of an anecdote to illustrate the prowess and talent of their chosen hero. In this case it is Dürer's ability to depict a scene with convincing similitude that is taken by Celtis to be a most praiseworthy talent. The abilities of artists at mimesis, or imitation of reality, had long been praised by classical writers.

Examining further humanist panegyrics one is struck by similarities in form, content and motive. There was a concerted effort to elevate Dürer as pre-eminent among artists. An excellent case in point is Erasmus of Rotterdam (1466–1536), who Dürer met while travelling in the Netherlands in 1521. The two men had great respect for each other, as shown by Dürer's engraved portrait of the Dutch humanist, and the eulogy that Erasmus composed for Dürer when informed of his death in 1528.[21] As Erwin Panofsky has pointed out, the response of Erasmus to Dürer, 'like that of all Northern humanists, was literary rather than visual, and his regard for Dürer, though unquestionably sincere, was born of respectful admiration rather than instinctive predilection'.[22] In essence, the whole eulogy is subordinated to the fact that Dürer could do in black and white what Apelles could only do with colour, a reference to Dürer's dominance in the field of printmaking. As 'the Apelles of black lines' Dürer's claim to fame rests on his not only being a painter, but a draftsman, woodcut designer and engraver. Erasmus also remarks: 'he who would spread colors on Dürer's prints would injure the work'.[23] Erasmus was also interested in theoretical works by Dürer, and advises that those who seek to understand the art of drawing and painting consult the 'book by Albrecht Dürer, written in German but very learnedly', certainly a reference to Dürer's *Unterweysung der Messung*.[24] His praising of Dürer's achievements continues as he describes Dürer as having emulated 'Pamphilus the Macedonian, who was proficient not only in literature but also geometry and arithmetic, who believed that art could never reach perfection without these disciplines.'[25] Clearly, this is a concerted effort to promote Dürer as having mastered science as well as art.

The Lutheran reformer Christopher Scheurl (1481–1542) referred to Dürer in publications of 1508, 1509 and 1515. He described Dürer as being greeted in Venice as 'a second Apelles', always valued for his skill in imitating nature, and the ability to make people believe the reality of what lay before them in paint. Scheurl describes Dürer as so skilled in depicting reality that he fooled servants by painting spider's webs, which they then tried in vain to brush away.[26] Another theologian who played a significant role in the protestant Reformation was Philipp Melanchthon (1497–1560), who was also familiar with Dürer and extolled his virtues. His is perhaps the most personal of the all the humanists' claims about Dürer:

> I remember that Albrecht Dürer, the painter, a man excelling in talent and virtue, used to say that when a youth he liked bright and florid pictures, and that he could not choose but rejoice when he contemplated the brilliancy and variety of his coloring. But that after he began to view Nature as an old man and endeavored to look upon her native face, then he understood that her simplicity was the greatest glory of art.[27]

Melanchthon's commentary carries an almost conversational tone, suggestive of his familiarity with Dürer and, significantly, placing an emphasis upon colour. This is important evidence of appreciation of Dürer not only as a printmaker, but also as a painter.

The earliest biography of Dürer was written by Johann Neudörfer (1497–1563), a scribe, accountant and master of calligraphy in Nuremberg. In 1547, Neudörfer composed his tome (which he claimed to have written in eight days) about the lives of artists and craftsmen who stemmed from Nuremberg.[28] The text contains several factual errors, for example the claim that Dürer was born in Hungary, and that Dürer had worked with Martin Schongauer in Nuremberg. We now know that Dürer's father (rather than Dürer himself) was born in Hungary, and Schongauer was never active in Nuremberg, nor did Dürer ever have the opportunity to work with him.[29] Two decades had passed between the death of Dürer and Neudörfer's composition, and while these errors have resulted in scholars taking him less than seriously, his work is certainly reflective of the historiography of the period and deserves due consideration. While he may have been the first, Neudörfer was certainly not the last to make factual errors about Dürer's biography, nor should such errors be taken to mean that the entire text is irrelevant. Neudörfer was ultimately concerned with establishing a tradition of art-making distinct to Nuremberg. He offers important observations about the early market for Dürer's works, noting for instance that the expense of obtaining Dürer's engravings and woodcuts was very high.[30] He seems to have been impressed by print collections, and notes that when available in sufficient number, and organized properly, prints could be used to portray an artist's entire career. This is early evidence of a historical attitude toward collecting prints, which were more accessible than paintings and could be used to represent an artist's development.

Also significant is the fact that Neudörfer was the calligrapher who was responsible for the inscriptions on Dürer's *Four Holy Men* (1526), inscriptions that were originally affixed to the bottom of the panels.[31] These inscriptions reproduce biblical passages from a recent translation of the Bible by Martin Luther (the so-called September-Testament of 1522), and include a warning against 'false prophets'. The first line of both are references to the Apocalypse of St John (22:18 ff.), followed by a reproach to the secular powers not to conceal the divine word in seductive human interpretation, and that everyone should take the warning of the 'four excellent men' to heart. The *Four Holy Men* has been interpreted by scholars as representing Dürer's personal religious credo, largely because of the inscriptions, and as exemplifying his support of Luther's reformation. According to Neudörfer, it was also Dürer's intention to represent the four temperaments in the panels: sanguine (John), choleric (Mark), phlegmatic (Peter), and melancholic (Paul), with each temperament corresponding to one of the four ages of life.[32] The *Four Holy Men* will be discussed further in later chapters: for now, the important thing to note is that Neudörfer's added inscriptions have been pivotal in interpretations of these paintings, and that it is important that early written (and sometimes confused) commentary on Dürer not be simply labelled as topoi or dismissed.

Further testimony can be found in the writings of the German humanist and poet, Joachim Camerarius (1500–1574), who was an admirer of Dürer's theoretical writings, and translator of Dürer's posthumous publication, *Treatise on Human Proportion* (Nureemberg, 1528), into Latin in 1532.[33] The educational reforms of Camerarius are well known – in 1526 Camerarius was appointed as the teacher for Greek and Latin at the newly founded gymnasium in Nuremberg; in 1535 he was called to Tübingen, where he helped in the reorganization of the university; and from 1541 until his death, he lectured at the University of Leipzig. Camerarius was skilled in translations, having rendered Herodotus, Homer, and Sophocles into Latin. In his translation of Dürer's treatise, he prefaces the work with praise for Dürer's high moral character, highly placed patrons, mathematical and scientific ability. For Camerarius, Dürer's greatest accomplishment lay in the manner in which he approached art from a more scientific perspective: 'With Albrecht all was ready, certain, and at hand, because he had brought painting into the fixed track of rule and recalled it to scientific principles.'[34] This is a significant early perception of Dürer in which he is seen as able to balance both artistic and scientific pursuits, another aspect of his reception in the seventeenth century.

It is important to consider Dürer's influence outside of the German lands as well. The Flemish artist Lambert Lombard (1506–1566) founded one of the first academies of art in the Low Countries. In a letter dated April 27th, 1565 from Liège, he wrote to Vasari on the subject of the history of art in Germany, including of course Dürer. Significantly, Lombard seems to have relied a great deal upon the tradition of Italian artistic biography, which in its turn depended for many points on Pliny the Elder's chapters concerning the history of art. Lombard's account is replete with the topoi of the humanists, and he gives the development of art a highly linear progression, much as in the first edition of Vasari's *Lives of the Artists*, which was certainly familiar to him. Lombard describes Dürer as 'wholly enchanting', an artist who was 'supported by knowledge of geometry, optics, rules and proportions'; he suggests further that

> truly we must render him undying thanks for leading us to the gate of perfection in art; he worked by the sweat of his brow for his goal, as much with his writings as with his works of art as all Italy knows well.[35]

Lombard's account demonstrates not only that interest in Dürer in the Low Countries was developing (and for that matter, and by his own admission, in Italy as well), but his account is also a crucial piece of reception that illustrates how topoi were not merely oft-repeated phrases. Indeed, topoi continued to serve the purpose of strengthening an artist's reputation even as the century continued.

In the case of Dürer, these topoi were also used to establish that he was equal to his Italian counterparts. Another Flemish writer who demonstrates the wide appeal of Dürer, as well as supporting the esteemed position Dürer was being elevated to in the history of art as it developed north of the Alps, is Dominicus Lampsonius (1532–1599). Originally from Bruges, Lampsonius was one of the first humanists in the north to write extensively on art. He studied painting under Lambert Lombard (discussed above), and published a biography of his master in 1565.[36] In this biography Lampsonius made no secret of his preference for Italian art, especially in terms of design and a furthering of antiquarian interests, and he valued greatly the grandeur of Italian history painting.[37] However, as was so often the case, an exception was made for Dürer, for whom Lampsonius had a great enthusiasm. Sharing in this enthusiasm was Lampsonius' friend, the geographer Abraham Ortelius; it is likely thanks to the collection of Ortelius that Lampsonius came to be so familiar with Dürer's work.[38] In a long letter to Ortelius, Lampsonius gave his opinions of Dürer, and argued that Dürer's greatness was measured by his talents in the graphic arts.[39] Lampsonius describes Dürer as dry in manner, and not completely natural. At the same time, Lampsonius consciously promoted and advanced Dürer against what hitherto had been declared the superiority of Italy.

Lampsonius' contribution to the development of a northern art history is significant, especially as manifest in his contribution to the very important print series, *Pictorum aliquot celebrium Germaniae inferoris effigies* (1572). The print series depicts valued and esteemed artists from the Low Countries, to which Lampsonius contributed the laudatory verses. In a recently published and important article, Sarah Meiers discusses this series as 'a valued tribute to Northern artists, a tribute which has been sourced again and again by those artists' successors'.[40] The series does not include Dürer, since it focuses exclusively on artists from the Low Countries.[41] However, the verses composed by Lampsonius do reveal a great deal about the development of a distinctly northern art history, and importantly, these verses were later incorporated by Karel van Mander into his *Schilderboeck*.[42] As pointed out by Meiers, 'for Lampsonius, the strength of a Northern artist rested in his mechanical skill and not in his creative vision unless, of course, that artist emulated the inspired designs of Italian High Renaissance masters'.[43] However, as pointed out in the letter from Lampsonius to Ortelius (discussed above), Dürer seems to have been an exception to this rule.

Hitherto it has been stressed that Dürer was seen as a paragon for those writing about art north of the Alps. Of course, Dürer was written about by the Italians as well. In the second edition of his *Lives of the Artists* (1568), Vasari included Dürer, describing him as a Flemish artist active in Antwerp, an obvious factual error. Vasari also described the perfection of Dürer's printmaking techniques – it seems that Dürer's paintings were practically unknown to him.[44] It should be noted that it was thanks to the texts of both Lambert Lombard (1565) and Dominicus Lampsonius (1564) discussed above that Vasari had any information about Dürer at all.[45] Another important sixteenth-century Italian writer who discussed Dürer is Giovanni Paolo

Lomazzo (1538–1600). The theoretical attitudes of this Lombard artist are often posited as having had greater importance than his paintings. His *Trattato della Pittura, Scultura e Architettura* (1585) is far more theoretical than Vasari's essentially biographical text. Lomazzo's treatise, in which criticism and theory are combined, rapidly gained widespread popularity on the continent.[46] Lomazzo praises Michelangelo, Titian, Raphael and Leonardo; as for artists from the north, Lomazzo praises only Dürer whose engravings are especially deemed worthy of imitation. This praise for Dürer is important in the context of reception, since in the art theory of the seventeenth century, Lomazzo's treatise was the most significant and widely read, if the number of editions of his writings can be taken to be any indication. His promotion of Dürer should not be underestimated in terms of the impact it would have had.

Lomazzo also relied upon Dürer's treatise on proportion, and states as much himself:

> since my purpose is to handle this matter exactly, it shall not be amiss, briefly to touch upon the art of proportion delivered by Albert Dürer ... I may not omit it, because it hath the authority of so famous a man, in the skill of painting, as Germaniae cannot match again.[47]

Yet in other passages Lomazzo shows a somewhat ambiguous attitude toward Dürer. While he has high praise for his theoretical efforts, he laments that he did not study in Italy, and describes him as having a somewhat 'barbarian manner'. He does, however, praise those who imitate Dürer's works, stating that they will get great advantage from it

> not only because of diligence or patience, but also because of the sure mathematical procedure ... and because of his knowledge of sciences, which he possessed in highest degree, and which necessarily accompany art and must be connected with it.[48]

Clearly, Dürer's prowess in mathematics was an emerging theme at the end of the sixteenth century, as well as the suggestion that imitation of his works was a sound and valid enterprise.

Some of the factual errors found in Vasari are repeated in the work of Karel van Mander (1548–1606), who was determined to posit Dürer as a paragon for a distinct northern history of art. Of course, the organization and intent of van Mander's *Schilderboeck* (1604) is similar to that of Vasari's *Vite* (1568), and it seems likely that van Mander relied in part on the information he obtained from Vasari's text. Van Mander had visited Nuremberg in 1577 was generally better informed than his predecessors about Dürer, and does state correctly Nuremberg as Dürer's birthplace. However, Martin Schongauer is cited as Dürer's teacher, and the year of Dürer's birth is given as 1470, a repetition of factual errors of previous writers. Yet for the purposes of reception, it is significant that the *Schilderboeck* includes Dürer as the most exemplary of northern artists, with van Mander referring to Dürer as a 'poetic painter'.[49]

The *Schilderboeck* appeared at the climax of the revival of interest in Dürer, and was a conscientious attempt to construct or reveal a northern tradition of art-making as distinct from the Italian. Van Mander praises Dürer for having accomplished so much left to his own devices. Significantly, he does not mention in a derogatory manner the often repeated observation that Dürer lacked contact with Italian art.[50]

Most importantly, Van Mander describes an almost cult-like veneration of works by Dürer. For example, he discusses Dürer's *Heller Altar* (1509), which stood in the Dominican church in Frankfurt until 1614, as being so popular that monks charged substantial fees for opening it to visitors on weekdays, a practice usually reserved for the veneration of religious relics and sites of pilgrimage. He states further that "it is almost unbelievable how much money this painting yields to the monks of the monasteries through the tips given and the drinks bought by gentlemen merchants, travelers and others interested in art to whom this painting is disclosed".[51] This is a telling statement about the significance of Dürer's altarpiece *in situ*, and early modern links between viewership and economic profitability, as much as the cult of Dürer that was rapidly developing. Dürer himself had participated in this long-standing tradition of paying to view famous altarpieces, and while in Cologne in 1520 he had paid a small sum to have Stefan Lochner's *Altar of the Patron* Saints opened.[52] In his diaries for his trip to the Netherlands (which he undertook between 1520–21), Dürer further describes paying a charge to view more paintings, stating: 'There I saw Rudgier [Rogeir van der Weyden's] painted *cappeln* and paintings by a great old master; there I gave the boy 1 st. to opon them up.'[53] Dürer's testimonials are indicative of precedents for the paid viewings his own paintings would experience subsequent to his death, the link between art and commerce of course still very much in effect to this day.

The theme of veneration of Dürer's work is continued in the writings of Matthias Quad von Kinckelbach (1557–1613), a well-travelled writer from a noble but impoverished Nuremberg family. In his *History of the German Nations*, published in 1609, Kinckelbach describes how

> Dürer's manuscripts and other plainly designed drawings on paper and parchment are regarded by artists and other admirers as holy things, his panels and paintings are displayed and preserved as the highest and noblest relics, so that for several, one must pay money simply to see and scrutinize them.[54]

This statement gives pause for thought. Yes, Dürer's altarpieces had very real ecclesiastical functions, and would have been venerated during acts of devotion. However, Kinckelbach's inclusion of Dürer's drawings and manuscripts in his list of 'holy things' is noteworthy, as is the suggestion that to view works by Dürer was a very real privilege, indeed one worth paying for. Recorded almost one century after the death of Dürer, the remarks of Kinckelbach attest to an intense appreciation not only of painted works by Dürer on public display, but also of his drawings and writings.

This public appreciation is also apparent in the writings of Johann Hauer (1586–1660), an engraver from Nuremberg who compiled several volumes about Nuremberg painters and craftsmen. Hauer also wrote a biography of Dürer that exists in two copies, one of which is in the Nuremberg Stadtsarchiv (and has been published and discussed by Andreas Tacke).[55] In addition, Hauer was responsible for preserving Dürer's Family Chronicle and Netherlandish travel journal. Hauer also experienced first-hand the gradual removal of the majority of Dürer's paintings from their original locations. The so-called 'Hauer-sche Manuskript' in Nuremberg is essential for understanding the manner in which Dürer's paintings were sought after by two of the most significant collectors of the Dürer-Renaissance, namely Maximilian I of Bavaria and Holy Roman Emperor Rudolf II. Hauer also details the 1636 sale of Willibald Imhoff's collection of works on paper by Dürer. The details of the removal of a number of Dürer's paintings, including the purchase of Dürer's major altarpieces (the *Adoration of the Trinity* was purchased in 1585, the *Paumgartner Altar* in 1613, the *Heller Altar* in 1614, and the *Four Apostles* in 1627), are all detailed by Hauer (as will be discussed further in Chapter 2).[56]

The final writer to be considered here is Joachim Sandrart (1606–1688) whose *Teutsche Academie* was published in 1675, with a second volume appearing in 1679.[57] Sandrart moved to Nuremberg in 1674 where he remained until his death in 1688. Sandrart's interest in forging a distinct history of Northern art making is shown not only in his writings, but also by the fact that he founded an academy of art in Nuremberg. While in Nuremberg, Sandrart purchased Dürer's tomb and renovated the Pirckheimer epitaph, added a coat of arms and the inscription that is there to this day. He published for the first time Dürer's Family Chronicle. Referring to Dürer as the 'universal master', Sandrart was also the first to provide information on the imitations that arose in conjunction with Dürer's works and style.[58] As pointed out by Bernard Ley, Sandrart 'did not object to fakes or pastiches either on ethical or artistic grounds, but discusses Dürer forgers, copyists and pasticheurs ... with encyclopedic seriousness'.[59]

According to one historian, the Dürer-Renaissance reached its height and also came to an end with Sandrart's 1675 *Teutsche Akademie*.[60] Dürer would not fare so well in the academic writings of the eighteenth century, and became associated with Gothic art by critics for whom this term had deeply negative connotations. Perhaps this is best foreshadowed by Roger de Piles (1636–1709) and his system for designating the perfect painter. In his *Cours de Peinture par Principe*, published in 1708, de Piles subdivides painting into four fundamental properties: composition, drawing, colour, and expression. In an appendix to this volume, he publishes a table in which he grades each of these properties on a scale between zero and twenty. The totals of each category are then added together, and a numeric value assigned to each painter. On the de Piles scale, Dürer receives 36 points, compared to Raphael with 65, Rubens with 65, Poussin with 53, Rembrandt with 50, Leonardo with 49, and Michelangelo with 37.[61] It has been suggested that de Piles looked upon this as a sort of game, while his contemporaries considered it a 'clever way to classify genius'.[62]

Dürer's eighteenth-century reception merits a study in its own right. For now, it will do well to note that for the sixteenth and seventeenth century commentators discussed above, Dürer was considered to be a superior artist in written commentaries on art, and used to elevate the status of northern art in particular. Also significant to his early reception are the various commemorative portraits, and appropriations of his self-portraits, which resulted in Dürer becoming one of the most internationally recognized of all artists. As such, Dürer came to be appreciated not only in the writings of the humanists and art theorists of the north, but also through the propagation of his likeness.

Commemorating Dürer in Portraiture

Dürer can be cited as anomalous in the history of art not only for the number of times that he depicted himself, but also as an artist whose features came to be widely recognized due to numerous depictions by others. Joseph Heller, in his nineteenth-century catalogue of works by Dürer, lists approximately 115 images after Dürer's likeness.[63] This is likely more than of any other artist in early modern art history. The transmission of Dürer's features in graphic reproductions and paintings certainly contributed to his fame. Moreover, these images can tell us a great deal about the emergence of the cult of the artist in the early modern period.

Other curious episodes highlight the manner and speed with which Dürer's likeness was treated with veneration. A group of artists opened Dürer's grave the day after his burial, exhumed his corpse, and fashioned a plaster cast out of his face and hand. This cast took pride of place in the collection of Duke Maximilian I of Bavaria, only to be destroyed in a fire in 1729. Another object that attained a similar relic-like status was a lock of Dürer's hair supposedly cut from Dürer's head two days after his death. The hair is now on display in the Vienna Academy of Art and has a provenance much like a painting.[64]

The humanist practice of personal commemoration reached a zenith with the veneration of Albrecht Dürer in the writings of the humanists during his lifetime and soon after his death, as discussed above. Yet the vast majority of commemorative medals and portraits date to the second half of the sixteenth century, as opposed to immediately after his death. The earliest portraits of Dürer are typical in their adherence to classical motifs and show the artist in profile. We will consider a number of these commemorative images, what they can reveal about the veneration of Dürer, and their reception. Not all of the artists discussed are well known to us today; however, when possible, some relevant details about their background will be provided. Again, a roughly chronological approach is observed, with the aim of characterizing the reception of Dürer's likeness in the studied period.

One of the earliest commemorative portraits of Dürer was created by the Augsburg artist Hans Schwarz (1492–1535). Schwarz's original single-sided medal of Dürer first appeared in 1520, and again in 1528, with a new inscription and as a commemoration of Dürer's death.[65] The boxwood model that Schwarz used for cutting the medal is found today in the Herzog-Anton Ulrich Museum, Braunschweig – however no examples cut from this original model have survived in good condition. Instead, Schwarz's medal is known to us thanks to the many posthumous copies, or 'aftercasts', one of which can be found in the British Museum (Figure 1). Given the dating of the original medal, it is possible that Schwarz worked in part from an actual sitting with Dürer. As Giulia Bartrum points out, Schwarz also perhaps based his medal in part on Dürer's 1500 self-portrait, and indeed there are some similarities in the hair, features and fur-trimmed robe.[66] It has been argued that this is the most accurate likeness of Dürer that exists. The popularity of this particular medal is indicative of a high demand for, and interest in, Dürer's likeness.

Another early portrait of Dürer was created by Mathias Gebel (1500–1574), who was granted citizenship in Nuremberg in 1523 and is described in the city archives as a woodcarver. This is the second medal of Dürer produced in the artist's lifetime (Figure 2), and given that Gebel struck the medal in 1527 before Dürer died, it is possible that the medal was commissioned by Dürer himself.[67] This was the definitive portrait of Dürer in his old age: shown in profile, the flowing hair has been trimmed. Like the earlier Schwarz medal, the Gebel medal was reissued in 1528 as a commemorative piece. We know that Gebel's medal was highly influential, not only due to the numerous impressions thereof, but also because of a woodcut that borrows from it directly (Figure 3). This woodcut, created by Nuremberg artist Erhard Schön (*c.*1491–1542), was extremely popular as a likeness of Dürer. A comparison with Gebel's medal shows that Schön based his portrait on Gebel's prototype: the profile, dress, hair and features are all similar. The impression has the title 'Portrait of Albrecht Dürer in his Old Age – 56th year.' The text below discusses the high esteem in which Dürer's work was held by princes far and wide and the importance of his work to craftsmen of the mid-sixteenth century. Although he was not a part of Dürer's studio, Schön was deeply familiar with Dürer's work and associated with Dürer's students.[68] Schön specialized in printed portraits of notable figures; however his 1528 woodcut of Dürer is his best-known work. The woodcut proved to be very popular: it was reprinted at least eight times during the sixteenth century alone, and there are also a number of coloured impressions.[69]

By the time this woodcut was made, Dürer had an international reputation, and reprints were being issued in response to the high demand for likenesses of him. It is difficult to state with certainty how these images were used; however, the proliferation of Dürer's likeness certainly suggests that his esteem was growing not only amongst theoreticians and humanists (as discussed in the preceding section), but also for those who would have been able to purchase prints, and an avid buying public. Nor was this proliferation restricted to Dürer's hometown. The Danish draughtsman and printmaker, Melchior Lorck (*c.*1527–1583) created an engraved portrait of Dürer, dated to 1550, that has also experienced a significant reception (Figure 4).[70] Lorck had travelled in Germany in the 1540s, and it has been assumed that during this trip he would have seen Dürer's 1500 self-portrait and borrowed from it in order to create his likeness of Dürer. It also seems plausible that Lorck incorporated aspects of the earlier depictions by both Schwarz (Figure 1) and Schön (Figure 3), making his portrait an amalgamation of types. In the Lorck depiction, the profile, as well as the fur collar, bears a marked similarity to the Schwarz medal. Moreover, the eyes in the Lorck's depiction of Dürer can be compared to the eyes of Schön's Dürer; suggesting that Lorck created an amalgamation of the two earlier works. Why is this significant? The answer is twofold. First, Lorck's use of the two earlier works suggests their accessibility and the heightened interest in Dürer's features. Secondly, in combining aspects of two images into one, Lorck shows himself to be operating under a pictorial principle that was central to the reception of Dürer in the seventeenth century; namely, the use of several models to create an improved image.

Lorck's refined depiction of Dürer is also of importance because it was so often imitated. An engraving by an anonymous artist, now in the British Museum, clearly imitates Lorck's depiction (Figure 5). The rope-like curls, the wide-eyed expression, the distinctly shaped nose, carefully trimmed beard, and stylish fur collar are identical. The subject is in profile once again. However, this artist has chosen the more conventional circular format in emulation of antique medals. Dürer's northern roots are stressed in the inscription 'Albertus Dürerus Noricus', as are his achievements as an artist, as 'pictor eminentis'.[71] Again, we can see at work here the pictorial principle of imitation, since the anonymous artist has combined motifs from Lorck, as well as antique medals, in order to show Dürer as an eminent artist.

It is beyond the scope of this section to delve into all aspects of the commemoration of Dürer through portraiture in the sixteenth and seventeenth centuries. As noted above, there are more likenesses of Dürer than of any other artist. These five selected examples demonstrate several important principles. First, the appreciation of Dürer was not restricted to written sources. Artists, through the creation of portraits, contributed to the esteem in which Dürer was held. Secondly, Dürer's northern origins are stressed in these artistic renditions as well. And thirdly, Dürer was an artist whose features came to be unusually well known, likely a contributing factor in the international dissemination of his reputation. This brings us to the following point: how accurate were these commemorative portraits? Dürer of course is well known for his creation of a series of self-portraits. This is not to suggest that the artists who created commemorative portraits would have been aware of these self-portraits. On the contrary, we can assume in most cases (with the possible exception of the Lorck portrait) that they were not. For this reason, it is important to characterize what we can of the reception of Dürer's self-portraits in a separate section, a consideration to which I now turn.

Appropriating Dürer's Self-portraits

The pictures included thus far can be categorized as commemorative, as they were often created in a spirit akin to the eulogies of the humanists. I now turn to a consideration of imitative works after Dürer's self-portraits, moving the discussion firmly into the territory of imitations and emulations of Dürer's own works and style. I discussed above how Melchior Lorck used several motifs from two different images in order to create his depiction of Dürer. In this section on self-portraiture, we must be aware of the possibility of imitative inclinations such as Lorck's, but in a slightly different way: when artists imitated Dürer's self-portraits, they were borrowing from Dürer himself. On the one hand, the commemorative portraiture of the preceding section is essential for illustrating the great esteem in which Dürer was held. On the other hand, the imitation of self-portraiture is concerned more emphatically with imitation of the artist proper, an essential consideration in this history of Dürer reception.

To begin, it is necessary to situate Dürer's self-portraits. It is well known that Dürer carefully fostered and propagated his own image and stature during his lifetime.[72] The sheer quantity of self-portraits by his hand is astonishing: three autonomous paintings, a watercolour, and six drawings. In addition, he included his self-portrait in four large-scale compositions *in assistenza* (as a bystander in a larger religious scene), usually holding an inscription or *cartellino* indicating his authorship and northern origins.[73] Until Rembrandt no artist depicted himself as often as Dürer, and his self-portraits represent an especially unique achievement in the history of art. Dürer's projection of himself in a socially advantageous manner, and as an eminent painter worthy of respect, is a central theme to be reckoned with in his reception. Much like the attention he gave over to his Family Chronicle, Dürer attended to visually documenting his self with great care and attention, indicative once again of his interest in leaving to posterity accurate records of his persona. His presentations of 'self' are highly calculated, and use clothing and posture to great effect.[74]

Dürer's earliest self-portrait, his silverpoint drawing at the age of 13, has taken a central role in discussions of an emerging self-consciousness during the Renaissance, and the emergence of the 'artist genius', by now fully emancipated from the medieval guild system (Figure 6). Dürer's precocious rendering of his features as a young boy, executed in the difficult medium of silverpoint, has rightfully been commented upon as utterly unprecedented, and perhaps even the oldest existing child's drawing in the Western tradition.[75] Also included by the hand of Dürer is the following inscription: 'This I drew from a mirror in the year 1484, when I was still a child. Albrecht Dürer.' This inscription indicates not only Dürer's pride in his artistry at such a young age, but also a confidence that this feat of drawing would be of interest to others.

Attesting to an early appreciation of Dürer's drawing is a copy now in the British Museum in London (Figure 7). Executed in brush and wash, the copy carefully imitates Dürer's technique, emulating the precociousness of the youthful style. Also imitated is the inscription, which has been altered slightly and states the following: 'On February 4th 1576 I made this portrait from the image drawn by the widely famous Dürer inscribed in his own hand thus: "This I drew from a mirror in the year 1484, when I was still a child".' This copy has been attributed to Hans Hoffmann (1530–1592), a German painter and draftsman, one of the chief imitators and emulators of Dürer's works and style in the period under scrutiny.[76] Especially noteworthy is that Hoffmann is usually cited as the main proponent of the Dürer-Renaissance, the historiography of which was detailed in the introduction. Very little biographical information is known about Hoffmann. His training has not been recorded, he is known to have been active in Nuremberg, and was first mentioned in the 1576 Nuremberg records as a painter and citizen of the town. He lived there until 1584, when he was called by Duke Wilhelm of Bavaria to the court in Munich. In 1585, he was named imperial painter at the court of Rudolf II in Prague, where he received an annual salary of 100 thalers until his death. When in Nuremberg he made copies and imitations for Hans Hierohymous Imhoff, Willibald Imhoff, and other Nuremberg collectors, including Paulus Praun. Hoffmann was described by a contemporary as a painter who could imitate Dürer's work so convincingly that it was almost impossible to distinguish a copy from the original. These collectors and Hoffmann as a painter will be discussed in Chapters 2 and 3 respectively.[77] For now, it is important to note that even a self-portrait by Dürer as an adolescent in training had been deemed a work worthy of copying, signifying a deep interest in Dürer's artistry and persona.

The first autonomous painted self-portrait by Dürer dates to 1493, when Dürer was 22 (Figure 8). This self-portrait was created after Dürer had undertaken a series of travels, which came to an end in 1493 when he returned to Nuremberg for his marriage to Agnes Frey. The painting was originally on vellum, and at some point was transferred to linen and pasted onto the panel. Since the painting was on vellum, it would have been easy for Dürer to roll it up during his travels. In the latest interpretation of this self-portrait, Jeroen Stumpel and Joelein van Kregten argue that the eryngium that Dürer is holding indicates the uncertainties of his years as a journeyman; Dürer depicted the eryngium without roots, and in sixteenth century herbals the eryngium is described as easily separating from its roots and being prey to the winds.[78] Stumpel and van Kregten suggest that Dürer chose to portray himself as 'the uprooted person he must have been during these beginnings of his career'.[79] Previous interpretations have focused on the inscription on the painting – 'My affairs will go, as it stands above' – as an indication of Dürer's need (and possible reluctance?) to return to Nuremberg for his marriage to Agnes Frey, with the eryngium a symbol of his sexual potency, a flower described in some sources as an aphrodisiac.

Regardless of which interpretation is ascribed to, it can be agreed that Dürer has chosen to depict himself here in an elevated manner. The significance of clothing in late fifteenth-century Nuremberg cannot be underestimated as a visual manifestation, or disavowal, of the social order.[80] 'Kleiderordnungen', or sumptuary laws were very specific as to what citizens could or could not wear. In the painting, it is clear that Dürer has paid a great deal of attention to the rendering of his clothing. His collarless shirt is finely trimmed in ribbon and gold embroidery, and his shirt is bound with laces. The fabrics appear to be of fine quality and are meticulously rendered, with fashionable slashes on the coat. Clearly, Dürer considered himself to be above the provision of the Nuremberg council that stated 'henceforth no male person, citizen or denizen of this city except doctors of the law and knights, shall wear in any part of his garb any strings, borders or lace, which are made wholly or in part of gold.'[81] There were also regulations that described fancy shirts as evidence of extravagance, and ruled that no jacket was to be cut too deeply, or left open. Dürer's clothing in this self-portrait would have been considered inappropriate to his social position, as he has fashioned himself more according to the dictates of the nobility and court society than to his own profession of artist.

The whereabouts of Dürer's painting are unknown between 1493 and 1847.[82] It is impossible to determine what collector had interest in the painting for this period of time. However, its reception is attested to by an almost exact copy of the painting, now in Leipzig.[83] It is identical in composition to the original, apart from the absence of the inscription. What distinguishes it is the fact that it is painted on panel, while as already mentioned the original was on vellum and transferred to canvas. Perhaps this copy was created out of concern for the stability of the painting's state. Either way, the existence of a copy usually attests to a heightened interest in the original. Executing a copy was a difficult and painstaking process, and rarely one entered into lightly or on a whim.

Dürer's efforts toward social elevation in his 1498 *Self Portrait* are even more pronounced (Figure 9). This painting also shows how clothing was used to construct a persona, or to express the desire for status and rank. Dürer's own writings attest to his interest in clothing and various curiosities. He wrote to friends such as the humanist Willibald Pirckheimer about pieces of clothing he obtained on his journeys, once bragging about several fine French and Spanish coats he had purchased.[84] His clothing was a sign of his worldly experience and a means to showing an eminent status. In his 1498 *Self-portrait*, Dürer explicitly presents himself as a young courtly nobleman. Again, Dürer is wearing expensive clothes. He has included a fashionable hat, with a meticulously groomed beard, at the time typically an attribute of older men. His hair is long, contrary to sumptuary law, and parted in the middle. His elegantly gloved hand is particularly significant: a denial of the artisan as labourer, and an explicit attempt to uphold the image of the artist as a gentleman. It is well known that Dürer fashioned this image to lay claim to his social position as a successful and cosmopolitan northern artist, and to challenge the perception of artists as craftsmen. His trip to Venice prior to the creation of this self-portrait had a great impact on him, for while there he took note of the higher social standing accorded to Italian artists. Harsh linearism and precise detail are coupled with a determined stare and clenched fist that seem appropriate for Dürer's self-fashioning as a successful painter. Clearly, Dürer considered himself an exception to the social position normally accorded to northern artists.

The painting would come to be in the possession of a very significant collector, Thomas Howard, the Earl of Arundel (1585–1646). In 1636 the Earl, who was functioning as ambassador of Charles I of England, traveled through Nuremberg on his way to Vienna, leading an embassy from the English king to the Holy Roman Emperor Ferdinand II in Vienna. During this trip, he remarked that he was disappointed to find that 'Herre in this town (Nuremberg) there being not one scratch of Albrecht Dürer's paintings in oyle to be sold, though it were his country.'[85] Arundel's remark reveals not only his emphatic interest in acquiring works by Dürer, but also how thorough Dürer collectors such as Maximilian of Bavaria and Rudolf II of Prague had been. The exception was the 1498 self-portrait, which was presented to the Earl as a gift to the King in 1636, along with a portrait of Dürer's father. Arundel asked Wenceslaus Hollar (1607–1677), an engraver from Bohemia who had spent many years in the service of the Earl in England, to create an etching after the self-portrait (Figure 10).[86] In Hollar's etching the landscape and sitter have been replicated faithfully. The inscription along the bottom states that the etching was made in Antwerp from a painting in the collection of Arundel.[87] Hollar has also included Dürer's monogram and the date on the window ledge. He has added Dürer's original inscription in a place different from the original painting, beneath the sleeve and in imitation of Dürer's handwriting: 'I made this after my image when I was twenty-six years old.' Arundel had a long-standing practice of having the items in his collection etched or engraved, and he requested that Hollar create etchings after other artists as well.[88] This was an important moment of reception for Dürer, given that his reputation in England was not necessarily as high as on the continent.

Another copy of the 1498 self-portrait is intriguing for its retrospective qualities, as much as being a sort of hybrid of quotations, since it also refers to Dürer's earlier 1493 self-portrait with the eryngium. This painting by an anonymous artist (Figure 11), is now in the Herzog-Anton Ulrich Museum. It is a simplified version of the original: the fine details have been reduced in the hair and clothing, the window ledge and fine alpine landscape are not included. In other words, all the Italian elements have been removed. Another significant change in this depiction is that Dürer is now shown holding a flower, a *Maiglöckchen*, making this copy in form and composition a hybrid of Dürer's 1493 and 148 self-portraits. The increased linearism and cut-out quality are more indicative of a late Gothic sensibility. The inscription states that it is a portrait (*imago*), and appears to have been constructed in a commemorative spirit, although Dürer's death is incorrectly stated as 1527. These pictorial quotations of Dürer's self-portraits are indicative of a firm awareness of his oeuvre, and an almost retrospective or nostalgic impulse in style and composition.

Such hybrid works are amongst the most fascinating to emerge from the Dürer-Renaissance. In another combination of multiple Dürer figures (Figure 12), it is fascinating to imagine just how the anonymous painter made decisions as to these visual quotations. As noted previously, such amalgamations were often considered as attempts to improve upon sources. In this case *three* self-portraits by Dürer are used as models: the 1493 and 1498 self-portraits, and the self-portrait that Dürer included in the *Feast of the Rosegarlands* (1506). The anonymous painter has taken the most striking elements of each of his models and created a hybrid Dürer. The positioning of the sitter is identical to that of the 1498 self-portrait, as is the distinctive right arm with its striped sleeve shown resting on a ledge. However, instead of the gloved right hand clasping the left, the right hand has been lifted from the 1493 self-portrait and holds once again the eryngium. Moving upward, the fur-trimmed robe and facial features in this sizeable panel are recognizable from Dürer's self-portrait in *The Feast of the Rosegarlands*. This depiction of Dürer exemplifies how artists sometimes chose to amalgamate aspects of different Dürer self-portraits into one composition. Such amalgamations are indicative of important pictorial principles of imitation common in the sixteenth and seventeenth centuries.

It is also noteworthy that in addition to these amalgamations, there was also an impulse toward isolating the self-portraits that Dürer had included in his own large-scale compositions. To dwell for a moment on Dürer's self-portrait *in assistenza* in the *Feast of the Rosegarlands* before proceeding to its copies: in this painting, Dürer shows himself in half-length format, wearing a richly designed and colourful mantle with fur trim (Figure 46). He holds a *cartellino* upon which his German origins and the date 1506 are stressed. The *Feast of the Rosegarlands* was Dürer's main commission while he was in Venice, and this was the painting that established his international reputation. Of all the self-portraits *in assistenza*, this was the most duplicated one, and Lucas Kilian (1579–1637), one the most important engravers in central Europe, used it as a source at least three times. Kilian had an esteemed reputation himself, he came from a family of engravers that remained active until well into the eighteenth century.[89] His engraving of Dürer dated to 1608 (Figure 13) is perhaps the best known appropriation of Dürer's likeness, as indicated by countless copies that came thereafter. In fact, Kilian's engraving is twice removed from Dürer. As the inscription states, Kilian engraved it after the copy of the *Feast of the Rosegarlands* by Johann Rottenhammer (1564–1625), a German painter who lived and worked in Venice between 1589 and 1606. In fact, Kilian's engraving was created in the same year that Rottenhammer made his copy of the painting, indicating the especially emphatic interest in Dürer's likeness around 1600. Moreover, Kilian's engraving was used by Joachim von Sandrart for his depiction of Dürer in his *Teutsche Academie* (1675), already discussed in the preceding section as perhaps the most concerted attempt to enshrine Dürer in a pantheon of northern artists toward the end of the seventeenth century. In the engraving, Kilian has preserved the half-length composition of Dürer's self-portrait; the clothing, hair and facial features are richly depicted and highly detailed, as if Kilian has taken a microscopic look at the *Feast of the Rosegarlands,* since the original figure is proportionally speaking quite small.

The popularity of Kilian's print is further evidenced by an imitation by Francis Delaram (active *c.*1615–24). Delaram was likely of Netherlandish origin, but his short career was spent in London, mostly in creating portraits and frontispieces.[90] Delaram crops Kilian's image so that only the head and upper collar are shown and includes a decorative curtain that surrounds the image, as if this were a theatrical production (Figure 14). The engraving was also destined to become the frontispiece of a book, as indicated by the title inscribed underneath: *A Booke of the Arte of drawing according to ye order of Albert Dürer, Jean Cozyn and other excellent Picture-makers, describing ye true proportions of Men, Women & Children.* This early English drawing book, published between 1652 and 1685 in five editions, and again in two editions of 1718 and 1731, includes plates illustrating the parts of the human body that are in part derived from Dürer's *Four Books on Human Proportion* (1528).[91] This is a remarkable instance of the use of Dürer's features as a selling point in England, as well as the interest in his theoretical writings.

Another highly inventive use a Dürer self-portrait can be seen in *Dürer before a Panaroma of Nuremberg,* by an anonymous artist from the late seventeenth century (Figure 19). Here, Dürer's self-portrait from the *Adoration of the Trinity (Landauer Altarpiece)* of 1511 (Figure 15) is the model. The artist has been extricated from his original surroundings, an open field with mountains in the distance, and placed in front of a cityscape of Nuremberg. Dürer's Nuremberg origins are thus clearly emphasized visually, as well as in the short biography contained in the inscription. While the picture is dated 1553, it has been surmised that this version is a copy and stemming from the seventeenth century. It is also signed HSL, which has led scholars to conclude that it is likely a copy of a lost work by Hans Lautensack (1520–1566) of Bamberg, who was known for his etched landscapes. He also carved moulds for portrait medals; thus he was well versed in commemorative works. Often he positioned Nuremberg patricians before a landscape; Dürer had definitively attained an elevated social status to be included in the category of patrician.[92]

The final self-portrait to be considered is Dürer's 1500 *Self Portrait* (Figure 16). Wearing a richly designed fox fur coat that would typically be worn by members of the aristocracy, Dürer's public face for posterity was complete. As has been much discussed elsewhere, what is especially striking about this self-portrait is its confronting and fully frontal composition, and the manner in which Dürer stares unflinchingly at the viewer. There is no precedent for this painting in portraiture, which until then had for the most part been restricted to images of noblemen in profile. More importantly, until Dürer's 1500 *Self-portrait,* the frontal pose had been reserved for images of Christ. There has been much debate as to Dürer's intentions when creating this self-portrait, and whether it is to be read as a pious emulation of Christ, or stands as an assertion of the freedom and autonomy of the artist.[93] In either reading it is the affinity between Dürer's pose and depictions of Christ in the Byzantine tradition as *Salvator Mundi* – depictions in which Christ is shown in the act of blessing – that has been noted by many scholars.[94] As an artist working in a religious context that had powerful injunctions against self-regard, the possibility that Dürer's self-presentation involved drawing parallels between his own life and that of Christ can be interpreted along the lines of *imitatio Christi*, or the practice of imitating Christ as a way to piety (as advocated in the sixteenth century). This *Self-portrait* was in Dürer's possession until his death, and his depiction could have been intended as a personal statement of faith. The idea of achieving piety through emulation of Christ was a powerful one in Renaissance Germany.

The belief that Dürer might have been attempting to equate himself with Christ stems in part from later uses of this self-portrait by artists during the seventeenth century. After Dürer's death his self-portrait was placed in the Nuremberg town hall. Georg Vischer used the self-portrait as a model for his depiction of *Christ and the Adulterous Woman*, painted in 1637 while in the employ of Duke Maximilian I of Bavaria (Figure 17). The figure of Christ in the centre of the image is based on the likeness of Dürer, with the same long hair, beard, piercing eyes, and hand raised in the gesture of a blessing. Thus, it is important to note that the assumption that Dürer sought to portray himself as Christ has a visual history in itself. Vischer's appropriation of Dürer would have been recognized, for as we have seen Dürer's face became well known in the sixteenth and seventeenth centuries due to the numerous images of his likeness. Vischer's *Christ and the Adulterous Women* is indicative of a context in which Dürer's works, and by extension his likeness, were used as a prototype worthy of being imitated.

The final image to be discussed in this chapter is Lucas Kilian's so-called *Double Portrait* of Dürer from 1617 (Figure 18). This engraving neatly summarizes all the characteristics that have been identified as forming part of the Dürer-Renaissance, the historiographic problem with which this book began. As has already been noted, Kilian was certainly one of the best known of the engravers in central Europe, and it can be assumed that his *Double Portrait of Dürer* was well known from the time of its creation. In this skilfull and highly finished engraving he has made a commemorative tribute to Dürer. Often referred to as the *Ehrentempel* (temple of honour), the engraving shows two figures, both representing Dürer, standing in the foreground of what has alternately been described as a classical temple, memorial arch, or altar. While an argument could be made for each, it seems more appropriate to say that the architecture is fanciful and combines elements of all three prototypes. This engraving was designed as a tribute to Dürer almost a century after his death, and the architecture overall has the appearance of commemoration. The inscription above the temple refers to Dürer as the first among German painters and gives authorship of the print to Lucas Kilian. There are tidy references to Dürer's family name – the roots of 'Dürer' lie in the word *Tür* (German for door) – and appropriately, in the festooned oval crest above the arch, an open door is depicted.

Significantly, both of the Dürer figures are appropriations of self-portraits that Dürer himself included in two of his major altarpieces: the *Adoration of the Trinity* and the *Heller Altar*. Kilian draws attention to this appropriation himself in the inscription below. The use of these two self-portraits indicates not only Kilian's knowledge of two of Dürer's major commissions, but also the manner in which Dürer's features had become well known and were central to his seventeenth-century reception. As we have seen throughout this chapter, Dürer carefully fostered his own image in his lifetime with his self-portraits and detailed autobiographical writings. It can hardly be a coincidence that there are more seventeenth-century portraits of Dürer than of any other artist.

Kilian's assimilation of these elements within his engraving illustrates the creative manner in which seventeenth-century artists used motifs from works by Dürer, as well as Dürer's paragon status. This engraved double portrait highlights the diversity of Dürer, his capacity to work in both a theoretical and practical capacity, the idea of Dürer as eminent artist and scientist, as much as the reverence in which he was held. Dürer is shown as having mastered the art of proportion on the left side of the print, symbolized by the compass he is holding, and as an exemplary graphic artist and painter on the right, suggested by numerous attributes including the painter's palette suspended above him as well as the model of a nude on the table before him. Overall, the engraving epitomizes the Dürer-Renaissance in a number of ways. First, it stands as a tribute to the artist, who had been dead for almost 100 years. Secondly, it exemplifies the manner in which aspects of Dürer's artistry were assimilated to create new images, in this case Kilian's use of two separate self-portraits by Dürer. Thirdly, the altarpieces in which these self-portraits appeared are the *Adoration of the Trinity* and the *Heller Altar*: the former acquired by Rudolf II in Prague in 1585, the latter acquired by Maximilian I in Munich in 1614. Kilian has thus brought together, in a sense, the two biggest proponents of the Dürer Renaissance. And finally, the engraving is a stark claim for Dürer as not only a pre-eminent artist, but as a scientist as well. It is clear that through contemporary writings and a proliferation of his image, both in portraiture and self-portraiture, Dürer had attained the status of a paragon in the period under scrutiny.

Notes

1 Jan Białostocki, Dürer and His Critics 1500–1971: *Chapters in the History of Ideas Including a Collection of Texts* (Baden-Baden: Valentin Koerner, 1986).

2 Hans Rupprich, ed., *Dürer-Schriftlicher Nachlass* (Berlin: Deutscher Verein für Kunstwissenschaft, 1956), vol.1, pp. 27–34.

3 This point is also made by Jane Campbell Hutchison in her *Albrecht Dürer: A Biography* (Princeton: Princeton University Press, 1990): p. 3.

4 This copy is now also lost. It was known because of the Nuremberg book dealer Friedrich Campe (1776–1846) who edited an edition of Dürer's autobiographical writings, and had in his possession the Petzolt manuscript (which was possibly Dürer's original). Two other copies survive: one transcribed by Nicholaus Paul Helffreich (d.1684), a member of the Nuremberg City Council, see Bamberg, Staatliche Bibliothek, J.H.Msc.art.50,III.12; and one in the Nuremberg Stadtbibliothek, Will-Nor.III 915b and 916 fol.pap. Both of these were copied from the same archetype.

5 Joachim von Sandrart, *Academie der Bau-, Bild- und Mahlerey-Künste von 1675. Leben der berühmten Maler, Bildhauer und Baumeister*, compiled by Rudolf Arthur Peltzer (Munich: G. Hirth, 1925).

6 No written records survive for Dürer's bachelor's journey, the itinerary of which has been subjected to much scholarly speculation. It has been surmised that Dürer stopped in some or possibly all of the following cities, Xanten, Wesel, Kalkar and Bocholt. See Campbell Hutchison, *Albrecht Dürer*, pp. 27–39, for a thorough account of Dürer's journeyman years.

7 For Dürer's trips to Italy, the literature is extensive: see primarily André Chastel, 'Dürer à Venise en 1506', in *Giorgione e l'humanesimo veneziano,* edited by Rodolfo Pallucchini (Florence: L.S. Olschki, 1981), pp. 459–463; Josef Meder, 'Zur ersten Reise nach Venedig (1494–95)', *Jahrbuch der Kunsthistorischen Sammlungen des Allerhöchsten Kaiserhauses* 30 (1911): pp. 183–227. For Dürer's presence in Venice see especially Fritz Koreny, 'Venice and Dürer', in *Renaissance Venice and the North: Crosscurrents in the Time of Bellini, Dürer and Titian*, edited by Bernard Aikema and Beverly Louise Brown (New York: Rizzoli, 1999): pp. 240–249; this publication includes other useful essays on the topic. The most recent contribution to the subject of the influence of Italian art on Dürer is Katherine Luber Crawford, *Albrecht Dürer and the Venetian Renaissance* (New York: Cambridge University Press, 2005).

8 Dürer likely traveled to the Netherlands in order to secure employment from Charles V, the newly crowned emperor. For Dürer's travels in the Netherlands see Fedja Anzelewsky, ed., *Albrecht Dürer aux Pays-Bas, son voyage 1520–21, son influence* (Brussels: Palais des Beaux-Arts, 1977); Albert Châtelet, 'Dürer und die nördlichen Niederlande', *Anzeiger des Germanischen Nationalmuseums* (1975): pp. 52–64; Philip Troutman, *Albrecht Dürer: Sketchbook of his Journey to the Netherlands, 1520–21* (London: Elek, 1971); Julius Held, *Dürers Wirkung auf die niederländische Kunst seiner Zeit* (The Hague: M. Nijhoff, 1931).

9 Hans Rupprich, *Dürer-Schriftlicher Nachlass*, vol. 1, p. 185. For further information on the pre-Columbian art seen by Dürer, see Linda Duychuk, *Dürer and Vera Cruz* (unpublished M.A. Thesis: University of Wisconsin-Madison, 1989).

10 For a general discussion of the increasing mobility and trade of art see Pamela H. Smith and Paula Findlen, *Merchants and Marvels: Commerce, Science and Art in Early Modern Europe* (New York, London: Routledge, 2002).

11 Białostocki 1986, p. 15.

12 Rupprich, *Dürers-Schriftlicher Nachlass.*

13 Franz Fuhse, 'Zur Dürerforschung im 17. Jahrhundert', *Mitteilungen aus dem Germanischen Nationalmuseum* (1895): pp. 66–73.

14 The painting has long been referred to as *The Four Apostles,* although as has been pointed out in numerous publications, this is an incorrect designation, since two of the four figures painted by Dürer are evangelists: Mark and John. Henceforth, the painting will also be referred to as *The Four Holy Men.*

15 David Price, *Albrecht Dürer's Renaissance: Humanism, Reformation, and the Art of Faith* (Ann Arbor: University of Michigan Press, 2003).

16 For a discussion of sixteenth-century comparisons of Dürer with Apelles, see Jan Białostocki, 'Alter Apelles', in *Dürer and His Critics 1500–1971: Chapters in the History of Ideas Including a Collection of Texts* (Baden-Baden: Valentin Koerner, 1986): pp. 15–36; Heinz Lüdecke and Susanne Heiland, 'Deutsche Humanisten und Reformatoren', in *Dürer und die Nachwelt* (Berlin: Rütten & Loening, 1955). For two overviews on Apelles used as a literary device in artistic biography see Ernst Kris and Otto Kurz, *Legend, Myth and Magic in the Image of the Artist: A Historical Experiment* (New Haven: Yale University Press, 1979); David Cast, *The Calumny of Apelles: A Study in the Humanistic Tradition* (New Haven: Yale University Press, 1981).

17 Catherine M. Soussloff, 'Imitatio Buonarroti', *Sixteenth Century Journal* 20/4 (1989): p. 581.

18 Białostocki 1986, p. 16.

19 For biographical information on Celtis see Dieter Wuttke, *Humanismus als Integrative Kraft: die Philosophia des deutschen 'Erzhumanisten' Conrad Celtis: eine ikonologische Studie zu programmatischer Graphik Dürers und Burgkmairs* (Nürnberg: H. Carl, 1985).

20 Białostocki 1986, p. 18.

21 The eulogy was inserted in Erasmus' *Dialogus de recta Latini Graecique sermonis pronuntiatione* (1528). On this eulogy see Erwin Panofsky, '"Nebulae in Pariete"; Notes on Erasmus' Eulogy on Dürer', *Journal of the Warburg and Courtauld Institutes* 14(1/2) (1951): pp. 34–41.

22 Panofsky 1951, p. 37.

23 Panofsky 1951, p. 37.

24 Albrecht Dürer, *Unterweysung der Messung mit dem Zirkel und Richtscheit*, facsimile of the 1525 edition (Zürich: Dietikon, 1966).

25 Panofsky 1951, p. 36.

26 Białostocki 1986, p. 17.

27 Melanchthon continues: 'He said that he was no longer an admirer of his own works, as once he had been, but that he rather groaned in looking at his paintings and thinking of his own infirmity.' As translated in Białostocki 1986, p. 34.

28 Johann Neudörfer, *Des Johann Neudörfer schreib- und rechenmeisters zu Nürnberg nachrichten von künstlern und werkleuten daselbst aus dem jahre 1547, nebst der fortzetzung des Andreas Gulden, nach den handschriften und mit anmerkungen hrsg. von G.W.K. Lochner*, compiled by G.W.K. Lochner (Wien, W. Braumüller, 1875).

29 Hans Kauffmann for instance does not take Neudörfer seriously; Kauffmann 1954, p. 23.

30 Neudörfer 1547/1875, p. 133, p. 138.

31 For the most detailed discussion of the paintings, including important technical examinations, see Gisela Goldberg, Bruno Heimberg and Martin Schwae, eds, *Albrecht Dürer: Die Gemälde der Alten Pinakothek* (Heidelberg: Braus, 1998): pp. 479–559.

32 Neudörfer 1547/1875, p. 133, p. 138.

33 Stephan Kunkler, *Zwischen Humanismus und Reformation: der Humanist Joachim Camerarius (1500–1574) im Wechselspiel von pädagogischem Pathos und theologischem Ethos* (Hildesheim: Olms, 2000).

34 Białostocki 1986, pp. 21–22.

35 Białostocki 1986, p. 52.

36 Dominicus Lampsonius, *Lamberti Lombardi apud Eburones pictoris celeberrimi vita. Pictoribus, sculptoribus, architectis, allisque id genus artificibus utilis et necessaria* (Bruges, 1565).

37 Jochen Becker, 'Zur Niederländischen Kunstliteratur des 16. Jahrhunderts: Domenicus Lampsonius', *Nederlands Kunsthistorisch Jaarboek* 24 (1973): pp. 45–61, at pp. 46–47.

38 For further details on Lampsonius see Becker, 'Zur Niederländischen Kunstliteratur des 16. Jahrhunderts'.

39 Quoted in Iain Buchanan, 'Dürer and Abraham Ortelius', *The Burlington Magazine* 124 (1982): p. 735.

40 Sarah Meiers, 'Portraits in Print: Hieronymous Cock, Dominicus Lampsonius, and *Pictorum aliquot celebrium Germaniae inferioris effigies*', *Zeitschrift für Kunstgeschichte* 69 (2006): pp. 1–16, at p. 16.

41 Meiers argues that more than likely Hieronymous Cock (1518–1570) was the conceiver of the series (described by Meiers as a 'paradigmatic' sixteenth-century printmaker). Meiers 2006, p. 1.

42 Meiers 2006, p. 2.

43 Meiers 2006, p. 4.

44 Giorgio Vasari, *Lives of the Most Eminent Painters, Sculptors, and Architects: Translated from the Italian of Giorgio Vasari*, translated by Jean Paul Richter (London: H.G. Bohn, 1907).

45 Sharon Gregory, *Vasari and Northern Prints: An Examination of Giorgio Vasari's Comments on, and Uses of Woodcuts and Engravings by Martin Schongauer, Albrecht Dürer and Lucas van Leyden*. Unpublished M.A.Thesis (Kingston: Queen's University, 1992).

46 Giovanni Paolo Lomazzo, *Trattato dell'Arte della Pittura, divisio in VII libri, nei quali si contiene tutte la Teoria e la Practica di essa Pittura* (Milan, 1584). It was also reprinted in the following year.

47 Giovanni Paolo Lomazzo, *A Tracte Containing the Artes of Curious Paintinge and Buildinge*, translated by Richard Haydocke (Oxford: Joseph Barnes, 1598): p. 39.

48 Białostocki 1986, p. 55.

49 The phrase in the Dutch is '*Poetelijk schilder*'. For van Mander's discussion of Dürer, see Carel van Mander, *Schilder-boek,* translated by Hessel Miedema (Doornspijk: Davaco, 1994–1999), vol.1, fols. 207v–210r.

50 Białostocki 1986, p. 54.

51 'Het is verwonderlijck, en schier onghelooflijck, wat dit stuck den Monicken oft het Clooster Iaerlijcx opbrengt, en nut is, alleen van de vereeringhen oft drinckpenninghen, die voor het ontsluyten oft toonen, van Heeren, Coopluyden, reys volck, en Const-liefdige worden gheschoncken: dit was gedaen van hem A. 1509.' Van Mander 1604/1999, fol. 209r.

52 Jane Campbell Hutchison, *Albrecht Dürer: A Biography* (Princeton: Princeton University Press, 1990), p. 150.

53 Hutchison 1990, p. 160.

54 'Von den Künsternen und andern admiratoribus fur Heiligthumb verwaret.' Cited in Białostocki 1986, p. 23.

55 Germanisches Nationalmuseum, Archiv (Rst Nürnberg XII/44). The other copy of the manuscript is in Bamberg; however the Bamberg manuscript is not in Hauer's writing, See Andreas Tacke, '*Der Mahler Ordnung und Gebräuch in Nürmberg*': *Die Nürnberger Maler(zunft)bücher ergänzt durch weitere Quellen, Genealogien und Viten des 16., 17. und 18. Jahrhunderts* (München, Berlin: Deutscher Kunstverlag, 2001): p. 126, n. 415.

56 The *Adoration of the Trinity (the Landauer Altar)* was purchased 1585 by Rudolf II, the *Paumgartner Altar* was purchased 1613 by Maximilian I, the *Heller Altar* was purchased 1614 by Maximilian I, and the *Four Apostles* was purchased in 1627 by Maximilan I.

57 Sandrart, *Teustche Academie der edlen Bau-*. On Sandrart see also Henry Ley, 'Dürer and the 17th Century', *Essays on Dürer* (Manchester: University of Manchester Press, 1973); Christian Klemm, *Joachim von Sandrart: Kunst Werke und Lebens Lauf* (Berlin: Deutscher Verlag für Kunstwissenshaft, 1986).

58 Sandrart 1675/1925, p. 255.

59 Ley 1973, p. 107.

60 'Die Dürer-Renaissance findet in Sandrarts Artikel in der Teutschen Akademie ihren Abschluß und Wissenschaftlichen Niederschlag. Mit der fortschretenden Aufklärung sinkt im Gefolge des Vordringes französicher Kultur das Ansehen Dürers zusammen mit der der Gotik . Dürers Kunst wird als altfränkisches Wesen mit nachsichtigem Lächeln betrachtet, bis sie im Zeitalter der Empfinsamkeit und des Sturmes und Dranges wieder entdeckt wird.' Ludwig Grote, 'Vom Nachleben Dürers: Beiträge zur Kunst der Epoche von 1530 bis 1650', *Anzeiger des Germanischen National-Museums* 1940–1953, p. 6.

61 Roger de Piles, *Cours de Peinture par Principe*, facsimile of 1708 edition with a preface by Jacques Thuillier (Paris: Gallimard, 1989).

62 Jacques Thuillier, 'Préface', in Piles, p. 1.

63 For the different artists who depicted Dürer in print see B.T. Ross, 'Prints depicting Albrecht Dürer', *Record of the Art Museums of Princeton University* 31 (1971): pp. 72–75. Ross also cites Joseph Heller as listing 115 depictions of Dürer.

64 Joseph Leo Koerner discusses both of these episodes: *The Moment of Self-Portraiture in German Renaissance Art* (Chicago: University of Chicago Press, 1993): pp. 249–250.

65 The most useful literature on the medals is Matthias Mende, *Dürer Medaillen: Münzen, Medaillen, Plaketten von Dürer, auf Dürer, nach Dürer* (Nuremberg: Verlag Hans Karl, 1990); for this particular medal see Mende 1990, no. 16; also Lüdecke/Heiland 1955, no. 16.

66 Bartrum, *Albrecht Dürer and his Legacy*, p. 84.

67 Lüdecke and Heiland 1955, no. 16b; Frankfurt 1981, no. 45; Mende 1990, no. 34; London 2002, no. 11.

68 For example, he worked with Hans Springinklee on the *Hortulus animae* (published in Nuremberg 1515 by Anton Koberger); Springinklee is known to have lived in the Dürer house as a pupil. Lüdecke and Heiland 1955, no. 17; Adam von Bartsch, *The Illustrated Bartsch*. 22 volumes. [Originally published as *Le peintre graveur* in 1922] (New York: Abaris Books, 1978), 156; London 2002, no. 12.

69 One of these reprints was created by Andrea Andreani (1558/9–1629) and includes the following inscription in Italian: 'Andrea Andreani of Mantua cut this print in 1588 in Siena.' Andreani was an Italian designer who specialized in chiaroscuro. Dürer's religious prints in particular were immensely popular and widely copied well into the sixteenth century in Italy, particularly by

Florentine artists. See the exhibition catalogue Bartrum, ed., *Albrecht Dürer and his Legacy*, p. 87; for coloured impressions see Gmelin 1983, no. 11.

70 Bartrum, ed., *Albrecht Dürer and his Legacy*, no. 14.

71 Bartrum, ed., *Albrecht Dürer and his Legacy*, no. 15.

72 For full-length treatments of Dürer's self-portraits see Koerner, *The Moment of Self Portraiture;* Hugo Kehrer, *Dürers Selbstbilnisse und die Dürer-Bildnisse* (Berlin: Gebr. Mann, 1934). For discussion of self-portraits in general see Joanna Woods-Marsden, *Renaissance Self-Portraiture: The Visual Construction of Identity and the Social Status of the Artist* (New Haven, London: Yale University Press, 1998).

73 For a detailed discussion of *cartellinos* in Venetian painting, see Louisa C. Matthew, 'The Painter's Presence: Signatures in Venetian Renaissance Pictures', *The Art Bulletin* 80/4 (1998): pp. 616–648. As pointed out by Matthew, 'a *cartellino* is any form of fictive paper carrying an inscription' and was used most often as a form of promotion, or in order to increase recognition. By the second half of the fifteenth century, this form of signature had become a convention in Venice. Matthew 1998, p. 633.

74 There can be no doubt that the autonomous self-portraits were carefully constructed. Each can be understood in part in terms of the social and cultural significance attached to various pieces of clothing, as Volker Manuth has argued: see Volker Manuth, 'Dürer ein Dandy? Beobachtungen zum Kostum des Künstlers', in *Aus Albrecht Dürers Welt. Festschrift für Fedja Anzelewsky*, edited by Bodo Brinkmann, Hartmut Krohm and Michael Roth (Turnhout: Brepols, 2001): pp. 165–171.

75 The standard reference for Dürer's drawings remains Friedrich Winkler's catalogue; for this drawing see Friedrich Winkler, *Die Zeichnungen Albrecht Dürers*, 4 volumes (Berlin, 1936–9), vol. 1, no. 1.

76 For the most thorough treatment of Hans Hoffmann see Kurt Pilz, 'Hans Hoffmann: Ein Dürer-Nachahmer aus der 2. Hälfte des 16. Jahrhunderts,' *Mitteilungen des Vereins für Geschichte der Stadt Nürnberg* 51 (1962): pp. 236–272.

77 The Dürer drawing was included in the Imhoff inventory of 1588. Hoffmann's drawing is dated 1576, which means that Hoffmann would have executed his copy of Dürer's drawing while it was still in Nuremberg, where he would have had access to all the Dürer drawings and prints in the Imhoff collection. The Imhoff inventory of 1588 is reproduced in Fritz Koreny, *Dürer and the Plant and Animal Studies of the Renaissance* (Vienna: Albertina, 1985): pp. 261–262. The entry for the Dürer drawing reads as follows: 'Self-Portrait of Albrecht Dürer done when still a child in silverpoint', Koreny 1985, p. 262. The inventory for the Imhoff collection has also been published, in its original language, in Hendrik Budde, *Die Kunstsammlung des Nürnberger Patriziers Willibald Imhoff unter besonderer Berücksichtigung der Werke Albrecht Dürers* (Münster: LIT Verlag, 1996); this is a very important source on all aspects of the Imhoff collection, and includes the original inventory documents.

78 Jeroen Stumpel and Joelein van Kregten, 'In the name of the thistle: Albrecht Dürer's self-portrait of 1493', *Burlington Magazine* 1186 (2002): pp. 14–18.

79 Stumpel and Kregten 2002, p. 18.

80 For the important details on the significance of clothing in Renaissance Nuremberg, see Jutta Zander-Seidel, *Textiler Hausrat – Kleidung und Haustextilien in Nürnberg von 1500–1650* (München: Deutscher Kunstverlag, 1990); Liselotte C. Eisenbart, *Kleiderordnungen der deutschen Städte zwischen 1350 und 1700* (Göttingen: Müster Schmidt, 1962).

81 Quoted in Jean C. Wilson, 'Enframing Aspirations: Albrecht Dürer's Self-Portrait of 1493 in the Musée du Louvre', *Gazette des Beaux-Arts* 126 (1995): p. 155.

82 For the history of the painting, see Anzelewsky 1991, pp. 118–119.

83 The copy was included in Lüdecke and Heiland 1955, p. 433.

84 'Item mein frantzossicher mantell lest ewch grossen mein welscher rockh awch'; Rupprich 1956, vol. 1, p. 55. 'Mehr hat mir herr Erasmus geschenckt ein spanioleins mantelle'; Rupprich 1956, vol. 1, p. 152.

85 Cited in Vienna 1994, Karl Schütz, 'Die Dürerrenaissance des späten 16. und 17. Jahrhunderts', in *Albrecht Dürer im Kunsthistorischen Museum*, exhib. cat. (Wien: Kunsthistorisches Museum, 1994): p. 55.

86 Richard Pennington, *A Descriptive Catalogue of the Etched Works of Wenceslaus Hollar 1607–1677* (Cambridge: Cambridge University Press, 1982), p. 238, no. 1390; see also Bartrum, *Albrecht Dürer and his Legacy*, pp. 90–91.

87 'Wenceslaus Hollar Bohemus fecit ex Collectione Arundeliana, A o. 1645. Antverpiae'.

88 Hollar also made etchings after Holbein. See Johannes Urzidil, *Wenceslaus Hollar, der Kupferstecher des Barock* (Vienna: R. Passner, 1936).

89 For details on Kilian, see Thomas DaCosta Kaufmann, *Drawings from the Holy Roman Empire: A Selection from North American Collections 1540–1680* (Princeton: Princeton University, 1982) p. 104.

90 London 2002, no. 17.

91 London 2002, no. 17.

92 Hannover 1979, Hans Georg Gmelin, *Dürerrenaissance um 1600: Im Blickpunkt,* edited by (Hannover: Niedersächsische Landesgalerie, 1979), no. 1.

93 Koerner describes it as the most programmatic and self-conscious of Dürer's works, constructed with a particular idea of reception in mind. He claims that the image is rife with codes of authorship and intended as a preparation for posterity, and that 'Dürer was the great original for German Renaissance art, the transforming instance that all later talents within the tradition endeavored to emulate, imitate, avoid or distort.' Koerner 1993, p. xvi.

94 Charles D. Cuttler, 'Undercurrents in Dürer's 1500 Self-portrait', *Pantheon* 50 (1992), pp. 24–27; Daniel Hess, 'Dürers Selbstbildniss von 1500– "Alter Deus' oder Neuer Apelles?"', *Mitteilungen des Vereins für Geschichte der Stadt Nürnberg* 77 (1990): pp. 63–90; Donat de Chapeaurouge, 'Der Christ als Christus. Darstellungen der Angleichung an Gott in der Kunst des Mittelalters', *Wallraf-Richartz Jahrbuch* 48/49 (1987): pp. 77–96; Klaus H. Jürgens, 'Neue Forschungen zu dem Münchner Selbstbildnis des Jahres 1500 von Albrecht Dürer', *Kunsthistorisches Jahrbuch Graz* (1983): pp. 167–190; Fedja Anzelewsky, 'Dürers Selbstbildnis aus dem Jahre 1500', *Ars Auro Prior. Studia Joanni Białostocki Sexagenario Dicata* (Warsaw: 1981): pp. 287–290.

2

Collecting Dürer

Many presiding ideas about connoisseurship can be traced back to the manner in which works by Dürer made their way into various collections in the sixteenth and seventeenth centuries. Dürer himself participated in collecting works on paper, preserving drawings by Martin Schongauer and Raphael as objects valuable for their link to a particular master. Thus, before his own drawings and prints became prized as highly collectible items, Dürer himself acted as a connoisseur and collector. The collecting sensibility (discussed in this chapter) could of course enable creative copying (the subject of Chapter 3) as the case of Dürer himself again demonstrates – Dürer often recycled compositions by Martin Schongauer, the Housebook Master, Master ES, or Mantegna (as demonstrated by his pen drawing of Mantegna's *Battle of the Sea Gods*). A desire for preservation for posterity is discernible in how Dürer preserved his own works: in 1490 he began initialling all his drawings. No artist did this for centuries after.[1]

The migrations of Dürer's works occurred with great frequency in the seventeenth century. In addition to his more transportable prints and drawings, Dürer's altarpieces, which had served such important purposes *in situ*, were removed from their original locations. The endeavours of the great collectors of the period, especially Holy Roman Emperor Rudolf II, Maximilian I of Bavaria, and Archduke Ferdinand of Tyrol were so thorough that it became difficult to find Dürer's works in their original locations. After a visit to Nuremberg in 1636, Thomas Howard, Earl of Arundel, ambassador of Charles I of England, remarked that he was disappointed to find that 'herre in this town [Nuremberg] there being not one scratch of Albrecht Dürer's paintings in oyle to be sold, though it were his country'.[2] The removal of Dürer's works was also lamented by Johann Hauer (1586–1660), one of the earliest of Dürer scholars.[3] It is important to remember that a collector's gain comes at the loss of another, and why original owners would allow for the removal or purchase of their esteemed works by Dürer is an important question. It is noteworthy that at a time when Dürer was the subject of international admiration, the Nuremberg Rathaus gave up the *Four Holy Men*, the church of San Bartolomeo in Venice gave up the *Feast of the Rosegarlands*, and the Landauer Zwölfbrüderhaus gave up the *Landauer Altar*.[4] These works all served vital functions in their original locations, and their removal speaks to the power of the collectors of the period.

Collecting in the sixteenth and seventeenth centuries was of a political and competitive nature, as illustrated by the diplomacy often necessary for acquisitions. As art became increasingly mobile, the ambitions of collectors grew. The removal of paintings from their original locations at an increased rate, and the ease with which prints could be transported, both contributed to a burgeoning culture of collecting. An increased metropolitan outlook ensued amongst collectors in their efforts to obtain art that reflected their personal tastes and wealth, as well as their commitment to tradition and culture.[5]

In this context, the art of Dürer fast became a commodity essential to all the major collectors, especially north of the Alps, in the period immediately after his death and increasingly so in the seventeenth century. Dürer's paragon status, especially in central Europe, resulted in a rapid dissemination of his work due to the efforts of independent and princely collectors. This chapter will show how a major aspect of the Dürer-Renaissance is the increase in the activity of collecting Dürer. Apart from the major collectors to be discussed in what follows, there are other, lesser-known collectors who participated in this phenomenon. For example, Jan Terunzo, the Bishop of Wrocław, acquired Dürer's panel paintings of *Adam and Eve* (1507), now in the Prado in Madrid.[6] The inventory for the Elector of Saxony from 1587 shows the purchase of 182 Dürer prints, forming the core of a *Kunstkammer* that he founded in 1560.[7]

Mark McDonald has pointed out that 'whereas Dürer's impact on artistic production is easy to trace, how contemporary collectors viewed him is not so easy to ascertain'.[8] Unlike the humanists and theorists, it is rare to find a direct statement from a collector in the period under scrutiny. Instead, inventories and attempts at reconstructing collections must be relied upon for comprehending collecting practices. Provenance research and investigations into copies can also reveal a great deal. Thanks to this primary source material, it is possible to reconstruct who held major collections of Dürer prints during the sixteenth and seventeenth centuries, as well as to ascertain the major acquisitions of his painted works, particularly the altarpieces. By 1600 a huge proportion of Dürer's painted works were in either Prague or Munich, and by the late seventeenth century, Vienna would become another major repository for his works.

Dürer's place in major court collections of period testify to his increased status, and also the centrality of court culture to this narrative of Dürer's reception. The encyclopaedic qualities of *Kunstkammern*, as well as the tastes of individuals, are considered here. This will prepare the way for the discussion in Chapter 3 of the artistic appropriations that later occurred. The retrospective quality of the Dürer-Renaissance was not simply a consequence of art being accessible through prints; court culture and copies of painted works must also be considered as vital too. Moreover, it was the paintings and drawings that were collected by Maximilian I and Rudolf II that would lead to the most intriguing artistic appropriations of all. This chapter on collecting will be essential for outlining precisely who owned which works by Dürer, in order to understand what court artists would have had access to. The princely collectors are contrasted with the earlier collectors, mostly patricians, and especially those from Nuremberg, whose strong interest in the works of Dürer were usually directed toward obtaining complete sets of his prints, a more plausible and easily realized endeavour early on.[9]

It is to a consideration of the collecting of Dürer's works on paper that I now turn. It seems logical to begin with the works more easily accessible and transportable. Further, in terms of chronology, it was the prints by Dürer that became collector's items first (only later would Dürer's paintings migrate from their original locations). A thorough examination of Dürer in some print collections will aid in discerning the prevailing tastes and the reception of Dürer.

Early Collections of Dürer

For an understanding of the early propagation of Dürer's prints, it is necessary to turn to the activities of Dürer himself. In 1497 Dürer began to employ an agent, Contz Swytzer, who was empowered to handle his print sales in foreign lands. This contract (now preserved in the Nuremberg Stadtsarchiv) required that Swytzer sell the prints at the highest prices, and cautioned him not to linger where there was no money to be made. For his services Swytzer received a salary: one-half a Rhenish florin weekly, and three *pfund* in addition for expenses.[10] In 1500, another salesman by the name of Jakob Arnold was hired by Dürer. Arnold was engaged by Dürer in a legal contract that made provisions for Dürer to be compensated if the prints were damaged by Arnold during his travels.[11]

At the centre of the Holy Roman Empire and trade routes from north to south and east to west, Nuremberg was the ideal location for a graphic artist seeking to distribute his works. Moreover, Dürer could count on a steady supply of paper thanks to Nuremberg's paper mill, one of the first in the German lands, founded in 1390. Well-equipped, working in a city at a crossroads for many travellers, and with travelling salesmen in his employ – these are all reasons for the speed with which Dürer became an internationally acclaimed artist in his lifetime. As was discussed in Chapter 1, Dürer's reputation and character were tended to as a source of northern pride, and this unusually heightened interest is largely reflected in contemporary writings and the commemorative portraiture that emerged after his death. Of course, the proliferation of his prints also contributed to the esteem in which he was held. Dürer was celebrated as master of the graphic arts and was, in the words of Erasmus, '[t]he Apelles of Black Lines'.[12] Collecting graphic art was also attractive to the burgeoning professionals in urban centres. For example, Melchior Ayrer was a medical doctor from Nuremberg whose collection of prints was formed during the second half of the sixteenth century. Two inventories are extant for his collection, which contained a substantial number of engravings and woodcuts. When inherited by his son Julius, the collection was expanded by 20,000 sheets. A partial inventory of the collection was preserved by Joachim von Sandrart in his *Teutsche Academie* of 1675.[13]

Dürer prints were attractive to collectors not only because they exemplified a medium in which Dürer excelled, but also because they were more easily obtainable than painted works. The main sources for understanding the history of print collecting are inventories, which provide information about collecting preferences, schemes of organization and means of display. Apart from inventories, there is little remaining evidence, for as noted above, it is very rare to find a direct statement from a collector. During the sixteenth and seventeenth centuries accessibility to works of art may have increased due to the size and easily transportable nature of prints; however, ownership brought with it another set of problems. Organizing prints in an intellectually coherent and accessible manner was certainly a challenge for the collectors of the period, whose collections sometimes numbered in the thousands. Initially, two separate solutions to this problem developed. The first was to give priority to the subject depicted, and the second prioritized authorship and the region or school of origin of the print.[14]

It could be argued that the proliferation of Dürer prints contributed to emphasis on the latter, especially in the seventeenth century. An interest in authorship, which often involved an interest in the personality of the artist himself, resulted in a different organization scheme for prints. The evidence from the earliest collections suggests that less consideration was given to the artist or his origin, and the print was valued more as a depiction of a certain theme. The 1580 inventory for the collection of Geerard Grameye of Antwerp is arranged according to topics, such as classical, biblical, architectural, landscape.[15] In Nuremberg, Paul Beheim arranged his collection chronologically and in certain cases by theme.[16] The Strassburg collector Balthasar Kunäst used topical groupings, with some attention to national schools.[17] The organization of graphics according to subject would continue. Indeed, it has been suggested that such an approach was revitalized in the later seventeenth century 'when didactic and descriptive rationales for acquiring prints were stressed in the writings of critics and patrons'.[18]

Many scholars have noted that with Dürer came a shift in the overall history of the print collecting. Even in the collections organized topically, an exception was made by creating a separate category for his works. This point is stressed by Peter Parshall, who after examining a number of inventories in Antwerp concluded that a topical scheme dominated, with the exception of noted masters such as Dürer.[19] Arrangements according to artists and regional styles, as opposed to subject matter, became more prevalent as the preference for 'old masters' valued by the humanist scholars developed.[20] By the latter part of the century, a history of artists and styles was being recognized by those who had prints available to them in significant numbers. The surviving inventories for the Amerbach family of Basel illustrate this point well. The inventories of the collections from 1578-79 and 1586, contain mostly Swiss and German masters, and the collection was organized by artist and region, with the five thousand prints and drawings stored in cabinet drawers and portfolios. Basilius Amerbach began his collection with prints purchased in Venice, and the collection increased with his new emphasis on drawings, and included in his inventory 3356 intaglio prints, 525 woodcuts, and 1866 drawings.[21]

The principles of organization involved in the Amerbach inventory; namely, organizing by artist and school or region, became even more commonplace in the seventeenth century. Prints were seen as a way of having a comprehensive knowledge of an artist's career, reflective of a linear development and narrative. The culmination of this approach to collecting prints can be seen in the collection of Michel de Marolles, whose print collection was published in a 1665 catalogue, noting 123,000 prints by 6,000 artists and bound into 500 volumes. Each volume was compiled in separate sections by both artist and subject.[22] As Peter Parshall suggests, there is evidence that an encyclopaedic or topical arrangement 'may have been a particular preference of scholarly collections within the humanist milieu in contrast to the collections of the landed nobility'.[23] In other words, for those who had the means to obtain a larger quantity of prints, it was more likely that they would seek to obtain a large portion of a particular artist's oeuvre. It would also become common for collectors to assemble works by an individual artist into an album. Rembrandt, for example, had several books of works by Lucas van Leyden, Brueghel the Elder and Raphael.[24] Generally speaking, this was a period when collecting took on a more conspicuous importance. With the rise of printing houses in the Netherlands, print collecting would also experience an exponential rise. And as suggested by Peter Parshall, 'the value of the old master print would be firmly established by what modern historians have come to label the "Dürer-Renaissance"'.[25]

In what follows, I have treated in some detail the collections of Hartmann Schedel, Ferdinand Columbus and Abraham Ortelius. The collections of these three men are amongst the earliest to incorporate Dürer, and as such are relevant to this consideration of how Dürer came to experience such an emphatic reception in the period under scrutiny.

HARTMANN SCHEDEL (1440–1514)

There are no print collections from the early sixteenth century that have survived intact, and as a result it is impossible to gauge fully the manner in which they were organized and used. Some of the earliest points of reference for print collections are libraries. One of the earliest for which information is available is the library of Hartmann Schedel (1440–1514), which survives in part in the Staatsbibliothek in Munich.[26] Schedel was a native of Nuremberg who studied medicine in Leipzig and then Padua. After receiving his degree in 1466, he returned to Nuremberg. Schedel is best known for his publication of the Nuremberg *Weltchronik* in 1493. As editor-in-chief, with the printing undertaken by Anton Koberger, the woodcuts that Schedel assembled for the volume included prints by Michael Wolgemut and Hanns Pleydenwurff, masters of the Nuremberg workshop where Dürer served his apprenticeship. The *Weltchronik* was extremely popular, if the number of surviving copies is any indication: some 800 copies of the Latin edition still exist and 400 of the German edition. The most elaborate printed book of its time, it was illustrated with more than 1800 woodcuts.[27]

Schedel was also an avid book and art collector. His library consisted of 370 manuscripts (many of them copied by his own hand) and 670 printed books. The 1498 inventory of his library lists the following thematic order: works of grammar, logic, rhetoric, astronomy, astrology, mathematics and philosophy – clearly in adherence to the medieval division of wisdom into the *trivium* and the *quadrivium*. Also included are a variety of books relating to Schedel's studies in the humanities, medicine, surgery, and lastly, religion and theology. Schedel pasted a number of Dürer prints into the beginnings, end, and blank pages of the books. The effect is decorative and akin to the prayer books of the fifteenth century.[28] These earliest motives of print collecting were to be superseded, later, by more conscious collecting practices including those of Ferdinand Columbus.

FERDINAND COLUMBUS (1488–1539)

Born in Cordoba, the son of Christopher Columbus, Ferdinand Columbus served as a page at the court of Isabel and Ferdinand in 1494.[29] At the age of 14 he was sent to accompany his father on his fourth and final voyage to the New World. After his return to Spain in 1504, the younger Columbus travelled continuously through Europe on missions for the Spanish court. In 1519, Charles V employed Ferdinand as part of his entourage as he travelled through the Low Countries and then to Germany for his coronation. In 1520 Ferdinand took leave of the Emperor and travelled to Basel, Venice, Nuremberg and Frankfurt. It was during this journey that Columbus started collecting prints in earnest. He was a meticulous collector, and he inscribed the dates and places of purchase on his prints, which eventually numbered 3204. An inventory of his collection survives in Seville as a manuscript copy made in the nineteenth century.[30] This inventory has only recently been published and has received much attention as one of the earliest surviving print inventories. It has been the subject of careful study by Mark P. McDonald, who in a recent article has proposed that the reason for Ferdinand's increased interest in collecting prints lay in a possible meeting with Albrecht Dürer.[31] McDonald points out that in 1520 Dürer and his wife Agnes spent almost a year in the Netherlands at a time when Ferdinand was also there.[32] The main purpose of Dürer's trip was to meet Charles V, who Dürer hoped would confirm the pension awarded to him by Emperor Maximilian. Maximilian was also

Ferdinand's employer. It is highly likely, according to McDonald, that Dürer and Ferdinand would have encountered each other in Brussels.

Regardless of whether the two met or not, the inventory allows for a concise picture of the contents of Ferdinand's collection (which is no longer extant). Out of the more than 3,000 prints, 174 were by Dürer's hand, with the majority of these being woodcuts. This was by far the greatest number of prints of any single artist represented in the collection. Included was the *Life of the Virgin* series, the *Small Passion*, and the *Apocalypse*. In the inventory, 23 of the prints have a 'B' next to them, which McDonald interprets as an abbreviation of *Biblioteca*, indicating that these prints were kept in the library proper.[33] Significantly, the authorship of prints was important to Ferdinand. For many entries, Ferdinand adds in his own hand 'this print is truly made by Albrecht', most often after Dürer's AD monogram, leading McDonald to the conclusion that Ferdinand had 'intimate knowledge of the artist'.[34]

As for other aspects that determined the organization, there is attention given to size, subject, the number of figures depicted, and the clothing of the figures. For example, Dürer's *St. Michael Fighting the Dragon* is described as a '*pliegio* size print of four dressed male saints'.[35] In the Seville inventory with its more than 3,000 thousand prints, each print is described according to size and subject, with no indication of a personal preference, with the exception of prints noted to be 'truly by Albrecht Dürer'.[36] Ferdinand's collection not only shows the high regard in which prints were held in their first years of production, but also how Dürer was often an exception within organizational schemes.

ABRAHAM ORTELIUS (1527–1598)

The Antwerp geographer and humanist Abraham Ortelius maintained friendships with a number of Netherlandish artists, among them Peter Brueghel the Elder.[37] The reputation of Ortelius was largely founded on the publication of his *Theatrum Orbis Terrarum*, which contained 53 maps and was one of the first geographical atlases printed and the most accurate to that date. For two generations it would remain the most consulted atlas, and it was revised and translated a number of times. In 1573, largely because of the success of this text, Ortelius was given the title of 'Royal Geographer' by Philip II. After the death of Ortelius in 1598, his heirs continued to produce the *Theatrum* well into the seventeenth century.[38]

It was during the 1560s when preparing the *Theatrum* that Ortelius assembled his collection of Dürer prints. While it is true that Dürer left many works in the Netherlands during his travels there, it seems that by the 1560s his works were rather scarce.[39] In the records of Christopher Plantin, the main print dealer of Antwerp and a friend of Ortelius, numerous sales of Dürer prints to Ortelius are recorded. It seems that Ortelius paid for these in part by contributing copies of his *Theatrum* as well as illuminated maps.[40] Ortelius' collection of woodcuts, engravings, and one drawing (now lost) were bound into albums. Unfortunately, none of the albums have survived intact. In 1877 the print room in the Amsterdam Rijksmuseum came into the possession of a leather album with sixteenth-century binding that contained the Dürer prints owned by Ortelius (the contents have since been removed and added as individual sheets to the rest of the Rijksmuseum collection).[41] The album contained 100 engravings by Dürer, his woodcut portrait, and a pen and ink portrait of him. The bound volume (minus the prints) has an inscription by Ortelius stating that he compiled the collection in 1562.

The second Ortelius collection is in the Louvre in Paris, in two volumes of woodcuts.[42] Originally there was a volume of engravings; however, this has since dispersed. The two volumes of woodcuts are bound in large volumes with gold-embossed leather. There are inscriptions by Ortelius pasted in, including Pirckheimer's epitaphs, a note recording the inscription on Dürer's tomb, and a handwritten poem by the Hungarian humanist Johannes Sambucus.[43] Contained within the two volumes are 244 woodcuts by Dürer. They also contain Ortelius' engraved portrait and his handwriting, and are among the earliest albums of an individual artist to have survived almost intact. This is evidence of the Dürer revival affecting the Netherlands as well as central Europe, a revival that Ortelius participated in as both dealer and collector.[44]

Expanding Collecting Ambitions

From the middle of the century, the ambitions of collectors began to encompass not only Dürer's prints and drawings, but also his paintings, resulting in a wholesale removal of his major painted works. The ambitions of princely collectors such as Rudolf II and Archduke Maximilian would become paramount, as the reputation of Dürer grew. No imperial collection in central Europe was complete without a work by Dürer. The major collections of works by Dürer in Nuremberg, belonging to Willibald Imhoff and Paulus Praun, would later be dispersed, in part because of the demands of the princely collectors. However, there are inventories that attest to their contents in the seventeenth century before they were absorbed into the large scale *Kunstkammern*. In general, the larger the *Kunstkammer* was, the more complex its organization. The works of Dürer were often an exception to the more typical organizational schemes of the inventories, as we have already seen in several early print collections. In what follows, I consider in some detail the Imhoff family, Paulus Praun and Thomas Howard (Earl of Arundel), as significant Dürer collectors. These three collections illustrate how collecting ambitions were expanding as the century proceeded.

WILLIBALD IMHOFF THE ELDER (1519–1580)

Willibald Pirckheimer (1470–1530), who was Nuremberg's most important humanist and Dürer's close friend, gathered together in his lifetime an especially significant collection of Dürer's work.[45] This collection was greatly expanded by his heirs, most notably his grandson and successor, Willibald Imhoff the Elder, who during his lifetime owned the largest quantity of works on paper by Dürer ever assembled.[46] Imhoff acquired part of his collection through inheritance, his father Hans having married Willibald Pirckheimer's daughter Felicitas, who was heir to her father's collection. He also purchased a number of works from the widow of Dürer's brother Endres, thus adding some 130 works.[47] The collection that Imhoff left behind after his death in 1580 was one of the primary sources for those who sought works by Dürer. It contained originals and copies, and had strong holdings not only of prints, but also of drawings.[48] For Imhoff the Elder, trade was of paramount importance, and his collection was the basis of an art dealership. He sought to monopolize the market for Dürer's work, since the aspirations of most northern European collectors by mid-century included Dürer. This has led Peter Parshall to suggest that Imhoff was surely driven 'by a more practical motive than local pride'.[49]

The inventory is prefaced by a letter written by Imhoff's widow Anna to the Holy Roman Emperor Rudolf II, in which she describes the collection as

> the fruits of my dear deceased lord and husband's many years of diligence and labor, and brought together at great cost, and over many long years, and for which he was often offered large sums and great honors by Electors and Princes and even foreign Potentates.[50]

Further, she notes that Imhoff stated in his last will that the pieces

> remain forever in the house of the Imhoff family and to their honor and never to be moved from there. Several of his sons, those who were at home at the time, had to give their hands and word of honor to it.[51]

Clearly, Imhoff valued his Dürer treasures highly. However, Anna Imhoff goes on to state that 'setting all this aside, since his Imperial majesty shows gracious interest in these pieces, we do not wish to withhold them from him'.[52] She writes how Joachim König would personally deliver the art book separately, and that she arranged for the paintings to be packed carefully and delivered to Prague. The letter is dated December 30th, 1588.

This letter illustrates not only the value of the collection to Imhoff himself and his family, but also the persistence of a collector such as Rudolf II. As will be discussed later, it was exceedingly rare that his wishes in terms of collecting were thwarted. The Imhoff inventory, which follows Anna Imhoff's letter, was sent to Rudolf in order that he might peruse its content and choose those objects which he would like to include in his collection. As noted above, the dispersal of the collection began in 1580, in part due to Imhoff's death, in part due to the purchases of collectors, and likely in part due to the financial insecurities his inheritors faced during the Thirty Years War. Some of the Imhoff drawings form the basis of the collection now housed in the Albertina in Vienna, while the majority of prints with Imhoff provenance are now to be found in the Kunstsammlungen der Veste Coburg.[53]

It is apparent from the inventory that the collection was catalogued by artist rather than subject and was exceptionally strong in its Dürer holdings. Each entry has notations. The graphic collection was bound in albums, both prints and drawings alike, and the works were arranged primarily by size. Some 29 albums, mostly of Dürer's prints, along with works by German, Netherlandish, and Italian masters are recorded. Considerable importance in the notations for each entry is given to the authorship of the prints and there is a separate section for Dürer.

One of the most revealing documents about the Imhoff collection and how it was dispersed is the so called 'secret book' (*Geheimbüchlein*) which was written by different members of the family.[54] This document is unique in the history of collecting and extremely important for what it reveals about aspects of collecting works by Dürer. Made in the second quarter of the seventeenth century by Hans Hieronymous Imhoff, the inheritor of the remnants of the Imhoff collection, this book was intended for private family use only.[55] In contrast to his predecessors, Hans Hieronymous Imhoff was eager to sell the remainder of the collection at any cost and was rather dismissive of its contents in favour of largely practical concerns. He discusses

> these present hard times, when all our income is blocked, both in the business in which our father sank all his capital, and on the land because of the ruination of partnership, no sensible man could blame us if, to our better maintenance, we should decide to make some silver of these totally useless art pieces, among which are many watercolor paintings.[56]

Given the importance of the *Geheimbüchlein* to the history of collecting, it will do well to linger for a moment on some of its entries. Most significant is the fact that some entries include information about copies and forgeries. For example, one entry reads: 'a fine lion on vellum, admittedly with A. Dürer's mark painted underneath, but one feels that only Hans Hoffmann could have painted it'.[57] Apart from noting the existence of copies by Hoffmann, a great deal of consideration is given to the conditions of the works and their financial value, for instance in the following entry: 'A small wooden panel, showing a young man painted by Dürer 1507 – my late father valued it at 200 fl, my grandfather however, only at fl.16.'[58] The most astonishing entry is an admission of forgery, as an addendum to a comment about another depiction of the Virgin Mary in oil paints on wood: 'My father had Albrecht Dürer's mark painted underneath, but for all that one could not really believe that Albrecht Dürer painted it.' This is definitive evidence not only of the Imhoff support for Hoffmann, but also the family's attempts to sell his works as being by the hand of Dürer. Later, Imhoff notes with satisfaction after a sale in 1633 that 'certainly among all the pieces sold there was not a single important one, but for the most part small items painted in watercolor, among them many where there may well be doubt whether Albrecht Dürer really did paint them'.[59] Here is clear evidence that not all of the scores of drawings that have survived bearing Dürer's monogram are to be trusted as authentic, and that the Imhoff family knowingly sold some inauthentic works.

Much as Anna Imhoff had discussed the shipment of works to Rudolf II, a generation later Hans Hieronymous Imhoff now alluded to the collecting efforts of Archduke Maximilian I. Imhoff mentions how a number of works on paper that Rudolf II had previously declined were later sent to Maximilian I, who purchased them in 1630.[60] Also of importance are the claims that when some works were sent to Maximilian I they were declined because he

> considered many of them not to be originals, and returned them all (except for a small St. Jerome and a small panel, on which A. Dürer, before he became a great painter, had drawn three little faces, for which he paid 200 Reichstaler).[61]

This is evidence of the collector as connoisseur, as well as an awareness of the existence of copies, imitations and emulations.

As the *Geheimbüchlein* proceeds, up until the last dated entry of 1658, a number of different inks and writing styles are evident. The number of works by Dürer decreases, and the number of works by the Dürer imitator Hans Hoffmann increases. For example, a 1637 entry records the sale of a 'Saint Sebastian, small woodcut, supposed to have been done by Dürer, but no art expert is willing to accept it as such.' In the same sale, 'a beautiful wing, one foot high, painted on vellum by Hans Hoffmann's hand, Rth. 50.-'.[62] The Imhoff inventory is crucial for our understanding of how Hans Hoffmann came to be seen as a valued creator of works after Dürer. It is also an important documentation of just how influential collectors were in the dissemination of imitative works, as well as the burgeoning art market of the period.

PAULUS PRAUN (1548–1616)

As was discussed in the section on the Imhoff collection, the late sixteenth and seventeenth centuries saw the beginnings of an art market not only for works by Dürer, but also for the Dürer imitations by Hans Hoffmann. Whether or not the buyers were aware of this is unfortunately a question that cannot be answered in its entirety. However, we can look to another Nuremberg patrician and his collection in order to understand more fully how Hoffmann's work came to be situated in renowned art collections alongside works by Dürer.

Born of a noble Nuremberg family, Paulus Praun (1548–1616) was an erudite, well-travelled and educated merchant. Praun showed an early interest in art, traveling to Italy at the age of 15, when he began collecting fine art. He spent 15 years in Italy, during which time he secured, amongst other works, several drawings by Vasari. Praun also maintained several German contacts, many of whom assisted him in building his collection, including Jacob Springli in

Zürich, and in the German lands Jobst Amman. In addition, he consulted the two famous Nürnberg goldsmiths, Christoph Albrecht and Wenzel Jamnitzer. The latter is important for this discussion since Praun acquired most of his Dürer pieces from Jamnitzer, who had direct contact with Dürer's brother Endres. Praun divided his time between Nuremberg and Bologna, living in the latter from 1600 onwards, however in 1616 he moved his entire collection back to Nuremberg.[63]

In terms of works on paper, Praun's collection eventually included 13 volumes of drawings, 25 portfolios of engravings and woodcuts amounting to about 4–5,000 independent impressions. The collection was arranged by artists and national schools. The collection was thoroughly catalogued by Christophe Gottlieb von Murr in 1797 before its dispersal, and it is rather astonishing given the quality of works that it remained intact for that length of time.[64] When Praun died he left his collection in perpetual trust to his descendants, with the explicit request that the works be kept together forever. Much of the Praun collection was purchased by Miklós Esterházy (1765–1833) and can now be found in Budapest, in the Szepmuveszeti Muzeum.[65]

Praun acquired at least five Dürer paintings including: *Lot and His Daughters* (*c.*1496/1499), *Madonna and Child*, (*c.*1496/1499) and *Portrait of Michael Wolgemut or A Clergyman* (1516).[66] However, Praun's collection of works on paper by Dürer was not particularly strong. Perhaps this explains in part why he was such an avid supporter of Hans Hoffmann. It is quite likely that Praun was well aware of the contents of the Imhoff collection and the strength of their Dürer holdings. Perhaps, in the spirit of competition, or towards the aim of completeness, Praun sought out works by Hoffmann. These works could have acted as substitutions, or perhaps even viewed as improvements upon, the Dürer models. Praun owned 35 works by Hans Hoffmann, including his imitations of Dürer's drawings of a stag beetle, head of the Pope, and 12-year-old Christ. With the Praun collection, we realize that Hoffmann and his imitations and emulations of Dürer's works and style came to hold a privileged position in seventeenth-century collections as well.

THOMAS HOWARD EARL OF ARUNDEL (1585–1646)

At this point, we will consider one English collection towards the end of gaining insight into how avidly Dürer's painted works were being collected. The most important collector of Dürer's art in early seventeenth-century Britain was Thomas Howard, Second Earl of Arundel and Surrey. Arundel was well known for his patronage of Rubens and van Dyck as well as his expeditions to Greece and Turkey for antiquities.[67] He was also famous for his library, which has since been dispersed. He acquired the most important part of his book collection when he purchased the remainder of the Pirckheimer library in 1636 while in Nuremberg.[68] Some of the Dürer miniatures that Arundel acquired were cut out of the books to sell separately.[69] David Howarth has suggested that Arundel celebrated his connection to the great humanist

Pirckheimer by commissioning Rubens to paint his portrait in a style akin to Dürer's portrait of Pirckheimer.[70] In 1636, he travelled as English diplomat to the court of Ferdinand II, and on the way he stopped in Nuremberg in May; on his return in November of 1636 he stopped in Nuremberg again.[71] On this journey he employed Wenceslaus Hollar to engrave works they saw along the way, as well as landscapes.

Arundel was mentioned in chapter one as having acquired Dürer's 1498 self-portrait in 1636 on behalf of Charles I, King of England. The self-portrait, along with the painting of Dürer's father, had been presented to Arundel by the council of the city of Nuremberg, more than likely in a gesture of diplomacy. Arundel had copies of these portraits made for his own collection, in the form of etchings done in reverse by Wenceslaus Hollar (see Chapter 1). According to Volker Manuth, it is likely that the city council of Nuremberg presented the painting to Arundel for Charles I in order to secure his protection in case the Protestant city was attacked by the Catholic league.[72] During his visit to Nuremberg, Arundel had remarked with disappointment that 'Herre in this town there being not one scratch of Albrecht Dürer's paintings in oyle to be sold, though it were his country.'[73]Arundel's remark is telling for the thoroughness of the Dürer collectors, who by this point in time had acquired all the major altarpieces. The collecting frenzy surrounding Dürer was so thorough that it became difficult to find Dürer's works in his hometown of Nuremberg.

Collecting Dürer at Court

In the seventeenth century, Dürer's altarpieces were removed from their original locations and placed within some of the most expansive and significant collections of the period. Initially, his major altarpieces were situated in Nuremberg, Frankfurt, Wittenberg, Stendal and Venice. However, due to the efforts of the collectors to be discussed in this section, Munich, Prague and later Vienna became the cities in which the majority of Dürer's large-scale paintings were to be found by the sevententh century.

This section focuses on collections that had an even larger scope than those of Imhoff and Praun. While these Nuremberg patricians could boast of having in their possession numerous works by Dürer, and in the case of Praun, a scope that was international, there was no comparison in the period for the enormous collections assembled by Archduke Ferdinand of Tyrol, Holy Roman Emperor Rudolf II, and the Archduke of Bavaria Maximilian I. As will be shown, works by Dürer figured in these collections in very important ways.

For a richer understanding of the enormous scope of these collections we will draw attention to one of the earliest systematic treatments of collecting practices. In 1565, Samuel Quiccheberg (1529–1567) published his *Inscriptiones vel tituli theatri amplissimi*, the first attempt to outline the proper arrangement of a collection.[74] Quiccheberg's treatise was written under the patronage of

Duke Albert V of Bavaria, at whose court he had been present since 1553.[75] This treatise is the clearest expression from the period of encyclopaedic tenets of collecting. Organization was crucial in order to reflect an ordered environment. The tenets of Quiccheberg's system, as well as his background, are important for understanding why copies and imitative works after Dürer were created in these seemingly encyclopaedic contexts.

Born in Antwerp, Quiccheberg travelled with his family to Ghent, and then Nuremberg in 1540. He studied medicine and philosophy at the universities of Basel and Augsburg. Between 1550 and 1553, and was in charge of the famed Fugger collection, where his duties included arranging and classifying the collection. In 1553, as noted above, he was called to the court of Albert V of Bavaria in Munich, whose collection of antiquities, coins and paintings was well known. While in service at the court, Quiccheberg is known to have made numerous trips to see first-hand collections in Frankfurt, Rome, Padua and Bologna.[76]

Quiccheberg's contribution to museology is helpful for an understanding of the enormous collections to be discussed. In his '*Theatrum universum*', Quiccheberg divides collections into five separate classes,[77] each of which has ten or eleven further divisions. The first class deals with genealogies, and includes portraits of the founder of the collection, family memorabilia, and maps of territory. The second class involves what was then referred to as *artificialia*, which included statues, clocks, mechanical devices, vases, weights, measures, coins, medallions, portrait busts and miniatures. The third class involved the natural sciences, and items Quiccheberg refers to as *naturalia*, such as stuffed animals, skeletons, fossils, plants, metals and earths. Fourth were instruments and tools of science. And the fifth class, obviously of greatest import in the context of this discussion, was art: paintings, engravings, tapestries and furniture.

In a section entitled 'Digressiones', Quiccheberg expands upon the organization of the fifth class, and discusses the placement of prints within the collection. Not only is this the first systematized arrangement of an engraving collection but also, as Barbara Balsiger has suggested, this is the first time that engravings were considered to be works of art.[78] It is interesting to note that Quiccheberg adheres strictly to a topical arrangement. He suggests binding the sheets in volumes, and arranging them horizontally on a classified system of three shelves, including the following: on the first shelf, biblical subjects, warfare, portraits, genealogy; on the second, natural history, mythology, processions, costume, heraldry; and on the third, geography, architecture, numismatics and ornamental designs.

The point to be made here is that collecting in the sixteenth and seventeenth centuries, when embarked upon by individuals with limitless means at their disposal, was encyclopaedic in scope and involved the absorption of parts into a greater whole. While it is exceedingly difficult to establish a link between theory and practice, and it is likely that Quiccheberg's *Inscriptiones* was never followed exactly to the letter, his work nonetheless reflects the ideals to which collectors of the period aspired. The inventories of major collections illustrate this very well. Collections were organized as a microcosm reflecting the macrocosm of the world at large, and could also embody the personality of their founder. Great purpose was seen in organization, arrangement and content. It is for this reason that study of the inventories of the period are essential for understanding the intellectual climate in which these collectors found themselves.

There is some evidence that Quiccheberg, who began his career as the librarian of Jacob Fugger, exerted a direct influence on collectors. It is important to note that Quiccheberg was in close contact with the antiquarian and scholar Jacopo Strada.[79] Both were involved in the maintenance and development of the collection of Albrecht V in Munich. Strada would go on to influence important Habsburg collectors such as Ferdinand I and Maximillian II, who were, respectively, the grandfather and father of Rudolf II.[80]

Some of the most spectacular collections of art were created at the courts of the ruling Habsburg dynasty, whose domains included parts of today's Austria, Czech Republic, Germany, Hungary, Slovakia and Poland. These collections, the predecessors of modern museums and galleries, were referred to as *Kunst-* and *Wunderkammern*.[81] Encyclopaedic in scope, and containing objects of dissimilar origin and diverse materials on a universal scale, the collections were typically intended to showcase a panoramic education and broad humanist learning. As discussed above, included were *naturalia* (products of nature), *arteficialia* (products of man), and *scientifica* (the testaments of man's ability to dominate nature, such as astrolabes, clocks, automatons and scientific instruments). Inventories attest to the display of paintings and sculpture together with these objects, reflective of the scheme outlined by Quiccheberg. Moreover, within the context of the *Kunst-* and *Wunderkammern,* activities now considered disparate were linked together under universal patronage.[82] It is no coincidence that these all-encompassing attempts at collecting and classifying came in a period when voyages of exploration and the discovery of the different species of animals and plants of the new world impacted on keen observers. As suggested by Keith Thomas, 'between 1500 and 1800 ... there occurred a whole cluster of changes in the way in which men and women, at all social levels, perceived and classified the natural world around them'.[83]

Even with the organizing principles laid out by Quiccheberg, obviously it would be impossible for a *Kunstkammer* to contain everything. Telling in this capacity is Gabriel Kaltemarckt's advice to Christian I of Saxony on the formation of an art collection in 1587, and the very explicit suggestion that a canon was needed.[84] Kaltemarckt also proposed to have moulds made of ancient and modern sculpture to enrich the collections in Dresden, in other words, to procure copies with the aim of encyclopaedic completeness. Such procedures of having copies created may account for the practices inherent in the reception of Dürer within these collections, when copies and imitative works were frequently made, as will be discussed in Chapter 3. Generally speaking, the *Kunstkammer* was a way of delivering total knowledge through study of objects. Far from being a random list, an inventory can reveal a great deal as to the epistemology of those who created the collection. In what follows, the major *Kunstkammern* that contained works by Dürer are discussed in chronological order: the collections of Archduke Ferdinand of Tyrol, Holy Roman Emperor Rudolf II, and Maximilian I Archduke of Bavaria.

ARCHDUKE FERDINAND OF TYROL (1529–1595)

The Habsburgs were avid and consistent collectors of art.[85] One of the most significant Habsburg collections, indeed, one of the most significant collections of the period, was the *Kunstkammer* of Archduke Ferdinand of Tyrol. His collection is relevant not only in terms of its Dürer holdings, but also for the approaches to display and patronage it embodied. While the art gallery was perhaps less developed than later Habsburg collections, the manner in which Ferdinand maintained and organized his *Kunstkammer* in the Castle Ambras in Tyrol was emulated throughout central Europe. Its purpose and evolution have yet to be thoroughly investigated.[86]

Ferdinand was in charge of the administration of Bohemia between 1547 and 1563.[87] During his time in Prague, he began his collection of the armour of famous men that was to become a centrepiece of the Ambras display, as well as his series of portraits for a gallery of famous men and women. His collection of prints dates back to this Prague period. Ferdinand also acted as both architect and patron of one of the most spectacular Renaissance buildings north of the Alps, the Hvězda Villa (Star Villa), that can still be seen today in Prague.

In 1563–4, after receiving regency over Tyrol, Ferdinand negotiated the purchase of the Castle Ambras near Innsbruck, which he dedicated to his wife, Philippine Welser of Augsburg. He established his own *Kunstkammer* and much of the collection is still intact.[88] Initially the collection was in holding at the Hofburg in Vienna, and later in Prague. In 1567 he started to ship his collection from Prague to Ambras. In 1571, after the Spanish hall was completed, he moved the entire collection there. Although the earliest layout of his collection cannot be reconstructed with precision, it is certain that from the beginning the building intended for housing the *Kunstkammer* was separate from the rest of the castle complex.[89] He also built a library, armoury, and an antiquarium.

As a fervent admirer of Dürer, Ferdinand amassed a large print collection, which has since been dispersed. The oldest inventory for the contents of the collection, which dates from 1596, one year after his death, shows entries for about 7,000 prints. It should be noted that the Ambras collection attained a considerable reputation among the patrons and connoisseurs of the period. Thus far, the best evidence for the organization of these prints is the major inventory after Ferdinand's death in 1596.[90] The *Kunstkammer* had a number of cases in which the prints, and other items, were housed. In the case in which the graphic collection was housed, the prints had pride of place along with other lavish books, manuscripts and scrolls. Another case contained an atlas, zoological illustrations, and another set of print albums. There was a case for liturgical books, one for military books, and one for ancient history, court books and portraiture.[91]

As has already been noted, large print collections were often contained in volumes, and the way the prints were pasted into these albums allows us to see the organizational scheme at work. It is possible that given the placement of the print collection volumes amongst the other reference texts it was used as a reference source within the *Kunstkammer* scheme. Notably, neither the albums nor their inventoried arrangement conforms to a historical survey of artists and regional schools; however, as often happens in such inventories, the work of Dürer is a notable exception. There were three major albums containing works on paper in Ferdinand's collection. The first is a book bound in brown leather, put together in Mainz in 1560, containing 211 prints and 13 drawings by Dürer.[92] The album is ordered partly according to the size of the prints, and partly according to medium. Early on there is attention to topical matters. The best known of Dürer's prints form the first section. Included are *Adam and Eve, Nemesis, St. Eustace, Melancolia,* and *Knight, Death and the Devil.* There is a section for portraits that includes the depictions by Dürer of Erasmus, Melanchthon and Pirckheimer. Print series' such as the *Engraved Passion,* the small and large woodcut *Passion* series, and the *Apocalypse* series, are represented. Also included is Dürer's *Celestial Map.* As for drawings, perhaps the most noteworthy entry is Dürer's *Dream of the Flood* along with Dürer's description.[93] The second album contains only woodcuts by Dürer and is also bound in leather. The woodcuts are trimmed and some are of poor quality. Included are the *Large Passion* series, the *Apocalypse,* the *Trinity* woodcut, *Holy Family with Three Hares, Martyrdom of the Ten Thousand,* and others. A third album containing the *Apocalypse, Large Passion* and *Life of the Virgin,* also bound and containing 52 folios, is in better condition and well preserved.[94]

As assemblies of the best-known graphic artist of the century, these albums are evidence of the esteem in which Dürer was held within one of the most important collections of the period. Within the Ambras collection Dürer is the only artist who had an album devoted exclusively to his work, a collecting decision based on authorship. After Ferdinand's death the entire collection, along with the Castle Ambras, passed to his second son, the Margrave Karl von Burgau (1560–1618). Karl had little interest in art and the collection passed into neglect. The entire collection was purchased by Rudolf II in 1605. It remained at Ambras, however, until the death of Archduke Sigmund Franz in 1665.[95] At this time many of the codices were removed to Vienna; as a result, most of the print albums are now at the Albertina.

HOLY ROMAN EMPEROR RUDOLF II

Habsburg collecting practices would continue unabated for much of the seventeenth and eighteenth centuries. The Holy Roman Empire was still a unitary concept in name, and although clashes between the Spanish and Austrian factions were often in evidence, between 1438 and 1740 the Emperor was always a Habsburg.[96] The *Kunstkammer* developed and maintained by Rudolf II (1552–1612), who reigned as Holy Roman Emperor from Prague, was arguably the most extensive collection ever brought together by a Habsburg, almost incomprehensible in terms of scope and size.

Rudolf was the first son and successor of Maximilian II, and he ascended to the throne of Bohemia and Hungary in 1576 upon the death of his father. He was crowned Holy Roman Emperor in Vienna in 1578, and then in 1583 he officially named Prague as the imperial residential city.[97] The transformation of the Prague castle complex (Hradčany) into a seat for the empire had been underway for some time and was completed during Rudolf's reign. The city was transformed into an imposing metropolis, with the skyline of the castle dominating the town and with important buildings, such as the St Vitus cathedral and Old Royal Palace recalling Prague's past glory as the seat of Charles IV (1346–78). The Rudolfine period is often referred to as Prague's second golden age.[98] Along with this continued development of the city, Rudolf's court became a cosmopolitan hub of activity, and attracted many scholars, artists and scientists. Rudolf also developed the castle gardens extensively, which included a menagerie with live animals. Concurrently, he amassed a collection of the highest quality, carefully housed in buildings especially constructed for the purposes of displaying his *Kunstkammer*.

Contained in the collection were all the categories outlined by Quiccheberg: sculptures, medals, paintings, precious metals, stones, rare plants, minerals, scientific instruments, and many other items were included in Rudolf's collecting endeavours. There have been many detailed studies of the myriad of objects represented by the collection, as well as exhibitions that attest to the scope and quality of the activities of Rudolf's circle.[99] Acting as both patron and collector enabled Rudolf to develop his diverse collection at an unprecedented rate. Rudolf's collection, built up through inheritance, systematic acquisitions, gifts, diplomacy, purchases, and the work of court artists, has become increasingly well documented. While virtually nothing is known of the Imperial *Kunstkammer* before Rudolf moved to Prague, there are important primary sources that inform us as to its contents in the early seventeenth century. The most important of these sources is the inventory dated from 1607–1611, an inventory that is especially useful for understanding how a *Kunstkammer* was organized, as well as the manner in which the collection developed over time.[100] Some 3,000 objects are inventoried, although the collection likely contained more. The court artist Daniel Fröschl (1563–1613) was charged with maintaining the contents of the collection through this inventory, and his notations accompanying entries, as well as a number of sketches he included, are especially telling.

Here, only one aspect of the Rudolfine *Kunstkammer* will be considered in detail; namely, the holdings of works by Dürer. Indeed, the court of Rudolf II has acquired such a central position in discussions of the Dürer-Renaissance that some cite the beginning of Rudolf's reign in 1576 as the beginning of this phenomenon. Rudolf's active and enthusiastic interest in Dürer is directly attested to by his numerous acquisitions. A consideration of the works on paper by Dürer in the Rudolfine collection will be instructive as to the encyclopaedic thoroughness of his collection.

It is unfortunate that, for the most part, the attention to authorship in the inventory overrode the provision of descriptions of works in the case of Dürer's prints, and the entries are not as specific as, for example, those in the Imhoff inventory. Entry 2709, for instance, reads 'Albrecht Dürer holtz und kupferstich.' This is because most of the Dürer prints and drawings that Rudolf owned were bound into albums, and hence required only one entry. This makes sense, given both the size of Rudolf's collection, and the number of inventory entries required. In 1586 Rudolf purchased 250 Dürer sheets from the heir of the collection of Cardinal Granvella, who had been resident at the Spanish court in Madrid. This purchase was arranged by Rudolf's ambassador in Spain, Hans Khevenhüller, whose duties were not only of a political nature, as he was also charged with obtaining pieces for Rudolf's collection.[101] Further additions to the Rudolfine collection were made after the death of Willibald Imhoff in 1580, when the economic decline of the Imhoff enterprise in Nuremberg began, and the family offered to Rudolf a number of works by Dürer in exchange for the lordship of Petschau. While they did not receive their lordship, Rudolf did receive the works of art. In 1588 Rudolf acquired an album with drawings and watercolours by Dürer from the Imhoff family. Also acquired was Albrecht Dürer's *Buch der Menschlicher Proportionen* in folio and bound in red leather.[102]

Works by Dürer also came by other means to the court in Prague. The 1524 manuscript of Dürer's family history had survived in three handwritten copies, one of which belonged to the Nuremberg goldsmith Hans Petzolt (1551–1633), who is documented as having worked at Rudolf's court.[103] Closer to home, a large collection of paintings recorded in 1612 as part of the estate of the painter Jindřich Ekenperger, who lived in the Mala Strana in Prague, was reportedly sent by the citizens of the lesser town to the castle. Included was an unnamed painting by Albrecht Dürer.[104]

Paintings offer the most direct evidence of the heightened interest in Dürer at Rudolf's court. The difficulties and cost involved in the acquisition and transport of paintings, as well as the extremely high value placed upon them in a context in which works on paper were only starting to be accepted as works of art in themselves, made the addition of a high-quality painting to a collection something only the wealthiest and most prestigious of collectors could accomplish. The Dürer paintings that Rudolf brought to Prague included the *Adoration of the Trinity* (plate 1) acquired in 1585, the *Martyrdom of the Ten Thousand* acquired in 1600, and the *Feast of the Rosegarlands* (plate 3) acquired in 1603. Other Dürer paintings to be found in Rudolf's collection, for which the dates of acquisition are unknown, include *Adam and Eve*, the *Madonna with the Pear*, and the *Portrait of Johannes Kleeberger*.[105] All of these paintings are still firmly attributed to Dürer by contemporary scholars, making it tempting to suggest that Rudolf and his agents were discerning and had an eye for quality. Regardless, these acquisitions are especially telling of the taste for Dürer that had developed amongst the most prominent collectors.

The shift of Dürer's painted works from their original locations in churches and chapels to the Rudolfine court is of great importance. Two of his most significant acquisitions were the *Adoration of the Trinity* and the *Feast of the Rosegarlands*. Primary sources give an especially detailed picture of the measures that Rudolf went to in his pursuit of these paintings. Examining each of these acquisitions in detail will contribute to this characterization of Rudolf's collecting tendencies. It will also show how works painted for ecclesiastic settings were shifted out of their contexts in the period under scrutiny. The reverence accorded to these works in their original locations was considerable, and not just because they were by Dürer. They served important ecclesiastic functions *in situ*. Thus, the question arises: how was their removal and acquisition by Rudolf made possible? Each of these paintings will now be considered in turn, including some commission details and histories of reception to show the value placed on Dürer paintings in their original location.

The *Adoration of the Trinity* (plate 1), painted by Dürer in 1511, is now in the Kunsthistorisches Museum in Vienna (without its original frame and behind glass). It was originally housed in the chapel of the *Zwölfbrüderhaus* (house for 12 brothers) in Nuremberg. This was a home for 'twelve aged and indigent' citizens of Nuremberg, to use Panofsky's expression, and was founded in 1501 by Mattias Landauer and Erasmus Schiltkrot, two wealthy and devout merchants.[106] Landauer moved into the home himself in 1510. When the chapel for the *Zwölfbrüderhaus* was completed in 1508, Dürer was asked not only to paint an altarpiece, but also to create a frame for the work, as well as a sketch for the stained glass in the chapel.[107] The chapel was dedicated to the Trinity and All Saints, and this determined Dürer's programme. The painting can be considered to contain three levels, the topmost depicting God in imperial garments, holding the crucified Christ, with numerous angels and saints surrounding the scene; then the middle register which shows earthly worshipers of ecclesiastic and royal background, as well as laymen; and finally below the entire scene is a self-portrait of Dürer *in assistenza*, standing small and alone, with a vast, luminous, and rather empty landscape rolling into the distance.[108]

In 1584, when the Nuremberg council sent their syndicate Joachim König to Prague to discuss legal matters, Rudolf II used the opportunity to express his wish to acquire this painting. The Emperor's insistence that he obtain the original is well documented in letters exchanged between Nuremberg and Prague. In the name of Rudolf II, Sigmund Viehauser dealt with Joachim

König, and both corresponded with the Nuremberg council from Prague. Rudolf's wish was declined in a response on 21 November 1584, in which the council stated that great difficulties would be encountered in meeting with this request. A few days later, König sent another letter in which the wishes of the emperor were repeated, and it was suggested that the costs of having a copy made would be covered and the copy given in place of the original to Nuremberg. Once again, the Nuremberg council sought to keep the painting by claiming that the difficulties and length of time needed to make a good copy would be too great. König, unhappy with this, wrote again from Prague, and stated decisively that it did not matter whether the council wanted to give the painting or not, and warned of the consequences of disobeying such a powerful ruler. On 16 December 1584, the Nuremberg council argued that yet another obstacle was the Landauer foundation itself, the *Zwölfbrüderhaus* charity house for which the painting had originally been created, and that the original context of the painting should be respected. The impatient Emperor again pushed König, and on 24 December the purchase was finalized, with another statement that disobeying the will of the Emperor would result in political consequences for the city of Nuremberg. Thus, the painting was acquired after five months of diplomatic negotiations.[109]

Noteworthy in this correspondence are the insistence that the original painting be brought to Prague, the suggestion that a copy could be made to replace the original and, finally, the statement that disobeying the will of the Emperor would result in political consequences for the city of Nuremberg. As for the responses from the Nuremberg council, it is telling that an argument was made for keeping the painting *in situ*, since the Zwölfbrüderhaus charity was the place for which the painting had originally been created.

Yet ultimately the demands of Rudolf were met. In March of 1585 the *Adoration of the Trinity* was brought to Prague, with Rudolf giving financial compensation of 700 florins to the Landauer foundation. This compensation was received by Tobias Panntzer, the guardian of the Landauer foundation which had existed since 1510 and remained effective as a charity house and place of worship until 1808. Disregard for the original context of the painting was twofold: the frame which Dürer had designed for the painting and which was an important aspect of its iconography was left in Nuremberg (now in the *Germanisches Nationalmusem*). Johann Hauer (1586–1660), the Nuremberg engraver and perhaps the earliest of Dürer researchers (discussed in Chapter 1), who wrote of the depletion of Dürer's works from Nuremberg, particularly emphasized the move of the *Adoration of the Trinity* to the court in Prague.[110] Hauer's distress at the removal of works by Dürer from Nuremberg emphasizes the fact that the acquisition by Rudolf II would have had a dramatic impact on those involved with the *Zwölfbrüderhaus*.

Another major Dürer acquisition that also sheds light on the processes involved in procuring important paintings is the *Feast of the Rosegarlands* (plate 3), a painting that also had a significant history of use in its original location.[111] The *Feast of the Rosegarlands* was, of course, Dürer's main commission during his stay in Venice in 1506. Dürer started work on the painting in February of 1506, and completed it in September of that same year. Painted for the church of San Bartolomeo, the picture depicts the cult of the rosary and the Coronation of the Virgin as Queen of Heaven, surrounded by highly individualized figures. In his letters from Venice to Willibald Pirckheimer, Dürer described the numerous visitors to the church who wished to see the painting, including the Doge of Venice and Giovanni Bellini, the latter deeply impressed by Dürer's mastery of colour.[112] The painting reportedly had such an impact on the public that Dürer was later offered a position as an official painter in Venice, a position that he turned down.[113]

The altarpiece was placed in the church of San Bartolomeo, where a chapel was used and maintained by the members of the Fondaco dei Tedeschi, an organization for German expatriates in Venice. Having an altarpiece painted by a native son likely meant a great deal to them: patriotism cannot be underestimated in this context. This was the first time that Dürer included his self-portrait in an altarpiece, and in the *cartellino* he stresses his northern origins. Further, the Fondaco dei Tedeschi was rebuilt after the fire of January 1505, and it is likely that the church would have had added significance as a place of worship thereafter. Attendance and maintenance of the chapel in San Bartolomeo was a vital aspect of the social cohesion and patriotism of the numerous Germans in Venice, most of whom were merchants involved in the shipment of goods between Venice and the German lands.[114]

Thus, great value was placed upon the *Feast of the Rosegarlands* in its original context where it functioned as an altarpiece. Significant in terms of the painting's reception is the role that it played in the activities of the Scuola dei Rosario (the Confraternity of the Rosary) whose members met in the chapel where the painting was housed.[115] This confraternity attests to the high level of corporate pride and organization on the part of German community in Venice, as well as being one of the earliest and most important promoters of the cult of the rosary. Like other confraternities under the secular jurisdiction of the Venetian government, the Scuola del Rosario placed great emphasis on the acts and objects of devotion as opposed to acts of practical charity.[116] As the main altarpiece for the confraternity, Dürer's painting would have had a significant role in activities of the scuola, at least in its inception. Like other confraternities, the scuola focused devotional activities on altars in churches and chapels. For example, account books for the confraternity of the goldsmiths (Scuola degli Orefici) for 1540–43 show that up to half of the income of the scuola might be spent on items connected with devotion.[117] Some sort of altarpiece would have formed a standard part of the permanent furniture of virtually every confraternity altar. This was partly a matter of lending public expression to the members' religious devotion, and of providing a practical means for concentrating the minds during services.

As noted above, the *Fondaco dei Tedeschi* burned down in January, 1505, and a year later Dürer wrote a letter dated 6 January 1506 stating that he had received the commission to execute an altarpiece for the Germans in Venice.[118]

Dürer's altarpiece was thus commissioned during the heightened ecclesiastic needs of the German community in Venice. It is improbable that a century later, the German community would have declined to such an extent that the cult of the rosary or their main altarpiece was no longer seen as important. Indeed, the church of San Bartolomeo is documented as implementing a feast of the rosary in 1573. Peter Humfrey's examination of account books reveals how much emphasis was placed on the acts and objects of devotion associated with these confraternities.[119]

In spite of its importance *in situ*, one century after its completion, the *Feast of the Rosegarlands* was removed from the church in Venice and transported to Prague. In this case, the agent acting on Rudolf's behalf was Bernardo Rosso, who was the envoy who conducted the lengthy transactions with the church of San Bartolomeo, and the painting was purchased for the Rudolfine collection on 10 March 1606, for 900 ducats. Joachim Sandrart described the transport of the painting from Venice to Prague, and how the image was: 'carefully wrapped in rags and much cotton wool and baled in wax cloth. At the emperor's orders, it was carried on poles by a group of strong men all the way from Venice to the Imperial Residence in Prague.'[120] The painting is included in the 1621 inventory.[121]

These are just two examples of Rudolf's acquisitions of significant works by Dürer. Both were greatly valued in their original contexts and replaced by copies. This throws into sharp relief the demand for copies, not as attempts at forgery, but for functional purposes. It is sometimes easy to forget when studying the dispersal of Dürer's works that great esteem was granted to the works *in situ*, and that they often played important liturgical roles. Yet the fact remains that around 1600, there was also a heightened interest in Dürer as an artist, and there were concerted efforts to own works by his hand. Thus, courtly collecting practices and copying become central themes in the reception of Dürer's works.

The provenance of the other paintings by Dürer in Rudolf's collection are not as easy to document. A major source was the Imhoff collection in Nuremberg. It is likely that the *Madonna with the Siskin*, now in Berlin, was purchased from the Imhoff collection in 1588, as it is documented in the Imhoff inventory prior to a number of purchases by Rudolf.[122] The same can be said for the *Portrait of Johannes Kleeberger* – the sitter in this portrait was Willibald Imhoff's stepfather. It is highly likely that this painting was purchased in 1588 as well.[123] The *Adoration of the Magi*, now in the Uffizi in Florence, was originally given to Rudolf as a gift from Kurfurst Christian. The *Martyrdom of the Ten Thousand*, originally in the collection of Friedrich the Wise, was acquired in 1600.[124] Another Dürer painting in the Rudolfine collection was the *Adam and Eve* now in the Prado.[125]

In addition to employing art agents and royal diplomats in his efforts to obtain original works, Rudolf seems to have encouraged artists in his employ to reckon with Dürer's artistry. The evidence for this, which will form the subject of Chapter 3, can be seen in works by the court artists Hans Hoffmann, Daniel Fröschl, Georg Hoefnagel, Aegedius Sadeler and Antonio Abondio.

Much of Rudolf's Dürer collection is now in Vienna.[126] After Rudolf's death, the most precious items were brought to Vienna by Rudolf's brother and successor Mathias. During the Swedish invasion of the seventeenth century, much of Rudolf's collection was dispersed to the court of Queen Christina in Sweden. Not every court held Dürer in such high regard: Queen Christina was uninterested in Dürer's work, and has been documented as stating that she was prepared to trade all the works of Dürer and those of other German masters for just one Raphael painting; and that even doing this was according them too much honour. Clearly, the tastes of a patron and collector are central to discussions of reception.

ARCHDUKE MAXIMILIAN I OF BAVARIA (1573–1651)

The Dürer holdings in Prague were matched only by the collection of Archduke Maximilian I of Bavaria, who certainly equalled Rudolf in his enthusiasm for Dürer.[127] Like Rudolf, Maximilian had a strong family tradition of collecting preceding him. The Wittelsbach princes who came before him, such as Wilhelm IV (1508–1550), Albrecht V (1550–1579) and Wilhelm V (1579–1597), strongly advocated collecting and establishing *Kunstkammern*. Maximilian was the son and successor of the latter, first as a duke in 1597, and then becoming Archduke of Bavaria in 1623, with his court based in Munich. When Maximilian inherited the Wittelsbach dynasty he was 25 years old.[128]

In his *Kunstkammer*, Maximilian also developed and maintained a print collection. The sheets were housed in the *Kunstkammer* proper, rather than the library, a practice that corresponds to a scheme developed by Archduke Ferdinand of Tyrol. However, unlike the arrangements at Ambras where the prints were all contained in albums, the Munich *Kunstkammer* also stored prints, drawings, paintings on parchment and maps in drawers. This was noted by the Augsburg patrician Phillip Hainhofer (1578–1647) in his seventeenth-century travel diary, written during his travels in Bavaria between 1611 and 1613.[129] Maximilian purchased a number of drawings from the Imhoff collection, including Dürer's sheets with a stag beetle, a number of heads from his studies of proportion, and the prayer book of Kaiser Maximilian I.[130]

The collection that Maximilian inherited after his father's death contained one work by Dürer: the painting of *Lucretia* (1518) that has remained in Munich ever since.[131] Maximilian began his collecting endeavours almost immediately after acquiring his title. His first major purchase was Dürer's *Glimm Lamentation* (1500) from the Imhoff collection in 1598, for which the Imhoffs asked 1000 gold gulden.[132] The painting was brought to Munich in 1598. Maximilian also acquired at some point before 1607 Dürer's *Virgin with the Carnation* (1516). All of these paintings have remained in Munich (now in the Alte Pinakothek).

Another phase of collecting paintings began in 1612, when Maximilian expressed interest in acquiring Dürer's *Paumgärtner Altar* (1504), which at that point was still *in situ* in the church of St Catherine (*Katharinenkirche*) in Nuremberg. This church belonged to the convent of Dominican nuns in Nuremberg, and Dürer's panel originally stood on the east wall of the south transept.[133] Depicted on the central panel is the Adoration, with Mary, Joseph and angels, and shepherds approaching from the background. In the foreground are members of the donor family, the Paumgärtners. The altarpiece has two wings, depicting St George and St Eustace (possibly with the features of Stephan and Lucas Paumgartner). It has been proposed that the central panel first stood in the church without the wings, possibly as a donation of the children (Stephan and Lucas) in memory of their parents, who had died.[134]

It is important to understand the details of this picture in light of the over-painting that occurred when it eventually came into Maximilian's possession. The manner in which the side panels in particular were altered by the hand of an anonymous artist will be discussed in Chapter 3. For now, we will establish the painting's acquisition history, which also gives hints as to what would occur: namely, the collector's wish to have a painting altered. Moreover, this purchase is indicative of an almost competitive spirit between Maximilian and Rudolf in their acquisition attempts.

In 1612 Maximilian wrote to the City Council of Nuremberg that he wished to purchase the painting in its entirety: that is, all three panels. The council refused, stating that they had already declined such an offer from Rudolf II. Initially, Rudolf II was interested in obtaining it for his collection, and there is correspondence from Johann von Seebach to Hieronymous Paumgartner in 1597 about this. Rudolf hoped that Paumgartner would say a word in his favour to the Nuremberg *Rat*. There seems to have been some debate over the attribution at the time, referred to as 'schlechten gemalde' and not worthy of the Kaiser's interest.[135] It has been suggested, however, that Rudolf's initial interest spurred Maximilian's desire for the painting, and he dispensed a diplomatic team to Nuremberg in order to engage in negotiations for the altarpiece. From Munich he sent Eustachius Unterholzer, whose wife was from Nuremberg, and Burgmeister Wolf Löffelholz. He also demanded support of members of the Paumgärtner family situated in Munich.[136] Ultimately, as if fearing political consequences, the altar was sent to Maximilian.

However, the story does not end there. It is at this point that the services of Lukas Friedrich Beheim von Schwartzbach (1587–1648) were called upon.[137] Beheim was a Nuremberg patrician who would assist Maximilian with this and a number of future purchases of works by Dürer. Upon receipt of the Paumgärtner panels, Maximilian was not satisfied. While the central panel was signed by Dürer, it carried no date, and Maximilian dispatched Beheim to investigate whether the original altar construction, which had been left behind, had a date. The Archduke had been in possession of the panel for half a year, and wished to ascertain when Dürer had completed the painting.

Beheim investigated and came to the conclusion that the altar was earlier than the panel it had contained, especially considering that Barbara and Martin Paumgärtner, the figures depicted kneeling, had died shortly after Dürer was born. Beheim also concluded that the side panels depicting George and Eustace were not from the hand of Dürer at all.[138] This in part explains why Maximilian would later have no qualms about altering the side panels.

The pervasiveness and competitiveness of Maximilian is amply demonstrated by his other acquisitions. Another telling example in this regard is the *Heller Altar*, completed by Dürer in 1509, which had stood in the Dominican church in Frankfurt since its completion. This altarpiece was commissioned by Jakob Heller (1460–1522), a wealthy merchant, member of the town council, and mayor of Frankfurt.[139] It was the primary devotional image in the church, depicting both the Assumption and the Coronation of the Virgin. Again, Dürer included his self-portrait *in assistenza*. Discussion with Heller (he saved Dürer's letters) became so heated that Dürer offered to cancel and sell the altarpiece to someone else. Dürer received 200 florins instead of 130. The painting was dispatched to Frankfurt in 1509, but Dürer still felt insufficiently rewarded. This altarpiece is considered by scholars to be something of an ill-fated work, due to the bickering between Dürer and his patron Heller about the time of completion and price.[140] Nine letters by Dürer's hand attest to the problems.

Upon acquisition of the altarpiece in 1615, Maximilian made sure to acquire these letters as well. Further, he purchased the central panel alone, which was the only one painted by Dürer. Again, this acquisition seems to have had some competitive overtones to it. It was duly noted at the time of purchase that this was a painting that Rudolf II had attempted to procure for a long time, and that he had at one point offered 10,000 gold gulden for the painting.[141] There was a sense of prestige and accomplishment which seems to have accompanied Maximilian's purchases of paintings that Rudolf had also wanted for his collection.

It is fortunate that Maximilian had artists engage often in practices of copying, since the only way that we now know of the Heller altar is through a copy created by Jobst Harrich (*c.*1580–1617). The original middle panel acquired by Maximilian was destroyed in a fire at the Munich residence in 1729.[142] It should also be recalled that the *Heller Altar* served important functions in its original location. As pointed out above, this picture was extremely popular in its original location. This is confirmed by the reports of Karel van Mander.[143] Yet in spite of this popularity *in situ*, the will of the collector pervaded, and the *Heller Altar* was acquired by Maximilan I in 1614.

Maximilian's final collecting phase occurred between 1627 and 1630. During these years, three major paintings by Dürer would be added to his collection. Two were acquired in the year 1629: *Hercules and the Stymphalian Birds* (1500), and *St. Anne with Virgin and Child* (1519). The former is unusual in Dürer's oeuvre for its depiction of a mythological theme. There are hardly any details as to the history of its acquisition, and it is now on permanent loan from the

Alte Pinakothek to the Germanisches Nationalmuseum in Nuremberg. As for the *St. Anne with Virgin and Child ('Anna Selbdritt')* (1519) (plate 8), from the date of its creation until the time of its acquisition by Maximilian, the painting was in the possession of the Tucher family of Nuremberg. It was first in the collection of Leonhard Tucher (d.1568), who had received the painting from a contemporary of Dürer's, and the painting was described in his inventory as being by the hand of Dürer. It was recorded as having been cleaned once by Tucher's daughter and was never retouched. The painting then passed through the hands of three further Tucher descendants until it was sold to Maximilian I. Upon his initial viewing of the painting, Maximilian sent it back to the Tuchers because he thought it was a copy. However, Maximilian was a careful collector, and upon reconsideration he demanded to see the painting again. After it was packed in a crate and sent to Munich in 1630, it was purchased by Lucas Beheim on behalf of Maximilian for 500 reichstaler.

The final acquisition by Maximilian to be considered is Dürer's enigmatic depiction of the *Four Holy Men* (plate 5), Dürer's gift to the city of Nuremberg which had hung in the town hall since the artist's death.[144] It is noteworthy indeed that the city hall allowed this removal to occur, especially given the emphatic Dürer revival underway. It seems that political pressure and Maximilian's threat of repression caused them to change their minds. The *Four Holy Men* was acquired from the city of Nuremberg in 1627, a purchase facilitated by the patrician Lukas Friedrich Beheim, who has already being mentioned as the purchasing agent for Maximilian, especially when it came to acquiring works from Nuremberg. Beheim played a large role in the dispersal of the Dürer images that has yet to be fully investigated.[145] Also playing a role in the purchase was Augustin Haimbl, who was charged with maintaining the *Kunstkammer* of Maximilian (he is named *Kammerdiener* in the literature).[146]

Johann Hauer's remarks in relation to the *Four Apostles* are extremely significant for what they tell us about the processes involved in making copies of pictures, and the great lengths to which powerful collectors would go to ensure that they were obtaining the original works by Dürer. Hauer describes how after having a copy of the painting made by Georg Vischer, Maximilian sent his *Kammerdiener* Haimbl to compare the original with the copy, in order to ensure that he was receiving the real requested treasure.[147] It was Haimbl who made the Archduke's wish to acquire the two panels known to the city starting in 1526, and engaged in negotiations, stating that if Nuremberg declined the consequences for the city would be enormous.[148] The proud reply of the city council discusses the honour bestowed upon them by the interest and affection of Maximilian for the panels, and for the native son Dürer, and that it was understandable that he would seek to obtain the originals, as the picture was completed with 'particular diligence'.[149] In return for the panels, the city had political demands, namely, certain privileges that would be bestowed upon Nuremberg providing some security for its future.

At this point, the middleman Beheim stepped in and secured the purchases. Further, the original inscriptions were then, by Maximilian's command, sawed off the original and attached to the Vischer copy which then remained in Nuremberg.[150] As already noted above, the inscriptions on the *Four Holy Men* included sayings from Luther's translation of the Bible and were considered heretical by Maximilian, a devout Catholic.

In total, Maximilian collected 11 paintings by Dürer, the majority of which are still in Munich in the Alte Pinakothek. It is clear that Maximilian was uninterested in obtaining Dürer's self-portraits, or any other portraits for that matter.[151] However, Maximilian was very interested in biographical details of Dürer, as attested to by his acquisition of the letters involved in the commission of the *Heller Altar* and his preservation of the copy of Dürer's diary of his journey to the Netherlands.[152] There is evidence of a competition with regard to Rudolf II, as shown by the numerous self-satisfied mentions of the Emperor failing where Maximilian had succeeded. As with Rudolf, little attention was paid to the functions that the paintings of Dürer had in their original locations, especially with regard to the altarpieces.[153] Overall, Maximilian's collecting practices, as they involved Dürer, exemplify the reverence in which the artist was held at the court in Munich. As at the court of Rudolf II, the practices of imitation and emulation in which the court artists would engage will be the subject of Chapter 3.

Conclusion

During the late-sixteenth and early-seventeenth centuries there was a large-scale dispersal of works by Dürer. Early collectors, such as Hartmann Schedel, Ferdinand Columbus and Abraham Ortelius, focused on acquiring full sets of Dürer's prints. An examination of the place of Dürer within these print collections is instructive for understanding changes in the development of print collections as a whole, for even within collections having topical schemes, Dürer is consistently treated as a separate category. This foreshadows the manner in which authorship would take a dominant role in the organization of collections. This presumably happened in part due to an increase in biographical literature on artists, and an increased interest in the role of the artist as representative of a distinct historical tradition. As was demonstrated in Chapter 1, a substantial amount of literature was devoted to Dürer and he was often named with pride as a northern artist.

The scope and ambitions of later collectors such as Willibald Imhoff, Paulus Praun and Thomas Howard, Earl of Arundel, expanded to include Dürer's painted works. Imhoff and Praun developed their print collections with great intensity. There was clearly an acknowledgement of a distinct tradition of art-making as exemplified by Dürer and, within these collections, Imhoff and Praun are always quick to highlight works by Dürer: there is evidence of a heightened demand for Dürer, and there is notation for copies of originals. In the Imhoff inventory, there are some cases of attempts to pass off copies as originals by Dürer. Imhoff's heirs were extremely important as the suppliers to the demand for Dürer, and much of Dürer's work on paper can be traced back to the Imhoffs. As for the Earl of Arundel, his acquisition of two painted works by Dürer for King Charles I of England exemplifies the international scope of the reception of Dürer.

Finally, through focus on the enormous *Kunstkammern* of Archduke Ferdinand of Tyrol, Rudolf II, and Maximilian I, the height of interest in Dürer has been documented. The collection of Ferdinand was an important precursor in terms of organization, and other central European collectors based their own upon his example. The scope of Rudolf and Maximilian was limitless, and as they focused their collecting ambitions on the painted works of Dürer, especially his altarpieces, there was a gradual removal of religious works by Dürer from their original locations. A competitive quality can be discerned in their efforts, since works by Dürer were so deeply valued and held pride of place within the burgeoning *Kunstkammern* of the period. How court artists in their employ appropriated these work by Dürer is the subject of the next chapter.

Notes

1 Joseph Leo Koerner, 'Albrecht Dürer: A Sixteenth-Century Influenza', in Giulia Bartum, ed., *Albrecht Dürer and his Legacy* (London: The British Museum Press, 2002), p. 26. For important new work on Dürer's collecting habits, see Jeffrey Chipps Smith, 'Albrecht Dürer as Collector', *Renaissance Quarterly* 64/1 (2011): pp. 1–49.

2 Andreas Tacke, *'Der Mahler Ordnung und Gebräuch in Nürmberg': Die Nürnberger Maler(zunft)bücher ergänzt durch weitere Quellen, Genealogien und Viten des 16., 17. und 18. Jahrhunderts* (München, Berlin: Deutscher Kunstverlag, 2001): p. 124; William Crowne, *A True Relation of all the Remarkable Places and Passages Observed in the Travels of the Right Honourable Thomas Lord Howard, Earle of Arundell 1636* (London: Henry Seile, 1636).

3 The Hauer manuscripts in the Nuremberg Stadtsarchiv have recently been published: see Tacke 2001, pp. 120–125.

4 For the *Four Apostles* (1526) see Anzelewsky 1971, no. 184; for the *Feast of the Rosegarlands* (1506) see Anzelewsky 1971, no. 93; for the *Adoration of the Trinity (Landauer Altar)* (1511) see Anzelewsky 1971, no. 118.

5 For general remarks on the history of collecting in central Europe at this time, see: Joseph Alsop, *The Rare Art Traditions: the History of Art Collecting and its Linked Phenomena Wherever These Have Appeared* (New York: Harper & Row, 1982); Niels von Holst, *Creators, Collectors, and Connoisseurs: The Anatomy of Artistic Taste from Antiquity to the Present Day* (New York: Putnam, 1967).

6 Ivo Hlobil and Eduard Petrů, *Humanism and the Early Renaissance in Moravia* (Olomouc: Votobia, 1999): p. 174. The panels are now in Madrid, Museo del Prado. See Anzelewsky 1971, no. 103 and no. 104.

7 This Kunstkammer was founded in 1560, and the Dresden *Kupferstichkabinett* would later emerge from its holdings. This is discussed by V. Hanatsch, 'Beiträge zur Älteren Geschichte der Kurfürstlichen Kunstkammer zu Dresden', *Neues Archiv fur Sächsische Geschichte und Altertumskunde* 23 (1902): pp. 230–237.

8 Mark McDonald, 'Humanist Transmissions: Dürer, Erasmus and the Print Collection of Ferdinand Columbus', Conference paper for *Albrecht Dürer and his Legacy* (London: British Museum Press, 2004): p. 1.

9 Other Nuremberg collectors of Dürer's prints include: Wenzel Jamnitzer, Melchior Ayrer, Paulus Praun, Paul Behaim, Johann Christoph Harsdörffer, Martin Peller, Philipp Scherl. See Theodor Hampe, 'Kunstfreunde im Alten Nürnberg und ihre Sammlungen', *Mitteilungen des Vereins für Geschichte der Stadt Nürnberg* 16 (1904): pp. 57–124.

10 See Rupprich 1956, vol. III, p. 448. The contract is preserved in Nuremberg Stadtarchiv, Lib. Cons.K, fol. 132v. See also Jane Campbell Hutchison, *Albrecht Dürer: A Guide to Research* (New York and London: Garland Publishing Inc., 2000): p. 50.

11 Hans Rupprich, *Dürer-Schriftlicher Nachlass* (Berlin: Deutscher Verein für Kunstwissenschaft, 1956), vol. 1, p. 244. Jacob Arnold's brother, the local painter Hans Arnold, vouched for his trustworthiness on the contract. See also Hutchison 1990, p. 57.

12 Erasmus' eulogy for Dürer is translated and quoted in Panofsky, '"Nebulae in Pariete"', at p. 37.

13 For the inventory see Joachim von Sandrart, *Academie der Bau-, Bild- und Mahlerey-Künste von 1675. Leben der berühmten Maler, Bildhauer und Baumeister*, compiled by Rudolf Arthur Peltzer (Munich: G. Hirth, 1925): pp. 316–318. For remarks on Melchior Ayrer see Peter Parshall, 'The Print Collection of Ferdinand, Archduke of Tyrol', *Jahrbuch der Kunsthistorischen Sammlungen in Wien* 78 (1982): pp. 139–184, at p. 141.

14 David Landau and Peter Parshall hint at these issues toward the end of their full-length treatment of Renaissance prints in *The Renaissance Print 1470–1550* (New Haven: Yale University Press, 1994): p. 367. For more general remarks on the history of collecting prints see W.W. Robinson, 'The Passion for Prints: Collecting and Connoisseurship in Northern Europe during the Seventeenth Century', *Printmaking in the Age of Rembrandt, Exhibition Catalogue* (Boston, Museum of Fine Arts, 1980): pp. xxvii–xxviii. For another comprehensive source on early print collecting, see Stephan Brakensiek, *Vom 'Theatrum Mundi' zum 'Cabinet des Estampes': Das Sammeln von Druckgraphik in Deutschland 1565–1821* (Hildesheim, Zürich and New York: Olms, 2003).

15 Jean Denucé, *De Antwerpsche 'Konstkamers'* (Antwerp: De Speigel, 1932): p. 7.

16 W. Schwemmer, 'Aus der Geschichte der Kunstsammlungen der Stadt Nürnberg', *Mitteilung des Vereins für Geschichte der Stadt Nürnberg* 40 (1949): p. 124.

17 Gabriel von Térey, 'Eine Kunstkammer des 17. Jahrhunderts', *Repertorium für Kunstwissenschaft*, 19 (1896): pp. 31–35.

18 Robinson 1981, pp. xxvii–xxviii. Even well into the nineteenth century, museum print cabinets were arranged as topographical repositories rather than according to schools, styles, or individual masters.

19 'The work of particular artists tends to be recorded in Antwerp inventories primarily in cases of noted masters of an earlier generation such as Lucas van Leyden or Albrecht Dürer.' Parshall, 1982, at pp. 141–142.

20 Parshall 1982, p. 144.

21 Otto Fischer, 'Geschichte der Öffentlichen Kunstsammlung Basel', *Festschrift zur Eröffnung des Kunstmuseums Basel* (Basel, 1936): pp. 1–25, at p. 25.

22 L. Metcalf, 'A Prince of Print Collectors: Michel de Marolles, Abbé de Villeloin', *Print Quarterly* 2 (1912): pp. 316–340.

23 Parshall 1982, p. 141.

24 Iain Buchanan, 'Dürer and Abraham Ortelius', *The Burlington Magazine* 124 (1982): pp. 734–741, at p. 741.

25 Landau/Parshall 1994, p. 365.

26 Schedel's library was purchased by Hans Jacob Fugger in 1552. In 1571 the contents went, along with other Fugger holdings, to Albrecht V of Bavaria. See R. Stauber, *Die Schedelsche Bibliothek*, edited by O. Hartig (Freiburg, 1908): pp. 78–80. The most important source on Schedel as a collector of prints is Béatrice Hernard, *Die Graphiksammlung des Humanisten Hartmann Schedel* (Munich: Prestel, 1990).

27 For discussion of the genesis and reception of the Nuremberg, *Weltchronik*, see Landau and Parshall 1994, pp. 38–42.

28 For discussion of Schedel's practice of pasting prints into his books, see Parshall 1982, p. 140.

29 For biographical details about Ferdinand Columbus, as well as details about his collection, I have relied on the work of Mark P. McDonald. See Mark P. McDonald, '"Extremely curious and important!": Reconstructing the Print Collection of Ferdinand Columbus', in *Collecting Prints and Drawings in Europe, c. 1500–1750*, edited by Christopher Baker, Caroline Elam, and Genevieve Warwick (Aldershot: Ashgate, 2003): pp. 37–54; McDonald, 2004; McDonald, *The Print Collection of Ferdinand Columbus (1488–1539): A Renaissance Collector in Seville* (London: British Museum Press, 2004).

30 The original is lost. The nineteenth-century manuscript is in the Biblioteca Columbina in Seville, inv. no. 1890-1-7-20.

31 See footnote 27 in this chapter for bibliographic citations for McDonald's work.

32 'From July to late October 1520, there were regular opportunities for Ferdinand and Dürer's paths to cross. Their first point of contact might have been in Brussels where Dürer arrived on August 27 and stayed 5 days. Ferdinand was there for periods in June, July and in August. Ferdinand and Dürer's itineraries corresponded at several points after that. Both were in Aachen in late October and in Cologne in November.' McDonald 2004, p. 1.

33 McDonald 2004, p. 2.

34 McDonald 2004, p. 2.

35 According to McDonald, *pliegio* (300/380 × 200/300 mm) was one of seven size categories. McDonald 2004, p. 2.

36 McDonald 2004, p. 2.

37 See A.E. Popham, 'Peter Breugel and Abraham Ortelius', *The Burlington Magazine* LIX (1931): pp. 184–188.

38 Iain Buchanan, 'Dürer and Abraham Ortelius', *The Burlington Magazine* 124 (1982): pp. 734–741, at p. 734.

39 Buchanan points out that the main evidence for this scarcity of Dürer prints is found in the letters and account books of Christopher Plantin. In 1567 Plantin wrote to Francisco Gentili of Padua that it was difficult and expensive to get good prints by Dürer. Plantin also sold prints to Ortelius. Buchanan 1982, p. 735.

40 Buchanan 1982, p. 735.

41 Buchanan 1982, p. 735. The album measured 42 × 32.5 cm. Unfortunately these prints carried no individual marks, and it is now impossible to state with certainty which prints belonged to the Ortelius album. Duplicates are recorded as having been sold. However, the original album was described in detail in a report by the Director of the Print Room in 1877, as well as an accessions inventory of 1878. Based on these inventories, the album is described in detail by Buchanan.

42 The collection was first described in the possession of William Six in 1734, when it consisted of two volumes, one of engravings and the other of woodcuts. Between 1808–24 Count von Fries had the collection reorganized into three volumes, one volume of engravings, and two of woodcuts. In 1851, the contents of volume one (the engravings) were sold separately and dispersed. The two albums that remained were acquired by the Louvre in 1911 at the Huth sale by Baron Edmund de Rothschild. Buchanan 1982, p. 739.

43 For biographical details about Sambucus, see Hans Gerstinger, *Die Briefe des Johannes Sambucus (Zsambosky) 1554–1584* (Vienna: Österreichische Akademie der Wissenschaften, Philosophische-Historische Klasse, 1968). A Hungarian scholar, Sambucus was interested in Dürer's Hungarian roots (Dürer's father was Hungarian).

44 Buchanan refers specifically to a 'Dürer revival' that occurred 40 years after Dürer visited the Netherlands. Buchanan 1982, p. 735.

45 Kurt Pilz, 'Willibald Pirkheimers Kunstsammlung und Bibliothek' in *Willibald Pirkheimer 1470/1970: Dokumente, Studien, Perspektiven*, edited by B. Glock and I. Meidinger-Geise (Nuremberg: Glock & Lutz, 1970): pp. 93–110.

46 Much of the relevant information on Imhoff has been published in Horst Pohl, ed., *Willibald Imhoff, Enkel und Erbe Willibald Pirckheimers* (Nürnberg: Stadtsarchiv Nürnberg, 1992).

47 Parshall 1982, p. 140.

48 Anton Springer, 'Inventare der Immhoff'schen Kunstkammer zu Nürnberg', *Mitteilungen der kaiserlichen königlichen Central Commission zur Erforschung und Erhaltung der Baudenkmale* 5 (1860): pp. 352–357.

49 Parshall 1982, p. 141.

50 The Imhoff inventory as well as the *Geheimbüchlein* are translated in their entirety in Fritz Koreny, *Albrecht Dürer and the Animal and Plant Studies of the Renaissance*, translated by Pamela Marwood and Yehuda Shapiro (Boston: Brown, 1988); for this passage see p. 261.

51 As translated in Koreny 1988, p. 261.

52 As translated in Koreny 1988, p. 261.

53 Josef Meder, *Dürer-Katalog. Ein Handbuch über Albrecht Dürers Stiche, Radierungen, Holzschnitte, deren Zustände, Ausgaben und Wasserzeichen* (Vienna: Gillhofer, 1932; reprint New York: Da Capo Press, 1971); Coburg 1975, Kunstsammlungen der Veste Coburg, *Meisterwerke europäischer Grafik*

15.-18. Jahrhundert aus dem Besitz des Kupferstichkabinettes Coburg: Kataloge der Kunstsammlungen der Veste Coburg (Coburg: Kunstsammlungen der Veste Coburg, 1975).

54 The most important publication on the topic is Hendrik Budde, *Die Kunstsammlung des Nürnberger Patriziers Willibald Imhoff unter beseonderer Berücksichtigung der Werke Albrecht Dürers* (Münster: LIT Verlag, 1996).

55 Koreny 1988, p. 17.

56 Koreny 1988, p. 263.

57 Koreny 1988, p. 264.

58 Koreny 1988, p. 264.

59 Koreny 1988, p. 263.

60 Anton Ernstberger, 'Kurfurst Maximilian I und Albrecht Dürer: Zur Geschichte einer grossen Sammlerleidenschaft', *Anzeiger des Germanisches National-Museums 1940–1953* (1954): pp. 143–196, at p. 164.

61 Koreny 1988, p. 263.

62 Fritz Koreny points out that the description of the 1649 sale was not written by Hans Hieronymous Imhoff himself 'but (presumably at his dictation) by another hand of rather younger style; the marginal notes and additions to this section, however, also the 1658 entries, are written by himself in ever deteriorating hand writing.' Koreny 1988, p. 266.

63 For biographical information on Paulus Praun, see Peter Fleischmann, 'Anmerkungen zum Patriziat und zu Kunstsammlungen des 16. Jahrhunderts in Nürnberg', in *Kunst des Sammelns: Das Praunsche Kabinett. Meisterwerke von Dürer bis Carracci,* edited by Katrin Achilles-Syndram (Nuremberg: Verlag des Germansichen Nationalmuseums, 1994): pp. 13–24.

64 Christophe Gottlieb von Murr, *Description du Cabinet de Monsieur Praun à Nuremberg* (Nuremberg: J.T. Schneider, 1797).

65 In 1801, the descendants of Praun decided to sell the collection through an art dealer named Friedrich Frauenholz, who sold only part at auction in 1802.

66 Rainer Schoch, '"Die kostbare unter allen nürnbergischen Kunstkammern", Glanz und Ende des Praunschen Kabinetts', in *Kunst des Sammelns. Das Praunsche Kabinett. Meisterwerke von Dürer bis Carracci,* edited by Katrin Achilles-Syndram (Nuremberg: Verlag des Germansichen Nationalmuseums, 1994): p. 33.

67 On Arundel as a collector see David Howarth, *Lord Arundel and His Circle* (New Haven and London, 1985); Mary F.S. Hervey, *The Life, Correspondence & Collections of Thomas Howard, Earl of Arundel* (Cambridge: Cambridge University Press, 1921).

68 Linda Levy Peck, 'Uncovering the Arundel Library at the Royal Society: Changing Meanings of Science and the Date of the Norfolk Donation', *Notes Rec. Royal Society of London* 52/1 (1998): p. 6.

69 Erwin Rosenthal, 'Dürer's Buchmalereien fur Pirckheimers Bibliothek', *Jahrbuch der Preussischen Kunstsammlungen* 49/3 (1929): pp. 1–54.

70 Howarth 1984, pp. 156–157.

71 Albert Gümbel, 'Die englische Mission des Grafen von Arundel in Nürnberg, Mai und November 1636', *Archivalische Zeitschrift* 11 (1904): pp. 100–117.

72 See also Howarth 1985, p. 202.

73 Crowne, *A True Relation*, p. 12ff. (May 1636) and p. 55f. (November 1636).

74 Samuel Quiccheberg, *Der Anfang der Museumslehre in Deutschland: das Traktat 'Inscriptiones, vel, Tituli Theatri Amplissimi' von Samuel Quiccheberg, 1565,* with commentary from Harriet Roth (Berlin: Akademie Verlag, 2000).

75 For further analysis of Quiccheberg see the unpublished doctoral thesis from the University of Pittsburgh by Barbara Balsiger, *The Kunst- und Wunderkammern: A Catalogue Raisonné of Collecting in Germany, France and England, 1565–1750* (Ann Arbor, Michigan: University Microfilms International, 1989), especially pp. 517–527 for her discussion of Quiccheberg.

76 Balsiger 1989, p. 518.

77 Balsiger 1989, pp. 523–524.

78 Balsiger 1989, p. 524.

79 Dirk Jacob Jansen, 'Example and Examples: The Potential Influence of Jacopo Strada on the Development of Rudolphine Art', in *Prag um 1600: Beiträge zur Kunst und Kultur am Hofe Rudolfs II.* Eds. Jürgen Schultze and Hermann Fillitz. (Freren: Luca Verlag, 1988): pp. 132–146, at p. 135.

80 Jansen 1988, p. 133 and p. 135.

81 Essential literature on these collections includes: Susan Crane, ed., *Museums and Memory* (Stanford: Stanford University Press, 2000); Susanne Konig-Lein and Alfred Walz, eds, *Weltenharmonie: die Kunstkammer und die Ordnung des Wissens* (Braunschweig: Herzog Anton Ulrich-Museum Braunschweig, 2000); Lorraine Daston, *Wonders and the Order of Nature, 1150–1750* (New York: Zone Books, 1998); Horst Bredekamp, *The Lure of Antiquity and the Cult of the Machine: the Kunstkammer and the Evolution of Nature, Art, and Technology*, translated by Allison Brown (Princeton: Markus Wiener Publishers, 1995); Andreas Grote, ed., *Macrocosmos in Microcosmo: die Welt in der Stube: zur Geschichte des Sammelns 1450 bis 1800* (Opladen: Leske and Budrich, 1994); ; Marcin Fabianski, 'Iconography of the Architecture of Ideal *Musaea* in the Fifteenth to Eighteenth Centuries', *Journal of the History of Collections* 2/2 (1990): pp. 95–134; Paula Findlen, 'The Museum: Its Classical Etymology and Renaissance Geneaology', *Journal of the History of Collections* 1/1 (1989): pp. 59–78; Oliver Impey and Arthur MacGregor, *The Origins of Museums: The Cabinet of Curiosities in Sixteenth- and Seventeenth-century Europe* (Oxford: Clarendon Press, 1985); Elisabeth Scheicher, *Die Kunst- und Wunderkammern der Habsburger* (Vienna: Molden Editions, 1979); Julius von Schlosser, *Die Kunst- und Wunderkammern der Spätrenaissance. Ein Beitrag zur Geschichte des Sammelwesens* (Braunschweig: Klinkhardt and Biermann, 1978).

82 On the politics of display and patronage, see Thomas DaCosta Kaufmann, *The Mastery of Nature: Aspects of Art, Science and Humanism in the Renaissance* (Princeton: Princeton University Press, 1993).

83 See Keith Thomas, *Religion and the Decline of Magic* (New York: Scribner, 1971): p. 1. It is beyond the scope of this chapter to delve further into the more philosophical aspects of these collections. However, I would consider a comparison between the principles of the *Kunstkammer* and the memory theater of Giulio Camillo as an important line of research for the future. Camillo's memory theater is discussed with great eloquence by Francis Yates. See Francis Yates, *The Art of Memory* (Chicago: University of Chicago Press, 1966).

84 Barbara Gutfleisch and Joachim Menzhausen, '"How a Kunstkammer should be formed": Gabriel Kaltemarckt's advice to Christian I of Saxony on the formation of an art collection, 1587', *Journal of the History of Collections* 1 (1989): pp. 3–32.

85 For details on the Habsburgs, see R.J.W. Evans, *The Making of the Habsburg Monarchy, 1550–1700* (Oxford: Clarendon Press, 1979).

86 There are parallels to be found in other collections in Poland, Prussia, Hungary, and Austria. There has already been some study of this very important collection: see Jiří Pešék, 'Obrazy a grafiky a jejich majitele v předbělohorské Praze', *Umění* 39 (1991): pp. 369–383; Alfred Auer, 'Die Sammeltätigkeit Erzherzog Ferdinands II. in Böhmen', in *Kaiser Ferdinand I. 1503–1564. Das Werden der Habsburgmonarchie* (Wien: Kunsthistorisches Museum, 2003), ed. Georg Johannes Kugler, pp. 297–306; Elizabeth Scheicher, 'The Collection of Archduke Ferdinand II at Schloss Ambras: its Purpose, Composition and Evolution', in *The Origins of Museums: The Cabinet of Curiosities in Sixteenth- and Seventeenth-century Europe,* edited by Oliver Impey and Arthur MacGregor (Oxford: Clarendon Press, 1985): p. 181.

87 For biographical details on Ferdinand see Josef Hirn, *Erzherzog Ferdinand II. von Tirol. Geschichte seiner Regierung und seiner Länder*, 2 volumes (Innsbruck: Wagner, 1885/88). Ferdinand's son and successor as emperor from 1564, Maximilian II, had more to do with local construction in Bratislava (Poszony, Pressburg), which replaced Buda as the capital of Hungary after the Ottoman invasion.

88 Alfred Auer, 'Das Inventarium der Ambraser Sammlungen aus dem Jahre 1621, II.Teil: Bibliothek', *Jahrbuch des kunsthistorischen Museums Wien* II (2001): pp. 281–345; Christian Gries 'Erzherzog Ferdinand von Tirol: Konturen einer Sammlerpersönlichkeit', *Frühneuzeit-Info* IV (1993): pp. 162–173.

89 Scheicher 1985, p. 181.

90 Boeheim, A., 'Verlassenschaftsinventar des Erzherzogs Ferdinand von Tirol, Mai 30, 1596, Innsbruck', *Jahrbuch der Kunsthistorischen Sammlungen des Allerhöchsten Kaiserhauses in Wien* X/2 (1889): pp. i–x.

91 Parshall 1982, pp. 139–184.

92 Kunstbuch Albrethen Dürers von Nürmberg (Inv. 5127–37).

93 For a description of the album contents see Parshall 1982, p. 148.

94 Parshall 1982, p. 149.

95 Parshall 1982, p. 142.

96 R.J.W. Evans, *Rudolf II and His World: A Study in Intellectual History* (Oxford: Clarendon Press, 1973), p. 10. Rudolf had become head of a vast empire 'with a constitution that was so complex as to be largely unfathomable even to its rulers, a rigid hierarchy through Electors, bishops and other ecclesiastics, secular princes of various kinds, and free cities down to the smallest *Reichsritter* ... where legal disputes regularly took decades to resolve, yet for all that a living organism where appeal to the highest authority was always possible.' See also p. 73.

97 The most extensive biographical study of Rudolf II remains Evans 1973 (see note above). For a history of the castle complex see Eliška Fučiková, 'Prague Castle under Rudolf II, His Predecessors and Successors', *Rudolf II and Prague: The Court and the City* (London: Thames and Hudson, 1997): pp. 2–71.

98 Fučiková 1997, p. 15.

99 Two major exhibitions aptly demonstrated the diversity and quality of Rudolf's collection, and the accompanying publications are indispensable for any understanding of the Rudolfine court. For the essays that accompanied the exhibition held in 1997 in Prague, see Eliška Fučiková, ed., *Rudolf II and Prague: The Court and the City* (London: Thames and Hudson, 1997); for the essays accompanying the 1988 exhibition in Vienna and Essen, see *Prague um 1600: Beiträge zur Kunst und Kultur am Hofe Rudolfs II*, eds. Jürgen Schultze and Hermann Fillitz (Freren: Luca Verlag, 1988).

100 Rotraud Bauer and Herbert Haupt, 'Die Kunstkammer Kaiser Rudolfs in Prag: Ein Inventar aus den Jahren 1607–1611', *Jahrbuch der Kunsthistorischen Sammlungen in Wien* 72 (1976): pp. xi–xxxvii. There are also inventories for 1619 and 1621 (which have not been published).

101 Bauer and Haupt 1607/11, p. 13.

102 Bauer and Haupt 1607/11, p. 13.

103 Hutchison 1990, pp. 4–5.

104 Zikmund Winter, Řemeslnictvo a zivnosti XVI. *věku v Čechách,1526–1620* (Prague: Ceské akademie císaře Františka Josefa, 1909): pp. 209–210. See also Michal Šroněk, 'Sculpture and Painting in Prague, 1550–1650', in *Rudolf II and Prague: The Court and the City* (London: Thames and Hudson, 1997): pp. 353–375, at p. 365.

105 The dates of Dürer's completion of these paintings are: *Adam and Eve* (1507), *Adoration of the Trinity* (1511), *Martyrdom of the Ten Thousand* (1508), *The Feast of the Rosegarlands* (1506), *Madonna and the Pear* (1526), *Johannes Kleeberger* (1526).

106 Erwin Panofsky, *The Life and Art of Albrecht Dürer* (Princeton: Princeton University Press, 1955): p. 125.

107 The stained glass is now in the Berlin Schlossmuseum. The frame is in Nuremberg, Germanisches Nationalmuseum.

108 For a thorough discussion of the painting see Anzelewsky 1991, no. 118.

109 Vienna 1994, *Albrecht Dürer im Kunsthistorischen Museum,* edited by Karl Schütz and Rotraud Bauer (Wien: Kunsthistorisches Museum, 1994): p. 55.

110 Hauer'sche Manuskript (Germanisches Nationalmuseum, Archiv Rst. Nürnberg XII/44) Bl. 27r; see Tacke 2001, p. 122.

111 See especially Andrew John Martin, ' "...Dass er nicht nachgelassen, bis ihm solches Blat aus der Kirche verwilligt worden." Der Erwerb von Albrecht Dürers Rosenkranzfest Durch Rudolf II', *Umění* 46 (1998): pp. 175–88.

112 William Martin Conway, compiler/translator, *The Writings of Albrecht Dürer* (New York: Philosophical Library, 1958): pp. 211–212.

113 Peter Humfrey, 'La Festa del Rosario di Albrecht Dürer', *Eidos: Rivista di Cultura* 2 (1988): p. 14.

114 Louisa C. Matthew, 'Working Abroad: Northern Artists in the Venetian Ambient', in *Renaissance Venice and the North: Crosscurrents in the Time of Bellini, Dürer and Titian,* edited by Bernard Aikema and Beverly Louise Brown, (New York: Rizzoli, 1999): pp. 61–69, at p. 61.

115 The cult of the rosary was a Dominican form of devotion that recommended the saying of prayers. One rosary contained 165 five beads: this represented the saying of 150 'Hail Marys' and 15 'Our Fathers'. The beads were said to represent an actual wreath of white and red roses, such as those depicted in Dürer's painting on the heads of the donors. The small white beads represented the saying of the Hail Mary prayer, and the large red beads the Our Father prayer. The circle of the rosary represented the unity of the Christian community.

116 Peter Humfrey, 'Competitive Devotions: The Venetian *Scuole Piccole* as Donors of Altarpieces in the Years around 1500', *Art Bulletin* 70/3 (1988): pp. 401–423, at p. 403.

117 Humfrey 1988, p. 403.

118 Domenico Romanelli, 'The Fondaco dei Tedeschi', in *Renaissance Venice and the North: Crosscurrents in the Time of Bellini, Dürer and Titian*, edited by Bernard Aikema and Beverly Louise Brown (New York: Rizzoli, 1999): pp. 77–81, at p. 77.

119 Humfrey 1988, p. 403.

120 Sandrart 1675/1925, 1: 223.

121 Martin 1998, p. 176.

122 Vienna 1994, p. 51. This painting was made around the same time as the *Feast of the Rosegarlands* while Dürer was in Venice, and Dürer brought it back with him to Nuremberg. It was in the possession of Hans Imhoff in the second half of the sixteenth century.

123 Vienna 1994, p. 51.

124 Kauffmann 1940–53, pp. 25–26.

125 Vienna 1994, pp. 50–51.

126 The Kunsthistorisches Museum in Vienna and the Albertina now hold 8 paintings and 140 drawings and watercolours by Dürer that were originally held in the *Kunstkammer* of Rudolf. See Vienna 1994, p. 51.

127 Gisela Goldberg has done extensive research on the collection of Maximilian. See Gisela Goldberg, 'Münchner Aspekte der Dürer Renaissance unter besonderer Berücksichtigung von Dürers Tier und Pflanzenstudien', *Jahrbuch der Kunsthistorischen Sammlungen in Wien* 82/82 (1986/1987): pp. 179–188; Gisela Goldberg, 'Zur Ausprägung der Dürer Renaissance in München', *Münchner Jahrbuch der Bildender Kunst* 31 (1980): pp. 129–176 (this publication includes an inventory of the collection); Gisela Goldberg, 'Dürer-Renaissance am Münchner Hof', *Um Glauben und Reich. Kürfurst Maximilian I: Beiträge zur Bayerischen Geschichte und Kunst 1573–1657*, edited by Hubert Glaser (Munich: Hirmer, 1980): pp. 318–322.

128 For a biographical sketch of Maximilian, and important observations about his collecting practices involving Dürer see Ernstberger 1954, pp. 143–196.

129 *Des Augsburger Patriciers Philipp Hainhofer Beziehungen zum Herzog Philipp II. Von Pommern-Stettin. Correspondenzen aus den Jahren 1610–1619 im Auszuge mitgehelt und commentiert von Dr. Oscar Doering. Quellenschriften für Kunstgeschichte und Kunsttechnik des Mittelalters und der Neuzeit,* compiled by Oscar Doering (Vienna: Verlag von Carl Graeser, 1894). Included is commentary from his trips to Eichstadt, Munich and Regensburg in the years 1611, 1612 and 1613.

130 Ernstberger reprints the inventory offered by Imhoff to Maximilian in 1630. Ernstberger 1954, p. 175.

131 For the inventory see Josef Weiss, 'Kurfürst Maximilian von Bayern als Gemäldesammler. Neue archivalische Beiträge', *Historisch-politische Blätter für das katholische Deutschland* 142 (1908): pp. 545–569.

132 Schwemmer 1949, p. 97.

133 Goldberg, Heimberg and Schwae, p. 5.

134 Goldberg, Heimberg and Schwae 1998, p. 5. As pointed out in this essential publication, the panels and painting techniques of the wings differ from the central panel. The curators of the Alte Pinakothek also outline the damage that the painting endured after an acid attack in 1988.

135 Vienna 1994, p. 53.

136 As cited in Ernstberger 1954, p. 148. Ernstberger quotes extensively from the correspondence of Beheim, dated 1630. In the Germanisches Nationalmuseum there is an archive exclusively devoted to Lucas Beheim, containing his *Kopierbücher*, 1622–1648.

137 Joseph Eduard Wessely, 'Das Manuscript von Paul Beheim's Kupferstichkatalog im Berliner Museums', *Repertorium für Kunstwissenshcaft* 6 (1883): pp. 54–63.

138 'Ganz von einer anderen Hand.' Beheim, as quoted in Ernstberger 1954, p. 165.

139 For a discussion of the commission see Panofsky 1955, pp. 123–125. Only the central element depicting the Assumption and Coronation of the Virgin was executed by Dürer himself.

140 The letters are dated August 28 (1507), March 19 (1508), August 24 (1508), November 4 (1508), March 21 (1509), July 10 (1509), July 14 (1509), August 26 (1509), and October 12 (1509). For a discussion of the contents of these letters, see Hutchison 1990, pp. 99–105.

141 'von Kayser, Khönig und Potentaten, darnach lang vnd vilfaltig getracht worden...' Karel Van Mander put together the first list of Dürer's paintings, including 14 works. Cited in Joseph Leo Koerner, *The Moment of Self-Portraiture in German Renaissance Art* (Chicago: University of Chicago Press, 1993): p. 49.

142 Panofsky 1955, p. 123.

143 As described by Karel van Mander in 1604, 'Het is verwonderlijck, en schier ongheloofiijck, wat dit stuck den Monicken oft het Clooster Iaerlijcx opbrengt, en nut is, alleen van de vereeringhen oft drinckpenninghen, die voor het ontsluyten oft toonen, van Heeren, Coopluyden, reys volck, en Const-liefdige worden gheschoncken: dit was gedaen van hem A°. 1509.' Carel van Mander, *Schilder-boek,* translation and notes by Hessel Miedema (Doornspijk: Davaco, 1994–1999): fol. 209r.

144 See Anzelewsky 1991, no. 66.

145 This is also noted in Tacke 2001, p. 123, n.397. Beheim is discussed in Ernstberger 1940–53, pp. 143–196; however the extensive Beheim archive, which includes Beheim's personal correspondence and a copious amount of letters, merits further research.

146 Haimbl's full title is 'Kurfürstlicher Durchlaucht in Bayern Kammerdiener und Kunstverwalter'. Ernstberger 1954, p. 150.

147 See Tacke 2001: he cites the Hauer'sche Manuskript, folio 27r.

148 Ernstberger 1954, p. 150. Nürnberg Stadtsarchiv, Beheimarchiv Nr. 1670, Lukas Friedrich Beheim an Johann Christoph Neustetter, Nürnberg 1727 November 1627.

149 '... mit sonderm Fleiß von seiner Hand gefertigtes Gemäl.' Nürnberg Stadtsarchiv, Briefbücher Nr. 246 (1627), fol. 707 ff. Nürnberg an Kurfürst Maximilian I von Bayern. Nürnberg, 27 August/6 September, 1627. Cited in Ernstberger 1954, p. 190, n. 26; pp. 150–151.

150 See Tacke 2001. Hauer'sche Manuskript, folio 27r.

151 Dürer's 1500 self-portrait, and Dürer's portraits of Oswalt Krell and Michael Wolgemut were all in Nuremberg during Maximilian's collecting sweep.

152 Only a single page of the original manuscript has survived. There are also two existing and complete copies made in the late-sixteenth or early-seventeenth century by professional scribes. When Dürer died Pirckheimer's grandson Willibald Imhoff still had the original. It was last mentioned in 1620.

153 Important work has been done on the reception of the altars by Felix Steinraths, *Albrecht Dürers Memorialtafeln aus der Zeit um 1500: Holzschuher-Epitaph-Glimm'sche Bewinung-Paumgärtner-Altar; Rezeption, Forschungsstand und offene Fragen* (Frankfurt am Main: Lang, 2000).

3

Appropriating Dürer

The previous chapter established that a number of sixteenth- and seventeenth-century collectors, especially Rudolf II in Prague and Maximilian I in Munich, had strong interest in the art of Albrecht Dürer. Through provenance research and the use of inventories, one important aspect of the reception of Dürer in the early modern period was firmly established: concentrated collecting of his drawings, prints and paintings. A chief characteristic of the Dürer-Renaissance was the removal of Dürer's paintings from their original contexts, and the movement of his prints and drawings to disparate locations.

This chapter focuses on the artistic reception of Dürer. Having pinpointed where works by Dürer could be found, the investigation now turns to creative borrowings including copies, imitations and emulations of Dürer's art: in short, the early modern appropriation of Dürer. Access to works by Dürer would have occurred in a number of ways; for example, artists attached to a particular court circle would have had the opportunity to view paintings housed there. In some instances albums including Dürer's prints were in circulation, and of course individual prints were distributed on an international scale.

A central argument here is that copying and forgery must be distinguished from imitation and/or emulation. The creation of a faithful and direct copy was considered to highly instructive and at times pedagogically directed endeavour, a way of adopting a master's style, almost as if the master was guiding the pupil's hand. In other instances a copy could be created in order to replace and important work of art *in situ*, another mode of production identified in Chapter 2, in particular in relation to Dürer's altarpieces. As for forgeries, perhaps the most famed artist to use Dürer's compositions for profit, without altering them at all, is Marcantonio Raimondi. Raimondi was not the only artist to engage in this sort of activity, but it is also important to note, and central to this discussion of the Dürer-Renaissance, that copying and forgery were only two of the modes of creation associated with Dürer's reception. To understand this, one needs look no further than seventeenth-century art writers, who held that artists were thought to have the ability to single out and choose praiseworthy examples from the past for imitation, thus allowing for the creation of a *new* manner of painting.[1] The choice of a model was deeply significant and could often be influenced by a patron. Solutions to problems of pictorial composition could be understood not only by absorbing the accomplishments of past artists, but by also necessarily improving upon them.[2] In short, the impulse of imitation and emulation – which can be neatly packaged as appropriation – had strong currency in the seventeenth century. There will always be debate as to the extent to which theory and practice can be said to overlap. While it may be impossible to directly document artistic intent, particularly with works by lesser-known artists, there is striking evidence for an emphasis in the images as well as the writings of the seventeenth century on imitation as a means of creating a new *maniera* of painting.

Art historians have long been adept at pinpointing influence, often with the aim of consolidating the body of work that can be attributed to a particular artist. Moreover, the transmission of motifs is a long-standing means of showing continuity in the history of art, demonstrating how a style was fostered or reacted against, and establishing where dependencies exist. Within this framework of influence, the tendency has often been toward a dismissal of more imitative works as passive and unoriginal.[3] What will be stressed here is how the imitative impulse was valued in the seventeenth century, especially in court contexts. Certain cases of imitation involved highly competitive motivations that were often deeply appreciated. A significant point to be made is that many of these imitative works were not thought of as insignificant or lesser, and that the imitative works themselves often occupied important positions within burgeoning seventeenth-century collections. It will be emphasized that many of the works ensuing from the Dürer-Renaissance were often charged with significant functions.

Laying emphasis on Dürer in this regard is not to suggest that his oeuvre was the only one imitated in the seventeenth century. Other noteworthy examples of artistic imitation could be cited for the sixteenth and seventeenth centuries. There are works by Rubens that evoke Titian, for example. When Rubens painted his portrait of *Helene Fourment*, he was paying homage to Titian's *Girl in Fur*. The painting by Rubens can hardly be considered a copy, but rather is a second presentation of the same theme. This particularly emphatic example of imitation is to be understood in the terms of the ideas of imitation prevalent in the sixteenth and seventeenth centuries: as creative assimilation with the aim of a new presentation.[4] King Philip IV of Spain, a well-educated lover of the arts and collector, paid 900 gulden and upwards for pictures by Titian. However, he paid double this amount for pictures by Rubens after Titian. This happened not because Rubens was valued more – Titian was highly valued by Habsburg collectors – rather, such a picture had double value because it was imbued with the talents of both Titian and Rubens. In other words, the idea of Titian was formulated in the speech of Rubens in a genuine and authentic imitation (sometimes referred to as a quotation). Rubens also imitated works by Raphael, using single figures or groups from Raphael's compositions and employing them in his pictures. Often, his borrowings were worked in so carefully that the imitation of Raphael was not immediately apparent.

In Italy at the end of the sixteenth and into the seventeenth century, the Italian Renaissance masters were avidly imitated as well. Another well-known example of one artist imitating another is Gianlorenzo Bernini, whose artistic references to the works of Michelangelo are prominent and by no means hidden. Rather, the quotations are proudly acknowledged. In her essay 'Imitatio Bounarroti', Catherine M. Sousloff discusses the repeated comparisons between Bernini and Michelangelo in numerous seventeenth-century sources, and how the papal patron Maffeo Barberini encouraged his court artist Bernini to cultivate his genius and become the Michelangelo of his century.[5] The use of an earlier artist's reputation was a common way of constructing a prominent position for seventeenth-century artists. This can also be seen in biographies from the period, wherein rhetorical devices were used to elevate individuals. In the sixteenth century it was commonplace for artists, including Dürer, to be compared to Apelles, the Greek painter active in the fourth century who was reckoned to be the most praiseworthy and exceptional painter to have lived (see Chapter 1 for the references to Dürer as a new Apelles).

By the seventeenth century, with a new artistic tradition being established, the comparison with Renaissance artists, as opposed to Apelles, was the new commonplace. Albrecht Dürer was one artist frequently used as the new measuring stick. To cite just one example, Georg Flegel (1566–1638), the Moravian-born artist who earned an esteemed reputation as a still-life painter in Frankfurt, was compared to both Apelles and Dürer on the occasion of his death. In his epitaph his Moravian origins are stressed, his success as a nature painter, and kinship with both Apelles and Dürer: 'Moravia bore me and Olmütz raised me. With the secrets of nature, I, her devoted admirer the blessed protege of the arts, Georg Flegel, truly have I been a second Apelles and Dürer.'[6] It is certain that at least one of Dürer's nature studies was well known to Flegel. In his *Still Life with Stag Beetle* (1635), Flegel has depicted an untouched meal of bread, fish, green onions and wine, toward which a stag beetle advances from the bottom left corner (Figure 81). The stag beetle is a depiction of (and improvement upon in terms of realism) Dürer's study of a stag beetle from over a century before. The stag beetle was one of Dürer's most copied animal studies (Figure 76). For the purposes of this chapter, note that Flegel's placement of the beetle in a scene and his use of and improvement upon Dürer's model are indicative of the manner in which a number of artists of the seventeenth century sought to align themselves with Dürer's reputation and pictorial ideas. No works survived by Apelles, making comparison with him rhetorical. On the other hand the seventeenth-century artist who aligned himself with a Renaissance predecessor such as Dürer had actual models to contend with, and often chose to present imitations in a very prominent manner.

In other words, Flegel's appropriation of Dürer is quite different from Marcantonio Raimonidi's copies of Dürer, or other uses of Dürer that can be more appropriately described as forgeries. The Dürer frenzy reached such heights in the sixteenth and seventeenth centuries that when existing originals were not enough to satisfy the demand, numerous forgeries came into existence. We have already seen how Hans Hieronymous Imhoff noted in 1634 when selling works to a Dutch merchant, that Dürer's signature had been added to several drawings even when there were insufficient grounds to believe that Dürer had painted them, and admittedly for the purpose of fetching a higher price.[7] Flegel's appropriation is quite different. He uses a Dürer motif with the full knowledge that his borrowing or quotation would be recognized as such; his epitaph is suggestive of his seeking to align himself with Dürer's artistry and reputation. The creative idea of Dürer, and its execution and improvement upon by another artist, was valued. Like the many Renaissance artists who had been fixated on imitating the antique, seventeenth-century artists imitated the new paragons that had emerged. In short, the awareness of having fostered and created an important artistic tradition worthy of imitation finds its expression in the Dürer-Renaissance, which was more than a concerted attempt to revive and enshrine Dürer.

It is noteworthy that of the works to be discussed fewer are dated to the sixteenth century, with the majority dated to the seventeenth century. With the exception of Hans Baldung, few works by Dürer's pupils have been included. The primary purpose of this chapter is not to discern the influence of Dürer on those associated with his studio, the three journeymen named Hans: Hans Süss von Kulmbach (1485–1522), Hans Schäufelein (1482–1539), and Hans Baldung (1484–1585).[8] In fact, Dürer's relationship with these pupils reflects a rather hands-off approach (atypical for the period) that perhaps contributed to their rapid developments as independent artists. By 1503, these three young journeymen are documented as part of Dürer's studio. As Jane Campbell Hutchison has pointed out,

> Dürer broke with tradition in permitting his journeymen to accept independent commissions as time allowed, even while they were still indentured to him … tradition was broken, as well, when Dürer's students were permitted to develop their own styles, rather than simply being set to copy the work of the master.[9]

At a time when Dürer was increasingly involved in the graphic arts and his commissions for Holy Roman Emperor Maximilian I, his pupil Hans Süss von Kulmbach undertook numerous commissions for the city of Nuremberg and was a key figure in shaping the city's church interiors (for example the eastern choir of St Sebaldus). By 1511 he had opened his own workshop.[10] Hans Schäufelein, active in Dürer's workshop from 1503–1507, was permitted to sign certain works of his own as early as 1504.[11] Hans Baldung, who was referred to by Dürer as 'Grienhans' in order to distinguish him from the other Hans, was the most successful in developing his own style, and is today counted as an artist of great versatility and imagination.[12] Dürer himself, writing in 1528, argued *against* the necessity of learning through copying, and disparaged those artists who 'only imitated others'.[13]

It appears the latter pupil heeded the advice of his master especially well. In fact, several examples show how rather than imitate, Hans Baldung Grien in fact appropriated Dürer in a subversive and highly critical manner. Not only does this support the idea that when compared to standard Renaissance workshop practices, Dürer's was contrary in its flexibility and permissiveness, but also will serve to illustrate how appropriation is a term better suited to much of the pictorial evidence to the Dürer-Renaissance, as opposed to copying. No one reflected more upon his teacher's example than Hans Baldung. Unlike his fellow journeymen, he did not come from a long line of artisans: the Baldungs were lawyers, doctors, university professors and high government officials. After working in Dürer's workshop around 1503, Baldung seems to have been keen to subvert some of his teacher's ideals. Unlike the classical proportions, balance and harmony of Dürer's art, we see in Baldung the familiar becoming strange and eerie, and there is a direct confrontation with subject matter that is usually treated with apprehension. Here we have an artist who was intrigued by the occult, and the characters of demons and witches are to be found in many of his prints. Baldung set up his own workshop in 1509 in Strasbourg, and in the works that emerged from that context we see a marked emphasis on the gruesomeness and inevitability of death. In his paintings colour is expressly discordant and illogical, full of the sickly greens that had inspired Dürer to give him the nickname 'Grien Hans'.

Baldung subverted Dürer's classical idealism on a number of occasions, and nowhere more brazenly than in his prints of horses, the animal who symbolized the passions most often in Renaissance.[14] As an accompaniment to his tract on the human figure, Dürer had once planned to write a theoretical tract on the proportions of the horse including his *Small Horse* of 1505 (Figure 19). He presents us with a muscular horse and his groom, all arranged according to a spatial central perspective, confined and contained within a classical barrel-vaulted space. Order and rationality abound. The muscular horse raises his foreleg, and is firmly in synch with the groom who accompanies him. The winged helmet and shoes indicate that it is Mercury, another reference to classicism. The burning vase in the background is an eternal fire alluding to human reason. In other words, unbridled passion, in the form of the horse, has been tamed by the force of human reason, as symbolized by Mercury and the eternal fire.

Now let us consider Hans Baldung's subversion of Dürer's prototype, created very soon as a response in 1512 (Figure 21). There is no more barrel vault, only a knotted tree and an open background. The groom must try to bridle the horse and is having great difficulty. The horse is obviously more powerful and resistant, and there is a corresponding tension in the forms of the tail, the bulging veins, and the gnashing teeth. Literally, the groom is being swept off his feet. For Baldung, the horse is no longer a representation of perfect proportions, noble restraint and calm dignity. On the contrary, the horse for Baldung is the accomplice of sorcery and the passions unleashed. The struggle between the groom and the horse gives a terrifying intensity to the portrayal, the crisis of the situation palapable as opposed to Dürer's resolute calm. The chief point to be made with this pictorial comparison is that when Baldung appropriated Dürer, he would fully have expected this to be recognized and reflected upon. He subverts the classicism and idealism of Dürer's vision. Rather than being a simple transmission of a past motif, this appropriation forces us to consider both Dürer's prototype and Baldung's subversion. What does an appropriation do? It makes the past patently and brazenly evident to us as a past. For whatever reason, Baldung has reformulated Dürer's horse in a discordant manner, and removed it from its balanced and harmonious existence.

Let us consider another study of horse proportions by Dürer, the *Large Horse* (Figure 20). Notice the monumental size of the horse's body, its stable position and calm expression, a balanced temperament. Classicism is again firmly in place, as indicated by the solid Doric column. While the horse is standing calmly and firmly on the ground, the warrior with him is striding energetically, in control of the creature he has tamed. Once again, form, control, idealism and proportion reign. Baldung's *Groom Bewitched* can be interpreted as a radical subversion of Dürer's vision (Figure 22). The well-formed and irked horse is clearly in charge. His groom lies flat on the floor behind him, clearly unconscious. The groom's tools – the pitchfork and comb – lie in disarray on the floor. A hag, possibly a witch, leans in across the window ledge and waves a flaming torch, possibly with the intent of arson. Various interpretations as to how the groom became incapacitated have been proposed. Is he dead? Hypnotized or possessed by evil spirits? Drunk? My preferred reading is that the groom has been kicked violently by the horse. This is a terrifying appropriation of Dürer's scene, a complete reversal of the role of passion. Nature and man can no longer be seen as peacefully coexisting, indeed, they are completely out of joint. Malevolent forces are now at play, as represented by the witch. Horses frequently symbolize the passions in Renaissance art, but rarely so powerfully and violently as in the series of prints by Baldung.

Again it should be stressed that Baldung would fully have appreciated that his audience would recognize his appropriation of Dürer's horses. Collectors of prints were adept at identifying parallels with the earlier creations, as John Shearman has convincingly argued in his majestic *The Power of Images: Studies in the History and Theory of Response*. The issue at stake thus becomes, not *did* Baldung intend for his subversion to be recognized, but rather *why*? I have noted that in both instances there is a focus on occult forces, and this leads to a consideration of how these artists' contexts differed from Dürer's. The fact that Dürer had travelled to Italy twice and assimilated the lessons of the Italian Renaissance accounts in part for his pervasive classicism. The same cannot be said of Baldung, who did not travel as Dürer did, and who chose to revert to the mystical elements that had dominated much Northern Renaissance art prior to the Renaissance. Equally, the tensions and the aftermath of the Protestant Reformation could have been felt and expressed by the younger artist in different ways. Fears of malevolent forces were not uncommon during the political and religious upheavals of the reformation, and Baldung, who died in 1545, would have experienced these changes to a far greater extent than Dürer, who died in 1528. Was Baldung reflecting on the subversion of social and political order, by subverting the more peaceful vision of his artistic prototype? Also, recall that the overwhelming example set by Dürer meant that appropriations of his work would have an added dimension of recognition. Rebelling against such a master could bring notoriety of its own.

Some art historians have lamented the fact that Dürer died he did not leave behind a 'legitimate' successor. This is in part because some of the artists who worked with him (such as Hans Baldung) and those immediately subsequent to his death used his motifs in a creative manner that can more rightfully be described as appropriation. The expert on Dürer's plant and animal studies, Fritz Koreny, discusses this with respect to three other artists known to have worked with Dürer on a number of commissions, Georg Pencz (1500–50), and the brothers Barthel Beham and Hans Sebald Beham, the so-called 'Little Masters of Nuremberg' (thus named because of their small-scale prints). Koreny writes that 'they may have been working in his style, but not one of them can be labeled as a disciple in the true sense'.[15] Perhaps this is why, in one of the earliest Dürer monographs ever written, the art historian Moritz Thausing described Hans Hoffmann and other Rudolfine artists, whose activities were several generations removed from Dürer, as epitomizing a 'posthumous Dürer school'.[16] As has already been discussed in the introduction to this book, it is important to distinguish between initial and later reception.

While Dürer may not have left behind, to use Koreny's phrase, a 'true disciple', the numerous artistic quotations of his work demonstrate a fascinating range of dependencies and adaptations. The seventeenth-century artists who imitated Dürer made a conscious decision to bring a predecessor, from whom they were removed by several generations, into focus. In doing so artists acknowledged and thereby highlighted a prior tradition of art-making. This was a means to create and stress a distinctive art historical lineage. Perhaps this is why the term 'influence' which can have passive connotations, is a less appropriate term than 'appropriation', which implies an active choice.

These later borrowings of Dürer include not only motifs, but also entire compositions that were altered and varied. None of his pictorial ideas were immune to this imitative impulse, including his monogram. The use of a symbol or monogram in art had its origin with the coat of arms from the mid-thirteenth century and was initially used to identify property. In the early fifteenth century the practice was appropriated from other crafts by graphic artists, largely because of the new economic demands involved in the trade of prints, works of art that were not financed by commission and enjoyed a wide distribution.[17] Dürer was one of the first artists to consistently indicate ownership through the use of a monogram. In his lifetime Dürer had fostered a proprietary relationship to his work, especially to his graphic oeuvre, and he initialled his drawings at a time when few others did so.[18]

During the Dürer-Renaissance monograms were sometimes added by collectors, as noted in the case of Hans Imhoff. At the same time, it is important to note that artists themselves would sometimes include the Dürer monogram. Before Dürer's generation, copyists almost never included the monogram of the original artist on copies; rather, they would sign only with a monogram of their own. As pointed out by Lisa Oehler,

> The initials AD, as they appear frequently in works by artists of the period, can signify a range of dependencies. When it is not simply an optimistic or deceptive addition, by the orders of later collectors, the monogram can identify a work as the product of Dürer's shop rather than his own hand, as seems to be in the case of certain images bearing the monogram.[19]

The Dürer monogram could also used by artists as a sign of respect or homage. There is evidence of a competitive spirit, in which case the imitative artist was eager for the original source to be known to the viewer, in order to demonstrate how the image had been improved. This was certainly the case when artists would include their own monogram, as well as that of the source. Such creations must be distinguished from outright forgery because the intention was not deception. It will perhaps be necessary to revise Anton Springer's remark, that 'the history of Dürer's works is simultaneously the history of the most spectacular forgeries of all time'.[20] Works often characterized as 'forgeries' are in need of fresh consideration.

This chapter is not an exercise in connoisseurship – no new attributions have been made, nor is there any instance where debate with an accepted attribution arises. Inherent is a respect and acknowledgement of the very crucial work done by the scholars who have differentiated the oeuvre of Dürer from his imitators. Perhaps the best way of characterizing this chapter is to state that the focus is firmly upon images known to be imitations from the time of their inception, especially within the contexts of the courts of the sixteenth and seventeenth centuries.

I would like to make a brief note about the organization of the chapter subsequent to this point. In the next section, Contexts for Appropriation, I discuss some literary sources that invoke theories of imitation. It becomes possible to distinguish between copying, imitation and emulation. However, it is also important to recognize that the lines between these modes of production were often blurred. This is essential background for my consideration of the vast trove of images that can be associated with the Dürer-Renaissance. In order to give some coherence to the discussion, I have found it useful to subdivide the images according to the Dürer source used by the artists, an organizing feature that has already been used in Chapter 2, where there was a rough progression from prints, to drawings, to paintings. This organizing principle is also reflected in the appendix of illustrations.

Prints by definition existed in multiple copies, were the most easily transportable and accessible of images, and in the case of Dürer, had international distribution. It will come as no surprise that Dürer's prints were his most imitated works. Because there are so many imitations in existence, it has been possible to consider only some of them. I have chosen some of the most striking examples, and in a wide array of media, in order to characterize the range of motivations that were involved: forgery, pedagogy, retrospection, emulation, transformation and internationalization, with each of these concepts considered in a subsection. Overall, the intention of the section on prints is not to provide an exhaustive catalogue of all the imitations of Dürer's prints, but rather to show that imitative works often arose due to diverse and rich epistemological concerns, and should not in every case be dismissed, as they have been in the past, as passive or unoriginal. Rather, they are an important source of information about art-making and the values of collectors in the period under scrutiny

The reception of Dürer's drawings was of a different order than the prints, since drawings obviously exist in one original state. This brings us to the context of the courts, where the drawings had become important collector items. Access to the drawings would have been more limited than to the prints. The numerous and divergent uses made of Dürer's drawings are especially intriguing, and range from straightforward copies to engraved versions. We know that some of Hans Hoffmann's drawings after Dürer were greatly valued by his patron Rudolf II, as were Aegedius Sadeler's engraved versions. This is interesting evidence of the value placed upon Dürer's pictorial ideas, as well as an inclination toward engraving the contents of a collection. Examining the use of Dürer drawings as sources also heightens our awareness of the roles that individual artists played in the reception of Dürer.

The final section is a consideration of imitative works after Dürer's paintings. Access to works by Dürer on panel became increasingly difficult in the late sixteenth century because avid collectors such as Rudolf II in Prague and Maximilian I in Munich had gone to such great lengths to obtain a vast quantity of Dürer originals. The imitative works after Dürer's paintings were most often created as a replacement for an original. In other cases, there are strong currents of the emulative tendency, as artists sought to work in the style of Dürer. The manner in which Dürer's works were treated in Chapter 2; namely, bringing them together according to where they resided in the seventeenth century, guides the organization for the copies, imitations and emulations created after them. For example, the *Adoration of the Trinity* and the *Feast of the Rosegarlands* will be found in the same section, as will the imitative works after them, because both paintings were brought to Rudolf's court in the seventeenth century. This allows for an understanding not only of the range of the results, but also the contexts of collecting and subsequent creation. The courts were extremely fertile for this phenomenon: the patron-collectors who obtained numerous works by Dürer would often foster Dürer imitation.

This examination of artistic quotations and dependencies will show that the reception of Dürer is indeed a peculiar case, for which perhaps the only other comparable example is the manner in which Raphael was revered in France and Italy.[21] It is safe to say that the appropriations that emerged in conjunction with Dürer's artistry have few precedents in the history of art, and are a fascinating case study in early modern appropriation.

Contexts for Appropriation

Ideas of imitation during the Renaissance have been analysed extensively in other disciplines of the humanities, especially music, poetry and literature.[22] In his essay on techniques employed by court composers, Howard Mayer Brown describes imitation as 'one of the most widespread practices in all branches of artistic endeavor in earlier and indeed in modern times. Composers as well as poets and painters learned their craft by imitating older masters'.[23] Brown describes cases of composers modelling new pieces directly on old ones and adding one or more voice to a pre-existing piece. He offers evidence for musicians who alluded to other compositions they thought were related to their own.[24]

Within the realm of poetry, the classical treatises that were studied urged imitation as a pedagogical exercise. Indeed, it has been suggested with regard to poetry that 'the burning issue in the fifteenth century, and well into the sixteenth, was not what is imitation? or should we imitate? but *whom* should we imitate?'[25] Further, as noted by Thomas Greene, 'the first half of the sixteenth century produced the most vigorous and sustained debate over the proper modes and goals of imitation ever witnessed on the European continent'.[26]

The article 'Versions of Imitation in the Renaissance' by G.W. Pigman is a useful starting point for investigations into how broad and diverse approaches to past models could be.[27] Pigman points out that in imitative texts the possibility of identifying the model is often challenging. What emerges, says Pigman, is 'the major hermeneutical problem of the possibility and importance of assessing authorial intention'.[28] Identifying an earlier model is only part of the problem, for then the investigator must gauge the extent to which understanding the motivation behind the imitation is possible. Pigman highlights the difficulties of discovering and analysing these relations.[29] Another essay that proves useful as broad discussion of imitation is Wolfgang Götz's 'Historismus: Ein Versuch zur Definition des Begriffes' (An Attempt to Define the Idea of Historicism).[30] As Götz suggests, the intentions behind imitation are varied: he discusses artistic methods used in the 'service' of historicism, and argues that the re-activation of past motifs signifies a distinct ideology that merits further investigation in the realm of the visual arts.[31]

These publications are a useful entry point for understanding the nuances of imitation that existed in the sixteenth and seventeenth centuries. In other words, the diversity of approaches toward past works of art are highlighted.

A number of texts have addressed this issue in relation to art-making in Italy. A recent publication that details early approaches to imitation is Ellen Perry's *Aesthetics of Emulation in the Visual Arts of Ancient Rome,* in which the author characterizes Roman strategies for the appropriation of Greek culture, and importantly, characterizes emulation (as opposed to only imitation) as an important motivation amongst Roman artists.[32] As for the Renaissance, a number of considerations of artists' attitudes toward copying ancient Roman models have been published. Most recently, the 2003 anthology *The Rediscovery of Antiquity: the Role of the Artist,* includes, amongst other things, sections on Michelangelo and Greek sculpture, Mantegna's use of ancient models, and the importance of Etruscan antiquities in the Tuscan Renaissance.[33] *Drawing and Painting in the Italian Renaissance Workshop* by Carmen Bambach includes sections on traditions of copying, as well as the censure of copying.[34] Another anthology that includes important essays on practices of copying, in this case in fifteenth-century Florence, is *Artistic Exchange and Cultural Translation in the Italian Renaissance City*; of particular importance is the second chapter in which Michael O'Malley details copying practices and marketing strategies in a fifteenth-century Florentine painter's workshop.[35] Also relevant are treatments of copyists for individual artists, especially Alfred Moir's *Caravaggio and his Copyists*.[36]

While there is no similar book-length treatment of the theory and practice of copying north of the Alps in this period, important scholarship has been done on practices of copying prints in the north. The importance of reproductive prints has recently come to prominence as a topic of scholarly discussion, as demonstrated by the 2005 publication of *Paper Museums: The Reproductive Print in Europe, 1500–1800*.[37] This significant publication includes considerations of imitation and invention, as well as a detailed analysis of creativity and authenticity in early print culture. Lisa Pon in her recent discussion of Marcantonio Raimondi's use of Dürer's prints has characterized 'a renaissance culture of copying'.[38] John Shearman has invoked the audience that would readily have been able to understand and identify parallels with earlier creations, in his *Art and the Spectator in the Italian Renaissance,* a significant contribution to ideas of reception.[39] And David Freedberg has drawn attention to images often considered lesser due to their imitative qualities in his *The Power of Images: Studies in the History and Theory of Response*.[40] Freedberg focuses his analysis on the practice of copying powerful devotional images, which involved different motivations than those under scrutiny here. However, Freedberg's treatment is instructive for the manner in which he draws upon images hitherto qualified as lesser in the typical hierarchy of images. Issues of pedagogy, competition and homage, are all distinguished entities that merit investigation. These closely related impulses are akin to the ideas being discussed in contemporary texts.

I now turn to a survey of some of the most prevalent ideas on imitation in the period under scrutiny that will prepare the way for the discussion of the imitative images that emerged in conjunction with Dürer. As has been pointed out above, the vast trove of images that imitate some aspects of Dürer's artistry are important for investigations into functions of imitation and a characterization of artistic climate. Imitative images are charged with meaning and raise important questions about ownership, collecting, artistic production and audience that merit further investigation. I begin with the ideas of some classical authors on imitation, and proceed chronologically to the seventeenth century. My intention is to merely highlight works that could possibly have been read by the scholars and artists of the sixteenth and seventeenth centuries, thus characterizing a small aspect of the intellectual climate in which the Dürer imitators were working.

To begin, we should recall that imitation was a major issue not only for artists of the period, but also those whose work was textually based. An example of the debate surrounding the classical treatises on rhetoric by Cicero (106–46BC), statesman of ancient Rome, illustrates this well. Cicero was considered to be the greatest of the Latin orators, and his works were highly esteemed and held up as the stylistic model for prose in the Renaissance. His works on rhetoric such as *De Oratore* and *De Inventione* were rediscovered in their complete forms in the early fifteenth century and were well known to the German humanists (Philipp Melanchthon, discussed earlier, had translated Cicero) as well as to the Italian humanists. In the 1520s Pietro Bembo (1470–1547), the famed Italian cardinal and scholar, and Giovanni Pico della Mirandola (1463–1494), also a famed humanist scholar, exchanged pamphlets on the subject of Cicero. Bembo argued that Cicero was the only classical author worthy of imitation, while Pico wanted to broaden the repertoire. The point is that imitation was an accepted and encouraged practice, and that discussions did arise as to who was worthy of such treatment.[41]

Once a model was chosen, the issue then became: how to imitate? A central tenet was that the source or model was to be transformed. An ancient writer who proves significant is Seneca (54–39BC), another Roman writer also famous for his works on rhetoric. His discussion of imitation in the *Epistulae Morales* involves perhaps the best-known metaphor for the transformative, or active aspect of imitation: the analogy of the poet with a bee collecting honey.[42] First, Seneca discusses how some investigators are uncertain whether bees collect honey from flowers, or whether they change what they gather into honey by some process of their own. Does their skill lie in gathering, or in the making? Seneca then goes on to strengthen his advice to imitate bees through reference to another image of transformation, digestion. The bees do indeed convert flowers into honey by a process, similar to the way digestion involves a conversion. In other words, Seneca is arguing for transformative imitation, not merely eclectic gathering. He acknowledges this by arguing that bees create honey by a process, similar to digestion in men, and in like fashion, when the poet imitates, he also transforms.[43] The bee is active as it transforms what it has borrowed into something new. Seneca also points out that there are indeed some poets who merely collect, without transforming.

Macrobius (395–423), the Roman grammarian, also discusses imitation. He focuses on one aspect of Seneca's bee metaphor, that the bees collect honey from different flowers into order to transform each individual part into a whole. He advocates a 'rearranging of previous material', transforming the model to produce something with its own identity. Macrobius is concerned with organization, not with transformation: 'I too will entrust whatever I have sought in my diverse reading to my pen so that under its direction my reading may coalesce into an orderly arrangement.'[44] This coalescing is not the transformation of pollen into honey, in which the pollen loses its identity and becomes something else, but the changing of individual parts into an organized collection. Macrobius conceives of imitation as a sort of redistribution – for him making something different means setting it in a new context. Of course after the gathering is complete, something new must emerge. Perhaps the best expression of this is taken from Petrarch (1304–1374), the humanist who wrote 'take care that what you have gathered does not long remain in its original form inside of you: the bees would not be glorious if they did not convert what they found into something different and something better'.[45]

The Dutch humanist and theologian, Erasmus (1466–1536), who befriended Dürer during his trip to the Netherlands, also engaged in the discussion of imitation. Erasmus derided those who used only Cicero as a model, calling them 'apes of Cicero'.[46] Instead he argues for imitation that has an active component. He uses Cicero as a starting point for delving into ideas of imitation, and suggests that it is important to have several models when engaging with the past: 'I approve an imitation that is not too limited to one model from whose features one does not dare to depart', an imitation that excerpts 'the most eminent' and 'which transfers what it finds into the mind itself, as into the stomach, so that transfused into the veins it appears to be a birth of one's intellect, not something begged and borrowed from elsewhere.'[47] This digestive analogy suggests that in order to imitate properly one must also disguise. Erasmus states plainly that 'if we wish to imitate Cicero successfully, we must above all disguise our imitation of Cicero'.[48] It is at this point that Erasmus also distinguishes between following, imitation and emulation:

> the follower walks in the footsteps of another and is a slave to his model ... An imitator, however, desires to say not so much the same things as similar ones – in fact sometimes not even similar, but rather equal things. But the emulator strives to speak better, if he can.[49]

Aspects of competition now enter the picture, as the emulator does not want to disguise the relationship because the victory over the model cannot be appreciated without recognition of it.

At this point we shift from treatments of literary texts to art theory proper. The thoughts of some Italian theorists of the sixteenth century will prove especially relevant.[50] The critical writings of the artist Giovanni Paolo Lomazzo

(1538–1600) are always cited as greater in importance than his paintings. This Lombard painter became blind and passed from the practice to the theory of art. His treatise on painting, *Trattato dell'arte della pittura*, was published in Milan in 1584 and rapidly gained widespread popularity on the continent.[51] It is instructive for what it tells us about who was deemed worthy of imitation. Lomazzo gave considerable importance to both genius and fantasy, and talent and skill are taken to be equal. In this regard Michelangelo, Titian, Raphael and Leonardo are praised as having both talent and skill; from the north, only Dürer is praised and deemed worthy of imitation. This is important, for in the art theory of the seventeenth century, Lomazzo's treatise was the most significant and widely read.[52]

Another writer who specifically discusses *imitatio* is the lesser known Bartolommeo Ricci (1490–1569), whose text *De Imitatione Libri Tres* has particular import for the visual arts.[53] Published in Venice in 1545, Ricci gives the most explicit discussion of divergent forms of imitation. In his discussion of Virgil, Ricci states: 'I attribute to imitation that which belongs to emulation. For although following, imitation and emulating are three entirely different species, they are similar and do belong to one class.'[54] This is a tripartite division of imitation that allows for the differences between copying and emulating. The first division, 'following', is the gathering or borrowing of phrases, sentences, and passages which amounts to a transcription of the models into the text. Past models are used for a new work and are not transformed, but are introduced to a new context. As Ricci explains, the second division, 'imitation', involves a situation in which the differences between text and model are at least as pronounced as the resemblances. Imitation is intended more as homage, includes clear reference to models, and uses borrowed materials prominently. Respect and the acknowledgement of an equal are involved. And finally the third category, 'emulation', involves a more critical reflection on, or even correction of, the model, often involving an awareness of the historical distance between present and past. In emulation, ingenious uses of the model are seen as evidence of skill. Emulation goes beyond imitation and implies a challenge to the model. In other words, there are receptive and productive aspects to emulation.[55] Ricci uses the metaphor of bees digesting, and the resemblance of father to son, as support for his analysis.

Emulation was thus seen as a very important means of expression. It is difficult as always to document artistic intention. However, as we shall see in what follows, the vast trove of images that emulate aspects of Dürer's artistry certainly attests to interest in this form of imitation. What is interesting about emulation is that it deliberately calls attention to its source. In doing so, there is an active and decisive quality to emulation, less apparent than in a more straightforward copy. In emulation, the relationship between past and present is not disguised: indeed, it is highlighted. Having considered some of the essential literary sources on imitation, I now turn to a consideration of the most essential primary source of all: the imitative artistic works that used Dürer prints as source material.

Appropriations of Dürer Prints

There has been a long-standing interest in distinguishing between prints by Dürer and prints by his imitators.[56] Given that the copying of Dürer prints began in the artist's lifetime, and that numerous highly exact copies exist, the approach of the connoisseur is made especially difficult. Comprehensive print catalogues, which allowed for the critical comparison of original and copy were compiled late in the eighteenth and early nineteenth centuries, and arose largely due to the burgeoning art market with its focus on originality, as well as the desire to make public large print collections formed during the eighteenth century. The most important of these catalogues was compiled by Adam von Bartsch (1757–1821), who organized prints according to schools, including Flemish, Dutch, German and Italian. He included 250 prints by Dürer, and several known copies. In the nineteenth century, Joseph Heller (1758–1849) compiled what is still known as the principal catalogue raisonné of hitherto known copies after Dürer, in *Das Leben und die Werke Albrecht Dürers* (1827). Josef Meder (1857–1934) discusses the technical processes employed by copyists, the functions of copying, and especially the prints executed for what he refers to as forgery.[57]

These sources are indispensable, yet they are focused on copying perceived from the perspective of pedagogy and forgery, and importantly, do not include emulative works. A central argument of this chapter is that the artistic reception that arose in response to Dürer in the late-sixteenth and seventeenth centuries was highly diverse in intention, and, as will be shown in what follows, this diversity is represented in the realm of print as well.

A basic observation that guides the discussion is that Dürer's prints were especially well known and endured many forms of imitation because they were transportable and by definition existed in multiple forms. It will be shown that while copying took precedence in the early sixteenth century, it was the forms of competition and emulation that would develop as the century proceeded. I consider the following categories in reference to the use of Dürer's prints as sources: forgery, pedagogy, retrospection, transformation and emulation.

FORGERY

Copies after prints by Dürer have been known since at least 1494.[58] Of particular importance in the history of printmaking is the length to which Dürer went to protect what he saw as his property. One of the earliest forms of copyright can be attributed to him. With a privilege granted by the Emperor Maximilian I, Dürer considered it his legal right to protect his work, and especially the use of his monogram. This proprietary relationship is best expressed in the 1511 edition (the second of Dürer's *Life of the Virgin*):

> Beware, you envious thieves of the work and invention of others, keep your thoughtless hands from these works of ours. We have received a privilege from

> the famous Emperor of Rome, Maximilian, that no one shall dare to print these works in spurious forms, nor sell such prints within the boundaries of the Empire ... Printed in Nuremberg, by Albrecht Dürer, painter.[59]

It is well known, and was certainly known to Dürer, that the Italian engraver Marcantonio Raimondi (*c.*1480–1534), who trained in Bologna and later worked in Venice and Rome, made numerous copies especially of Dürer's *Life of the Virgin* series. In total Raimondi made about 70 copies of Dürer's prints, and often included Dürer's monogram. According to Vasari, Dürer complained to the Venetian senate about being plagiarized, whereupon it was decided that 'Marc Antonio could no longer use the name or the above mentioned signature of Albrecht in his works.'[60] While Vasari's statements cannot be verified entirely, it is true that Dürer had complained in a letter to Pirckheimer about Italian artists forging his work, claiming that such artists were his enemies.[61] Another instance of prints as the subject of a court case appears in the records of the Nuremberg council of 1512, and runs as follows:

> The foreigner, who sold prints before the town hall, some with Albrecht Dürer's monogram that were fraudulently copied from him, shall be bound by oath to remove all said monograms and sell none of them here, and if he refuses, all his said prints shall be confiscated as counterfeit (am falsch), and taken into the hands of council.[62]

The legal discourse in Dürer's day held that the works were considered forgeries if they had the monogram.[63]

As Raimondi's use of Dürer's prints shows, the early sixteenth century was a time of reflection upon ownership, as well as upon the nature of the medium of print. Reproducibility, it was realized, could also lead to duplicity. As Dürer's prints were disseminated in the seventeenth century, the opportunities for artists to use his work in a variety of capacities increased greatly. What needs to be stressed is the diversity of intentions behind imitative works. Raimondi's forgery of Dürer and the imitations and emulations of the Dürer-Renaissance are phenomena separated by several generations. Yet the tendency remains to label all imitative works as plagiarism or forgery. The discourse of Dürer's day must be differentiated from the later context in which emulation was an encouraged practice. A central feature to both is the manner in which Dürer's monogram was appropriated. However, it must be stressed that this appropriation was not always done with the aim of fooling the buyer.

Indeed, even Raimondi did not always create his copies to the end of deception. *Virgin Worshiped by Angels and Saints* is one of the final prints of the *Life of the Virgin* series. On the original version, Dürer included his monogram in the bottom of the scene underneath a *putto* that is playing at the feet of the Virgin. While Raimondi's version of the same scene is often described in the literature as an exact copy, his version is an engraving whereas Dürer's is a woodcut. The difference between these techniques should not be underestimated, and it is rather remarkable how similar Raimondi's version appears. Another reason why caution must be exerted before referring to this imitative work as a strict forgery is that Raimondi carefully included not only Dürer's monogram (in the same spot as on the original woodcut), but has also included his own: the initials MAF appear on the base of the candlestick holder on the left side of the print. These initials represent Raimondi's acknowledgment of his own work: 'Maracanotio Raimondi Fecit' (Marcantonio Raimondi made this).

Another example of Raimondi's imitative work is his engraving after a woodcut from Dürer's *Small Passion* series. The *Small Passion* was a series of 37 woodcuts that was published in 1511, and the eleventh woodcut depicts *Christ taken Captive*. Again, in his copy Raimondi engraved Dürer's woodcut with exacting precision. There is one exception: where on the original a Dürer monogram appears in the bottom right corner, Raimondi has inserted an empty *cartellino*. This exemplifies Raimondi seeking to avoid the consequences of using Dürer's monogram in a fraudulent manner.

Reproductive works such as these have traditionally been derided in the secondary literature. It is clear that there was a demand for Raimondi's engravings after Dürer, if the existing quantities are to be taken as indicative. Before the invention of photography, reproductive prints were the only medium by which pictorial images of works of art could be passed on to a wide audience. Famous works could be transmitted from workshop to workshop. Lacking the modern convenience of illustrated reference books, young artists could learn from the portfolios of sketches collected by their teachers. Therefore, reproductive prints became desired by artists, and prints of high quality were at a premium.[64] This brings us to the second consideration in this section on Dürer's prints as sources; namely, issues of pedagogy.

PEDAGOGY

Some of the most prevalent impulses that lay behind the copying of prints by Dürer were pedagogical in nature. Not all exact copies were created with the intention to deceive, as the indications of both source and authorship show in numerous cases. Some artists specialized in copying Dürer's prints earlier in their careers and later branched into other endeavours, as the example of the Wierix brothers from Antwerp demonstrates. Hieronymous Wierix (1553–1619) and Jan Wierix (1548–1618) both copied works by Dürer on a number of occasions. They reflect how in the large Antwerp print workshops, children learned at a young age to use the burin and engrave other people's designs in copper to very high standards. Drawing one's own inventions was not a priority. The brothers Wierix were capable at the ages of 12 and 16 respectively of cutting technically perfect copies of Dürer engravings, but seldom – even later – made prints after their own designs. As suggested by J.H. Merck when discussing Jan Wierix, 'The beautiful Dürer copies by Wierix are, however, in no way deceitful because the young man invariably attached his signature

... Nor did he try to keep slavishly to Dürer's manner.'[65] In total the Wierix brothers made about 50 engravings after Dürer's prints.

Consider how Dürer's master print *Knight, Death and the Devil* from 1513 (Figure 23) was used as a prototype. This print was especially well known, and during his trip to the Netherlands in 1520–21, Dürer sold at least one impression of this engraving, and gave one away. We know that the print was admired already by the art critics of the sixteenth and seventeenth centuries.[66] A number of copies were made after this engraving. Around 1564, Jan Wierix at the age of 16 created a copy that is faithful with the exception of a few small details (Figure 24). While the dimensions are almost exactly the same, the print has been reversed (as is so often the case), and in the original cartellino, the date 1564 has been added, leaving no doubt as to the later execution of this copy. This is a case of Dürer's works being an instructive tool, given Wierix's age, and the fact that he included the accurate date of creation and left off Dürer's monogram.

RETROSPECTION

Painted copies of Dürer's prints were frequently made throughout the sixteenth and seventeenth centuries.[67] While many museums have painted copies after Dürer's works in their collections, such painted copies, a characteristic feature of the so-called Dürer-Renaissance, have hitherto received less than thorough scrutiny. There is a tradition amongst print experts to regard painted additions as lesser works. Indeed, to the modern viewer, seeing Dürer's prints coloured in such a fashion is rather startling. Scholars have traditionally argued that Dürer himself would never have coloured a print. However, it could be suggested that the colouring of prints was a direct result of the Dürer-Renaissance. Hans Georg Gmelin has argued that because by 1600 Dürer's paintings were no longer available to aristocratic collectors, they commissioned hand-painted impressions of his prints as surrogates.[68] It also seems likely that these coloured prints were part of a retrospective impulse: artists, and perhaps also their audiences, were accustomed to the coloured manuscripts that had been prevalent for centuries. The colouring of prints can be seen as a harkening back to this tradition of art-making. Sometimes coloured prints are imbued with a retrospective quality that evokes a previous era of illuminated manuscripts. This referral to past techniques can be illustrated with the coloured impressions of Dürer's woodcuts from the *Apocalypse Series* (1498) which he published as a book, the first occasion in the history of Western art of a book being both published and illustrated by an artist.[69] Motifs from this series can be found in Peruvian frescoes, Iranian manuscripts and Spanish stained glass. Given these numerous adaptations it is perhaps not surprising that coloured versions also exist.[70] There is a certain sense of irony that accompanies these images, because the *Apocalypse* series is often cited by scholars as the moment when Dürer's innovations in the medium of woodcut freed prints from the need for colour. Indeed, this is the series for which the most coloured versions exist.

It is interesting to note that often the identity of the colourist can be ascertained. With Dürer's engravings, there are some impressions that can very positively be identified as having colour added by the Mack family of Nuremberg. For example, Hans Mack was listed in the 1573 Nuremberg council records as a painter of manuscripts.[71] Another Mack family member who engaged in colouring prints by Dürer was Georg Mack the Elder (1556–1601) a miniaturist, painter and printer. There are seven sheets coloured by Mack the Elder, all mounted on parchment and including his GM monogram, dating to 1588. In the late-fifteenth and sixteenth centuries in northern Europe, hand-coloured engravings were mounted in manuscripts as replacements for the more costly and labour-intensive illuminations that had decorated manuscripts since the middle ages.[72] In short, colouring techniques for prints have a development and a history of their own. Yet overall it must be argued that coloured prints are most often imbued with a retrospective impulse, harking back to the illuminated manuscripts of the medieval period. Dürer may have been considered the artist who freed line from its need for colour; however, the addition of colour to his most widely distributed works, his prints, speaks to a demand for colour, and a retention of elements of what had traditionally been seen as a realm of colour, the illuminated devotional manuscript. Other books that had a tradition of being coloured include hymn books. Between 1520 and 1562, the illuminator Fabian Pulér was employed at the workshop of Jan Táborsky (1500–1572) of Klokotská Hora. Pulér combined styles found in southern Germany and the Danube basin with patterns taken from Dürer – about 50 such hymn books survive.[73] While painted prints are often considered a sort of hybrid art form, they give rise to an interesting question, as to the value of objects that have been altered or adapted by a subsequent artist. It is essential to recognize the value placed on these coloured prints as important collector's items, much like their black and white sources.

Often, colouring would occur on Dürer's best known prints. *St. Jerome in his Study* from 1514 is without a doubt one of Dürer's best-known works; as indicated by his diaries, during his travels in the Netherlands in 1520–21, Dürer sold or gave away this print more frequently than any other (Figure 25). A seventeenth-century coloured version of the print has been attributed to Domenicus Rottenhammer (active *c.*1594–1640) due to the initials DR in the bottom left corner (Figure 26). Rottenhammer seems to have had a career as a colourist, and there are at least 12 sheets attributed to him in the print collection in Coburg, and several in Berlin.[74] For his coloured version of *St. Jerome*, Rottenhammer layered transparent washes and body colours in order to achieve a multidimensional painterly effect. Dark shades are applied to the hatched areas, and gold is used to emphasize contours. The frequency of gold highlights suggests that this would have been a highly valued sheet. Moreover, the bright and transparent tones, for example the pink floor, yellow table and violet stonework, have led to the suggestion that this palette closely resembles one used in Rudolfine Prague, which of course was a key site of the Dürer-Renaissance.[75]

EMULATION

Thus far, cases have been examined that involved more or less direct copies. Imitations were discussed as being created with a view to forgery and pedagogy, or retrospection through the addition of colour to prints. Other cases of dependency of artists on prints by Dürer are less clear-cut and defy these categorizations. It is helpful to discuss these works as emulations, works often characterized by an attempt to either pay homage to Dürer, or even as ways to enter into a sort of imagined competition with him.

To emulate is to acknowledge a source while transforming it at the same time. The use of Dürer's St Jerome support the point that emulation had strong currency in the sixteenth century when it came to the use of Dürer's print. Wolfgang Stuber (active late sixteenth century), a relatively unknown engraver, created a work that follows Dürer's closely, altering the features of Jerome in order to represent Martin Luther (Figure 27). In doing so, Stuber clearly changed the meaning of the print, using Dürer's pictorial idea to the end of charging a known individual with new meaning. The print can be interpreted as equating Luther with Jerome, as a reference to the importance of both figures as biblical translators of importance (Jerome translated the Bible from the original Hebrew and Greek into the Latin Vulgate, while Luther translated into High German). Other alterations include the *cartellino* on which Dürer's monogram has been replaced with Stuber's initials, again indicative of an open acknowledgement of the source. The meaning of the print has clearly been altered; Dürer has been used as a source, in order to layer a new meaning on a historical figure.[76]

Another variation on Dürer's engraving, also of note from the perspective of emulation, is a work by Lucas Cranach the Elder (1472–1553), in which the features of Jerome have again been altered to depict yet another historical figure, in this case Cardinal Albrecht of Brandenburg (Figure 28). Cranach was Dürer's contemporary, although he outlived Dürer by 25 years. The cardinal's vestments lie on a table in the foreground. Further additions include the numerous animals scattered throughout the room. Further, Cranach's work is an oil painting that is roughly three times the size of Dürer's original. It is an emulative work that has transformed the source in both subject and medium.[77]

Cranach also appropriated Dürer's *Melencolia I* (Figure 29), and the result is an image that can hardly be considered a copy (Figure 30). In Dürer's prototype, what had prior to the Renaissance been the least desirable of the four temperaments is personified in a sobering and stoic manner. The angelic figure is weighed down by profound thoughts, yet she is unable to continue in her creative enterprise, having been afflicted with melancholy, the humour that could incapacitate artists and artisans. Amidst various unused tools, she holds a compass but does not seem to be able to manipulate it. Other scattered accessories hint at her plight: the magic square, in which each row of numbers adds up to 34, is a talisman against negative forces; the scales are equalized because there has been no progress in any direction; and time has been suspended at midday in the hourglass. The enormous polyhedron with its awkward shape is possible to conceptualize, but constructed only with great difficulty, the sphere in the foreground is seemingly immovable, and what is its purpose? These monolithic structures again accentuate the problematic nature of action after conceptualizing.[78]

Moving to Cranach's appropriation, we see that the core elements of Dürer's engraving have been maintained yet transformed. Prior to becoming the painter of the Protestant Reformation, Cranach was well known for his interest in the occult, and often portrayed witchcraft in negative ways. Initially everything seems quite innocent. The putti frolic and play, and the angelic figure is now engaged in whittling. Several accessories, such as the impossible polyhedron, the hourglass of mortality, and the magic square have been removed. The removal of the latter especially indicates that darker forces are no longer kept at bay. As if to make this explicit, Cranach shows personifications of the apocalypse and darker forces thundering through a threatening storm cloud. Melencolia herself is in a sort of contemplative state or perhaps even a trance, and a legion of riders appears in the sky, witches who are riding the animals of the hunt. Is Melencolia herself now representative of evil forces, as opposed to simply being affected by them? Overall, we can see that Dürer's more contemplative vision has been subverted through Cranach's appropriation.

Another prototype for artists was Dürer's 1502 engraving *Nemesis* or *Large Fortune*, in which the classical Goddess of retribution is depicted carrying a goblet and bridle (representing reward and castigation). With her wings, she also bears resemblance to the figure of Fortune, and stands confidently on a globe (Figure 31).[79] Urs Graf (1485–1527/9) created a bold drawing that clearly draws from Dürer's prototype in composition and theme, but also departs in significant ways (Figure 33). Graf, who was born in Solothurn and died in Basel, was highly versatile and perhaps the most gifted artist of the Renaissance in Switzerland.[80] In Graf's woodcut version of *Nemesis*, the theme has been significantly altered. The classical goddess of retribution has been replaced by a courtesan in a state of undress, bejewelled and with fine ribbons in her hair and adorning her legs. Dürer's composition is turned on its head, literally: the figure is now rotated 45 degrees, and instead of holding a chalice, she now holds an open hourglass and a pendant.[81] This is clearly an emulation of Dürer involving the transformation of the source, and the gearing of the image toward a different and more explicitly sexual meaning.

One of the most intriguing of Dürer's emulators is Heinrich Aldegrever (1502–1555–61), the German engraver, painter and designer. Like Graf, Aldegrever also borrowed the female figure from *Nemesis* in his *Respice Finem* (Figure 32), but the borrowings did not stop there, and in fact, *Respice Finem* holds multiple Dürer quotations. The hourglass that Aldegrever's figure holds has been quoted directly from Dürer's *Melencolia*, and also possibly the celestial phenomenon in the background. The skull is a quotation of *St. Jerome*. Though Aldegrever was dependent on Dürer, he is free and loose in his interpretation. He used multiple works by Dürer to create a fresh piece, an appropriation of Dürer as opposed to a simple copy. Further, he acknowledges his source in a clever manipulation of the Dürer monogram, replacing the D with a G, in order to indicate his surname Aldegrever. Clearly, Aldegrever had no intention of passing this work off as a piece by Dürer, but rather sought to invoke Dürer.[82]

Finally, I would like to consider some aspects of the work of Hendrick Goltzius (1558–1617), who must be given special consideration in this section for the manner in which he used Dürer's prints as source material, as well as the esteem and reputation that his emulative works enjoyed in his lifetime. Largely self-taught, Goltzius was born near the town of Venlo, and moved to Haarlem, then a center for panel painting, around 1577.[83] At the age of 24, Goltzius opened his own publishing house. As a reproductive printmaker he also published dozens of copies after antique sculpture. He issued more than 200 of his own sheets at his firm in Haarlem. Thanks to his ability to design his own prints, he was able to break the monopoly of the Antwerp print publishers and set up an independent, international print business in Haarlem.[84]

In his review of the 2003 Goltzius exhibition held in Amsterdam, Christopher Heuer refers to Goltzius as a 'ventriloquist' of the styles and techniques of older Italian and German artists. He further points that 'when Goltzius made proper engravings and woodcuts, which he did enthusiastically and prodigiously, he often mimicked established styles in an idiom of his own'.[85] It is these emulative works that are of greatest relevance for the purpose of this chapter, works that embody Goltzius' references to, and appropriations of, the past.

In 1594, Goltzius created six engravings for a *Life of the Virgin* series. The series was dedicated to Duke William V of Bavaria, from whom Goltzius received a gold chain with an engraved portrait as a reward.[86] Each of the six prints emulates a distinct Renaissance hand: Raphael, Parmigianino, Bassano, Barocci, Dürer and Lucas van Leyden. Goltzius extracted recognizable elements from works by these masters and then organized them to make six completely new compositions of his own. Leaving no doubt as to his intentions, Goltzius signed each engraving, thereby stamping the series as his.

These examples are important not only for understanding a particular strategy of making prints, but also for what they can reveal to us about the impetus of appropriation, and the extent to which imitative works were valued. Examining the reception of these engravings one is struck by the admiration and value placed upon them in context. The engraving that emulates Dürer is obviously of greatest interest here, namely the fourth engraving in Goltzius' *Life of the Virgin* series which depicts the *Circumcision of Christ* (Figure 37). It will be recalled that Dürer depicted the same subject in his own *Life of the Virgin* series which was published in 1505 (Figure 36). The first thing to note is that the Dürer source is a woodcut, and the Goltzius emulation is an engraving. In an amazing display of virtuosity and playfulness, Dürer's grouping has been rotated 45 degrees as if to firmly state that the viewer is now looking at Dürer with fresh eyes, thanks to the added hand of Goltzius.[87] While the subject matter and style are similar, there are notable differences. Goltzius incorporates Dürer's distinct *cartellino* for his monogram, however he places his own HG monogram and the date 1584 inside. Further, Goltzius has taken the central group in Dürer's engraving and transposed it into a setting of his choice, the St Bavo church in Haarlem. He has also included a self-portrait, behind the priest, looking at the viewer.

In Karel van Mander's *Schilderboeck*, printmaking receives attention in two instances: in reference to Dürer, and in relation to Goltzius' *Life of the Virgin* series. Van Mander pays careful attention to how Goltzius imitated Dürer in *The Circumcision* engraving, and his lengthy statement is significant and worth considering in its entirety:

> [Goltzius] had very witty practical jokes played, in particular with the print of the *Circumcision*, engraved in the style of Albert Dürer, and in which Goltzius' self portrait appears, this along with his mark, he had burned out with a red-hot coal or iron and repaired again, after that he smoked and crumpled it as if it were very old and had been made on this earth for elsewhere, was eagerly seen with great admiration and pleasure by artists and art lovers who had knowledge of these things, and was also bought at a high price by some who were happy that they had been able to obtain such a piece by the art-full Nuremberger, which had never been seen before. It was of course very funny that the master was praised everywhere way above himself; for when it was said or asked whether Goltzius could have made something like that, some people, who were not poor in art, replied that it was the best by Albert Dürer that they had ever seen. Some further asserted that Albert had engraved a particular which, when he died, he specified should remain hidden for a hundred years after his death and it could have been printed only if his work was then still appreciated – and that this must be none other than this print. When then, after many rumors and much claptrap, the print was shown and came before the eyes of these people in its entirety and freshly printed, they stood (as the saying goes) with egg on their faces and were ashamed and bewildered for their being so cocky. Some became angry and blamed those who had played the joke.[88]

In van Mander's account, a playful attitude is stressed. Goltzius used his prowess as a printmaker to attempt to pass his version of the *Circumcision* off as a long-lost print by Dürer, going so far as to falsely age the print to the end of deceiving his viewers. Even those with some knowledge of art-making ('not poor in art') had been fooled, and were angry when the deception was revealed. And so, van Mander is quick to add, this audience had set Goltzius above Dürer without realizing it, for they had habitually said that Goltzius could never match the past master.

What does this passage tell us about attitudes toward emulation? If we are to accept van Mander's description as accurate, Goltzius not only created an emulation in the style of Dürer, he also attempted to pass his work off as an original by Dürer. However, I stress once again the playfulness that pervades van Mander's account. It is not as if Goltzius wanted to sell the engraving in a fraudulent manner: rather, he has used it to demonstrate his prowess as an engraver, to uphold van Mander's contention that he matched the talent and skill of Dürer, and could perhaps even surpass the past master.

As suggested by Lawrence W. Nichols,

> this game of imitation and borrowing makes the series a fascinating puzzle for print connoisseurs. With utter self assurance, Goltzius appears to have been inviting collectors to take their [works] by Dürer and Lucas from their cupboards, and to look for similarities and differences.[89]

Goltzius was a major printmaker of the period, known internationally, and his career was prolific. He showed a definitive interest in the preservation of heritage, as demonstrated in 1602 when he and Van Mander prevented the Leiden City Council from selling Lucas's triptych of *The Last Judgment* to the agents of Rudolf II, because they were determined that the triptych not be shipped to Prague. This action has been referred to as one of the earliest known instances of the protection of national heritage.[90] With his own considerable collection, Goltzius was certainly interested in the tradition of printmaking established by his predecessors, especially Dürer. His emulative works after Dürer were imbued with pride and recognition that a market existed for such tributes to his predecessors. Nor should playfulness be underestimated, for it was often as part of an intellectual game that the seventeenth-century artist engaged with those who had created before him. Indeed, at times it seems as if there was no limit to the numbers of appropritaions that Dürer followers would engage in. Consider for example the fanciful polytych by Erhard Schön (Figure 47) which includes no fewer than five Dürer motifs.

TRANSFORMATION

There are examples of Dürer's prints being transformed into media that he himself never worked in, especially sculpture.[91] Ebert Wulff (died 1608/9) for example is known to have transformed Dürer motifs into sculpture on a number of occasions. Born into a German family of sculptors, Wulff and his successors used prints as models for decorations and figural compositional sculptures.[92] In the Castle Brandys on the Elbe in Bohemia, there is a relief sculpture of the *Adoration of the Magi*, clearly based on Dürer's treatment of the same subject in his *Life of the Virgin* series. This polychrome and partly gilt marble stucco on a metal construction was likely executed around 1600, and probably commissioned by Rudolf II for the altar in the Chapel of the Three Magi in the Castle at Brandys, which was consecrated in the first decade of the seventeenth century.[93] The most influential print from Dürer's series of the

Life of the Virgin was his depiction of the *Death of the Virgin*, which Dürer added to the 1510 edition of the series (Figure 34). In stone relief, Georg Schweigger (1613–90) executed an intriguing imitative work after the Dürer print (Figure 35). Schweigger was a Nuremberg-based artist who spent his career there. Son of the sculptor Emanuel Schweigger, he was a major exponent of Dürer motifs and his work was avidly sought by Nuremberg patricians and German princes from Berlin to Vienna.[94] In this relief, he has signed with Dürer's monogram and inserted the date 1510. The panel is small and detachable and on the reverse his signature and the date 1642 appears. It is interesting to note how Schweigger adapted Dürer's composition to relief: the size of the room has been diminished, and a dog inserted in the foreground. Most significant is that while the composition is the same as the Dürer original, the subject differs: instead of depicting the death of the Virgin, the subject is the birth and naming of John the Baptist in two scenes. Well into the nineteenth century this relief was thought to be a work by Dürer.[95]

Some artists employed specialized painting techniques in their borrowings, again, rendering Dürer in media that he himself never employed. Martial Ydeux dit le Pape was an enameler active in the mid-sixteenth century who specialized in works in grisaille. He often used prints by Dürer as sources, including *Christ before Pilate* (Figure 38) from Dürer's *Small Passion* series, which he transformed into a grisaille plaque (Figure 39).[96] Enamel paintings using works by Dürer as models were created in France as evidenced in a triptych from the workshop of Pierre Reymond (active 1537–1584). Reymond ran a large and successful workshop in Limoges, and his enamels were in great demand. Using scenes from Dürer's *Engraved Passion* in the two upper scenes (*Christ Carrying the Cross* and *Entombment*) the triptych, which is dated to 1543, shows a clear dependence on prints by Dürer (Figure 40). The triptych was assembled in the nineteenth century (in its current frame) and the plaques may not have originally belonged together. Reymond's early work was very much dependent on Dürer and other sixteenth-century printmakers for subject matter. The workshop specialized in dining vessels and devotional works.[97]

Motifs from Dürer's prints are also in evidence in the maiolica dishes of the sixteenth century. Numerous workshops were involved in the production of these highly esteemed and much sought after tin-glazed earthenware items. The borrowings from Dürer are direct copies and would likely have given the products an additional value. A number of workshops specialized in this type of transformation of Dürer's works. At the court in Fontainebleau, France, painters of maiolica were keen on copying Dürer's prints.[98] For instance Bernard Palissy, artist and ceramicist to the French Court, discussed Dürer in his writings.[99] One example of a maiolica artist engaging with Dürer uses a woodcut from the *Small Passion* series, *Christ before Annas* (Figure 41) as a prototype.[100] Measuring 19 centimetres in diameter, the three figures are copied almost exactly, and the palpable tension and composition of the figures has translated well into the new medium (Figure 42). A notable difference is the complexity of the architectural background, developed in order to fill in the space where there are other figures in Dürer's print. There is a deep blue border, depicting putti riding dolphin heads.[101]

INTERNATIONALIZATION

The final examples to be considered in this section on appropriations of Dürer prints illustrates how we must always bear in mind aspects of geography when considering these copies. The British Museum has in its collection a small diptych that is contained in a silver gilt case (Figure 44). On the left-hand side is a late-sixteenth-century Limoges enamel, which bears a kinship in style to the work of Pierre Reymond, already described above as one who appropriated Dürer's prints. Indeed, the prototype used here is a work from Dürer's *Small Passion*, specifically *Christ Taking Leave of his Mother* (Figure 43), and the imitation is a straightforward and faithful one. On the right-hand side is a depiction of the Ethiopian Saint Abun Gabra Manfus Qeddus, executed as a gilded engraving.[102] The saint is shown with hands raised in prayer, wearing only a devotional scapular, and a robe that has been inscribed with fine lines, 'representing the belief that the Saint was clothed only in his own hair'.[103] Inscriptions testify to the identity of the saint. The work has not been dated with certainty, and only the range of sixteenth–nineteenth century is given – regardless, it is noteworthy indeed that a print by Dürer has been appropriated in an African context.

Also testament to the internationalization of Dürer is an appropriation that harkens from early modern India (Figure 46). The source is Dürer's engraving of the *Crucifixion* from 1511 (Figure 45). A careful study in brush and black ink with wash by Abu'l Hasan (1588 – after 1618) is demonstrative of the diversity of artists associated with the reception of Dürer (Figure 46). Hasan was the leading painter at the court of Emperor Jahangir in India, he specialized in miniatures and made his copy after Dürer's print in 1601, when he was still a child.[104] The drawing exemplifies how far the works of Dürer had travelled and the varied instructional uses they served.

Any discussion of the appropriation of Dürer's prints would be incomplete without acknowledgement of the most internationally received and widely dispersed of his entire print oeuvre, the *Rhinoceros* of 1515 (Figure 49). It is ironic that Albrecht Dürer's most widely distributed image of an exotic animal depicts a subject that he had never seen. Typically, Dürer's independent animal and plant studies are imbued with a rich sense of realism and were drawn from life. His sketch of a baboon, a lynx and a chamois in a garden in Brussels in 1521 indicate not only his interest in exotic animals, but also that he sought out opportunities to draw them. His studies of hares, beetles and various birds have been noted in the history of art for their veracity of detail and as a turning point in the history of scientific illustration (and will be discussed in the section on drawings). In Dürer's 'zoo' the rhinoceros remains unique and unlike his other animal studies for two key reasons. First, the extraordinary and bizarre details of the rhinoceros' appearance are suggestive of embellishment and fanciful creation on the part of the artist, unusual in the context of Dürer's other more faithful depictions of animals. And secondly, despite the creation of other more 'realistic' depictions of the rhinoceros, it was Dürer's print that became a point of reference for naturalists and the public alike, accepted as a true likeness of a rhinoceros, with attempts to replace it doomed to failure.

How do we know that Dürer did not see the animal? There is a wealth of detail surrounding the rhinoceros that arrived in Lisbon, Portugal on 20 May 1515, the first rhinoceros to reach Europe alive since the third century.[105] As was often the case with exotic creatures, the rhinoceros played an important role in court diplomacy and pageantry. Albuquerque, governor of Portuguese India had received the rhinoceros as a gift from Sultan Muzafar II, ruler of Gujarat. The governor in turn sent the animal, along with a cargo of spices, to his king in Portugal, Dom Manuel I, a ruler known (like so many others) for his exotic tastes. Shipped from the region of Cambaia in north-west India, one of the farthest of Portuguese colonies, it is remarkable that the rhinoceros survived the journey – the novelty of this event, and the anticipation and excitement felt at the court and amongst citizens of Lisbon cannot be underestimated.

How did Dürer come to depict the creature? The source for Dürer's image has been documented as a sketch by Valentine Ferdinand, a Moravian printer who was present in Lisbon when the animal was shipped there.[106] The usual claim is that a newsletter including the sketch by Ferdinand came into the possession of Dürer shortly after the arrival of the rhinoceros. Dürer then executed a drawing in brown ink after the image on which he included Ferdinand's original inscription that begins with the statement 'in the year 1515 there was brought to our king at Lisbon such a living-beast ... on account of its wonderfulness I thought myself obliged to send you a representation of it' (Figure 48). Dürer then created his woodcut, including Ferdinand's inscription, though slightly changed in an attempt to lend the image an air of authenticity, stating 'They call it a rhinoceros. It is represented here in its complete form.' It seems likely that Dürer intended for the print to have a wide distribution, since he used a wood block instead of a copper plate, thus allowing for a maximum number of impressions to be made.

This print, obviously intended for public consumption, widely distributed, and the only animal study that Dürer inscribed in such a manner, has also been described as the most idiosyncratic of his oeuvre. The rhinoceros appears to be dressed in a suit of armour and is covered in peculiar scales, with a variety of patterned plates covering its body, and a tiny dorsal horn that points to the letter 'r' in the rhinoceros label. Erwin Panofsky famously characterized the woodcut as follows: 'Dürer stylized the creature, bizarre in itself, into a combination of scales, laminae and shells, suggesting a fantastically shaped and patterned suit of armor.'[107] In the eighteenth century the naturalist James Parsons complained of Dürer's depiction because it was 'adorned with scales, scallops and other fictitious forms'.[108] In short, Dürer's rhinoceros has appeared to many commentators as far removed from 'the real thing'.

Why did Dürer, an artist who was obviously given over to realism in his studies of nature, create this depiction based on the work of another artist and inscribe it as he did? As Colin Eisler points out, Dürer's print 'is really a broadside, a journalistic scoop of a major event'.[109] As noted earlier, the excitement surrounding the arrival of the rhinoceros in Lisbon cannot be underestimated, largely because the rhinoceros was an unknown entity on European shores.

Dürer's idea of the rhinoceros remained a reference point for centuries to come. The wood block went into eight printings, seven of them posthumous. Two printings from the original wood block occurred in 1540 and 1550. In the seventeenth century the wood block came into the possession of Hendrick Hondius, a Dutch map printer, who prepared an additional wood block. The result is that numerous reproductions of the image as a print exist. Further, the sixteenth century was the burgeoning age of printed natural history texts, and a new emphasis was laid on the inclusion of images. Dürer's rhinoceros appeared in numerous natural histories, perhaps most significantly the Swiss doctor Conrad Gessner (1516–65) included the rhinoceros in his three-volume *Historiae Animalium* of 1555–58 (Figure 51), a text that is widely considered to be the beginning of modern zoology.[110] In the seventeenth centuryDürer's rhinoceros was included in zoological atlases. There is a notable dependence on not only the rhinoceros but also the other animals in Dürer's zoo in Sebastian Münster's *Cosmographiae* (1544). Indeed, writing in 1938 the art historian F. Winkler stated that school books had only then given up using Dürer's image of the rhinoceros in favour of more 'naturalistic' depictions.[111]

The invincibility of Dürer's rhinoceros in art and science persisted from the time of its inception despite the concurrent creation of other more 'naturalistic' depictions. One of these was a version by Hans Burgkmair, a friend of Dürer's, who also produced a woodcut of the rhinoceros that had arrived in Lisbon in 1515. Working in Augsburg, the relationship between Burgkmair's and Dürer's woodcuts is uncertain, although it is likely that Burgkmair had access to the same drawing as Dürer. What is certain is that Burgkmair's woodcut did not experience the same mass appeal as Dürer's – it survives in a single copy in the Albertina. Burgkmair's animal is decidedly less fanciful than Dürer's. There is no dorsal horn or armour, the skin sags less than gracefully, and the rhinoceros has none of the majestic and regal air of Dürer's. Instead it is shown with chains around its forelegs and sunken eyes. In 1579 the Flemish engraver Phillip Galle depicted another rhinoceros in a deeply naturalistic manner. Again, there is only one copy in existence.

Further attesting to the popularity of the print, and the manner in which Dürer had become *the* artist to appropriate in the seventeenth century, is the inclusion of the rhino in works by Pieter Coecke van Aelst (Figure 50), Joseph Boillot (Figure 52), John Dunstall (Figure 53) and Jan Griffier (Figure 54). The rhinoceros moves in these images from an imagined woodland setting, to being a decorative column, to a fight with his purported enemy the elephant, and back into a sober zoological treatise. The rhinoceros and its influence is especially demonstrative of the international and incredibly diffuse reception that Dürer's prints underwent not only during the so-called Dürer-Reniassance, but also with artists and scientists well into the nineteenth century.

Appropriations of Dürer Drawings

For the use of Dürer drawings as source material, the court of Rudolf II in Prague is especially significant. Given the abundance of works by Dürer at the court of Rudolf II, the artists who worked there had ample opportunity to see, paraphrase and quote from Dürer's work. Indeed, the *Kunstkammer* in Prague housed the largest collection of works by Dürer ever assimilated: this accounts in part for why artists at Rudolf's court would have made such extensive use of Dürer's art. The inventories from Prague show that the collection was maintained in an orderly, systematic and encyclopaedic fashion.[112] It is possible that the inventory was used as a sort of location guide for indicating where, amongst the vast array of items, works by a particular artist could be found. In the 1607 inventory, a number of entries relate to Dürer. Very clear distinctions are made between works known to be originals, and works known to be imitations. For example, one item is stated as a copy by Hans Hoffmann. In another entry, Aegedius Sadeler is named as a Dürer imitator. Imitative works by both of these artists will be considered in this section.[113] Interest in Dürer's drawings at the court can be documented not only through inventories, but also through the array of artistic appropriations (in like fashion to the section above on prints). This places greater emphasis on the collector, since drawings were only beginning to be seen as collector's items in the sixteenth and seventeenth centuries; to view a drawing was arguably more difficult than a print.

FIGURATIVE DRAWINGS

Motifs from the drawings were incorporated into other media. One example is the use of Dürer's drawing *Death of Lucretia* (1508), on blue paper, which can be traced through provenance research to the Prague court (Figure 55). In a bronze medal, measuring 52 mm, and created *c.*1580, an unidentified artist of the Rudolfine court quoted Dürer by including the head of his *Lucretia*, as well as the Dürer monogram and a date of 1508 (Figure 56). This imitative work was created in Prague when the drawing could be found in the collection there, that is between 1576 and 1612.[114]

It is especially telling when more than one artist used the same drawing as a source. This is indicative of a strong interest in the original, or perhaps a continued competition toward improving upon the image. Another example exists of a sixteenth-century medalist active at the court of Rudolf II using Dürer's *Death of Lucretia* drawing as a source. In a cast bronze plaque that has been attributed to Antonio Abondio (1538–91) the Dürer motif has been elaborated with the addition of two women, leading to suggestions that the image was intended to depict Venus and her attendants (Figure 57). Abondio, who began his service as medallist at Rudolf's court in 1576, was one of the only Italian medallists highly successful north of the Alps.[115] Abondio shows a deep understanding of the importance of his source material: he incorporated Dürer's monogram within a larger 'A', creating a clever double monogram, thus giving authorship to himself, as well as Dürer. Continuing the lineage of dependency on Dürer's source, Johann Friedrich Leonart (1633–1680) created a mezzotint that again shows a bust of Lucretia, and clearly used either the anonymous or the Abondio medal as its prototype (Figure 58). Leonart, a Belgian engraver who was active in Brussels, Nuremberg, Regensburg and Berlin, was also active in Prague around 1670, during which time he would have viewed the medals and perhaps even the Dürer protoptype.[116] Curiously, Leonart has also included the inscription 'Agnesi Alberti Düreri Conjux – J.F.L.' Leonart has thus imagined the identity of the figure to be Agnes Dürer, correctly stating her as Dürer's wife and also including the date of the original drawing. However, as noted in the most recent exhibition catalogue to display this mezzotint, 'it is likely that the identification of the sitter is a fantasy on the part of the engraver'.[117] Dürer's biography was of continued interest well into the seventeenth century.

Leonart's appropriation is indicative that even subsequent to the court of Rudolf II in Prague – Rudolf reigned 1576–1612 – the taste for imitations of Dürer had not gone out of fashion. Yet it is true that in terms of appropriations of Dürer's drawings, this court is indeed our richest source of information. One of the most noteworthy of the Dürer appropriations comes from the hand of Daniel Fröschl (1563–1613), an Augsburg-born painter in the employ of the court of Rudolf II in Prague who was responsible for the inventories for the Rudolfine collection, and was named Imperial miniaturist in 1603.[118] Prior to his service in Prague, Fröschl was active at the Medici court. It is also likely that he created some works for the famous Bolognese naturalist Ulisse Aldrovandi.[119] It has been pointed out that Fröschl was accustomed to making copies of famous works from the collection at the court of the Grand Duke of Tuscany, copies perhaps intended as gifts.[120] Active in Prague between 1601 and 1613, Fröschl engaged with the available works by Dürer on a number of occasions. This is especially evident in a miniature by Fröschl from 1604 (Figure 60), one that exhibits how multiple Dürer sources could be combined into one image. Using Dürer's drawing of the *Virgin and Child* of 1512 (Figure 59), Fröschl created what at first glance appears to be a faithful copy in watercolour. However, included in the bottom right corner of the image is another Dürer source: Dürer's first self-portrait, executed in silver point when the artist was 13 (Figure 6). Thus, the appropriation takes place on several levels. Fröschl has transformed Dürer's 1512 drawing into a coloured miniature, giving it a more finished quality. Further, Fröschl has inserted Dürer's self-portrait in the bottom right-hand corner as opposed to a monogram. This inspired addition, in one of the most interesting of the Dürer-Renaissance works, is Fröschl's means of identifying his source: an historical reference to the original artist. This is a very clear example of the manner in which Dürer motifs were appropriated and transformed at the court in Prague. Far from intending to deceive, Fröschl's work draws attention to the fact that he used a drawing that was housed in the Imperial collection. Moreover, it can be assumed that appropriations such as Fröschl's were valued in the context of the court, and were characteristic of the veneration of Dürer as the great 'original'. As shown with Fröschl's appropriation of two aspects of Dürer's artistry, artists would choose to imitate some or all elements of a given model, and transform and reject various aspects of their source. Dürer was recognized and valued as a source for artists, and by the end of the sixteenth century his art existed as a canon of art, one that was deemed worthy of assimilation.

In the section on appropriations of Dürer prints, the works were separated according to differing guises of appropriation – forgery, pedagogy, retrospection, emulation, transformation. Perhaps what is most fascinating, and readily identifiable in this focused section on appropriations of Dürer drawings, is that the same artist could also be involved in differing guises of appropriation, working in a multiplicity of modes all of which employed Dürer as a prototype. To understand this, the Rudolfine artists Hans Hoffmann, Aegeidius Sadeler and Jan Brueghel will be focused on extensively.

Hans Hoffmann (*c.*1530–92) has already been referred to on numerous occasions as the figure most readily associated with the Dürer-Renaissance.[121] It should be recalled that this Nuremberg-born artist had a wealth of experience with drawings by Dürer prior to his arrival at the court in Prague. In Nuremberg he created a number of direct copies after drawings by Dürer for Willibald Imhoff, likely as forgeries for financial gain at a time when the works of Dürer were amongst the most sought-after pieces of art north of the Alps.[122] Whether Hoffmann profited from this enterprise is unknown. At least five figural copies by Hoffmann have been dated to his Nuremberg period (between 1576 and 1584). *Man Aged Ninety-Three* is a technically impressive copy of Dürer's preparatory drawing for a painting of St. Jerome; *Head of a Pope*, in which Hoffmann skillfully copies Dürer's preparatory study for the pope from the *Feast of the Rosegarlands*; and finally *Head of an Apostle*, a copy of a preparatory study by Dürer for his *Heller Altar*.[123] In this final drawing, Hoffmann even imitated the support for the drawing, also using Venetian paper prepared with a bright blue ground, including Dürer's breezy depiction of knotting for a rode at the bottom left. In this copy, Hoffmann included the Dürer monogram and date of 1508, and imitated Dürer's technique and style to such an extent that earlier scholars assumed this to be a work by Dürer. Recall again that to create a convincing copy is by no means an easy feat. This can be demonstrated by comparison with the Dürer originals and Hoffmann drawings that are illustrated here.

A Dürer drawing to which we can assume Hoffmann had access is *Head of Christ* (Figure 61), a preparatory study for the figure of Christ in Dürer's painting *Christ Among the Doctors*. In his copy, Hoffmann has enlarged the subject slightly and created more effects in terms of shading and highlighting (Figure 62). The exacting qualities of Hoffmann's early copies can especially be seen in his use of Dürer's *Head of An Angel* (Figure 64), a preparatory study for *The Feast of the Rosegarlands*. Hoffmann's copy (Figure 65) was more than likely especially valued by the Emperor during his quest to obtain the original painting, which was documented in Chapter 2. These copies by Hoffmann illustrate his technical skills as well as an interest in creating copies after the Dürer originals found in the Imhoff collection, and later in the Rudolfine collection. Apart from creating technically proficient copies, Hoffmann also engaged with Dürer in an emulative manner, as will be highlighted below in the sections on animal drawings and paintings.

For now, I wish to characterize other ways in which the Dürer (and Hoffmann) drawings of heads were used by another Rudolfine artist, Aegidius Sadeler (1570–1629). Sadeler was an engraver, draughtsman and painter who was probably born in Antwerp, and later travelled with his father in 1587 to Prague. He was named imperial engraver at the court in 1597, and he resided in Mala Strana in the house that had belonged to the court painter Bartholomäus Spranger. After Rudolf's death he continued to serve in Prague under Rudolf's successor Mathias, and was one of the last of the Rudolfine artists. Sadeler died in Prague, and his works are often used to signal the end of the Rudolfine era.[124] He specialized in engravings, and while the tendency in the secondary literature is to refer to Sadeler's works as 'reproductive engravings', this is a modern construct that is anachronistic, as it was never used in the inventories of the period.[125] Nor should these works be referred to in a negative fashion.[126] To engrave pictures means to translate them; which is a challenge in much the same way as translating literary texts.[127]

Over 400 prints and drawings by Sadeler are known. His engravings after Dürer are amazing displays of virtuosity and skill, and more than mere projections of the original. As pointed out by Dorothy Limouze, Sadeler was able to transfer motifs to metal plates as mirror images without using the usual technique of 'engraving through'. As a result, the prints were the same way round as their models. Rudolf considered the copper plates from which Sadeler printed to be works of art in themselves and thus, together with Dürer's plates, they occupied a special place in the Prague *Kunstkammer*.[128]

Sadeler made several exceptional engravings after Dürer drawings in the collection. Especially noteworthy are his engravings of three different heads by Dürer, two of which we have just seen were copied faithfully as drawings by his predecessor Hoffmann, and certainly intended as companion collector's items.[129] To view these works as sets of three is demonstrative of a sort of chain of dependency, and leads one to speculate that the works would have been shown side by side, just as they have been reproduced here. Dürer's drawing of Christ (Figure 61) was engraved by Sadeler in 1598 (Figure 63);

Dürer's 1506 drawing of an angel (Figure 64) was also engraved by Sadeler in 1598 (Figure 66). In both cases the date of Sadeler's engraving, as well as the source for the engraving, are included in the inscription found at the bottom of the engravings in a memorial-type plaque. Sadeler always included a Dürer monogram, even when none had been present in the original. Another drawing acquired by Rudolf was *Head of an Apostle with Beard and Cap* (Figure 67), for which no copy by Hoffmann is extant, but which Sadeler engraved in 1597, again including an inscription as to his source as well as the dates (Figure 68).

These companion 'studies of heads' were all engraved by Sadeler when the original Dürer drawings were in the collection of Rudolf II, and when the Hoffmann drawings were likely present as well. As an additional tribute to Dürer, the memorial-type plaques on all three engravings are in the style of the plaques Dürer himself included in his own portrait engravings. These are some of the first sets of 'reproductive' engravings to be made after drawings, a practice that would continue into the seventeenth century, for example in the work of Wenceslaus Hollar. As both productive and reproductive, Sadeler's work is a significant example of how Rudolfine artists engaged with the work of Dürer in a range of borrowings and shifts in media. Sadeler interprets not only the picture itself and its composition, but also its intrinsic ideas and all the finest details. His appropriations included more than Dürer: he later engraved works by Lucas van Leyden, Raphael and Titian. He reproduced figural and landscape compositions of all Rudolfine painters. In the Rudolfine inventory, prints were regarded as works of art equal to paintings and drawings.[130] As with the coloured prints encountered earlier, reproductive engravings have traditionally been undervalued in historical scholarship, but in the context of the court this was not the case. Just as Rudolf was interested in Hans Hoffmann's ability to work in the manner of Dürer as opposed to creating forgeries intended to deceive, he employed Aegedius Sadeler toward the end of engraving the prized works in his collection. In both approaches, a reverence toward the past can be detected, heightened by a desire to improve upon it.

Another Dürer drawing that was part of the Rudolfine collection is the unfinished watercolour *Madonna with the Multitude of Animals* (Figure 69). The original work by Dürer, resplendent with animals, as this drawing seems to have had a special resonance at the Rudolfine court. This drawing depicts at least 20 different species including a dog, fox, parrot, crab, snail, butterfly, dragonfly, stag beetle, frog, owl and swan. The plant life is equally varied, and the same attention to detail is given over to the individual flowers. The image has been interpreted as Dürer's tribute to his medieval heritage, a summation of or last echo of the bestiary tradition.[131] Indeed, given the presence of the Madonna and Child, as well as numerous plants typically associated with her in Christian iconography, such as irises and peonies, it would seem that the animals are being fused with meaning as well through their association with traditional Christian imagery. In the words of Dagmar Eichberger, the animals

> peacefully coexist in an environment which recalls life before the fall ... in this idyllic portrait of the world, humankind is in harmony with nature, for the image of the Virgin and Child among the multitude of animals seems to offer spiritual peace in a time of upheaval and change.[132]

Eichberger takes the argument one step further, and suggests that in this drawing Dürer created a microcosmic image of the world that reflected his notion of an ordered universe. In this instance, the process of designing an image corresponded to the collector's aspiration to give shape to his collection in his cabinet.[133]

This is an intriguing way of situating this drawing, and an important allusion to the context in which it would have been found as artists at Rudolf's court made their way to Dürer by means of the drawings in the *Kunstkammer*. Attesting to artistic interest in this drawing is a painted copy after the original now in Rome in the Galleria Doria Pamphili (Figure 70). This copy is roughly one centimetre larger all around than the original, and has been attributed to Jan Brueghel the Elder (1568–1625).[134] Brueghel was the son of Pieter Brueghel I, the painter whose landscapes were of such great interest to Rudolf. It is likely that in 1604 when Brueghel visited the Prague court, Brueghel created this transformation of a Dürer drawing, probably at the request of the Emperor. In Brueghel's appropriation, Dürer's sketchy and unfinished drawing is reborn as a colourful tableau. The slight enlargement in dimensions has led to the suggestion that Rudolf commissioned Brueghel's copy as a protective cover for the original Dürer drawing.[135] Alternatively, it is possible that Rudolf wished to see how Dürer's unfinished drawing would have looked if 'completed'. While at the Prague court, Brueghel worked with more than one Dürer source housed there. Again in 1604, Brueghel used Dürer's *Road to Calvary* of 1505 toward the end of an artistic assimilation. The Dürer original, which is in very poor condition and now in the Uffizi, is a chiaroscuro drawing with white and black washes depicting the Passion of Christ on Galgotha. The Brueghel painting, also in the Uffizi, copies this drawing into paint faithfully. Inscribed on the stone in the lower left corner are Dürer's monogram and an inscription stating that the picture was invented in 1505 and made again in 1604 by Brueghel.[136] As with the *Madonna with the Multitude of Animals* painted copy, the Brueghel painting of *Road to Calvary* is about 2 centimetres larger than Dürer's drawing, suggestive that as with the previous transformation, Rudolf asked Brueghel to create this tableau as a protective covering for the Dürer chiaroscuro drawing in his collection. It also seems plausible that Rudolf was encouraging, as he did with so many of his court artists, an imagined competition with, or homage to, Dürer. The fact that Aegedius Sadeler also engraved the *Madonna with the Multitude of Animals* (Figure 71) certainly supports this interpretation. Indeed, Rudolf as collector and patron seems to have held Dürer drawings of animals in especially high regard, as will be shown in the next section.

ANIMAL DRAWINGS

Dürer was especially interested in depicting the natural world, and his attentiveness to the wondrous, coupled with fresh observation, is further attested to by his own collecting tendencies. As pointed out by Dagmar Eichberger, that Dürer not only drew but also collected rare and exotic items himself later in his life has not received much attention to date.[137] However, Dürer's letters to Pirckheimer from Venice, and the diary of the trip to the Netherlands, attest to an interest in collecting natural objects. Dürer made notations about many of the items he acquired, including the numerous gifts he received in exchange for portraits. A large portion of the gifts that Dürer received would be classified within a seventeenth-century collection as *Naturalia*: white and red branches of coral, 16 coconuts from India, feathers from India, a large tortoise shell, a branch of cedar, six snail shells, a large fish scale, two dried fish and precious stones. He also purchased numerous items, including a magnetic stone, a small tortoise, horns, shells and numerous claws of elk. Dürer also obtained ethnographic material on his journeys: from India he obtained a wooden shield, a small bag made from fish skin, various fabrics such as silk and cotton, three Chinese porcelain vases, a Turkish whip and a pipe carved from ivory. Also acquired were treasures from the new Indies, as well as rare and exotic food stuffs. Many of these items were gifts, but he did at times spend money, as the purchase of a carved ivory salt cellar from India demonstrates, since for this rare artefact Dürer paid the substantial sum of three gilders; for a small skull, also carved from ivory, he paid one gilder.[138] In the early sixteenth century, Antwerp was truly a centre for international trade, a place in which one could acquire all sorts of newly imported objects from the old and new world.

Given this wealth of objects that we know held Dürer's interest, it is unfortunate indeed that no inventories have survived for Dürer's house in Nuremberg: one can only imagine what curiosities he housed there. Dürer kept a close eye on his budget and was always concerned about being out of pocket. In this light, the purchase of a small live monkey, a so-called 'Meerkätzlein', for the price of four gilders is very significant. He had already studied this exotic animal 20 years earlier, probably during his first stay in Venice.[139] In Antwerp he and his wife also owned three live parrots, presented to them by the Portuguese merchant Rodrigo.[140]

In Dürer's lifetime, and well into the seventeenth century, collecting was a way of understanding the universe.[141] Dürer was an artist who very consciously observed and commented on what was happening around him, an impetus to which collecting is closely related. Between the acts of recording and collecting, a way of dealing with the flood of information was to try to organize it all. Collections increasingly were focused on *naturalia*, which included plants, animals, and minerals; *exotica*, ethnographic materials from distant places; and *artefacta*, the remaining man-made materials.

One of the first theoretical manuals to be published on how to organize materials in a *Kunstkammer* has already been discussed in the chapter on collecting: the *Inscriptiones* by Samuel Quiccheberg (1529–1567), a guide to establishing the ideal ducal collection, published in 1565.[142] According to Quiccheberg, the recording, analysis and investigation of nature was the highest goal of human activity. His recommendations were based upon his experiences as the keeper of the collection of Albrecht V of Bavaria, and focused upon a purpose-built, museum-like space, that was equipped with special tables and carefully constructed display cases in which contents would be stored. One of the most ideal reference points for such a collection is Archduke Ferdinand's Schloss Ambras, which included an extensive armoury, a *Kunstkammer* for art objects, a library and an antiquarium. The art collection contained objects made from gold, silver, ivory, alabaster, glass, corals, cast iron, porcelain, wood, as well as musical instruments, clocks, automats, books and pre-Columbian feathers. It is known that Ferdinand kept his collection in 18 cupboards consciously decorated with 8 different colours, and that the colours carefully reflected what was inside, a clever scheme for organization (see Chapter 2).

Ferdinand's collection and Quiccheberg's manual show that encyclopaedic collecting was widespread, and thought to be reflective of a certain conception of the universe: the universe was a macrocosm that could be understood through a microcosm of its parts, the collection. However, while ambitious and wealthy collectors such as Ferdinand could develop menageries and gardens, most collectors were not so fortunate. Rather than an entire menagerie, they would have perhaps a stuffed specimen, or if that was not possible, a faithful rendition of the desired species. It seems likely that a naturalistic image by Dürer could have been valued from this perspective as well, namely, as a vivid and accurate portrayal of an item which could not be obtained.[143]

These tenets of encyclopaedic collecting help us to understand why Dürer's nature studies were so often copied. The hitherto unprecedented number of nature studies from the hand of one artist, and also the unprecedented number of imitative images after these nature studies, are one of the most fascinating features of the Dürer-Renaissance. Due to the myriad of quotations and evocations of the animal and plant studies, there have been perpetual problems for Dürer scholars from the perspective of attribution. Joseph Heller, who compiled the first comprehensive catalogue of Dürer's works in 1827, pointed out the difficulties inherent in separating the works by Dürer's hand from those of his imitators. In his definitive study of Dürer's drawings published in 1939 Friedrich Winkler noted that the animal and the plant pictures were the hardest to judge.[144] The wealth of scholarship surrounding the 1971 celebrations of the five-hundredth anniversary of Dürer's birth did not bring much in the way of fresh evaluations of the nature studies.

It was the publication of Fritz Koreny's highly evocative and exhaustively researched *Albrecht Dürer and the Animal and Plant Studies of the Renaissance* in 1985 that shed the most extensive and pervasive light on this aspect of Dürer's oeuvre.[145] Published after the exhibition by the same name at the Albertina in Vienna, Koreny brought together the findings that had emerged from the thorough comparative work that the exhibition had enabled, as drawings associated with Dürer were brought from numerous collections to Vienna to be compared with the rich holdings at the Albertina. The watercolours depicting animals and plants that had been attributed to Dürer were gathered together, scrutinized, and evaluated as a group by scholars. Unlike the plant studies, a large number of these animal studies remained firmly attributed to Dürer. Moreover, it was shown that these authenticated watercolours had been copied, imitated, and emulated in the late-sixteenth and seventeenth centuries to a greater extent than any other group of works by Dürer. New attributions emerged, and while some may lament that the oeuvre of Dürer did decrease in favour of his most notable imitator, Hans Hoffmann, this outcome is highly provocative in terms of understanding the issues of imitation that were at play in the seventeenth century. As noted by Koreny, it appears that the works now accepted to be by Dürer are the very ones that were used most extensively as models in the seventeenth century.[146] Modes of copying are vital for understanding the ways in which Dürer's works became yardsticks for reality. And as we shall see, the extent to which copying occurred underscores the difference between the endeavours of a number of court artists and twentieth-century expectations of artistic originality and empirical observation of nature. As Lee Hendrix has argued, 'copying was ubiquitous in printed illustrated nature treatises and hand painted compendia of nature illustrations of the sixteenth century and also played a significant role in the growth of scientific knowledge'.[147]

We should note that there has been a tendency amongst scholars to caution against ascribing too great a significance to the Dürer animal studies. Elisabeth Trux argues that it is fallacious to posit Dürer's nature studies as the first autonomous animal studies.[148] She suggests that it is more important to situate Dürer historically, and to account for the influences on his explorations of the natural world. To this end James Ackerman suggests that it was fifteenth-century Italian naturalists, such as Pisanello, rather than any northern naturalism that stimulated Dürer, giving greater emphasis to works that Dürer would have encountered on his trips to Venice.[149] As pointed out by Dagmar Eichberger,

> the rise of naturalistic studies of nature in the early fifteenth century, first in Northern Italy and later in the southern Netherlands and Germany, prepared the way for the almost systematic exploration of the visible world which became a characteristic of Albrecht Dürer's large oeuvre of watercolors and drawings.[150]

However, it is a moot point here whether or not Dürer was one of the earliest artists to create autonomous animal drawings. When charting the reception of

Dürer's animals, it is undeniable that their influence was felt amongst artists and scientists alike in the seventeenth century. Regardless of the precedents for Dürer's work, irrespective of whether his were the first autonomous studies of animals, it is possible to qualify the reception of these works as especially intense. A number of exceptional animal studies by Dürer became prototypes for artists in their work, giving a heightened significance to the mechanisms of reception at play in this genre.[151]

To begin, the astonishing qualities of Dürer's animal studies must be highlighted. Dürer chose as his subjects animals that he would have encountered in Nuremberg, or those that he saw on his travels, presenting first hand and personal testimony as to what he witnessed. This is a significant shift away from the tradition of depicting the mythical or moralizing animals of the bestiary. Dürer also seems to have been uninterested in the very popular subjects of Aesop's fables, and he depicted few mythological creatures. As noted earlier, Dürer was a highly sensitive artist who was very much in tune with his surroundings. It is thus less than surprising that when he approached the animal world, he portrayed what was accessible. Indeed, when considered in their roles as preparatory studies, Dürer's animals can almost be thought of as a vast pictorial archive, more accessible than living models and he could make use of his studies at any point for inclusion in a large-scale painting.

Dürer was profoundly interested in the external and whole of what he saw. In his capacity as observational scientist, he performed no dissections. In conjunction with his studies of plants, the animal studies offer further evidence that inner workings were less important to him than surface appearances. Often, he carefully calculated the angle from which he showed his subject in order to give the maximum information.

Not only are Dürer's animal studies remarkable for their astonishing realism, they are remarkable for the number of times they were copied, imitated and emulated in the sixteenth and seventeenth centuries. Fritz Koreny goes so far as to suggest that in the period often qualified as the Dürer-Renaissance, Dürer's art became the yardstick or model after which artists created their studies, as opposed to artists seeking out nature for themselves.[152] Colin Eisler argues that Dürer's works 'were so close to the truth, so far beyond conventional ideas of beauty, that they were accepted as nature rather than art'.[153] While Dürer's nature studies are often considered by scholars in terms of being studies for larger compositions, and it is highly probable that this was the intention with which they were created, note that from the perspective of reception that during the late-sixteenth- and seventeenth-century these nature studies were appreciated as finished works in their own right. It is known, for example, that Dürer's sketchbook, as well as manuscripts with illuminations of birds and sea creatures by Jacopo Ligozzi, were bound together and accorded a special place in the Rudolfine *Kunstkammer*.[154] In the realm of animal studies, it is again the court of Rudolf II that provides the greatest evidence for reception.[155] Heightened interest in animals at the court can be documented in other ways as well. Rudolf had a menagerie, and the imperial *Kunstkammer* contained a wide variety of stuffed animal specimens.[156] These aspects of collecting were illustrated vividly in a manuscript known as the 'Rudolfine Bestiary', in which a vivid picture can be gained of the animals encountered at court.[157] Also present at the court were a number of figures important for the development of animal studies and zoology, including Anselmus de Boodt (1550–1632) who studied medicine in Heidelberg and Padua, and then spent 30 years as an advisor and physician to Rudolf II. The albums of de Boodt illustrate vividly how important animals were to the prevailing concepts of collecting.[158] Rudolf further fostered his interest in animals through the acquisition of a number of essential Dürer studies, including the *Hare*, *Blue Roller*, *Wing of Blue Roller*, and *Lion*.

As for the copies, imitations, emulations of these and other animal studies, two of the main contributors were also situated in Prague: Hans Hoffmann and Georg Hoefnagel. Hoffmann died in Prague in 1592, and that Hoefnagel arrived at the Prague court in 1594. It seems likely that Rudolf as a patron emphasized the continuity of their work. Hans Hoffmann (1530–1591) has repeatedly come up in these pages as the main proponent of the Dürer-Renaissance, and his biography has already been discussed in preceding sections. Georg Hoefnagel (1542–1600) was born in Antwerp, and was a well-travelled miniaturist who entered the service of Rudolf permanently in 1590. One of Rudolf's prized possessions was a book of miniatures created by Hoefnagel representing the animal kingdom, the *Four Kingdoms of Living Creatures*, which contained 1339 miniatures of animals and fishes created by Hoefnagel during his service at the Wittelsbach court.[159] After entering permanent service with Rudolf in 1590 Hoefnagel created a number of miniatures that quoted or imitated Dürer in some way, in a sense, continuing the work of Hans Hoffmann. Hoefnagel presented Rudolf with at least six books and numerous independent miniatures.[160] Hoefnagel expressed his interest in imitating Dürer in his writings as well. This is attested to in a poem by Hoefnagel, published by Thomas DaCosta Kaufmann, which was discovered in an album belonging to the Netherlandish merchant and poet Johannes Rademacher.[161] In the poem Hoefnagel elevates Dürer by stating that 'In one citizen the people of Nuremberg possess all things.'[162] For Hoefnagel, Dürer is the embodiment of the humanist ideal, a universal man capable of drawing upon the encyclopaedia of the arts.

Another significant artist for the depiction of animals at the Rudolfine court is the Augsburg-born artist Daniel Fröschl (1573–1613), who was named imperial antiquarius and curator of the Rudolfine collection in 1607. Confirmed as a miniature painter by Rudolf II in 1601, in 1604 he settled permanently in Prague, where new impulses to work were provided by the imperial collections. Fröschl made a number of miniature copies of the works of foreign masters, and was particularly interested in the work of Dürer, which he transformed and improved.[163] Like Hoffmann and Hoefnagel, the work of Fröschl in the genre of animal studies can be described as derived in part from the works of Dürer that he would have seen at the court of Rudolf II.

There are dozens of imitations of Dürer's *Blue Roller* and *Wing of Blue Roller*, and with no other animal study are the lines so blurred between copy and forgery. What is important is that there is evidence of Dürer's nature studies being made into a sort of artistic canon for artists to copy or imitate at the court of Rudolf II in Prague. Dürer's pictorial subject had become an established example. The Roller had come to be seen as a work of art and a prototype, valued as a model and frequently imitated. That a dead creature alone came to be viewed as a significant subject is indicative of an important artistic attitude that represents a step towards the genre of self-contained still life.

Dürer's *Hare*, signed and dated 1502, is a self-contained, figurative study (Figure 72). Its attribution to Dürer has never seriously been questioned, and it is one of the most popular works of Dürer's zoo, at least 15 copies are known from the seventeenth century.[164] In a deft homage, as much as a competitive spirit, Georg Hoefnagel appropriated the motif *Hare* into his work in *Hare, Raurackl, and Squirrel*, a miniature from the second volume of his four-volume illustrated natural history (Figure 73). For Hoefnagel, issues of zoology are combined with an attempt to document in an encyclopaedic fashion all the creatures of the universe, divided according to the four elements: fire, earth, air and water. His emphasis on encyclopaedism is symptomatic of the impetus behind the *Kunstkammer* as a whole. In the presence of other animals, Dürer's hare is not immediately noticeable. He sits next to a 'raurackl', a fanciful creature that combined a hare with the horns of a deer, which was deemed by hunters of the period to exist. The juxtaposition of real with fanciful is especially demonstrative of the lacing of fact with fiction, so peculiar to the natural history illustrations of the seventeenth century. Hoefnagel's appropriation is another example of the manner in which Dürer's models were incorporated into works with diverse themes, and he would use the hare on other occasions (Figure 74) Again, there is a shift in terms of medium and composition. From Dürer's study of an independent hare, Hoefnagel has created a miniature that is part of a construction of an encyclopaedic representation of all that exists in nature.[165]

Hans Hoffmann also created a number of variations on Dürer's hare prototype. Of the surviving copies and imitations of Dürer's hare, no fewer than six are by Hoffmann. Not one of them is totally faithful to the model, exemplifying Hoffmann's role as emulator very well. Perhaps the most noteworthy of Hoffmann's emulations occurred when he moved the animal from its white environment back into nature, surrounding it with grasses, wildflowers, insects and little animals, as in *Hare Among Grasses and Wildflowers in a Glade* (Figure 75). In this case, animals and plants are artistically arranged in a semicircle around the model, a sort of paraphrase that is symptomatic of the impetus behind the Dürer-Renaissance. The lighting of the scene is almost theatrical in effect, and not as one would expect in a darkened forest. It has been noted that the plants – including thistle, plantain, and bluebell – do not coexist in the natural world, further enhancing the imaginative engagement on the part of Hoffmann.[166] For this painting Rudolf II paid an unusually high sum of 200 guldens, indicating that as a patron Rudolf was pleased with Hoffmann.[167]

Hoffmann's art is richly suggestive of late sixteenth- and seventeenth-century thought about emulation. Emulation seems to have been promoted as a creative combining of received models, an accepting of tradition while simultaneously moving towards an improved image. The imitative impetus amongst artists seems to have been accorded a higher purpose than simply transcribing what lay before one's eyes. When an artist like Hoffmann copied Dürer, he would simultaneously paraphrase and rethink the motifs involved. The idea was to renew and uphold the tradition as represented by Dürer, borrowing while at the same time developing towards a higher goal. Moreover, in his depictions of hares, Hoffmann created images that were forerunners of what would become a widespread genre in seventeenth-century Netherlandish art, the animal piece.[168]

Dürer's 1505 study *Stag Beetle* is another one of his most popular and enduring studies, and one of his most often appropriated drawings (Figure 76). Stag beetles had appeared in German panel painting on many occasions prior to Dürer.[169] Hans Hoffmann copied it at least once, including on this occasion his own monogram HH and the date of his composition, 1574 (Figure 77). Georg Hoefnagel appropriated the *Stag Beetle* on no fewer than three occasions. The first is a version found on in a folio containing 80 miniatures with illustrations of insects (Figure 78). Hoefnagel's version is one of the most careful copies of a work by Dürer. He also executed a variation on the beetle that appears immediately after the stag beetle in the book of miniatures, a turning of the beetle to the left and an improvement on the beetle in terms of realism (Figure 79), and a depiction of the beetle with outstretched wings in the presence of a scorpion (Figure 80). Koreny describes this work as both in the style of Dürer and an inventive variation of the prototype.[170] Invoked was a careful arrangement of botanical and zoological specimens in overlapping relationships that involved scientific pretensions and visual appeal. Georg Flegel's *Still Life with Stag* Beetle incorporates Dürer's beetle amidst an imagined still life (Figure 81), and has already been discussed at the beginning of this chapter.

At the 1985 Albertina exhibition of Dürer's plant and animal watercolours, Fritz Koreny argued that in the realm of natures studies, Dürer acted as artist and scientist simultaneously.[171] With persistence and exactitude rendered in the swift medium of watercolour, Dürer carefully recorded subjects from nature at a time when science was entrenched in the realm of observation. In other words, since science was wholly descriptive in the sixteenth century, Dürer, due to his extensive and first-hand documentation of nature, can be counted a descriptive scientist. His interests were firmly in the external appearances of the specimens that he observed, rather than dissection to the end of seeing parts. Dürer's nature studies are thus on the threshold of the eventual examination, description and recording of plants and animals as an end in itself.[172]

Dürer's endeavours as a descriptive scientist are an important aspect of his reception. Most significant are the copies, imitations and emulations that arose in conjunction with his nature studies. Through a discussion of the myriad of borrowings after these nature studies, it can be seen that the impact of Dürer is perhaps even greater than hitherto perceived. His efforts also prepared the way for the development of still life as a genre. In the realm of animal studies, Dürer's precision can be seen as an important precursor to the efforts of zoologists in the next century. Clearly, it is essential to understand that, in some ways, Dürer acted as artist and scientist simultaneously, and was perceived as such by those upon whom he exerted such a strong influence.

Appropriations of Dürer Paintings

The issues involved with the dispersal and reception of Dürer's paintings are of a different nature than those outlined for prints and drawings as sources. Prints by definition are easily transportable and more readily accessible. Drawings were also easily transportable, although access was more restricted than with prints. Over the course of the sixteenth and seventeenth centuries, the majority of painted works by Dürer were removed from their original locations and placed in a variety of new contexts. The courts in Prague and Munich take on a paramount importance in this discussion. I begin with a discussion of a number of known copies of Dürer's paintings. This is followed by emulations created at the courts of Holy Roman Emperor Rudolf II, Archduke Maximilian I of Bavaria, as well as a discussion of the court of Archduke Leopold Wilhelm. It will be shown how these three locations fostered imitations and emulations of Dürer's works.

One principle that emerges is the emphasis placed upon pictorial ideas in the sixteenth and seventeenth centuries. By pictorial ideas, I mean the invention of new schemes and the solutions to problems of composition. The value placed upon this principle created a demand for copies. Making a good copy of a renowned work was not easy. Access to the original could prove to be a problem for the artist who wished to make a convincing copy. The overwhelming concern is, of course, the technical aspect: the imitation of another hand is a difficult and exacting process that is not always successful. In much the same way that connoisseurs evaluate the technical aspects of artists' original works, a qualitative aspect to the copies exists as well. Some copies are simply higher in quality than others. Further, given the reception of Dürer after his death and the high esteem in which his works were held, only well-versed collectors could afford to obtain originals when collecting. For others, copies had to suffice.

A number of painters active in Nuremberg executed copies after Dürer's paintings. Often, the motivation behind such works appears to have been the creation of a substitute in the absence, or expected absence, of the originals. As with prints, executing a copy could be a pedagogical exercise. There are a number of primary sources that describe in some detail the need for the creation of a copy after an original was acquired by a collector. This is especially evident in the Hauer manuscript, discussed in Chapters 1 and 2, in which Hauer discusses the creation of copies when originals were purchased by the main collectors of Dürer's paintings, Rudolf II and Maximilian I.[173]

As with prints, the practice of creating copies after Dürer's paintings began in Dürer's lifetime. Dürer painted the *St. Jerome* in Antwerp in March 1521 and presented the panel to his friend Rodrigo Fernandez d'Almada. The panel was displayed in the merchant's private chapel in Antwerp and was later taken back to Portugal, where it has remained to this day.[174] A number of copies of this painting are known. One copy was created by Georg Pencz (1500–1550), an artist who had worked in Dürer's studio.[175] Pencz's copy is still in Nuremberg. Two paintings created by Dürer that never left his hometown, and can be found there to this day in the Germanisches Nationalmuseum, are the companion pieces *Emperor Charlemagne* (1512/13) and the *Emperor Sigismund* (1511). The city council commissioned Dürer to create images of two figures integral to the history not only of the Holy Roman Empire, but also the place of Nuremberg within it. These paintings were commissioned to commemorate the *Heiltumsfest*, a celebration in Nuremberg around Easter time during which the coronation insignia (crown jewels) were exposed to public view. Dürer was asked to portray the personages who had figured most prominently in the history of the insignia: Charlemagne, the original owner of the insignia, and Sigismund, who had entrusted the insignia to Nuremberg. Charlemagne is depicted as larger in scale, somehow taller and grander, wearing a gothic crown, with an imposing scepter. Sigismund is dwarfed by four shields, and wears simple garments.

These paintings would have had great significance for the city of Nuremberg, and given their role in a very important civil ceremony, it is not surprising that they were not among the Dürer paintings that left the city. The historical importance of the figures depicted, as well as the great esteem granted to Dürer as an artist, would have made them of great relevance to any ruler within the Holy Roman Empire. It is likely for this reason that numerous copies of the paintings can be found in other cities that were vital to the Austro-Hungarian Empire, including Budapest and Vienna. Also in Vienna are two partial copies in bust format, an interesting retreat in form to a more antique way of representing historical figures. Dating to roughly 1600, these busts are of a high quality, and were once in the Ambras collection in Tyrol.[176] It seems likely that in this context they would have been viewed as essential reminders of historical figures of the Holy Roman Empire, reminders for which the copies could have served as well as the originals.

Consideration must also be given to the evidence of Hoffmann as emulator of Dürer's paintings. One drawing in particular created by Hoffmann during his Prague period shows his peculiar brand of recycling toward the end of creating a new image, more in the style of Dürer, rather than a copy after Dürer, is his drawing *Christ among the Doctors* (plate 11).[177] Hoffmann's authorship of this drawing is noted with his HH monogram, perhaps denoting a sense of pride in this emulative achievement. Hoffmann used at least two Dürer drawings that were preparatory studies for other paintings in order to create a fresh version of a subject that Dürer had already painted.[178] The result is a patchwork of dependency, and likely a competitive emulation created within a court circle in which creative assimilation of past artists seems to have been encouraged. A quick comparison with Dürer's painting of the same subject (plate 10) shows clearly that Hoffmann's drawing is not a direct copy of Dürer's painting. As has been discussed above, most of Dürer's works did not remain in their original contexts, and on some occasions, tracing their migrations poses particular problems. The original painting was in Rome at the end of the sixteenth century.[179] A trip by Hoffmann to Rome is not documented and seems unlikely given his numerous activities in Prague.[180] There are no early painted copies of the painting, however, a watercolour and several sketches after the painting existed, one of which is mentioned in the 1628 correspondence from Lukas Friedrich Beheim.[181] It is likely that Hoffmann knew of the Dürer painting from a drawing by a travelling artist, or possibly the painting was in a northern collection prior to being deposited in Rome.

The fact that Hoffmann likely did not see the original Dürer painting, coupled with the fact that motifs in the drawing had previously been copied by Hoffmann, indicate an intriguing episode of reception. In Hoffmann's free interpretation, he has reworked numerous elements of Dürer's drawings. While the overall composition of the painting is possibly based on a sketch of the Dürer painting, there are distinct variations. Christ is of course central to Hoffmann's drawing, as in Dürer's painting, and is surrounded by the authorities who question him. The hands of Christ are also gesturing in the same way as in Dürer's painting (a preparatory study is known for this gesture). From there, Hoffman has chosen different pictorial sources. There is the addition of the table in the foreground. The figures, while placed in the same spots for the composition, are a pastiche of other Dürer drawings. For the head of Christ, Hoffmann used a figure which he had previously copied (Figure 62), the head of an angel from Dürer's *Feast of the Rosegarlands*. The figure in the far left foreground seems to have been based in part on another Dürer character Hoffmann had already copied as well, the head of the Apostle from Dürer's *Heller Altar*. It is difficult to account for artistic intention; however, in this case it seems certain that Hoffmann intended to create a preparatory study using Dürer motifs, with the aim of painting a different version of a subject that Dürer had already painted.

It is noteworthy that there are two sixteenth-century versions of the subject of *Christ among the Doctors* that have remarkable similarities to Hoffmann's drawing. For these two paintings, there are regrettably more questions than answers. In an oil painting that has tentatively been attributed to Hoffmann, both Hoffmann's drawing and Dürer's painting are used as sources (plate 12). The painting has the date 1512; however, it is the opinion of this author that it should be dated later. For the figure of Christ, the painter has chosen to use the original figure in Dürer's *Christ among the Doctors*. However, the figure on the far left is as in Hoffmann's drawing. It also seems plausible to suggest a further case of emulation for a painting attributed to Jobst Harrich, *Woman Taken in Adultery* (plate 13). The overall plan of the composition is based on Dürer, and the third figure from the right is based on his study for an apostle for the *Heller Altar* (Figure 68). As noted previously, the dependencies in these three paintings are complex and merit further investigation.

I suggest that Hoffmann's activities changed upon entering the service of the Rudolf II in Prague in 1585. While in Nuremberg, Hoffmann seems to have created mostly copies. However, the emulative drawing he created for *Christ among the Doctors*, as well as the emulative animal studies discussed in the section above, are suggestive of a context in which imitation was encouraged not for the sake of duplicity, but rather in terms of homage or competition. Eliška Fučíková, a scholar of the court of Rudolf II, has suggested that the emperor made use of Hoffmann's expertise when in 1588 he was offered the famous Imhoff collection which consisted largely of Dürer's work.[182] It is highly likely that Hoffmann was able to distinguish originals from copies – after all many of them were his own copies – and thus save his patron unnecessary expenses. Fučíková also argues that the Dürer forgeries stemmed mostly from the German lands, while at the court of Rudolf II in Prague, these conditions for forgery did not exist to the same extent.[183] Instead, the evidence suggests that emulation of Dürer as a creative process was encouraged.

THE COURT OF RUDOLF II IN PRAGUE (1576–1612)

As discussed in Chapter 2, the *Feast of the Rosegarlands* painted by Dürer for the church of San Bartolomeo in Venice in 1506, was acquired by Rudolf II for his imperial court in Prague in 1606 (plate 3). It was transported to Prague and is the only painting by Dürer to have remained there. There is an exact copy of the painting, dated to 1600, now in the Kunsthistorisches Museum in Vienna. The dimensions of the original (162 × 194 cms) and the copy (160 × 193 cms) are almost identical. It is possible that the copy was made for Rudolf, as was common procedure for the time, when he initially experienced difficulty procuring the original, although this is not mentioned in the known correspondence surrounding the acquisition.[184] Or, it is possible that the copy of the painting was created as a brochure for the Emperor's approval, as a necessary step prior to purchase, as sometimes occurred in the period. This anonymous work is first documented as a copy after Dürer in the Vienna inventory in 1772.[185]

It was because of Rudolf's acquisition of this painting that at least one other copy came into existence, that by Hans Rottenhammer (1564/5–1625), which has not survived. In 1606 Rottenhammer was commissioned to replace the original after it was purchased by Rudolf II.[186] This is an excellent example of how high-profile artists were often called upon to create exacting copies, because Rottenhammer is a fairly well documented painter. Born in Munich, Rottenhammer had a prolific career as a well-travelled painter and draughtsman before his death in Augsburg. He has been described as 'standing in the vanguard' of the German artists, mainly from Bavaria, who journeyed to Italy and lived and worked in Venice.[187] Rottenhammer's use of colour signifies his absorption of the style of the great Venetian masters of the sixteenth century, and it is largely due to him that a distinctive south German style, with Italian overtones, can readily be discerned.[188] During his career he gained a considerable reputation as a painter of small devotional images and mythologies on copper, and included among his clients Cardinal Carlo Borromeo, the Duke of Mantua, and Rudolf II, for whom he also acquired and restored works of art.[189]

Another copy of the painting (plate 4) freely adapts Dürer's painting in terms of composition and iconography. Changing the format of the *Feast of the Rosegarlands* from a horizontal to a vertical composition, the dimensions of the copy (164 × 142 cm) vary from the original (160 × 193 cm). More significantly, the artist has made alterations to the figures gathered. On the left-hand side of the painting, the papal figure has been replaced with St Catherine of Alexandria, identifiable thanks to her attribute of the wheel. The Dominican saint (identified by some scholars as St Dominic himself) who is present in the background of Dürer's painting has been replaced by two small angels. Further to the left where one would find a grouping of angels in the Dürer orignal, one finds a large angel who indicates to the heavens. Also, the baldachin on which the Virgin was seated has been removed and replaced by a tree. At least one copy after this copy is known.[190] Apart from being documented later in the Ambras collection, nothing is known about the purpose of this copy and the details as to why the figures were altered. However, the removal of the Dominican saint, the prominent inclusion of St Catherine in the place of the papal figure, and the replacement of only some of the figures, highlight that the work must have been commissioned with specific intention. It seems highly likely that this copy would have had a votive or liturgical function, and functioning in some capacity as a dedication to St Catherine. At one point, there were three copies of the painting in the Imperial collections, proof that this was one of the most esteemed works in the Emperor's collection.

At Rudolf's court, Dürer was not the only artist after whom creative copies were made. For example, Joseph Heintz (1564–1609) made a copy of Parmigianino's *Cupid with Bow and Arrow* before Rudolf was able to acquire the original from Philip II in 1603. It is interesting to note that the original was later displayed together with the copy.[191] Heintz was well versed in copying, as Rudolf sent him to Rome on a number of occasions to make copies of antiquities. Jeremias Günther (active early seventeenth century), a painter at Rudolf's court, was named *Kammermaler* with a salary of 15 gulden per month in 1604. In 1616 he executed in oil for Rudolf a copy after Brueghel the Elder's

Three Peasants, as well as a copy of Brueghel the Younger's *Court Scene*: neither painting has survived.[192] He is also recorded as having executed a Crucifixion after Dürer which is also lost.[193]

THE COURT OF ARCHDUKE MAXIMILIAN I IN MUNICH (1597–1651)

Just as at Rudolf's court, numerous imitative works after Dürer's paintings stem from the court of Archduke Maximilian I of Munich, another major repository of Dürer paintings. There is even some evidence of competition between these two collectors: Maximilian acquired the *Paumgartner* altar in 1614, a painting that Rudolf had expressed interest in for some time. As discussed in Chapter 2, it is possible that Rudolf declined the purchase due to some debate over the quality of the painting, since it had been referred to in the correspondence as a 'bad painting' and not worthy of the Kaiser's interest.[194] When Maximilian expressed his interest in the painting, the Nuremberg Council pointedly stated that such an offer had already been declined, and from no less a personage than Emperor Rudolf II. Maximilian was undeterred, and after lengthy negotiations with the Paumgartner family, he acquired the painting in 1614.

Maximilian's dissatisfaction upon receipt of the painting must be noted, as well as the discussion prior to acquisition regarding quality. Half a year after he received the painting, Maximilian sent his envoy Lorenz Beheim to investigate the original altar construction. After his investigation Beheim concluded that the side panels depicting George and Eustace were not from the hand of Dürer at all.[195] This is a possible explanation as to why Maximilian had no qualms about altering the side panels. In 1630, both side panels were over-painted by an unknown court artist using motifs from engravings by Dürer. These results can be seen in an early photograph, taken before the removal of the over painting in 1903. In the over painted version, Dürer's figure of St George was changed from a solitary standing figure, to a knight standing with his horse in a detailed landscape. Dürer's figure of St Eustace was also embellished, and altered to the guise of Dürer's knight from the *Knight, Death and the Devil* engraving, also with a rich landscape in the background. It is as if the unknown painter at Maximilian's court sought to make the Dürer painting even more 'Dürerish' by incorporating Dürer motifs from his graphic oeuvre into the over-painting.

At least one exact seventeenth-century copy of the Paumgartner in its original state is known, likely the one created on the occasion of Maximilian's purchase of the original. The copy hangs in the Lorenzkirche in Nuremberg, and the painter is named as as Jobst Harrich (1579–1617).[196] Harrich's activities as copyist of Dürer are known especially in reference to his copy of the *Heller Altar*, which was another major acquisition by Maximilian in 1614, who purchased the middle panel from the Dominican church in Frankfurt in which it was originally situated.[197] After the acquisition Harrich, then in the employ of Maximilian, made a copy for the Dominican church as a replacement for the original that was sent to Munich.[198] Harrich's copy is the only way in which Dürer's painting is known to us today: the original was destroyed in a fire in 1729.

One of the most interesting and telling alterations of a painting was occasioned by Maximilian's acquisition of the *Four Holy Men* in 1627 (plate 5). Acquired by Maximilian almost one century after Dürer completed the painting and bequeathed it to the Nuremberg town hall, this depiction of four holy men was a personal statement on the part of the artist that would endure a significant shift in meaning in its new context.[199] In 1627 the painting was sent to Maximilian in Munich, and a copy was created that remained in Nuremberg and is still there to this day. The creation of this copy is described by Hauer, who states that Maximilian's court painter Georg Vischer was sent to Nuremberg to make a copy, which he did, before witnesses including Maximilian's *Kammerkunstler*, Augustin Hammel Haimbl.[200] Maximilian further requested that the original inscriptions on the bottom of the painting be sawed off and placed on the copy.[201] In a way, it is not difficult to imagine why, given the Protestant nature of the inscriptions and the new Catholic context into which the painting was entering. In the original inscriptions, Dürer posits a warning against 'false prophets' and 'not to accept human seduction for the word of God', quoting from Martin Luther's *Septemberbibel*. Maximilian, on the other hand, was a catholic and would likely have found the Protestant sentiments endorsed in the inscriptions less than appealing.[202] This speaks volumes as to his steadfast interest in Dürer: to Maximilian it was more important to have a work by Dürer's hand even if its religious credo was in contrast to his own. This episode of reception also reveals a great deal as to how paintings were altered to suit new needs in the seventeenth century.

By 1627 both the *Heller Altar* and the *Four Apostles* could be found at Maximilian's court in Munich. In an early seventeenth-century painting, entitled *Eleven Apostles*, an anonymous painter made use of both images to create a distinct and unusual emulation (plate 6). This large picture, measuring over two-and-a-half metres in height, combines figures from both the *Heller Altar* and the *Four Apostles* by Dürer. The figures of John, Peter, Mark and Paul are flanked by a grouping of three, respectively, who have been taken directly from the central panel of the *Heller Altar*. It is highly likely that the anonymous artist saw both paintings at Maximilian's court.[203] The effect is similar to Hoffmann's emulation of Dürer discussed above: using a number of different sources in one image, the artist created a work in the style of Dürer, as opposed to a straightforward copy.

Another curious picture from the court of Maximilian has been attributed with certainty to Georg Vischer is *Christ Carrying of the Cross* (plate 7). This painting contains many borrowings from Dürer. There is a definite sense of playfulness, as if Vischer is playing a game of hide and seek, challenging the viewer to identify motifs in a test of visual knowledge. In the eighteenth century, this painting was attributed to Dürer himself. This exemplifies how imitation often involved a myriad of sources. In Vischer's painting, the two riders in the background are quotations from Dürer's prints *Knight, Death and the Devil* and *St. George*. The figure in the foreground wearing a sheath for a dagger contains a Dürer reference: the dagger sheath has a small portrait of Dürer in profile. The general composition of the painting bears a resemblance to Dürer's *Martyrdom of the Ten Thousand*. As pointed out by Gisela Goldberg, other motifs in this curious painting have been taken from works by other painters, including Guido Reni, Quinten Massys, Martin Heemskerck and Jan Hemessen.[204] Goldberg has also discussed extensively other paintings in the Alte Pinakothek that were altered during the reign of Maximilian I.[205] It appears that Maximilian had a very 'hands on' approach in his attitudes toward works in his collection. If something did not quite appeal to his taste or sensibility, he would have it altered. Over-paintings were used to give new meaning to older subject matter.

Another important acquisition for Maximilian came in 1630, when Dürer's *St. Anne with Virgin and Child* of 1519 came to the court (plate 8). There exists a relatively exact copy that is close in terms of dimensions (the Dürer original measures 60 × 50 cms, the copy 76 × 59 cms) and colouration (plate 9). The major difference is that the anonymous copyist has chosen to include two additional figures in the scene. Flanking Anne in the background are the figures of Joachim and Joseph, the husbands of Anne and the Virgin, respectively. This creative appropriation, an active choice on the part of the anonymous artist to give a fuller consideration to the theme of family in his painting, is again indicative of an impetus towards making Dürer 'more Dürerish' at the court of Maximilian I.

THE COURT OF ARCHDUKE LEOPOLD WILHELM OF AUSTRIA (1614–62)

In order to understand a number of other copies of Dürer paintings executed in the seventeenth century, it is necessary to turn to the court of Archduke Leopold Wilhelm of Austria (1614–62). Leopold Wilhelm is one of the most important collectors of paintings in the Habsburg family. However, he was not mentioned in Chapter 2 as a significant Dürer collector because most of the works contained in his collection were copies. This episode of reception is significant for the phenomenon of the Dürer-Renaissance, and is examined below.

Leopold Wilhelm was a commander in chief of Imperial troops during the Thirty Years War, governed the Spanish Netherlands, and spent much of his life in Brussels. Recently, Renate Schreiber has published a detailed, and much needed, account of the Archduke.[206] She points out that the first exhibition on Leopold Wilhelm's collection was held in 2003, a collection comprising more than 800 works that has survived intact and forms an important part of the holdings of today's Kunsthistorisches Museum in Vienna.[207] Schreiber drew her details on Leopold from unpublished correspondence with his elder brother Emperor Ferdinand III, his confidant Count Johann Adolph von Schwarzenberg, and records from the archives in Vienna, Brussels,

Stockholm, and Česky Krumlov. From the letters to his brother, it is revealed that Leopold Wilhelm was personally involved in buying paintings, for his brother Ferdinand III in Vienna and later for himself.[208]

It is likely that Leopold Wilhelm's interest in Dürer has not been given much consideration in scholarship because the works contained in his collection are now known as copies. Seven months after Leopold Wilhelm's arrival in Brussels in 1647, he wrote to his brother that once he had a little bit of money, he would build a gallery in Brussels 'nach meinem humor' (in my own taste). Gustav Glück has published a thorough analysis of Leopold's collection that to date is the most detailed analysis of the *Kunstkammer* in Brussels.[209] Glück suggests that in inventories of the sixteenth century the name of Dürer was so significant that forgeries were created, a number of which Leopold Wilhelm acquired.[210] It should be recalled (continues Glück) that the Archduke was not as familiar with German art and that it is hardly surprising that he was unable to make wise decisions in this realm.[211]

Glück does not point out that it is equally as plausible that Leopold Wilhelm commissioned the imitative works. This is a tempting suggestion, and given what we have seen in terms of the activities at the courts in Prague and Munich, not entirely out of the realm of possibility. A significant point to be made here is that the Archduke's interest in Dürer should not be discounted: indeed, the imitative works that can be traced back to the context of Leopold Wilhelm's court are amongst the most intriguing of the Dürer-Renaissance.

It is now known that Leopold Wilhelm had no original Dürer paintings in his collection, despite what the inventories say. There were no Dürer paintings on the market at the time he began collecting. Altogether 30 pieces in the inventory were associated with Dürer's name: oil paintings, a painting on glass, drawings, a glass painting and sculpture. Fifteen were qualified in the inventory as Dürer originals. The other 15 were designated as copies and imitations. Not all of the 15 designated as originals have survived; however of the ones that did, none are authentic. In total, two drawings that were in the Duke's collection are still considered to be by Dürer's hand.[212] It is interesting to note that in the seventeenth century, many items of sculpture, as well as medals, were still attributed to Dürer in inventories, especially in the inventory of Leopold Wilhelm.

This is rich evidence of the manner in which imitative works were seen as essential to a collection. If collectors could not have the original painting, they at least could procure a very good copy. In the Archduke's collection, the objects that bore Dürer's name are colourful and varied. A number of these works can be found today in the Kunsthistorisches Museum in Vienna: a painting on glass with the Dürer monogram that depicts a scene from the *Life of the Virgin*; a drawing pasted onto wood and varnished like an oil painting that was included in the inventory as being by Dürer; and the counterfeit of Dürer by Eberhard Schön, which in the Archduke's inventory is attributed to Dürer.[213]

Most striking are the works in the Archduke's collection that are imitations of paintings that had already been acquired by other major collectors. Rudolf's acquisitions of the *Adoration of the Trinity* (plate 1) in 1585 and the *Martyrdom of the Ten Thousand* in 1600 have already been discussed. However, these paintings did not remain in Prague: both were dispersed to Vienna after the ascension of Rudolf's brother Mathias to the Habsburg throne, when the seat of the Imperial residence, along with many of the art treasures, were removed to Vienna (*c*.1612). Certainly, by the time Leopold Wilhelm was establishing his collection, both of the originals were in Vienna in the Imperial Residence of Emperor Ferdinand III, brother of Leopold Wilhelm. Demonstrative of the motivation toward completeness in collecting are the copies that Leopold Wilhelm commissioned of these major works by Dürer. In 1654, Johann Christian Rupprecht (1600–1654) created copies after both these paintings for the Archduke, copies that are now in the Kunsthistorisches Museum in Vienna. Rupprecht, a Nuremberg-born artist who died shortly after the completion of these copies, was called by Emperor Ferdinand III to Vienna, where his copies were executed, and he eventually ended up in Brussels.[214] It is likely that Ferdinand asked for the two panels to present to his brother Leopold Wilhelm for his gallery in Brussels. They are listed in the inventory of 1659.[215]

The motivation toward a complete *Kunstkammer* cannot be underestimated in this context. Leopold Wilhelm likely sought to have representations of two of the most famed altarpieces created north of the Alps. Rupprecht's copies are exacting and precise, especially his copy of the *Adoration of the Trinity*, in which the dimensions match exactly the original by Dürer, and every single detail has been painstakingly reproduced. The only exception is the *cartellino* of authorship. In the original, Dürer has included his name, the fact that he made this painting in 1511, as well as his monogram. On the copy, in addition to this information, Rupprecht has included the fact that he has imitated Dürer.[216] In openly acknowledging his source and using the term imitate, Rupprecht left little doubt as to the intention of this painting: it would have been valued as a direct copy of the Dürer original, or as an exercise in the skill of the imitator. In his copy of *Martyrdom of the Ten Thousand*, Rupprecht again includes his own identity and acknowledges Dürer as a source.

A final imitative work from the collection of Leopold Wilhelm is especially demonstrative of the inclination toward emulation that the court likely fostered. In one of the most unusual imitative works after Dürer, an anonymous artist transformed the *Adoration of the Trinity* into the wings of a triptych (plate 2). The middle panel for this work is missing. However, based on what remains, interesting observations can be made.[217] To look closely at the painting is to see a patchwork quilt of Dürer borrowings. Overall, the composition is based on the *Adoration of the Trinity*. However, the kneeling Emperor, the patricians and the cardinal, have all been borrowed from *The Feast of the Rosegarlands*. A group on the right has been taken from the *Heller Altar*. There are figures taken from *Christ among the Doctors*, and three females from the *Life of the Virgin* series. This is perhaps the most complex of all the Dürer emulations. It is as if the artist had all the works by Dürer in front of him and pieced them all together. The hint of nostalgia is strengthened when we consider that Dürer's *Adoration of the Trinity* was one of the first altarpieces north of the Alps that did not take the form of a triptych. In this copy there is a harking back to the past in terms of structure and content.

Conclusion

Of the known emulations in reference to Dürer, the most free-spirited quotations used his drawings and paintings as sources. This speaks to the context of the courts, where most of the Dürer paintings and drawings could be found. Indeed, the so-called Dürer-Renaissance found its greatest expression in the court circles. At the height of this phenomenon around 1600, significant centres such as Munich and Prague were involved not only in collecting Dürer, but also in patronizing and employing artists to emulate his works and style. Procedures of procuring copies were highly complex, and indicative of the changing role of art and art collecting in the sixteenth and seventeenth centuries.

Cases of dependency examined are not always clearly defined. Placing works into categories such as forgery, pedagogy, retrospection, emulation and copy is a difficult enterprise, especially given that the boundaries between these categories were not rigidly defined in the period under scrutiny. Roughly speaking, one could define a forgery by an intention to deceive, often for financial gain. Imitation is a mode of production, usually resulting in a more or less exact copy, in which the source is acknowledged. As for works characterized as emulations, these usually involve an assimilation or transformation of some aspect or motif from the source. Emulation is a special form of competitive imitation, in which the goal is to surpass the chosen model. This kind of artistic competition seems to have been considered to be the highest compliment an artist could pay another.

There is a need to give consideration to the epistemology of the period, an epistemology that accorded the term original a very different meaning than today. It is important to recognize copying as a valuable mode of production in the courtly circles of the sixteenth and seventeenth centuries. Moreover, the works discussed in this chapter attest to the widespread and diffuse interest in Dürer in the period, if only because the artists who engaged in these practices were of an international caliber and working in highly cosmopolitan atmospheres (such as the courts of Rudolf II in Prague and Maximilian I in Munich). Dürer's influence was not limited to the Netherlands and Italy, where it has most commonly been accounted for. Accounting for Dürer's reception means expanding the vision of what we perceive as important sites of art-making to include central Europe.

Notes

1 On this point see Charles Dempsey, *Annibale Carracci and the Beginnings of Baroque Style* (Glückstadt: Augustin, 1977); also Mary Ann Graeve Frantz, 'Taddeo Zuccaro as a Precursor of Annibale Carracci', *Essays in Honor of Walter Friedländer*, edited by W. Cahn (New York: Institute of Fine Arts, 1965): pp. 62–79.

2 Friederike Klauner discusses this positively as a form of 'Schöpferfreude',or delight in the creation that could accompany the process of making copies: 'Neue Gebiete schließen sich hier dem Kopierenden, dem Nachvollziehenden auf und lassen ihn fast einen Abglanz der Schöpferfreude nachempfinden.' Friederike Klauner, 'Dürers Werke in der Kopie', *Alte und moderne Kunst*, 16 (1971): pp. 14–18, at p. 14.

3 This is particularly the case in projects of connoisseurship in the nineteenth century, and even the first half of the twentieth century, where the focus was on making a case for the 'originality' of an artist. The definitive oeuvre catalogue of the early nineteenth century for Dürer was Joseph Heller, *Das Leben und die Werke Albrecht Dürers*, 2 volumes (Bamberg: E.F.Kunz, 1827). The first volume is biographical. The second volume is divided into two parts: the first deals with paintings, drawings, and sculpture attributed to Dürer; the second part deals with engravings and woodcuts, and includes an extensive list of copies. Heller's text is no longer relied upon; however, it is an essential and important episode of connoisseurship that indicates how attributions to Dürer have shifted (for example, Heller attributes a number of sculptures to Dürer, while today it is accepted that Dürer did not execute any sculptures).

4 '...schöpferisches Neugestallten und neu Überlegen...' Klauner 1971, p. 14.

5 Catherine M. Soussloff, 'Imitatio Buonarroti', *Sixteenth Century Journal* 20/4 (1989): pp. 581–602; for the reference to Barberini, which is taken from F. Baldinucci's *Life of Bernini*, see p. 587.

6 The Berlin Kupferstichkabinett houses all the known works on paper by Flegel, 110 watercolours that were received together. Thirty were lost in the Second World War. The epitaph quoted above is by Hendrick van der Borcht.

7 'The Imhoff Inventory'and 'The Imhoff Geheimbüchlein', *Albrecht Dürer and the Animal and Plant Studies of the Renaissance*, compiled by Fritz Koreny (Boston: Brown, 1988): pp. 261–266, p. 263.

8 For a discussion of Dürer's studio, see Jane Campbell Hutchison, 'The Master and his Journeymen',in *Albrecht Dürer: A Biography* (Princeton: Princeton University Press, 1990): pp. 108–118.

9 Hutchison 1990, p. 110.

10 Hutchison 1990, p. 109. See also Sigrid Walther, *Hans Süss von Kulmbach* (Dresden: Verlag der Kunst, 1981); Barbara Butts, *'Dürerschüler' Hans Süss von Kulmbach* (Ph.D. Thesis: Harvard University, 1985).

11 M.J. Liebman, 'Dürer und seine Werkstatt', in Ernst Ullmann, Günter Grau, and Rainer Behrends, eds, *Albrecht Dürer: Zeit und Werk* (Leipzig: Karl Marx Universität, 1971). A relatively recent monograph on Schäufelein has been published: Christoph Metzger, *Hans Schäufelein als Maler* (Berlin: Deutscher Verein für Kunstwissenschaft, 2002); the text was originally presented as the author's doctoral thesis at the University of Augsburg in 1999 and includes a catalogue raisonné.

12 Gert von der Osten, *Hans Baldung Grien – Gemälde und Dokumente* (Berlin: Deutscher Verlag für Kunstwissenschaft, 1983); *Hans Baldung Grien: Prints and Drawings*, edited by James H. Marrow and Alan Shestack (Chicago: University of Chicago Press, 1981).

13 Hans Rupprich, ed., *Dürer-Schriftlicher Nachlass*, 3 volumes (Berlin: Deutscher Verein für Kunstwissenschaft, 1956). 'Das musse ein gar sproder Verstand sein, der sich nicht traut, auch etwas Weiteres zu erfinden, sondern liegt allwegen auf der alten Bahn, nur andere imitiert, und nicht den Mut hat, weiter nachzudenken.'

14 For inspired discussion of these prints, and the guises of borrowings associated with Dürer in general, see Thomas daCosta Kaufmann,'Hermeneutics in the History of Art: Remarks on the Reception of Dürer in the Sixteenth and the Early Seventeenth Centuries', in *New Perspectives on the Art of Renaissance Nuremberg: Five Essays*, edited by Jeffrey Chipps-Smith (Austin: Archer M. Huntington Gallery, 1985): pp. 23–39.

15 'On reflection, we have to admit that we know of no nature study either by a pupil of Dürer's or by any one of the Little Masters; apart from Cranach, this applies to German art in general in the second quarter of the sixteenth century.' Fritz Koreny, *Albrecht Dürer and the Animal and Plant Studies of the Renaissance*, translated by Pamela Marwood and Yehuda Shapiro (Boston: Brown, 1988): p. 18.

16 Moritz Thausing, *Dürer: Geschichte seines Lebens und seiner Kunst* (Leipzig: E.E. Seemann, 1884).

17 Williamstown 1975, *Dürer Through Other Eyes: His Graphic Work Mirrored in Copies and Forgeries of Three Centuries (An exhibition prepared by students in the Williams College–Clark Art Institute graduate program in art history, March 14 – June 15, 1975* (Williamstown, Massachusetts: Sterling and Francine Clark Institute, 1975): p. 11.

18 Koreny 1988, p. 45. For more details on Dürer's monogram as a sign of ownership, see Joseph Koerner, 'Albrecht Dürer: A Sixteenth-Century Influenza', *Albrecht Dürer and his Legacy*, edited by Giulia Bartrum, (London: The British Museum Press, 2003): pp. 25–31.

19 Lisa Oehler, 'Das Dürermonogramm auf Werken der Dürerschule', *Städel Jahrbuch* 4 (1973), p. 38. Through a painstaking and thorough comparison, Lisa Oehler has compiled and compared a range of monograms and attempted to distinguish them.

20 Quoted in *Albrecht Dürer and his Legacy: The Graphic Work of a Renaissance Artist*. Edited by Giulia Bartrum (London: The British Museum Press, 2002): p. 24.

21 Jan Białostocki, 'The two worlds of arts: Dürer versus Raphael', *Dürer and His Critics 1500–1971: Chapters in the History of Ideas Including a Collection of Texts* (Baden-Baden: Valentin Koerner, 1986): pp. 73–90.

22 See especially Hermann Gmelin, 'Das Prinzip der Imitatio in der romanischen Literatur der Renaissance', *Romanische Forschungen* XLVI (1932): pp. 83–360; Thomas Greene, *The Light in Troy: Imitation and Discovery in Renaissance Poetry* (New Haven: Yale University Press, 1982): p. 171.

23 Howard Mayer Brown, 'Emulation, Competition and Homage: Imitation and the Theories of Imitation in the Renaissance', *Journal of the American Musicological Society* 35/1 (Spring, 1982): pp. 1–48, at pp. 8–9.

24 Brown 1982, p. 14.

25 *The Princeton Encyclopedia of Poetry and Poetics*, edited by Alex Preminger (Princeton: Princeton University Press): p. 380.

26 Greene 1982, p. 171.

27 G.W. Pigman, 'Versions of Imitation in the Renaissance', *Renaissance Quarterly* 33/1 (1980): pp. 1–32.

28 Pigman 1980, p. 15.

29 Pigman 1980, p. 2.

30 Wolfgang Götz, 'Historismus, Ein Versuch zur Definition des Begriffes', *Zeitschrift des Deutschen Veriens für Kunstwissenschaft* XXIV (1970): pp. 196–212.

31 Götz 1970, p. 212.

32 Ellen Perry, *Aesthetics of Emulation in the Visual Arts of Ancient Rome* (Cambridge: Cambridge University Press, 2005).

33 Fefjer, Fischer-Hansen and Rathje, eds, *The Rediscovery of Antiquity: The Role of the Artist* (Copenhagen: Museum Tusculanum Press, University of Copenhagen, 2003).

34 Carmen Bambach, *Drawing and Painting in the Italian Renaissance Workshop: Theory and Practice, 1300–1600* (Cambridge: Cambridge University Press, 1999).

35 Michael O'Malley, "Copying practices and marketing strategies in a late fifteenth-century painter's workshop," *Artistic Exchange and Cultural Translation in the Italian Renaissance City*, edited by Stephen J. Campbell and Stephen J. Milner (Cambridge: Cambridge University Press, 2004).

36 Alfred Moir, *Caravaggio and his Copyists* (New York: New York University Press, 1976).

37 *Paper Museums: The Reproductive Print in Europe, 1500–1800*, edited by Rebecca Zorach (Chicago: David and Alfred Smart Museum of Art, University of Chicago, 2005).

38 Lisa Pon, *Raphael, Dürer, and Marcantonio Raimondi: Copying and the Italian Renaissance Print* (New Haven: Yale University Press, 2004).

39 John Shearman, *Only Connect...: Art and the Spectator in the Italian Renaissance* (Princeton: Princeton University Press, 1992), p. 232.

40 David Freedberg, *The Power of Images: Studies in the History and Theory of Response* (Chicago: University of Chicago Press, 1989).

41 See Izora Scott, *Controversies over the Imitation of Cicero in the Renaissance: With a Translation of Letters between Pietro Bembo and Gianfrancesco Pico On Imitation, and a Translation of Desiderius Erasmus, The Ciceronian (Ciceronianus)* (Davis: Hermagoras Press, 1991).

42 As pointed out by G. W. Pigman, the 'apian metaphor' is the most familiar of all the images in writings on imitation. [In Latin *apis* means bee]. Pigman also notes, 'the apian metaphor is perhaps the most misleading *topos* because it is used to present two opposed conceptions of imitation: the poet as collector (following) and the poet as maker (imitation or emulation)', Pigman 1980, p. 4. For more on the apian metaphor see Jürgen v. Stackelberg, 'Das Bienengleichnis: Ein Beitrag zur Geschichte der literarischen *Imitatio*', *Romanische Forschungen* 68 (1956): pp. 271–293.

43 For a fuller discussion see *Seneca's Moral Epistles*, selected and edited with an introduction by Anna Lydia Motto (Wauconda, Illinois: Bolchazy-Carducci Publishers, 2001); see also Pigman 1980, pp. 4–5.

44 As quoted in Pigman 1980, p. 6.

45 Petrarch, *Familiarum rerum libri*, 1.8.23 (Translation from Pigman 1980, p. 7). See also Thomas M. Greene, 'Petrarch and the Humanist Hermeneutic', in *Italian Literature: Roots and Branches*, edited by Giose Rimanelli and Kenneth John Atchity (New Haven: Yale University Press, 1976): pp. 201–224.

46 Brown 1982, p. 38.

47 As translated in Pigman 1980, p. 8. See also Izora Scott, *Controversies over the Imitation of Cicero in the Renaissance: With a Translation of Letters between Pietro Bembo and Gianfrancesco Pico On Imitation, and a Translation of Desiderius Erasmus, The Ciceronian (Ciceronianus)* (Davis: Hermagoras Press, 1991).

48 As translated in Pigman 1980, p. 10; from Erasmus, *Ciceronianus* (1527).

49 As translated in Pigman 1980, p. 25; Erasmus, *Ciceronianus* (1527).

50 For a detailed discussion of the Italian art theorists see Philip L. Sohm, *Style in the Art Theory of Early Modern Italy*, (Cambridge: Cambridge University Press, 2001).

51 Giovanni Paolo Lomazzo, *Trattato dell'Arte della Pittura, divisio in VII libri, nei quali si contiene tutte la Teoria e la Practica di essa Pittura* (Milan, 1584). It was reprinted in the following year.

52 Reinhard Steiner discusses Lomazzo's treatise as a pioneering text for an artistic canon: see Reinhard Steiner, '"Idea del Tempio della Pittura": Giovanni Paolo Lomazzo und die Entstehung des 'Kanonschrift'', *Kunstforum International* 162 (2002): pp. 96–101.

53 Bartolomeo Ricci, *De Imitatione libri tres* (Venice, 1545). According to Pigman: 'To my knowledge only Bartolomeo Ricci, in his *De imitatione* first published in 1541, writes as if there were accepted divisions of the genis *imitatio* into species', Pigman 1980, p. 3.

54 Bartolomeo Ricci, *De Imitatione libri tres* (Venice, 1545), folio 43v.

55 See Carmelo Peter Comberiati, 'Aspects of Renaissance *Imitatio* in Musical Settings of the Mass Ordinary at Rudolf's Court', *Prag um 1600: Beitrage zur Kunst und Kultur am Hofe Rudolfs II.* Eds. Jürgen Schultze and Hermann Fillitz (Freren: Luca Verlag, 1988): p. 29.

56 See especially Nürnberg, 1978, *Vorbild Dürer: Kupferstiche und Holzschnitte Albrecht Dürers im Speigel der europaischen Druckgraphik des 16. Jahrhunderts (Ausstellung des Germanischen Nationalmuseums Nürnberg, 8. Juli bis 10. September 1978)* (Munich: Prestel Verlag, 1978).

57 Adam von Bartsch, *The Illustrated Bartsch*, 22 volumes [Originally published as *Le peintre graveur* in 1922], (New York: Abaris Books, 1978); Joseph Heller, *Das Leben und die Werke Albrecht Dürers*, 2 volumes (Bamberg: E.F. Kunz, 1827); Josef Meder, *Dürer-Katalog. Ein Handbuch über Albrecht Dürers Stiche, Radierungen, Holzschnitte, deren Zustände, Ausgaben und Wasserzeichen* (first published Vienna: Gillhofer, 1932, reprint New York: Da Capo Press, 1971).

58 For two excellent surveys of copies of Dürer's prints, see Williamstown 1975 and Nürnberg, 1978.

59 Translation from Joseph Leo Koerner, *The Moment of Self-Portraiture in German Renaissance Art* (Chicago: Chicago University Press, 1993), p. 213. The first edition was designed between 1503 and 1505, and contained seventeen woodcuts, with Dürer adding two more in 1510. The entire series was published in 1511.

60 For the latest discussion about this episode, see Lisa Pon, *Raphael, Dürer, and Marcantonio Raimondi: Copying and the Italian Renaissance Print* (New Haven: Yale University Press, 2004): pp. 39–43. The Vasari quotation is cited on p. 41.

61 Cited in Białostocki 1986, p. 55.

62 Cited in Koerner 1993, p. 209.

63 As suggested by Lisa Pon, 'there was a collision, then, between Dürer's efforts at constructing an artistic identity based on a sense of legal, authorial, possession of his artistic output, and an older system of producing printed texts and images that often did not valorize the originating author or artist above others in the production of the work'. Pons 2004, p. 58.

64 Walter Strauss, ed., *Hendrik Goltzius (1558–1617): The Complete Engravings and Woodcuts*. (New York: Abaris Books 1977): p. 11.

65 J.H. Merck, *Anmerkungen über einige der betrüglichen Copien von der Kupferstichen Albrecht Dürers* (1787) as quoted in Białostocki 1986, p. 153. A section on the Wierix brothers was included in the recent Goltzius exhibition: see Huigen Leeflang and Ger Luijten, eds, *Hendrick Goltzius (1558–1617): Drawings, Prints and Paintings* (Zwolle: Waanders Publishers, 2003): p. 33.

66 For example Vasari referred to it as 'an armored knight engraved with perfection'. In 1675, Joachim von Sandrart described the print as the 'Great Christian Knight'. Strauss 1972, p. 150.

67 For the best discussion of the colouring of prints in general see Susan Dackerman, *Painted Prints: The Revelation of Color in Northern Renaissance and Baroque Engravings, Etchings, and Woodcuts* (Baltimore: Baltimore Museum of Art, 2002).

68 Hans Georg Gmelin, 'Illuminierte Druckgraphik um 1600: ein Phänomen der Dürer-Renaissance?', *Städel-Jahrbuch* 9 (1983): pp. 183–209, at p. 186.

69 Few bound volumes of Dürer's book remain. The first edition was in German, a Latin edition was produced in 1498, and again in 1511. In the Rottenhammer version, the images are on one page, with text facing on the opposing page. This was unlike the illuminated manuscripts that preceded this work, in which text and image were more often than not intertwined on the same page. Dürer also issued a number of impressions of the 15 woodcuts as individual prints, which further increased circulation. The woodcuts that would have made up the Apocalypse series are typically seen as individual impressions. They are no longer seen as book illustration, but rather as autonomous works of art.

70 Colin Eisler discusses the dissemination of motifs from the *Apocalypse* series, especially the animals found therein: see Colin Eisler, *Dürer's Animals* (Washington: Smithsonian Institution Press, 1991): p. 21.

71 Dackerman suggests that these coloured prints were often included within albums for presentation as gifts or for use as prayer books; Dackerman 2002, p. 241.

72 Dackerman 2002, p. 242.

73 J. Krčalová, 'Renesanční malba v chechach a na Moravě' *Dějiny Českeho vytvarného umění: Od počatku renesanče do závyrku baroka II/I* (Prague, 1989): pp. 64–91, at p. 91.

74 Dackerman 2002, p. 239.

75 Dackerman 2002, p. 240.

76 Gmelin 1983, p. 91.

77 For a discussion of the painting, see Mark Ormond, ed. *John Ringling: Dreamer, Builder, Collector* (Sarasota: John and Mable Ringling Museum of Art, 1996), cat. no. 11.

78 For interpretations of the print, see the definitive two volume study by Peter-Klaus Schuster, *Melencolia I – Dürers Denkbild* (Berlin: Gebr. Mann, 1991).

79 For a discussion of the print, see Bartrum 2002, pp. 139–140.

80 A pen and ink copy of Dürer's *Nemesis* engraving by Graf's hand is known, which is similar in detail, with the exception of the substitution of Graf's birthplace Solothurn below the figure. Strauss 1972, p. 76.

81 Bartrum 2002, p. 34. See also Christian Müller, *Urs Graf. Die Zeichnungen im Kupferstichkabinett Basel* (Basel, 2002).

82 Aldegrever was a graphic artist from Westphalia who executed a number of ornamental designs, which make up about one-third of his engravings: these were intended for models for metalworkers, but also adapted by other craftsmen for enamel and for book illustration; see Thomas DaCosta Kaufmann, *Drawings from the Holy Roman Empire: A Selection from North American collections* (Princeton: Princeton Art Collection, 1982): p. 50.

83 For biographical details about Goltzius I have relied on the recent exhibition catalogue edited by Huigen Leeflang and Ger Luijten, *Hendrick Goltzius (1558–1617): Drawings, Prints and Paintings* (Zwolle: Waanders Publishers, 2003): pp. 33–34. Definitive works on Goltzius include: Otto Hirschmann, *Hendrick Goltzius* (Leipzig: Klinkhardt & Biermann, 1919); Otto Hirschmann, *Verzeichnis des Graphischen Werks von Hendrick Goltzius* (Leipzig: Klinkhardt & Biermann, 1921).

84 His publishing house reached the height of its productivity between 1586 and 1590, during which time he issued about 208 prints with a team of assistants who were responsible for 151 of them. Leeflang and Ger Luijten 2003, p. 34.

85 Heuer continues: 'Here the modernist repatriations of Mannerism ring true: Goltzius's was an art about art'; see Christopher P. Heuer, 'Hendrick Goltzius', *ArtForum* 40/5 (2003): p. 67.

86 Carel van Mander, *Schilder-boek*, translation and notes by Hessel Miedema (Doornspijk: Davaco, 1994–1999), folio 285r.

87 For a discussion of the print, see Bartrum 2002, cat. no. 232; and Leeflang and Ger Luijten 2003, cat. no. 75.4.

88 Carel van Mander, *Schilder-boek*, translation and notes by Hessel Miedema (Doornspijk: Davaco, 1994–1999), fol.284v.

89 Lawrence W. Nichols 'The Passion', in *Hendrick Goltzius (1558–1617): Drawings, Prints and Paintings*, edited by Huigen Leeflang and Ger Luijten (Zwolle: Waanders Publishers, 2003), cat. no. 80.

90 Leeflang and Ger Luijten 2003, p. 21.

91 For a full treatment of this subject see Frankfurt 1981, *Dürers Verwandlung in der Skupltur zwischen Renaissance und Barock*, edited by Herbert Beck and Bernhard Decker (Frankfurt: Museum Alter Plastik, 1981).

92 Hans Georg Gmelin, 'Vorbild und Rezeption: Motive aus Dürers Graphik in Kunstwerken der Niedersächsischen Landesgalerie', *Weltkunst* 54/6 (1984): pp. 699–702 at p. 701.

93 *Prag um 1600: Beiträge zur Kunst und Kultur am Hofe Rudolfs II*, preface by Eliška Fučiková(Freren: Luca Verlag, 1988): p. 164.

94 Bartrum 2002, cat. no. 240.

95 Richard Payne Knight, who bequeathed the piece to the British Museum in 1824, thought the work to be by Dürer himself. Bartrum 2002, cat. no. 240.

96 Bartrum 2002, cat. no. 211.

97 Bartrum 2002, cat. no. 216.

98 A forthcoming publication by C. Jenkins, *The Fontainebleau School of Printmakers*, will address maiolica interpretations of Dürer's prints; see also Bartrum 2002, p. 240.

99 Bernard Palissy's reference to Dürer was with regard to the *Life of the Virgin* series: he stated 'despite being of a fine design, there were so many impressions in circulation that they had become undervalued and were sold individually for a pittance'. Bartrum 2002, p. 240.

100 Bartrum 2002, cat. no. 202.

101 Bartrum 2002, cat. no. 208.

102 From the British Museum online database.

103 From the British Museum online database.

104 Bartrum 2002, cat. no. 217.

105 T.H. Clarke, *The rhinoceros from Dürer to Stubbs, 1515–1799* (New York: Harper & Row, 1986) Clarke is extensive in the detail he provides about not only the rhinoceros, but also the historical figures who played a part in its travels. Albuquerque was governor of Portuguese India from 1509–15, Sultan Muzafar II was ruler of Gujarat from 1511–26, and Dom Manuel I king of Portugal from 1495–1521. Clarke 1986, p. 16.

106 Clarke 1986, pp. 20–22.

107 Erwin Panofsky, *Life and Art of Albrecht Dürer* (Princeton: Princeton University Press, 1955), p. 192.

108 Quoted in T.H. Clarke, *The Rhinoceros: from Dürer to Stubbs, 1515–1799* (New York: Harper & Row, 1986), p. 22.

109 Eisler 1991, p. 270.

110 Other publications by Gessner include *Icones Animalium quadrupedum* (1553), *Historia quadrupedum oviparorum* (1554), *De avium natura* (1555), *De piscium aqautilium natura* (1558), *Horti Germaniae* (1561), and *De rerum fossilim figuris* (1565). He also compiled *Bibliotheca Universalis* (1545) – a catalogue of all writers who had ever lived (!) along with the titles of their works.

111 Winkler 1938, p. 625.

112 Rotraud Bauer and Herbert Haupt, 'Die Kunstkammer Kaiser Rudolfs in Prag: Ein Inventar aus den Jahren 1607–1611', *Jahrbuch der Kunsthistorischen Sammlungen in Wien* 72 (1976): pp. xi–xxxvii.

113 For example, a depiction of St Eustace is described as being by Sadler after Dürer ('Sadeler nach Dürer'). The miniaturist Daniel Fröschl (1563–1613) was charged with maintaining the Rudolfine collection. His notations in the margins are telling, since he usually acknowledges when an object is by Dürer, and provides helpful descriptions, for example: 'Ein kupfer von Albrecht Dürer ist unser frau mit dem kindl und hatt ein apfel in der lincken hand.' Bauer and Haupt 1976, p. 104.

114 The medal was included in the recent Dürer exhibition held at the British Museum in London, see Bartrum 2002, pp. 278–279.

115 For biographical information on Abondio, see Bartrum 2002, pp. 278–279.

116 M. Mende, 'Münzen, Medaillen, Plaketten von Dürer, auf Dürer, nach Dürer' Nuremberg, 1983, Figure 1, p. 114.

117 Bartrum 2002, p. 279.

118 Fröschl was named imperial *miniaturmaler* with a salary of 15 *gulden* per month on May 1, 1603. In 1607 he was named imperial *antiquarius*, and his salary was raised. Between 1607 and 11, it was Fröschl who was responsible for the creation of an inventory of the Kunstkammer: in 1611–12 he was named *Imperial Kammerdiener*. After Rudolf's death on 20 January 1612, he was arrested on suspicion of having been involved with Rudolf's negotiations with the Protestant Union. He died 16 October 1613. See Kaufmann 1988(a): p. 173.

119 See Lucia Tongiorgi Tomasi, 'Daniel Froeschl before Prague: his artistic activity in Tuscany at the Medici Court', in *Prague um 1600: Beiträge zur Kunst und Kultur am Hofe Rudolfs II* (Freren: Luca Verlag, 1988): pp. 289–298.

120 Fröschl also made a copy of the *Sacra Famiglia Canigiani* by Raphael, and some works by Michelangelo. See Tomasi 1988, p. 293.

121 Very little is known about Hoffmann's biography. The most comprehensive treatment to date is Kurt Pilz, 'Hans Hoffmann: Ein Dürer-Nachahmer aus der 2.Hälfte des 16. Jahrhunderts', *Mitteilungen des Vereins für Geschichte der Stadt Nürnberg* 51 (1962): pp. 236–272. Pilz does summarize the known facts: Hoffmann trained and worked in Nuremberg, and was first mentioned in the 1576 Nuremberg *Ratsverlässe* as a painter and citizen of the town. He lived there until 1584, when he was called by Duke Wilhelm of Bavaria to the court in Munich (reigned 1579–1597, died 1626). He was called to Prague in 1585, a call that was possibly arranged by Willibald Imhoff II. From 1585 he was court painter to Rudolf II, where he received an annual salary of 100 thalers until his death. Described as loyal and industrious, Hoffmann received high prices for his painted works according to the inventory.

122 In light of the evidence of the Imhoff inventory, it cannot be doubted that some of the works Hoffmann created were passed off as works by Dürer (see Chapter 2).

123 For illustrations and discussion of these copies, see Nuremberg 1994, pp. 189–199.

124 For Sadeler's biography see Dorothy Limouze, 'Aegedius Sadeler, Imperial Printmaker', *Bulletin of the Philadelphia Museum of Art* 85/362 (1989): pp. 2–24.

125 See Franz Wickhoff, 'Beiträge zur Geschichte der Reproducierenden Künste: Marcantons Eintritt in den Kreis Römischer Kunstler', *Jahrbuch der kunsthistorischer Sammlungen der allerhöchsten Kaiserhauses* 20 (1899): pp. 181–94.

126 This was signalled as early as 1803 when Adam Bartsch put together his multi-volume masterpiece, *Le Peintre-Graveur*. He argued that 'the print made by an engraver after a painter's design can be compared perfectly to a text translated into a language different from that of the author; and just as a translation cannot be exact except when the translator has become imbued with the author's ideas, in the same way a print will never be perfect if the engraver does not have the talent to seize the spirit of his original, and to render the value with the strokes of his burin'. Adam von Bartsch, *Le Peintre Graveur* (Vienna, 1803), vol. I, p. 3.

127 Cornelis Cort, for example, is documented as ceasing his work at the Hieronymous Cock print house in Amsterdam to relocate to Italy and become Titian's principle engraver. Meiers 2006, p. 5.

128 Bauer and Haupt 1976, pp. 104–106.

129 On these engravings, see Limouze 1990, pp. 143–148, 220–221.

130 In some instances prints were associated with the technological side of Rudolf's collection and grouped with the copper plates used for printing. Bauer and Haupt 1976, pp. 104–106.

131 Eisler 1991, p. 22.

132 Dagmar Eichberger, '*Naturalia* and *artefacta*: Dürer's nature drawings and early collecting', in *Dürer and his Culture*, edited by Dagmar Eichberger and Charles Zika (Cambridge: Cambridge University Press, 1998): p. 36.

133 Eichberger 1998, p. 37.

134 Ertz confirms Brueghel in Prague; see Klaus Ertz, *Jan Brueghel der Ältere (1568–1625)* (Köln: DuMont, 1985), pp. 436 and 439ff., cat. 108 and 109.

135 This would make sense, given that Dürer's drawing is roughly 2 cms smaller (58 × 40 cms) than Brueghel's painting (60 × 42 cms). For a thorough discussion of the possibility that the painting was intended as a cover, see Hirakawa Kayo, 'Dürer and Jan Brueghel the Elder: one aspect of the pictorialization of Dürer's drawings at the court of Rudolf II', *Aesthetics* 10 (2002): pp. 61–73.

136 AD [Albrecht Dürer] INVENTOR 1505 BRVEGHEL FEC.1604.

137 A summary of Dürer's collecting tendencies can be found in Eichberger 1998, p. 18. See also Jeffrey Chipps-Smith, 'Albrecht Dürer as Collector', *Renaissance Quarterly* 64/1 (2011): pp. 1–49.

138 Using Dürer's diaries and letters, Dürer's possessions are summarized in Eichberger 1998, p. 18.

139 Eichberger 1998, p. 28.

140 Eichberger 1998, p. 29.

141 There is a vast amount of scholarship on seventeenth-century collections. See especially Susanne König-Lein and Alfred Waltz, eds, *Weltenharmonie: die Kunstkammer und die Ordnung des Wissens* (Braunschweig: Herzog Anton Ulrich-Museum, 2000); Horst Bredekamp, *The Lure of Antiquity and the Cult of the Machine: the Kunstkammer and the Evolution of Nature, Art, and Technology*, Allison Brown, trans. (Princeton: Markus Wiener Publishers, 1995); Paula Findlen, *Possessing Nature: Museums, Collecting and Scientific Culture in Early Modern Italy* (Los Angeles: University of California Press, 1994); Ellinoor Bergvelt and Reneé Kistemaker, *De Wereld Binnen Handbereik: Nederlandse Kunst- en Rariteitenverzamelingen, 1585–1735* (Amsterdam: Amsterdams Historisch Museum, 1992); Barbara Balsiger, *The Kunst- und Wunderkammern: A Catalogue Raisonne of Collecting in Germany, France and England, 1565–1750* (Ph.D. Dissertation, University of Pittsburgh, 1989); Oliver Impey and Arthur MacGregor, *The Origins of Museums: The Cabinet of Curiosities in Sixteenth- and Seventeenth-century Europe* (Oxford: Clarendon Press, 1985); Elisabeth Scheicher, *Die Kunst- und Wunderkammern der Habsburger* (Vienna: Molden Editions, 1979); Julius von Schlosser, *Die Kunst- und Wunderkammern der Spätrenaissance. Ein Beitrag zur Geschichte des Sammelwesens*, 2nd edn (Braunschweig: Klinkhardt & Biermann, 1978).

142 Samuel Quiccheberg, *Der Anfang der Museumslehre in Deutschland: das Traktat 'Inscriptiones, vel, Tituli Theatri Amplissimi' von Samuel Quiccheberg*, with commentary from Harriet Roth (Berlin: Akademie Verlag, 2000).

143 Eichberger 1998, p. 18.

144 Joseph Heller, *Das Leben und die Werke Albrecht Dürers*, 2 volumes (Bamberg: E.F. Kunz, 1827); Friedrich Winkler, *Die Zeichnungen Albrecht Dürers*, 4 volumes (Berlin, 1936–9).

145 Koreny 1988.

146 Koreny 1988, p. 16.

147 Lee Hendrix, 'Natural History Illustration at the Court of Rudolf II', *Rudolf II and Prague: The Court and the City* (London: Thames and Hudson, 1997): p. 159.

148 Elisabeth M. Trux, *Untersuchung zu den Tierstudien Albrecht Dürers* (Würzburg: Ergon, 1993): p. 19.

149 'I suggest that Dürer discovered in Venice a tradition quite distinct from the one that had drawn him there, which had its roots in fourteenth-century Lombard model books of animals, birds, flora and fauna such as that of Giovannino de Grassi, and which was preserved by north Italian artists of the fifteenth century, most notably by Pisanello, whose drawings of animals from life and death must have exerted a strong influence toward the end of the century.' James Ackerman, 'Early Renaissance "Naturalism" and Scientific Illustration', *The Natural Sciences and the Arts: Aspects of Interaction from the Renaissance to the 20th century* (Stockholm: Almqvist and Wiksell International, 1985): p. 19.

150 Dagmar Eichberger, '*Naturalia* and *artefacta*: Dürer's nature drawings and early collecting', *Dürer and his Culture*, edited by Dagmar Eichberger and Charles Zika (Cambridge: Cambridge University Press, 1998): pp. 13–37, at p. 15.

151 On the tradition of still life painting as it relates to Dürer, see Sam Segal, 'Die Entstehung der Stilleben-Tradition im Hinblick auf Dürer', *Jahrbuch der Kunsthistorischen Sammlungen in Wien* 82/83 (1986): pp. 273–286.

152 Koreny 1988, p. 13.

153 Eisler 1991, p. 18.

154 Ilse Schimke, 'Der Dürerbuchmeister: Ein Buchbinder aus dem rudolfinischen Prag', *Archiv fur Buchbinderei* 42 (1982): pp. 75–80. The manuscript is now in Dresden, Sachsische Landesbibliothek, ms.147f.

155 As pointed out by Gisela Goldberg, the animal and plant studies were not a big part of the Munich Dürer-Renaissance; see Gisela Goldberg, 'Münchner Aspekte der Dürer Renaissance unter besonderer Berücksichtigung von Dürers Tier und Pflanzenstudien',*Jahrbuch der Kunsthistorischen Sammlungen in Wien* 82/82 (1986/1987): pp. 179–188, at p. 179. Eliška Fučíková also argues that the two cities had very different retrospective reactions to the work of Dürer, that in Munich the goal was to make Dürer even more 'Dürerish', while in Prague, the impetus was more varied; see Eliška Fučíková 'Umělci na dvoře Rudolfa II a jejich vztah k tvorbì Albrechta Dürera', *Umění* 20 (1972): pp. 146–166, at p. 160.

156 The concept of a menagerie had an established tradition with the Habsburgs, ever since Archduke Maximilian (1527–1576) constructed at Ebersdorf a place baptized as a menagerie. Bauer and Haupt 1976, p. 9.

157 *Le Bestiaire de Rodolphe II*, edited by Herbert Haupt, Thea Vignau-Wilberg, Eva Irblich, Manfred Staudinger (Paris: Editions Citadelles, 1990). Cod. Min 129 and 130 in Bibliotheque nationale, Paris.

158 As noted by Marie Christiane Maselis, this ensemble is 'rarely mentioned, never studied, never exhibited and nowhere reproduced, [it] has until recently enjoyed a hidden existence'. See Marie Christiane Maselis, *The Albums of Anselmus de Boodt (1550–1632) Natural History Painting at the Court of Rudolf II in Prague* (Ramsen: Bibermühle, 1999): p. 9.

159 There are two scholars who have done extensive work on Hoefnagel. See Lee Hendrix; *Joris Hoefnagel and the Four Elements: A Study in Sixteenth Century Nature Painting* (Unpublished Ph.D. dissertation, Princeton University, 1984); Thea Vignau-Wilberg, *Durch die Blume: Natursymbolik um 1600* (Munich: Staatliche Graphische Sammlung, 1991).

160 According to van Mander, his main patron during the period 1575–82 was Rudolf II by whom he was paid 400 gulden per year. Rudolf acquired in 1604 the *Four Elements* by Joris Hoefnagel (1542–1600), for which he paid 1000 florins. See the entry on Hoefnagel in Jürgen.Müller, *Concordia Pragensis: Karel van Manders Kunsttheorie im Schilderboeck: ein Beitrag zur Rhetorisierung von Kunst und Leben am Beispiel der rudolfinischen Hofkünstler* (Munich: Oldenbourg, 1993).

161 Thomas DaCosta Kaufmann, 'The Nature of Imitation: Hoefnagel on Dürer', *Jahrbuch der Kunsthistorischen Sammlungen in Wien* 82/83 (1986): pp. 163–178, at p. 163.

162 For the translation, see Kaufmann 1986, pp. 164–165.

163 Tomasi 1988, pp. 289–298, at p. 298.

164 Koreny 1988, p. 126.

165 Eisler 1991, p. 100.

166 Getty Museum online database.

167 Fritz Koreny and Sam Segal, 'Hans Hoffmann: Entdeckungen und Zuschreibungen', *Jahrbuch der Kunsthistorischen Sammlungen in Wien* 85/86 (1989/1990): pp. 57–65, at p. 60.

168 Kaufmann 1985, p. 26.

169 Often, they are interpreted as a symbol of Christ. Colin Eisler describes it as a sort of 'zoological lightening rod' that was thought to divert or absorb God's wrath. Eisler 1991, p. 136.

170 Koreny 1988, p. 126.

171 Koreny 1988. See also the papers that emerged from the symposium that accompanied the exhibition: Fritz Koreny, ed., *Albrecht Dürer und die Tier und Pflanzenstudien der Renaissance-Symposium. Die Beiträge der von der Graphischen Sammlung Albertina von 7. Bis 10. Juni 1985 veranstalteten Tagung* (Vienna: Jahrbuch der Kunsthistorischen Sammlungen in Wien, 1986).

172 For the literature on this transition, see *Plant, Animal and Anatomical Illustration in Art and Science: A Bibliographical Guide from the 16th Century to the Present Day*, compiled by Gavin D.R. Bridson and James J. White (Winchester: St. Paul's Bibliographies, 1990). For more recent discussion of the herbal manuscripts see Anna Pavord, *The Naming of Names: The Search for Order in the World of Plants* (New York: Bloomsbury, 2005).

173 Andreas Tacke, *'Der Mahler Ordnung und Gebräuch in Nürmberg': Die Nürberger Maler(zunft)bücher ergänzt durch weitere Quellen, Genealogien und Viten des 16., 17. und 18. Jahrhunderts* (München, Berlin: Deutscher Kunstverlag, 2001).

174 The painting is in Lisbon, Museo Nacional de Arte Antigua. Dürer wrote in his diary: 'I painted a Jerome carefully in oils and gave it to Rodrigo of Portugal'. See Anzelewsky 1991, cat. no. 162.

175 Pencz arrived in Nuremberg in 1523 whereupon he joined Dürer's workshop. For a discussion of Dürer's studio, see Hutchison 1990: pp. 108–118.

176 Another set of seventeenth-century copies is in a private collection in Switzerland.

177 This drawing was included in *Kunst des Sammelns. Das Praunsche Kabinett. Meisterwerke von Dürer bis Carracci*, edited by Katrin Achilles-Syndram (Nuremberg: Verlag des Germansichen Nationalmuseums, 1994), p. 18.

178 Dürer painted his *Christ among the Doctors* at the same time as *The Feast of the Rosegarlands*, that is, during his visit to Venice around 1505–6. *Christ among the Doctors* is a small panel, with brushwork that appears spontaneous and paint applied with broad and fluid strokes. Protruding from the book at the bottom left corner is a small bookmark, on which the Dürer monogram and the date 1505 are faintly visible. Underneath the date is the statement *Opus quinque dierum*, traditionally interpreted as Dürer's statement that the work had been completed in five days. This is a pointed reference to his inscription on *The Feast of the Rose Garlands*, on which he inscribed 'the work of five months'. Despite this declaration of speed, *Christ among the Doctors*, was based on a number of careful studies, including one of Christ's gesticulating fingers, and another of the head of Christ himself. Although not present on the original painting, two early copies of the panel have the word 'Romae' added to the inscription on the bookmark and have been used to argue that Dürer visited Rome late in 1506.It is possible that the *Opus Quinque Dierum* might be a later addition of a Dürer-Renaissance artist.

179 The original painting was in Rome's Galleria Barberini until its acquisition by Baron Heinrich von Thyssen-Bornemisza in 1935. Katrin Achilles-Syndram, ed *Kunst des Sammelns. Das Praunsche Kabinett. Meisterwerke von Dürer bis Carracci* (Nuremberg: Verlag des Germansichen Nationalmuseums, 1994): p. 18.

180 See Pilz 1962, p. 236 for a summary of Hoffmann's known activities; also Achilles-Syndram 1994, p. 18.

181 There are several known copies: one in Paris, two in Budapest, one in Frankfurt.

182 Fučíková 1972, pp. 146–166, at p. 147.

183 Fučíková 1972, p. 164.

184 The information that is verifiable is that Rudolf sent his secretary Bernardo Rosso to Venice to undergo negotiations with the church of San Bartolomeo, and on 10 March 1606, the painting was purchased for 900 ducats. See Vienna 1994, *Albrecht Dürer im Kunsthistorischen Museum,*edited by Karl Schütz and Rotraud Bauer (Vienna: Kunsthistorisches Museum, 1994): p. 53.

185 Vienna 1994, p. 130.

186 Rottenhammer's copy was in the collection of the Grimani family in Venice until the nineteenth century, but has not survived. For a recent discussion see Andrew John Martin, 'Die Kopie nach Dürers *Rosenkranzfest* aus dem Palazzo Grimani bei Santa Maria Formosa', *Studia Rudolphina* 6 (2006): pp. 64–66.

187 For biographical information on Rottenhammer see Kaufmann 1982, p. 98.

188 Kaufmann 1982, p. 98.

189 Kaufmann 1982, p. 98.

190 Schütz and Haupt 1994, p. 132.

191 Fučíková 1972, p. 146.

192 Kaufmann 1988 (a), p. 178.

193 'Weil auch ein Creuzigung Christi durch Albrecht Dürern von asherfarb und weiss gar mühlsamb gerissen, in oelfarb copiert worden, ist darauf wol verdient 100 taler.' Kaufmann 1988(a): p. 179.

194 Schütz and Haupt 1994, p. 53.

195 'Ganz von einer anderen Hand.' Beheim, as quoted in Ernstberger 1954, p. 165.

196 Hauer folio 27r: 'Albrecht Dürer Altarbalt bei St. Catherina haben auch ihr Durchlaucht in Bairn zu sich gebracht. Ist eine Copei, so Jobst Harrich gemacht, dahin gestelt worden. Die Copai, so in Franckfort in dern Predigermünchs Closter, hat auch Jobst Harrich, Burger und Mahler in Nurnberg, daselb im Closter copiert.' Tacke 2001, p. 123.

197 Hauer, folio. 27r', Albrecht Dürer gemahlte Himmelfahrt Mariae, so in dern Predigermunchs Closter zu Franckfort gestanden, hat der Herzog in Bairn auch zu sich gebracht und selbigen Brudern Predigerordens ein Stuck Gelds, solches jarlich zugeniessen, dafur geordnet hat.' Tacke 2001, p. 123.

198 Harrich's painting is now a pendant to Phillip Uffenbach's *Himmelfahrt Christi*, dated to 1599.

199 Dürer gave it to the Nuremberg Rathaus in 1526 'Zue seyner gedectnus'. It remained there until it was acquired by Maximilian. As outlined in Chapter 2, in the details of the acquisition, it is likely that the council had no choice but to relinquish the painting because of debts incurred during the Thirty Years War.

200 Tacke 2001, pp. 121–123.

201 Hauer, folio 27r: 'Auf dem obern Rathaußsaal im neüen Gebäu seind die vier Complectiones, so etwas grosser als Leben, von Albrecht Dürer fleissig und aufs Bestegemahlt, gestanden. Solche zu copiern hat der Herzog in Baiern einen Mahler namens [Georg] Fischer hierher geschickt, welcher solche, so noch vor Augen, alhier copiert. Als solche gefertigt, hat der Herzog in Bairn Herr Maximilian seinen Cammer kunstler Herrn [Augustin] Hammel [Haimbl] alhero geschickt, solche zu besichtigen, und zugleich begehrt, man wolle ihm die Originalia und Copia zugleich zu besichtigen uberschicken, welches dan geschehen. Da seind die Schrifften, so an denen Originalien gestanden, darvon herab geschnitten und an die Copien aufs Fleissigste angesetzt worden, welche Copien wider alhero gesandt und alhier an dern Original statt uf dem obern Rathaußsaal zu sehen sind gesetzet worden.' Tacke 2001, p. 123.

202 The inscriptions were written in Dürer's workshop, but not by Dürer himself, but rather, Johann Neudörfer, who knew Dürer well (see Chapter 1).

203 There have been some attempts to attribute this painting to Georg Vischer, however, according to Gisela Goldberg, this attribution cannot be confirmed, since as she points out, the brushwork is quite different from Vischer's copy of the *Four Apostles*. See Munich 1971, *Dürer-Renaissance: München, 7. Mai–29. August 1971*. Edited by Gisela Goldberg and Barbara Heine (Munich: Alte Pinakothek, 1971): p. 21.

204 Munich 1971, p. 21.

205 Gisela Goldberg, 'Veränderungen von Bildern der ersten Hälfte des 16. Jahrhunderts: Versuch einer Interpretation', *Städel-Jahrbuch* 9 (1983): pp. 151–182.

206 For biographical information on Leopold Wilhelm, see Renate Schreiber, *'Ein Galerie nach meinem Humor': Erzherzog Leopold Wilhelm* (Wien: Kunsthistorisches Museum, 2004). Leopold Wilhelm was the youngest son of the Emperor Ferdinand II (1578–1637) and Maria Anna of Bavaria (1574–1616).

207 Georg Kohlprath, 'Leopolds Liebe', *Weltkunst* 75/7 (2003): p. 103.

208 Kohlprath 2003, p. 103.

209 Gustav Glück, 'Falschungen auf Dürers Namen aus der Sammlung Erzherzog Leopold Wilhelms', *Jahrbuch der Kunsthistorischen Sammlungen des Allerhöchsten Kaiserhauses* 28 (1909–1910): pp. 1–35.

210 Glück 1909–10, p. 3.

211 Glück 1909–10, p. 3.

212 From the 1659 inventory, published in Glück 1909–10: 'Ein Stückhel, warinn vnnser liebe Fraw mit dem Jesuskindl auf dem Schosaz, vnndt der heyl. Joseph auff dem Tisch ligt vnndt shlafft, darbey die Engeln musicieren. Mit der Federn auf Papier gerissen vnndt mitt vndershiedtlichen Farben schattiert. Original von Albrecht Dürer.' Another piece is described as follows: 'Ein Stückhel warin eines alten, melancolischen Weibs Prustpildt vnndt ober ihrem Kopf ein rechte Hand mit einem Pixel. Auf weisz Papier mit der Feder gerissen. Von Albrecht Dürer.' Others are designated as 'Copia nach Albrecht Dürer'. A Kaiser bild is described as 'Nach Albrecht Dürer'. See Glück 1909–10, p. 4.

213 See Glück 1909–10, p. 7.

214 The following details are known about Rupprecht: his birth has been postulated to 1600. He came as 'fremder Flachmalergeselle' to Nuremberg, became a master there in 1634, and in 1651 went to Vienna. In the inventories for the court there are no payments to Rupprecht. Schütz and Haupt 1994, p. 148, and cat. no. 51.

215 Klauner 1971, pp. 14–18, at p. 18. In an engraving from 1661, after the *Martyrdom of the Ten Thousand*, it is stated that Leopold I had commissioned Nikolaus van Hoy to make a design after Dürer's painting, *at that time in his collection*.

216 AD.IMITAT.E.IOH.CHRIST./IAN.RUPERT.CIV/NORIB./ANN.MDCLIV.

217 Schütz and Haupt 1994, cat. no. 42. This painting is described elsewhere as 'Hoffmann's copy', see Kauffmann 1940–53, p. 56, no. 49.

Conclusion

Just as Dürer travelled internationally, so too did his art. Miniatures attest to the impact of Dürer during the golden age of Mughal art in India, especially at the court of Emperor Jhangir who reigned from 1605–27.[1] In Latin America, Dürer's prints were disseminated by Spanish missionaries.[2] His most important commission outside of his homeland, the *Feast of the Rosegarlands* (1506) painted for the church of San Bartolomeo in Venice, is perhaps the most important point of contact to occur between Italy and Northern Europe during the Renaissance.[3] During his trip to the Netherlands he often gave away prints or drawings as diplomatic gifts or in exchange for hospitality. Even when not travelling, Dürer sought to maintain his presence internationally, as shown by his contracts with two travelling salesmen charged with selling his prints abroad.[4]

The movement of Dürer's pictures and ideas, initiated during his lifetime, is at the core of how Dürer's influence was perpetuated in the seventeenth century, with interest in his works becoming increasingly diffuse and international. Moreover, Dürer was the greatest pioneer and exponent of printmaking techniques. Prints were easily transportable, allowing for influence to spread in an unprecedented fashion. Nor should it be forgotten that in the seventeenth century paintings were removed from their original contexts to a greater extent than ever before, due to a changing and emerging culture of collecting.

Removed from their original locations, and installed in new environments, Dürer's images were brought into new contexts and charged with different meanings. A picture that moves from a sixteenth-century church to a seventeenth-century court experiences changes of a geographical and temporal nature. As a result of displacement, the use of an image can change. Images can gain potency or become buried in obscurity. Inevitably images are involved in an evolution that requires the art historian to place less emphasis on origins and become attuned to a range of later contexts. This requires sensitivity to the newness of place and the fresh evaluations that can emerge there. One of the most noteworthy aspects of images is their potential to retain meaning long after creation and in diverse locations.

As an observer of the migrations of images, a task of the art historian is to reveal and respect contexts. Typically it is stated that images have an 'afterlife' – yet this implies demise. A more appropriate claim is that images have lives. Or to use the phrase of James Elkins, 'art historical images change meaning continuously, in accord with shifting contingencies of critical reception and historical circumstance'.[5]

Examining the work of an artist from the perspective of reception focuses attention on the values and interests of later audiences. Rather than prioritizing the creative act and its original location, reception allows us to consider the later uses that works undergo, with the aim of considering emerging cultures and epistemologies. To study reception is to place emphasis not only on the creator, but also what works tell us about their owners and audiences. Significantly, reception can reveal a great deal about attitudes toward the past, as much as our present perspectives. As suggested by the nineteenth-century historian Johann Gustav Droysen, 'That which was does not interest us because it was, but because in a certain sense it still *is*.'[6]

Clearly, Albrecht Dürer still *is*. Yet the diversity and prolific nature of Albrecht Dürer creates challenges for characterizing his reception. The works by his hand that have survived include some 100 oil paintings, 100 engravings, 400 woodcuts, 6 etchings, 1200 drawings, and 2 published theoretical works. To characterize the reception of all these works would require a much larger volume. However, we can and should consider what it means when past works are isolated or chosen for extensive quotations and paraphrases, when a published tract experiences numerous editions, and when an inventory reveals that an overwhelming number of entries bear one name. An essential step toward understanding past societies involves gauging what opinions existed regarding pictorial ideas. Even if it is impossible to write a comprehensive treatment of Dürer reception, it is certainly possible to highlight aspects of his oeuvre that had particular importance in a period under scrutiny.

In this book, I have explored only a short period in the five centuries of reception that Albrecht Dürer has experienced since his death. Between 1528 and 1700 the interest in Dürer was especially heightened. This is an episode of reception that is particularly revealing for what it tells us about a time and place. To say that the reputation of Dürer peaked, and that his works were held in high regard, especially at the very important cultural centres of Munich, Nuremberg and Prague, is to work toward characterizing the milieu of collecting, artistic production and scientific endeavours that existed in these locations in the sixteenth and seventeenth centuries.

Admittedly, this intensity of interest in a single artist for a limited period of time was an exception, rather than the norm. To quote Jane Hutchison, 'Dürer is certainly the only artist to have been honored by art historians with his own eponymous epoch – the Dürerzeit – and to have undergone a personal renaissance fifty years after his death.'[7] Yet idiosyncrasies should not be noted for the sake of omission. The term Dürer-Renaissance is oft-repeated, yet just as often misunderstood. It has, in the past, been dismissed as insignificant, a period in which artists lacked the insight to have their own pictorial ideas, and thus relied heavily upon Dürer. However, as has been shown through this exploration of aspects of art and collecting, there ought not to be such a quick dismissal of this episode of reception. The Dürer-Renaissance was diverse, impacted a number of important artists, and has genuine and significant importance for studies of early modern culture. Appropriation was a much-versed and important mode of production. This is shown by the number of times Dürer was quoted and paraphrased, not necessarily toward the end of falsification. Rather, imitation in many cases seems to have been an open and honest acknowledgement of historical fact, a building upon tradition, and exhibition of rich and deep understanding of Dürer as a predecessor.

It has been stated elsewhere that 'to be modern in the Renaissance was to show how much you knew about antiquity'.[8] In the early modern period, if the Dürer-Renaissance is any indication, being modern also involved knowledge of and invoking of one's more immediate predecessors. Since imitation was accorded such a high function, artists had to be receptive and productive simultaneously. In intriguing displays of ingenuity, artists engaged in playful competition with the past, and especially with Dürer. While this fashion may not have affected all artistic centres of the period, it certainly contributed to perceptions of Dürer's work and the ways in which succeeding generations were to receive him.

It is true that defining these attitudes with precision can be challenging. Yet the forms of imitation discussed in the context of Dürer reception do allow us to approach the epistemology of the period with some confidence. To use a phrase suggested by Dorothy Limouze, imitative works provide rich evidence of an 'earnest attitude' toward the past.[9] Not only are the imitations of Dürer important evidence of interest in his works and style, but they also demonstrated new interest in art historical traditions, 'a growing desire to record the cultural past that can be linked with the beginnings of art historical writing in northern Europe'.[10] Fostering a distinct tradition of art-making involved elevating Dürer as a celebrated and esteemed artist, a northern talent whose works were valued by any standards.

The compositions and motifs of artists have often been copied. However, with no other artist did this happen to such an extent as with Dürer. In the sixteenth and seventeenth centuries, Dürer's work served as a model for imitation and emulation, especially at the courts in Munich and Prague. In terms of artistic production, it is noteworthy that artists worked in several different capacities in their assimilation of Dürer. At this point it seems possible to conclude that the forms of imitation are evidence of a canonization of Dürer that had occurred in art as well as in literature. It also seems likely that the encyclopaedic motivations behind collections in this period often necessitated forms of imitation. As attempts to systematically contain and collect all that existed in nature, all that had been created by man, the *Kunstkammern* were considered to be incomplete without a representation of the oeuvre of the most revered northern European artists. Thus, court artists were likely encouraged to use the collections toward the end of creating imitations. Most significant is the idea that works that incorporated motifs from Dürer were not necessarily thought of as lacking originality or devalued.

Largely due to the emphasis on imitation, the early modern period is sometimes discussed as conservative and uncritical. This is suggested for example by Hans Baron, who claims that imitation 'presupposes that the model is thought to be superior to the imitator', hence contributing to a passive and unoriginal culture.[11] Statements such as Baron's are in need of revision. As has been shown with reference to the art of the Dürer Renaissance, pedagogy, retrospection, homage and competition are not passive forms of engagement. Emulation was often considered a way of improving upon the past. This phenomenon is richly suggestive of the manner in which imitation took many different forms in the sixteenth and seventeenth centuries.

Thus, even if the Dürer-Renaissance is qualified as idiosyncratic in nature, it should not be omitted from scholarly research for this reason. If one thing can be said as a result of this exploration, it is that it is necessary to count reception as a significant theme for understanding the lives and migrations of images. While written response is one way of gauging the reception of an artist, I have intentionally approached reception from another perspective by examining the artistic responses to Dürer, the varied ways his art was used and arguably abused by artists in the sixteenth and seventeenth centuries. As a way of encompassing all the variations and nuances of how artists borrowed from Dürer, ultimately, it is the concept of appropriation that becomes useful for this case study in reception.

My use of the term appropriation will perhaps surprise some, given that it is a term more readily employed in conjunction with the ready-mades of Dada artists or Pop Art, the photographs of Cindy Sherman or the paintings of Bacon's study of Velazquez. Didn't appropriation have its heyday in the 1980s? Why think about appropriation now, and why in conjunction with Dürer? To put it simply, the objects have been allowed to speak for themselves. In a range of media, works that are often pastiche-like in appearance and veritable patchworks of borrowings from Dürer lie buried in obscurity in numerous repositories. Traditionally dismissed as unimportant copies, they merit closer scrutiny because of how they exceed the passive connotations of the term imitation. If we take visual appropriation in its most basic sense to mean a deliberate acknowledgement and simultaneous transformation of a past model, the early modern works under scrutiny today certainly qualify. Instead of thinking about whether appropriation art has a future, I have sought to characterize its past. Arguably, appropriation has a much longer history than has hitherto been acknowledged.

Notes

1 See Amina Okada, *Indian Miniatures of the Mughal Court*, translated by Deke Dusinberre (New York: H.M. Abrams, 1992); and Bartrum 2002, no. 217.

2 'In Latin America his prints, due to the endorsements of Paleotti and Pacheco, were sent to accompany Spanish missionaries.' Jane Campbell Hutchison, *Albrecht Dürer: A Guide to Research* (New York: Garland Publishing Inc., 2000): p. 6.

3 A recent exhibition at the National Gallery in Prague considers in detail the creation, restoration and reception of the painting. See Prague 2006, *Albrecht Dürer: The Feast of the Rosegarlands 1506–2006*, edited by Olga Kotkova (Prague: Národní Galerie v Praze, 2006).

4 Hans Rupprich, *Dürer-Schriftlicher Nachlass*, 3 volumes (Berlin: Deutscher Verein für Kunstwissenschaft, 1956), vol. 1, p. 244 and vol. III, p. 448. These contracts are now preserved in the Nuremberg *Stadtsarchiv*, Lib.Cons.K, fol. 132 v.

5 James Elkins, 'Art History and Images That Are Not Art', *Art Bulletin* 77 (1995): pp. 553–571, see especially p. 564.

6 Johann Gustav Droysen, cited in H.G. Jauss, *Toward an Aesthetic of Reception*, University of Minnesota Press, 1982, p. 59.

7 Hutchison 2000, p. 12.

8 Colin Eisler, *Dürer's Animals* (Washington: Smithsonian Institution Press, 1991): p. 278.

9 Dorothy Limouze, 'Aegedius Sadeler (1570–1629): Drawings, Prints, and the Development of an Art Theoretical Attitude', *Prague um 1600: Beiträge zur Kunst und Kultur am Hofe Rudolfs II* (Freren: Luca Verlag, 1988): p. 187.

10 Dorothy Limouze, 'Aegedius Sadeler, Imperial Printmaker', *Bulletin of the Philadelphia Museum of Art* 85/362: pp. 2–24, at p. 7.

11 Hans Baron, 'The *Querelle* of the Ancients and Moderns as a Problem for Renaissance Scholarship', *Journal of the History of Ideas* XX (1959): pp. 3–22, at p. 6.

Bibliography

Some sources are essential to any attempt at Dürer scholarship, including two indispensable bibliographic sources. Matthias Mende's *Dürer Bibliographie* was published in 1971 on the occasion of the five-hundredth anniversary of Dürer's birth, and is a thorough and painstakingly cross indexed listing of *c*.10,000 publications on Dürer. Jane Campbell Hutchison's *Albrecht Dürer: A Guide to Research,* published a generation later, is very much a continuation of Mende's work, and contains all essential pre-1971 material, as well as the numerous publications from the Dürer Year 1971 celebrations that Mende was unable to include. Hutchison's annotated entries, and the location guide for Durer's works, are extremely helpful for navigation of the ever-increasing research on Dürer.

For catalogues of works of art by Dürer, which are after all the essential primary sources under investigation here, the scholar is faced with numerous publications: some are less trustworthy than others. For paintings, the catalogue raisonné (revised edition) by Fedja Anzelewsky is the standard monograph. Josef Meder's catalogue is one of many on Dürer's prints, but its meticulous treatment is unsurpassed and makes it the standard to which other publications must aspire. As for drawings, Friedrich Winkler's is in the opinion of many the most reliable and useful. Another indispensable publication for Dürer scholarship is Hans Rupprich's publication of Dürer's writings, which includes Dürer's theoretical publications, his unpublished writings, and letters written by his clients and contemporaries. Rupprich reproduced the original language and includes extensive footnotes that are highly instructive. Finally, Jan Białostocki's masterful *Dürer and His Critics 1500–1971* is the main source for Dürer reception. The text is richly suggestive and as already noted, and as already noted, a chief guide for the present volume. In order to give some order to the bibliography I have arranged the entries according to the following categories: essential sources, primary sources, secondary sources and exhibition catalogues.

Essential Sources

Anzelewsky, Fedja. *Albrecht Dürer. Das Malerische Werk*. Revised edition. 2 volumes. Berlin: Deutscher Verlag für Kunstwissenschaft, 1991.

Białostocki, Jan. *Dürer and His Critics 1500–1971: Chapters in the History of Ideas Including a Collection of Texts*. Baden-Baden: Valentin Koerner, 1986.

Hutchison, Jane Campbell. *Albrecht Dürer: A Guide to Research*. New York and London: Garland Publishing Inc., 2000.

Meder, Josef. Dürer-Katalog. *Ein Handbuch über Albrecht Dürers Stiche, Radierungen, Holzschnitte, deren Zustände, Ausgaben und Wasserzeichen*. First published Vienna: Gillhofer, 1932. Reprint New York: Da Capo Press, 1971.

Mende, Matthias. *Dürer-Bibliographie*. Wiesbaden: Harrassowitz, 1971.

Rupprich, Hans, ed. *Dürer-Schriftlicher Nachlass* 3 vols. Berlin: Deutscher Verein für Kunstwissenschaft, 1956.

Winkler, Friedrich. *Die Zeichnungen Albrecht Dürers*. 4 volumes. Berlin, 1936–9.

Primary Sources

Achilles-Syndram, Katrin. 'Die Kunstsammlung des Paulus Praun. Die Inventare von 1616 und 1719', *Quellen zur Geschichte und Kultur der Stadt Nuremberg (25)*. Compiled by Katrin Achilles-Syndram. Nuremberg: Stadtrat, 1994.

Auer, Alfred. 'Das Inventarium der Ambraser Sammlungen aus dem Jahre 1621', II.Teil: Bibliothek, *Jahrbuch des kunsthistorischen Museums Wien* II (2001): pp. 281–345.

Bauer, Rotraud and Haupt, Herbert. 'Die Kunstkammer Kaiser Rudolfs in Prag: Ein Inventar aus den Jahren 1607–1611', *Jahrbuch der Kunsthistorischen Sammlungen in Wien* 72 (1976): pp. xi–xxxvii.

Boeheim, A. 'Verlassenschaftsinventar des Erzherzogs Ferdinand von Tirol, Mai 30, 1596, Innsbruck'. *Jahrbuch der Kunsthistorischen Sammlungen des Allerhöchsten Kaiserhauses in Wien* X/2 (1889), pp. ccxxvi–cccxii. Compiled by Boeheim.

Crowne, William. *A True Relation of all the Remarkable Places and Passages Observed in the Travels of the Right Honourable Thomas Lord Howard, Earle of Arundell and Surrey1636*. London: Felix Kingston, 1637.

Dürer, Albrecht. *Unterweysung der Messung mit dem Zirkel und Richtscheit*. Facsimile of the 1525 edition. Zürich: Dietikon, 1966.

Dürer, Albrecht. *Von Menschlicher Proportion*. Facsimile of the 1528 edition. Nördlingen: Uhl, 1980.

Fischaler, Lorenz. 'Ein verzeichnis der im Jahre 1607 auf der Cammer Galeria Herzog Maximilians I. aufbewahrten Gemälde', *Der Zwiebelturm* 25/4 (11970): pp. 88–92.

Gümbel, Albert. 'Das Inventar der Scherlschen Kunstkamer in Nürnberg vom Jahre 1637', in *Mitteilungen des Veriens für Geschcihte der Stadt Nürnberg* 30 (1931), pp. 321–37. Compiled by Albert Gümbel.

Haiminsfeld, Melchior Goldast. 'Das Prager Tagebuch des Melchior Goldast von

Haiminsfeld, in *Abhandlungen und Vortrage herausgeben von der Bremer Wissenschaftlichen Gesellschaft* 5/4 (1931): pp. 220–276.

Hainhofer, Philipp. *Des Augsburger Patriciers Philipp Hainhofer Beziehungen zum Herzog Philipp II. Von Pommern-Stettin. Correspondenzen aus den Jahren 1610–1619 im Auszuge mitgehelt und commentiert von Dr. Oscar Doering*. Quellenschriften fur Kunstgeschichte und Kunsttechnik des Mittelalters und der Neuzeit. Compiled by Oscar Doering. Vienna: Verlag von Carl Graeser, 1894.

Hainhofer, Philipp. 'Philipp Hainhofers Reise-Tagebuch enthaltend Schilderungen aus Frankn, Sachsen, der Mark Brandenburg und Pommern im Jahr 1617', *Baltische Studien* 2 (1834).

Koreny, Fritz. 'The Imhoff Inventory'and 'The Imhoff Geheimbüchlein', in *Albrecht Dürer and the Animal and Plant Studies of the Renaissance*. Compiled by Fritz Koreny. Boston: Brown, 1988. pp. 261–266.

Lamspsonius, Dominicus. *Lamberti Lombardi apud Eburones pictoris celeberrimi vita. Pictoribus, sculptoribus, architectis, allisque id genus artificibus utilis et necessaria*. Bruges, 1565.

Lomazzo, Giovanni Paolo. *Trattato dell'Arte della Pittura, divisio in VII libri, nei quali si contiene tutte la Teoria e la Practica di essa Pittura*. Milan: Paolo Gottardo Pontio, 1584.

Lomazzo, Giovanni Paolo Lomazzo, *A Tracte Containing the Artes of Curious Paintinge and Buildinge*. Translated by Richard Haydocke. Oxford: Joseph Barnes, 1598.

Mander, Carel van. *Schilder-boek*. In English and Dutch. Translation and notes by Hessel Miedema. Doornspijk: Davaco, 1994–1999.

Moryson, Fynes. *An Itinerary: Amsterdam, Theatrum Orbis Terrarum*. Facsimile of 1617 edition. New York: Da Capo Press, 1971.

Murr, Christophe Gottlieb von. *Description du Cabinet de Monsieur Praun à Nuremberg*. Nuremberg: J.T. Schneider, 1797.

Neudörfer, Johann. *Des Johann Neudörfer schreib- und rechenmeisters zu Nürnberg nachrichten von künstlern und werkleuten daselbst aus dem jahre 1547, nebst der fortzetzung des Andreas Gulden, nach den handschriften und mit anmerkungen hrsg. von G.W.K. Lochner*. Wien, W. Braumüller, 1875.

Quiccheberg, Samuel. *Der Anfang der Museumslehre in Deutschland: das Traktat 'Inscriptiones, vel, Tituli Theatri Amplissimi' von Samuel Quiccheberg*. With commentary from Harriet Roth. Berlin: Akademie Verlag, 2000.

Ricci, Bartolomeo. *De Imitatione libri tres*. Venice 1545. Reprint. Paris: Apud Bernardum Turrisanum, 1557.

Sandrart, Joachim von. *Academie der Bau-, Bild- und Mahlerey-Künste von 1675. Leben der berühmten Maler, Bildhauer und Baumeister*. Compiled by Rudolf Arthur Peltzer. Munich: G. Hirth, 1925.

Springer, Anton. 'Inventare der Immhoff'schen Kunstkammer zu Nürnberg', in *Mitteilungen der kaiserlichen koniglichen Central Commission zur Erforschung und Erhaltung der Baudenkmale* 5 (1860): pp. 352–357.

Tacke, Andreas. *'Der Mahler Ordnung und Gebräuch in Nürmberg': Die Nürberger Maler(zunft)bücher ergänzt durch weitere Quellen, Genealogien und Viten des 16., 17. Und 18. Jahrhunderts*. München, Berlin: Deutscher Kunstverlag, 2001.

Vasari, Giorgio. *Lives of the most eminent painters, sculptors, and architects: translated from the Italian of Giorgio Vasari*. 5 volumes. Translated by Jean Paul Richter. London: H.G. Bohn, 1907.

Secondary Sources

Achilles, Katrin. 'Naturstudien von Hans Hoffmann in der Kunstsammlung des Nürnberger Kaufmanns Paulus II Praun', *Jahrbuch der Kunsthistorischen Sammlungen in Wien* 82/83 (1986): 243–259.

Achilles-Syndram, Katrin. *Die Zeichnungsammlung des Nürnberger Kaufmanns Paulus II. Praun (1548–1616)*'. Ph.D. Dissertation, Berlin, 1990.

Achilles-Syndram, Katrin, ed *Kunst des Sammelns. Das Praunsche Kabinett. Meisterwerke von Dürer bis Carracci*.Nuremberg: Verlag des Germansichen Nationalmuseums, 1994.

Ackerman, James. 'Early Renaissance "Naturalism" and Scientific Illustration', *The Natural Sciences and the Arts: Aspects of Interaction from the Renaissance to the 20th century*. Stockholm: Almqvist and Wiksell International, 1985.

Aikema, Bernard and Beverley Louise Brown. *Renaissance Venice and the North: Crosscurrents in the Time of Bellini, Dürer and Titian*. New York: Rizzoli, 1999.

Alpers, Svetlana. *The Art of Describing: Dutch Art in the Seventeenth Century*. Chicago: University of Chicago Press, 1983.

Alsop, Joseph. *The Rare Art Traditions: the History of Art Collecting and its Linked Phenomena Wherever These Have Appeared*. New York: Harper and Row, 1982.

Anzelewsky Fedja. 'Dürers Selbstbildnis aus dem Jahre 1500', Ars Auro Prior. *Studia Joanni Bialostocki Sexagenario Dicata*. Juliusz A. Chrościcki, ed. Warszawa : Państwowe Wydawn. Nauk., 1981. pp. 287–290.

Anzelewsky, Fedja. 'Dürer zwischen Symbolik und Naturwissenschaft', *Jahrbuch der Kunsthistorischen Sammlungen in Wien* 82/83 (1986): pp. 33–42.

Anzelewsky, Fedja. 'Pflanzen und Tiere im Werke Dürers. Naturstudien und Symbolik', *Jahrbuch der Kunsthistorischen Sammlungen in Wien* 82/83 (1986): pp. 33–42.

Auer, Alfred. Die Sammeltätigkeit Erzherzog Ferdinands II. in Böhmen, in *Kaiser Ferdinand I. 1503–1564. Das Werden der Habsburgmonarchie*. Ed. Georg Kugler. Wien: Kunsthistorisches Museum, 2003. pp. 297–306.

Baier, Lesley. *The Spread of Dürer's Woodcut Style: A Didactic Exhibition*. New Haven: Yale University Art Gallery, 1981.

Baldass, Ludwig. *Der Künstlerkreis Kaiser Maximilians*. Vienna: Anton Schroll, 1923.

Balsiger, Barbara. *The Kunst- und Wunderkammern: A Catalogue Raisonne of Collecting in Germany, France and England, 1565–1750*. Ann Arbor, Michigan: University Microfilms International, 1989.

Bambach, Carmen. *Drawing and Painting in the Italian Renaissance Workshop: Theory and Practice, 1300–1600*. Cambridge: Cambridge University Press, 1999.

Baron, Hans. 'The *Querelle* of the Ancients and Moderns as a Problem for Renaissance Scholarship', *Journal of the History of Ideas* xx (1959): pp. 3–22.

Bartrum, Giulia, ed. *Albrecht Dürer and his Legacy: The Graphic Work of a Renaissance Artist*. London: The British Museum Press, 2002.

Bartsch, Adam von. *The Illustrated Bartsch*. 22 volumes. [Originally published as *Le peintre graveur* in 1922]. New York: Abaris Books, 1978.

Becker, Jochen. 'Zur Niederländischen Kunstliteratur des 16. Jahrhunderts: Domenicus Lampsonius', *Nederlands Kunsthistorisch Jaarboek* 24 (1973): pp. 113–127.

Bedaux, J.B. and A van Gool. 'Breughel's Birthyear, Motive of an Ars/Natura Transmutation', *Simiolus* 7/3 (1974): pp. 133–156.

Bergvelt, Ellinoor and Kistemaker, Reneé. *De Wereld Binnen Handbereik: Nederlandse Kunst- en Rariteitenverzamelingen, 1585–1735*. Amsterdam: Amsterdams Historisch Museum, 1992.

Bergström, Ingvar. 'Hans Hoffmann's Oil-Painting *The Hare in the Forest*', *Prague um 1600: Beiträge zur Kunst und Kultur am Hofe Rudolfs II*. Freren: Luca Verlag, 1988. pp. 16–18.

Bialostocki, Jan. 'Vernunft und Ingenium in Dürers kunsttheoretischem denken', *Zeitschrift des Deutshcen Veriens fur Kunstwissneschaft* 25 (1971): pp. 107–114.

Bie, Cornelis de. *Het Gulden Cabinet*. Antwerp: Juliaen van Montfort, 1662.

Brakensiek, Stephan. Vom 'Theatrum Mundi' zum 'Cabinet des Estampes': *Das Sammeln von Druckgraphik in Deutschland 1565–1821*. Hildesheim, Zürich and New York: Olms, 2003.

Bredekamp, Horst. *The Lure of Antiquity and the Cult of the Machine: the Kunstkammer and the Evolution of Nature, Art, and Technology*. Translated by Allison Brown. Princeton: Markus Wiener Publishers, 1995.

Brown, Howard Mayer. 'Emulation, Competition and Homage: Imitation and the Theories of Imitation in the Renaissance', *Journal of the American Musicological Society* 35/1 (1982): pp. 1–48.

Bridson, Gavin D.R. and White, James J., eds. *Plant, Animal and Anatomical Illustration in Art and Science: A Bibliographical Guide from the 16th Century to the Present Day*. Winchester: St. Paul's Bibliographies, 1990.

Buchanan, Iain. 'Dürer and Abraham Ortelius', *The Burlington Magazine* 124 (1982): pp. 734–741.

Buchner, Ernst. *Bildnis der Spätgotik und der frühen Dürerzeit*. Berlin: Deutscher Verien für Kunstwissenschaft, 1953.

Budde, Hendrik. Die *Kunstsammlung des Nürnberger Patriziers Willibald Imhoff unter beseonderer Berücksichtigung der Werke Albrecht Dürers*. Ph.D. Dissertation. Berlin, 1990. Münster: LIT Verlag, 1996.

Budde, Hendrik. 'Das "Kunstbuch" des Nürnberger Patriziers Willibald Imhoff und die Tier- und Pflanzenstudien Albrecht Dürers und Hans Hoffmanns', *Jahrbuch der Kunsthistorischen Sammlungen in Wien* 82/83 (1986): pp. 213–241.

Busch, Renate von. *Studien zur Süddetschen Sammlungen des 16. Jahrhunderts*. Ph.D. Dissertation. Universitätsbibliothek Tübingen, 1915.

Butts, Barbara. *'Dürerschuler' Hans Süss von Kulmbach*. Ph.D. Dissertation. Harvard University, 1985.

Cartensen, Jens. *Über das Nachleben antiker Kunst bei Albrecht Dürer*. Ph.D. Dissertation. Freiburg im Breisgau: Albert-Ludwigs-Universität, 1982.

Cast, David. *The Calumny of Apelles: A Study in the Humanistic Tradition*. New Haven: Yale University Press, 1981.

Chapeaurouge, Donat de. 'Der Christ als Christus. Darstellungen der Angleichung an Gott in der Kunst des Mittelalters', *Wallraf-Richartz Jahrbuch* 48/49 (1987): pp. 77–96.

Chastel, André. 'Dürer à Venise en 1506', *Giorgione e l'humanesimo veneziano*. Edited by Rodolfo Palluchini. Florence: L.S. Olschki, 1981. pp. 459–463.

Chastel, André. 'Zu Vier Selbstbildnissen Albrecht Dürers aus den Jahren 1506 bis 1511', *Albrecht Dürer: Kunst im Aufbruch. Vorträge der Kunstwissenschaftlichen Tagung mit Internationaler Beteilung zum 500. Geburtstag von Albrecht Dürer*. Leipzig: Karl Marx Universität, 1972, pp. 37–46.

Châtelet, Albert. 'Dürer und die nördlichen Niederlande', *Anzeiger des Germanischen Nationalmuseums* (1975): pp. 52–64.

Chipps-Smith, Jeffrey, ed. *Nuremberg: A Renaissance City 1500–1618*. Texas: University of Texas Press, 1983.

Chipps-Smith, Jeffrey. 'Albrecht Dürer as Collector' *Renaissance Quarterly* 64/1 (2011): pp. 1–49.

Clarke, T.H. *The Rhinoceros from Dürer to Stubbs, 1515–1799*. New York: Harper and Row, 1986.

Comberiati, Carmelo Peter. 'Aspects of Renaissance *Imitatio* in Musical Settings of the Mass Ordinary at Rudolf's Court', in *Prag um 1600: Beiträge zur Kunst und Kultur am Hofe Rudolfs II*. Eds. Jürgen Schultze and Hermann Fillitz. Freren: Luca Verlag, 1988. pp. 27–32.

Conway, William Martin. *The Writings of Albrecht Durer*. New York: Philosophical Library, 1958.

Crane, Susan, ed. *Museums and Memory*. Stanford: Stanford University Press, 2000.

Cuttler, Charles D. 'Undercurrents in Dürer's 1500 Self-portrait', *Pantheon* 50, 1992, pp. 24–27.

Dackerman, Susan. *Painted Prints: The Revelation of Color in Northern Renaissance and Baroque Engravings, Etchings, and Woodcuts*. Baltimore: Baltimore Museum of Art, 2002.

Daston, Lorraine. *Wonders and the Order of Nature, 1150–1750*. New York: Zone Books, 1998.

Decker, Bernhard. 'Dürer-Nachahmungen und Kunstgeschichte – ein Problem am Rande? Dürer-Konstruktion eines Vorbildes, Gelingen, oder Mißlingen des Fortschritts', in *Dürers Verwandlung in der Skupltur zwischen Renaissance und Barock*. Edited by Herbert Beck and Bernhard Decker. Frankfurt: Museum alter Plastik, 1981. pp. 385–489.

Delen, A.J.J. 'Christoffel Plantin als prentenhandelaar', *De Gulden Passer* 10 (1932): pp. 1–24.

Dempsey, Charles. *Annibale Carracci and the Beginnings of Baroque Style*. Glückstadt: Augustin, 1977.

Denucé, Jean. *De Antwerpsche 'Konstkamers'*. Antwerp: De Speigel, 1932.

Duychuk, Linda. *Dürer and Vera Cruz*. Unpublished M.A. Thesis. University of Wisconsin-Madison, 1989.

Dworshcak, F. *Antonio Abondio: Medaglista e Ceroplasta (1538–1591)*. Trento: Collana Artisti Trentini, 1958.

Eichberger, Dagmar. '*Naturalia* and *artefacta*: Dürer's nature drawings and early collecting', in *Dürer and his Culture*. Edited by Dagmar Eichberger and Charles Zika. Cambridge: Cambridge University Press, 1998. pp. 13–37.

Eisler, Colin. *Dürer's Animals*. Washington: Smithsonian Institution Press, 1991.

Eisenbart, Liselotte C. *Kleiderordnungen der deutschen Städte zwischen 1350 und 1700*. Göttingen: Müster Schmidt, 1962.

Elkins, James. 'Art History and Images That Are Not Art', *Art Bulletin* 77 (1995): pp. 553–571.

Ernstberger, Anton. 'Kurfurst Maximilian I und Albrecht Dürer: Zur Geschichte einer grossen Sammlerleidenschaft', *Anzeiger des Germanisches National-Museums 1940–1953* (1954): pp. 143–196.

Ertz, Klaus. *Jan Brueghel der Ältere (1568–1625)*. Köln: DuMont, 1985.

Evans, R.J.W. *The Making of the Habsburg Monarchy, 1550–1700*. Oxford: Clarendon Press, 1979.

Evans, R.J.W. Rudolf II and His World: A Study in Intellectual History. Oxford: Clarendon Press, 1973.

Fabianski, Marcin. 'Iconography of the Architecture of ideal *Musaea* in the Fifteenth to Eighteenth Centuries', *Journal of the History of Collections* 2/2 (1990): pp. 95–134.

Fejfer, Jane, Fischer-Hansen, Tobias and Rathje, Annette, eds. *The Rediscovery of Antiquity: The Role of the Artist*. Copenhagen: Museum Tusculanum Press, University of Copenhagen, 2003.

Findlen, Paula. 'The Museum: Its Classical Etymology and Renaissance Geneaology', *Journal of the History of Collections* 1/1 (1989): pp. 59–78.

Findlen, Paula. *Possessing Nature: Museums, Collecting and Scientific Culture in Early Modern Italy*. Los Angeles: University of California Press, 1994.

Fischer, Hans. Conrad Gessner 1516–1565. *Universalgelehrter, Naturforscher, Arzt*. Zurich: Orell Füssli, 1967.

Fischer, Otto. 'Geschichte der Offentlichen Kunstsammlung Basel', *Festschrift zur Eroffnung des Kunstmuseums Basel*. Basel, 1936. pp. 1–25.

Fleischmann, Peter. 'Anmerkungen zum Patriziat und zu Kunstsammlungen des 16. Jahrhunderts in Nürnberg', in *Kunst des Sammelns. Das Praunsche Kabinett. Meisterwerke von Dürer bis Carracci*. Ed. Katrin Achilles-Syndram. Nuremberg: Verlag des Germanischen Nationalmuseums, 1994. pp. 13–24.

Freedberg, David. *The Power of Images: Studies in the History and Theory of Response*. Chicago: University of Chicago Press, 1989.

Fučíková, Eliška 'Prague Castle under Rudolf II, His Predecessors and Successors', in *Rudolf II and Prague: The Court and the City*. Eliška Fučíková, ed. London: Thames and Hudson, 1997. pp. 2–71.

Fučíková, Eliška. *Rudolf II and Prague: The Court and the City*. London: Thames and Hudson, 1997.

Fučíková, Eliška. 'Umělci na dvoře Rudolfa II a jejich vztah k tvorbě Albrechta Dürera', *Umění* 20 (1972): pp. 146–166.

Fučíková, Eliška. 'Historisierende Tendenze in der Rudolfinischen Kunst-Beziehungen zur Älteren Deutschen und Niederländischen Malerei', *Jahrbuch der Kunsthistorischen Sammlungen in Wien* 82/83 (1986): pp. 179–188.

Fuhse, Franz. 'Zur Dürerforschung im 17. Jahrhundert', *Mitteilungen aus dem Germanischen Nationalmuseum* (1895): pp. 66–73.

Garas, Klara. 'Zur Geschichte der Kunstsammlungen Rudolfs II', *Umění* 18 (1970): pp. 134–141.

Gerstinger, Hans. *Die Briefe Des Johannes Sambucus (Zsambosky) 1554–1584*. Vienna: Österreichische Akademie der Wissenschaften, Philosophische-Historische Klasse, 1968.

Gessner, Conrad. *Gistoria Animalium.* 4 volumes. Tiguri, apud C. Froschoverum, 1551–87.

Ginsburgh, Victor and Sheila Weyers. 'On the Contemporaneousness of Roger de Piles' *Balance des Peintres*', *Sublime Economy: On the Intersection of Art and Economics*. Edited by J. Amariglio, S. Cullenberg, J. Childers. London, Routledge, 2009.

Glück, Gustav. 'Falschungen auf Dürer's Namen aus der Sammlung Erzherzog Leopold Wilhelms', *Jahrbuch der Kunsthistorischen Sammlungen des Allerhöchsten Kaiserhauses* 28 (1909–1910): pp. 1–35.

Gmelin, Hans Georg. 'Vorbild und Rezeption: Motive aus Dürers Graphik in Kunstwerken der Niedersächsischen Landesgalerie', *Weltkunst* 54/6 (1984): pp. 699–702.

Gmelin, Hans Georg. 'Illuminierte Druckgraphik um 1600: ein Phänomen der Dürer Renaissance?', *Städel-Jahrbuch* 9 (1983): pp. 183–209.

Gmelin, Hermann. 'Das Prinzip der Imitatio in der romanischen Literatur der Renaissance', *Romanische Forschungen* XLVI (1932): pp. 83–360.

Götz, Wolfgang. 'Historismus, Ein Versuch zur Definition des Begriffes', *Zeitschrift des Deutschen Veriens für Kunstwissenschaft* XXIV (1970): pp. 196–212.

Goldberg, Gisela. 'Dürer-Renaissance am Münchner Hof', *Um Glauben und Reich. Kurfürst Maximilian I: Beiträge zur Bayerischen Geschichte und Kunst 1573–1657*. Ed. Hubert Glaser. Munich: Hirmer, 1980. pp. 318–322.

Goldberg, Gisela. 'Zur Ausprägung der Dürer Renaissance in München', *Münchner Jahrbuch der Bildender Kunst* 31 (1980): pp. 129–175.

Goldberg, Gisela. 'Veränderungen von Bildern der ersten Hälfte des 16. Jahrhunderts: Versuch einer Interpretation', *Städel-Jahrbuch* 9 (1983): pp. 151–182.

Goldberg, Gisela. 'Münchner Aspekte der Dürer Renaissance unter besonderer Berücksichtigung von Dürers Tier und Pflanzenstudien', *Jahrbuch der Kunsthistorischen Sammlungen in Wien* 82/82 (1986/1987): pp. 179–188.

Goldberg, Gisela, Heimberg, Bruno and Schwae, Martin. *Albrecht Dürer: Die Gemälde der Alten Pinakothek*. Heidelberg: Braus, 1998.

Graeve Frantz, Mary Ann. 'Taddeo Zuccaro as a Precursor of Annibale Carracci', *Essays in Honor of Walter Friedländer, Marsyas*. Edited by W. Cahn. New York: Institute of Fine Arts, 1965. pp. 62–79.

Greene, Thomas. *The Light in Troy: Imitation and Discovery in Renaissance Poetry*. New Haven: Yale University Press, 1982.

Greene, Thomas M. 'Petrarch and the Humanist Hermeneutic', in *Italian Literature: Roots and Branches*. Edited by Giose Rimanelli and Kenneth John Atchity. New Haven: Yale University Press, 1976. pp. 201–224.

Gregory, Sharon. *Vasari and Northern Prints: An Examination of Giorgio Vasari's comments on, and uses of woodcuts and engravings by Martin Schongauer, Albrecht Dürer and Lucas van Leyden*. M.A. Thesis. Kingston: Queen's University, 1992.

Gries, Christian. 'Erzherzog Ferdinand von Tirol: Konturen einer Sammlerpersönlichkeit', *Frühneuzeit-Info* IV (1993): pp. 162–173.

Grote, Andreas, ed. *Macrocosmos in Microcosmo: die Welt in der Stube: zur Geschichte des Sammelns 1450 bis 1800*. Opladen: Leske and Budrich, 1994.

Grote, Ludwig. 'Vom Nachleben Dürers: Beiträge zur Kunst der Epoche von 1530 bis 1650', *Anzeiger des Germanischen National-Museums* (1940–53). Berlin: Verlag Gebr. Mann., 1954.

Gümbel, Albert. 'Die englische Mission des Grafen von Arundel in Nürnberg, Mai und November 1636', *Archivalische Zeitschrift* 11 (1904): pp. 100–117.

Gutfleisch, Barbara and Menzhasuen, Joachim. '"How a Kunstkammer should be formed": Gabriel Kaltemarckt's advice to Christian I of Saxony on the formation of an art collection, 1587', *Journal of the History of Collections* 1 (1989): pp. 3–32.

Hampe, Theodor. 'Kunstfreunde im Alten Nürnberg und ihre Sammlungen', *Mitteilungen des Vereins für Geschichte der Stadt Nürnberg* 16 (1904): pp. 57–124.

Hanatsch, V. 'Beiträge zur Alteren Geschichte der Kurfürstlichen Kunstkammer zu Dresden', *Neues Archiv fur Sächsische Geschichte und Altertumskunde* 23 (1902): pp. 230–237.

Haupt, Herbert. 'Neue Quellen zur Kunst- und Kunstgeschichte am Hofe Kaiser Rudolfs II. In Wiener Archiven', *Prague um 1600: Beiträge zur Kunst und Kultur am Hofe Rudolfs II*. Freren: Luca Verlag, 1988. pp. 105–109.

Haupt, Herbert Haupt and Thea Vignau-Wilberg and Eva Irblich & Manfred Staudinger, eds. *Le Bestiaire de Rodolphe II*. Paris: Editions Citadelles, 1990.

Heimbürger, Munna. *Dürer e Venezia*. Rome: Ugo Bozzi Editore, 1999.

Held, Julius. *Dürers Wirkung auf die niederländische Kunst seiner Zeit*. The Hague: M. Nijhoff, 1931.

Heller, Joseph. *Das Leben und die Werke Albrecht Dürers,* 2 volumes. Bamberg: E.F. Kunz, 1827.

Hendrix, Lee. 'Natural History Illustration at the Court of Rudolf II', *Rudolf II and Prague: The Court and the City*. Ed. Eliška Fučíková. London: Thames and Hudson, 1997. pp. 157–171.

Hendrix, Lee. Joris *Hoefnagel and the Four Elements: A Study in Sixteenth Century Nature Painting*. Unpublished Ph.D. dissertation, Princeton University, 1984

Hernard, Béatrice Hernard. *Die Graphiksammlung des Humanisten Hartmann Schedel*. Munich: Prestel, 1990.

Hervey, Mary F.S. *The Life, Correspondence and Collections of Thomas Howard, Earl of Arundel*. Cambridge: Cambridge University Press, 1921.

Hess, Daniel. 'Dürers Selbstbildniss von 1500– "Alter Deus' oder Neuer Apelles?"' *Mitteilungen des Vereins für Geschichte der Stadt Nürnberg* 77 (1990): pp. 63–90.

Heuer, Christopher P. 'Hendrick Goltzius', *ArtForum* 40/5 (2003): p. 67.

Hirn, Josef. *Erzherzog Ferdinand II. von Tirol. Geschichte seiner Regierung und seiner Länder. 2 volumes*. Innsbruck: Wagner, 1885/88.

Hirschmann, Otto. *Hendrick Goltzius*. Leipzig: Klinkhardt and Biermann, 1919.

Hirschmann, Otto. *Verzeichnis des Graphischen Werks von Hendrick Goltzius* Leipzig: Klinkhardt and Biermann, 1921.

Hlobil, Ivo and Petrů, Eduard. *Humanism and the Early Renaissance in Moravia*. Olomouc: Votobia, 1999.

Honeiger, Cathleen. 'The Reception of Correggio's *Loves of Jupiter*', in *Coming About: A Festschrift for John Shearman*. Edited by Lars R. Jones and Louisa C. Matthew. Cambridge: Harvard University Art Museums, 2001. pp. 191–197.

Holst, Niels von. *Creators, Collectors, and Connoisseurs: The Anatomy of Artistic Taste from Antiquity to the Present Day*. New York: Putnam, 1967.

Holub, Robert C. *Reception Theory: A Critical Introduction*. London and New York: Methuen, 1984.

Howarth, David. *Lord Arundel and his Circle*. New Haven: Yale University Press, 1985.

Howarth, David. Ed. *Thomas Howard, Earl of Arundel: Patronage and Collecting in the Seventeenth Century*. Oxford: Ashmolean Museum, 1985.

Humfrey, Peter. 'La Festa del Rosario di Albrecht Dürer', *Eidos: Rivista di Cultura* 2 (1988): pp. 4–15.

Humfrey, Peter. 'Competitive Devotions: The Venetian *Scuole Piccole* as Donors of Altarpieces in the Years around 1500', *Art Bulletin* 70/3 (1988): pp. 401–423.

Hutchison, Jane Campbell. *Albrecht Durer: A Biography*. Princeton: Princeton University Press, 1990.

Hutchison, Jane Campbell. '"Ehrlich gehalten nah und feren": Five Centuries of Dürer Reception', in *Albrecht Dürer: A Guide to Research*. New York and London: Garland Publishing Inc., 2000. pp. 1–24.

Impey, Oliver and MacGregor, Arthur. *The Origins of Museums: The Cabinet of Curiosities in Sixteenth- and Seventeenth-century Europe*. Oxford: Clarendon Press, 1985.

Jansen, Dirk Jacob. 'Example and Examples: The Potential Influence of Jacopo Strada on the Development of Rudolphine Art', in *Prag um 1600: Beiträge zur Kunst und Kultur am Hofe Rudolfs II*. Eds. Jürgen Schultze and Hermann Fillitz. Freren: Luca Verlag, 1988. pp. 132–146.

Jauss, Hans Robert. *Toward an Aesthetic of Reception*. Minneapolis: University of Minnesota Press, 1982.

Juren, Vladimir and Lubomir Konečny. 'Beiträge zur Rezeptionsgeschichte des Nemesis Kupferstichs von Albrecht Dürer', *Bulletin of the National Gallery in Prague* 2 (1993): pp. 36–41.

Jürgens, Klaus H. 'Neue Forschungen zu dem Münchner Selbstbildnis des Jahres 1500 von Albrecht Dürer', *Kunsthistorisches Jahrbuch Graz* (1983): pp. 167–190.

Kauffmann, Hans. 'Dürer in der Kunst und Kunsturteil um 1600', *Anzeiger des Germanischen National-Museums* (1940–1953): pp. 18–60.

Kaufmann, Thomas DaCosta. 'Hermeneutics in the History of Art: Remarks on the Reception of Dürer in the Sixteenth and the Early Seventeenth Centuries', in *New Perspectives on the Art of Renaissance Nuremberg: Five Essays*. Edited by Jeffrey Chipps-Smith. Austin: Archer M. Huntington Gallery, 1985. pp. 23–39.

Kaufmann, Thomas DaCosta. *Court, Cloister and City: The Art and Culture of Central Europe 1450–1800*. Chicago: University of Chicago Press, 1995.

Kaufmann, Thomas DaCosta. *Drawings from the Holy Roman Empire: A Selection from North American collections*. Princeton: Princeton University, 1982.

Kaufmann, Thomas DaCosta. 'The Nature of Imitation: Hoefnagel on Dürer', *Jahrbuch der Kunsthistorischen Sammlungen in Wien* 82/83 (1986), pp. 163–178.

Kaufmann, Thomas DaCosta. *The School of Prague: Painting at the Court of Rudolf II*. Chicago and London: The University of Chicago Press, 1988 (a).

Kaufmann, Thomas DaCosta. '"Gar lecherlich": Low-life Painting in Rudolfine Prague', *Prague um 1600: Beiträge zur Kunst und Kultur am Hofe Rudolfs II*. Freren: Luca Verlag, 1988 (b). pp. 33–38.

Kaufmann, Thomas DaCosta. *The Mastery of Nature: Aspects of Art, Science and Humanism in the Renaissance*. New Jersey: Princeton University Press, 1993.

Kayo, Hirakawa. 'Dürer and Jan Brueghel the Elder: one aspect of the pictorialization of Dürer's drawings at the court of Rudolf II', *Aesthetics* 10 (2002): pp. 61–73.

Kehrer, Hugo. *Dürers Selbstbildnisse und die Dürer-Bildnisse*. Berlin: Gebr. Mann, 1934.

Kemp, Martin. 'Naturally Natural: Albrecht Dürer's Studies of Animals', *Nature* 420 (2005): p. 744.

Kemp, Martin. *Visualizations: The Nature Book of Art and Science*. Berkeley: University of California Press, 2000.

Kemp, Wolfgang. *Der Anteil des Betrachters: Rezeptionsästhetische Studien zur Malerei des 19. Jahrhunderts*. Munich: Mäander, 1983.

Kemperdick, Stephan. *The Early Portrait: From the Collections of the Prince of Liechtenstein and the Kunstmuseum Basel*. Munich: Prestel, 2006.

Killermann, Sebastian. A. *Dürers Werk. Eine natur- und kulturgeschichtliche Untersuchung*. Regensburg: Druck und Kommission bei der Vormals Manz'schen Buchdruckerei und Verlag Regensburg, 1953.

Klauner, Friederike. 'Dürers Werke in der Kopie', *Alte und Moderne Kunst* 16 (1971): pp. 14–18.

Koerner, Joseph Leo. 'Albrecht Dürer: A Sixteenth-Century Influenza', in *Albrecht Dürer and his Legacy*. Edited by Giulia Bartrum. London: The British Museum Press, 2002. pp. 18–38.

Koerner, Joseph Leo. *The Moment of Self-Portraiture in German Renaissance Art*. Chicago: University of Chicago Press, 1993.

Kohlprath, Georg. 'Leopolds Liebe', *Weltkunst* 75/7 (2003): p. 103

Konečný, Lubomír. 'Zeuxis in Prague: some Thoughts on Hans von Aachen', *Prague um 1600: Beiträge zur Kunst und Kultur am Hofe Rudolfs II.* Freren: Luca Verlag, 1988. pp. 147–155.

König-Lein, Susanne and Waltz, Alfred, eds. *Weltenharmonie: die Kunstkammer und die Ordnung des Wissens*. Braunschweig: Herzog Anton Ulrich-Museum Braunschweig, 2000.

Koreny, Fritz. 'Venice and Dürer', in *Renaissance Venice and the North: Crosscurrents in the Time of Bellini, Dürer and Titian*. Edited by Bernard Aikema and Beverly Louise Brown (New York: Rizzoli, 1999): pp. 240–249.

Koreny, Fritz. *Albrecht Dürer and the Animal and Plant Studies of the Renaissance*. First published 1985. Translated by Pamela Marwood and Yehuda Shapiro. Boston: Brown, 1988.

Koreny, Fritz, ed. *Albrecht Dürer und die Tier und Pflanzenstudien derRenaissance Symposium. Die Beiträge der von der Graphischen Sammlung Albertina von 7. Bis 10. Juni 1985 veranstalteten Tagung*. Vienna: Jahrbuch der Kunsthistorischen Sammlungen in Wien, 1986.

Koreny, Fritz and Sam Segal. 'Hans Hoffmann – Entdeckungen und Zuschreibungen', *Jahrbuch der Kunsthistorischen Sammlungen in Wien* 85/86 (1990): pp. 57–65.

Kotkova, Olga. '"The Feast of the Rosegarlands": what remains of Dürer?', *Burlington Magazine* CXLIV (2002): pp. 4–21.

Kotrborá, M.A. 'Obraz Ružencové slavnosti Albrechta Dürera', *Umění* 19 (1971): pp. 588–599.

Krčalová, J. 'Renesanční malba v chechach a na Moravě' *Dějiny Českeho vytvarného umění: Od počatku renesanče do závyrku baroka II/I* (Prague, 1989): pp. 64–91

Kris, Ernst and Kurz, Otto. *Legend, Myth and Magic in the Image of the Artist: A Historical Experiment*. New Haven: Yale University Press, 1979.

Kuchynka, A. 'Manuál Pražského Pořádku Malířského z Let 1600–1656', *Památky Archaeologické* 27 (1915): pp. 24–36.

Kurth, Wili, ed. *The Complete Woodcuts of Albrecht Durer*. New York: Dover Publications, 1963.

Kurz, Otto. 'Umělcké Vztahy Mezi Prahou a Persií za Rudolfa II', *Umění,* XIV (1966): pp. 461–487.

Kuspit, Donald B. 'Dürer's Scientific Side', *Art Journal* 32/2 (1972): pp. 163–171.

Kutschbach, Doris. *Albrecht Dürer. Die Altäre*. Stuttgart/Zürich: Belser Verlag, 1995.

Kugler, Georg. 'Rudolf II. als Sammler', *Prague um 1600: Kunst und Kultur am Hofe Rudolfs II.* Freren: Luca Verlag, 1988: pp. 9–21.

Kunkler, Stephan. *Zwischen Humanismus und Reformation: der Humanist Joachim Camerarius (1500–1574) im Wechselspiel von pädagogischem Pathos und theologischem Ethos*. Hildesheim: Olms, 2000.

Klemm, Christian. *Joachim von Sandrart: Kunst Werke und Lebens Lauf*. Berlin: Deutscher Verlag für Kunstwissenshaft, 1986.

Landau, David and Parshall, Peter. *The Renaissance Print 1470–1550*. New Haven: Yale University Press, 1994.

Leeflang, Huigen and Ger Luijten, eds *Hendrick Goltzius (1558–1617): Drawings, Prints and Paintings*. Zwolle: Waanders Publishers, 2003.

Levey, Michael. 'Dürer and England', *Anzeiger des Germanischen Nationalmuseums* (1970): pp. 157–164.

Ley, Henry. *Essays on Dürer*. Manchester: University of Manchester Press, 1973.

Lhotsky, Alphons. 'Die Geschichte der Sammlungen', in *Festschrift des Kunsthistorisches Museums zur feier des fünfzigjährigen Bestandes*. Wien: Verlag Ferdinand Berger, Horn, 1941. Volume 2.

Liebman, M.J. 'Dürer und seine Werkstatt', in *Albrecht Dürer: Zeit und Werk*. Edited by Ernst Ullmann, Günter Grau, and Rainer Behrends. Leipzig: Karl Marx Universität, 1971.

Limouze, Dorothy. 'Aegedius Sadeler (1570–1629): Drawings, Prints, and the Development of an Art Theoretical Attitude', *Prague um 1600: Beiträge zur Kunst und Kultur am Hofe Rudolfs II*. Freren: Luca Verlag, 1988. pp. 183–192.

Limouze, Dorothy. 'Aegedius Sadeler, Imperial Printmaker', *Bulletin of the Philadelphia Museum of Art* 85/362 (1989): pp. 2–24.

Limouze, Dorothy. *Aegedius Sadeler (c.1570–1629): Drawings, Prints and Art Theory*. Ph.D. dissertation. Princeton, 1990.

Luber Crawford, Katherine. *Albrecht Dürer and the Venetian Renaissance*. New York: Cambridge University Press, 2005.

Lüdecke, Heinz and Susanne Heiland. *Dürer und die Nachwelt*. Berlin: Rütten and Loening, 1955.

Manuth, Volker. 'Dürer ein Dandy? Beobachtungen zum Kostum des Künstlers', in *Aus Albrecht Dürers Welt, Festschrift für Fedja Anzelewsky*, edited by B. Brinkmann and M. Roth. Turnhout: Brepols, 2001. pp. 165–171.

Marrow, James H. and Alan Shestack, eds. *Hans Baldung Grien: Prints and Drawings*. Chicago: University of Chicago Press, 1981.

Martin, Andrew John. 'Durers Rosenkranzfest und eine Fuggergrablege mit einem Gemälde von Battista Franco in San Bartolomeo di Rialto: Zu den verwirrenden Angaben in Francesco Sansovinos *Venetia citta nobilissima et singolare* (1581)', *Studia Rudolphina* 6(2006): pp. 59–63.

Martin, Andrew John. 'Die Kopie nach Durers *Rosenkranzfest* aus dem Palazzo Griman bei Santa Maria Formosa', *Studia Rudolphina* 6 (2006): pp. 64–66.

Martin, Andrew John. '"...Dass er nicht nachgelassen, bis ihm solches Blat aus der Kirche verwilligt worden." Der Erwerb von Albrecht Dürers Rosenkranzfest Durch Rudolf II', *Umění* 46 (1998): pp. 175–188.

Maselis, Marie Christiane. The Albums of Anselmus de Boodt (1550–1632) Natural History Painting at the Court of Rudolf II in Prague. Ramsen: Bibermühle, 1999

Matthew, Louisa C. 'Working Abroad: Northern Artists in the Venetian Ambient', *Renaissance Venice and the North: Crosscurrents in the Time of Bellini, Dürer and Titian*, edited by Bernard Aikema and Beverly Louise Brown, New York: Rizzoli, 1999. pp. 61–69.

Matthew, Louisa C. 'The Painter's Presence: Signatures in Venetian Renaissance Pictures', *The Art Bulletin* 80/4 (1998): pp. 616–648.

McDonald, Mark P. '"Extremely curious and important!": Reconstructing the Print Collection of Ferdinand Columbus', in *Collecting Prints and Drawings in Europe, c. 1500–1750*. Edited by Christopher Baker, Caroline Elam, and Genevieve Warwick. Aldershot: Ashgate, 2003. pp. 37–54.

McDonald, Mark P. *The Print Collection of Ferdinand Columbus (1488–1539): A Renaissance Collector in Seville*. London: British Museum Press, 2004.

Meder, Josef. 'Zur ersten Resie nach Venedig (1494–95)', *Jahrbuch der Kunsthistorischen Sammlungen des Allerhöchsten Kaiserhauses* 30 (1911): pp. 183–227.

Meiers, Sarah. 'Portraits in print: Hieronymus Cock, Dominicus Lampsonius, and "Pictorum aliquot celebrium Germaniae inferioris effigies"', *Zeitschrift für Kunstgeschichte* 69 (2006): pp. 1–16.

Melanchthon, Philip. *Dispositio orationis quam pro Archia poeta Cicero habuit* Nuremberg: Methiam Scharffenberg, 1537.

Mende, Matthias. *Dürer Medaillen: Münzen, Medaillen, Plaketten von Dürer, auf Dürer, nach Dürer*. Nuremberg: Verlag Hans Karl, 1990.

Metcalf, L. 'A Prince of Print Collectors: Michel de Marolles, Abbé de Villeloin', *Print Quarterly* 2 (1912): pp. 316–340.

Metzger, Christoph. *Hans Schäufelein als Maler*. Berlin: Deutscher Verein für Kunstwissenschaft, 2002.

Moir, Alfred. *Caravaggio and his Copyists*. New York: New York University Press for College Art Association, 1976.

Mulcahy, Rosemarie. *Philip II of Spain, Patron of the Arts*. Portland: Four Courts, 2004.

Müller, Christian. Urs Graf. Die Zeichnungen im Kupferstichkabinett Basel. Basel, 2002.

Müller, Jürgen. *Concordia Pragensis: Karel van Manders Kunsttheorie im Schilderboeck: ein Beitrag zur Rhetorisierung von Kunst und Leben am Beispiel der rudolfinischen Hofkünstler*. Munich: Oldenbourg, 1993.

Münster, Sebastian. *Cosmographiae Universelle*. Basle: H. Pierre, 1552Nagel, H. 'Ein Bayernfürst sammelt Dürer. Kurfürst Maximilian I als Kunstsammler', *Unser Bayern; Heimatbeilage der Bayerischen Staatszeitung* 20/3 (1979): p. 22.

Neuwirth, Josef. 'Rudolf II als Dürer Sammler', *Xenia Austriaca*, 1883. pp. 185–225.

Neubert, Eberhard. *Albrecht Dürer: Pflanzen und Tiere*. Leipzig: E.A. Seemann, 1960.

Neumann, Jaromír. 'Kleine Beitrage zur Rudolfinischen Kunst',*Umění* 18 (1970): pp. 142–170.

Neumann, Jaromir. *Karel Skreta 1610–1674*. Prague: Jizdarna Prazskeho Hradu, 1974.

Neumann, Jaromír. 'Rudolfinske Umění I',*Umění* 25 (1977): pp. 400–448.

Neumann, Jaromir. 'Rudolfinske Uměni II. Profily Malířu a Sochařu',*Umění* 26 (1978): pp. 303–347.

Nichols, Lawrence W. 'The Passion', in *Hendrick Goltzius (1558–1617): Drawings, Prints and Paintings*, edited by Huigen Leeflang and Ger Luijten. Zwolle: Waanders Publishers, 2003.

Nuti, Lucia. 'The Urban Imagery of Georg Hoefnagel', in *Prague um 1600: Beiträge zur Kunst und Kultur am Hofe Rudolfs II*. Freren: Luca Verlag, 1988. pp. 211–217.

Oehler, Lisa. 'Das Dürermonogramm auf Werken der Dürerschule', *Städel Jahrbuch,* 4(1973): pp. 37–80.

Okada, Amina. *Indian Miniatures of the Mughal Court.* Translated by Deke Dusinberre. New York: H.M. Abrams, 1992.

O'Malley, Michael. *Artistic Exchange and Cultural Translation in the Italian Renaissance City.* Eds. Campbell, Stephen J. and Stephen Milner. Cambridge: Cambridge University Press, 2004.

Ormond, Mark, ed. *John Ringling: Dreamer, Builder, Collector* (Sarasota: John and Mable Ringling Museum of Art, 1996)

Osten, Gert von der. *Hans Baldung Grien – Gemälde und Dokumente.* Berlin: Deutscher Verlag für Kunstwissenschaft, 1983.

Oszczanowski, Piotr and Jan Gromadzki. *Theatrum Vitae et Mortis: Grafika, rysunek I malarstwo książkowe na Śląsku w latach ok. 1550– ok.1650* Wrocław: Muzeum Historyczne, 1995.

Palissy, Bernard. *Oeuvres Complètes.* Edited by Keith Cameron and Marie-Madeleine Fragnard. Mont-de-Marsen: Editions InterUniversitaires, 1996.

Panofsky, Erwin. 'Dürer as a Mathematician', *The World of Mathematics,* volume 1. Edited by J.R. Neuman. New York: Simon and Shuster, 1956. pp. 603–621.

Panofsky, Erwin. *Das Leben und die Kunst Albrecht Dürers.* Princeton: Princeton University Press, 1943. Translated into the English 1955.

Panofsky, Erwin. '"Nebulae in Pariete": Notes on Erasmus' Eulogy on Dürer', *Journal of the Warburg and Courtauld Institutes* 14/2 (1951): pp. 34–41.

Parshall, Peter. 'Albrecht Dürer and the Axis of Meaning', *Allen Memorial Art Museum Bulletin* 50/1 (1997): pp. 4–31.

Parshall, Peter. 'The Print Collection of Ferdinand, Archduke of Tyrol', *Jahrbuch der Kunsthistorischen Sammlungen in Wien* 78 (1982): pp. 139–184.

Pavord, Anna. *The Naming of Names: The Search for Order in the World of Plants.* New York: Bloomsbury, 2005.

Pass, Gunther. 'Dürer und die Wissenschaftliche Tierdarstellung der Renaissance', *Jahrbuch der Kunsthistorischen Sammlungen in Wien* 82/83 (1986): pp. 57–67.

Patty, James S. *Dürer in French Letters.* Paris: Champion-Slatkine, 1989.

Pav, John I. 'Wenceslaus Hollar in Germany, 1627–1636', *The Art Bulletin* 55/1 (1973): pp. 86–105.

Pešék, Jiří Pešék. 'Obrazy a grafiky a jejich majitele v předbélohorské Praze', *Umění* 39 (1991): pp. 369–383.

Peck, Linda Levy. 'Uncovering the Arundel Library at the Royal Society: Changing Meanings of Science and the Date of the Norfolk Donation', *Notes and Records of the Royal Society of London* 52/1 (1998): pp. 3–24.

Pennington, Richard. *A Descriptive Catalogue of the Etched Works of Wenceslaus Hollar 1607–1677.* Cambridge: Cambridge University Press, 1982.

Perry, Ellen. *Aesthetics of Emulation in the Visual Arts of Ancient Rome.* Cambridge: Cambridge University Press, 2005.

Pigman, G.W. 'Versions of Imitation in the Renaissance', *Renaissance Quarterly* 33/1 (1980): pp. 1–32.

Piles, Roger de. *Cours de Peinture par Principe*. Facsimile of 1708 edition with a preface by Jacques Thuillier. Paris: Gallimard, 1989.

Pilz, Kurt. 'Hans Hoffmann: Ein Dürer-Nachahmer aus der 2. Hälfte des 16. Jahrhunderts', *Mitteilungen des Vereins für Geschichte der Stadt Nürnberg* 51 (1962): pp. 236–272.

Pilz, Kurt. 'Willibald Pirkheimers Kunstsammlung und Bibliothek', in *Willibald Pirkheimer 1470/1970: Dokumente, Studien, Perspektiven*. Edited by B. Glock and I. Meidinger-Geise. Nuremberg: Glock and Lutz, 1970. pp. 93–110.

Pohl, Horst. Willibald *Imhoff, Enkel und Erbe Willibald Pirckheimers*. Nürnberg: Stadtarchiv Nürnberg, 1992.

Pon, Lisa. *Raphael, Dürer, and Marcantonio Raimondi: Copying and the Italian Renaissance Print*. New Haven: Yale University Press, 2004.

Pope-Hennessy, John. 'Nicholas Hilliard and Mannerist Art Theory', *Journal of the Warburg and Courtauld Institutes* 6 (1943): pp. 89–100.

Popham, A.E. 'Peter Breugel and Abraham Ortelius', *The Burlington Magazine* LIX (1931): pp. 184–188.

Preminger, Alex, ed. *The Princeton Encyclopedia of Poetry and Poetics*. Princeton: Princeton University Press, 1974.

Price, David. *Albrecht Dürer's Renaissance: Humanism, Reformation, and the Art of Faith*. Ann Arbor: University of Michigan Press, 2003.

Robinson, W.W. Robinson. 'The Passion for Prints: Collecting and Connoisseurship in Northern Europe during the Seventeenth Century', *Printmaking in the Age of Rembrandt, Exhibition Catalogue*. Boston, Museum of Fine Arts, 1980.

Romanelli, Domenico. 'The Fondaco dei Tedeschi', *Renaissance Venice and the North: Crosscurrents in the Time of Bellini, Dürer and Titian*, edited by Bernard Aikema and Beverly Louise Brown. New York: Rizzoli, 1999. pp. 77–81.

Rosenthal, Erwin. 'Dürer's Buchmalereien für Pirckheimers Bibliothek', *Jahrbuch der Preussischen Kunstsammlungen* 49/3 (1929): pp. 1–54.

Ross, B.T. 'Prints depicting Albrecht Dürer', *Record of the Art Museums of Princeton University* 31 (1971): pp. 72–75.

Rowlands, John. 'Prints and Drawings', in *Sir Hans Sloane: Collector, Scientist, Antiquary Founding Father of the British Museum*, edited by Arthur MacGregor (London: British Museum Press, 1984), pp. 245–263.

Rupprich, Hans. 'Das literarische Bild Dürers in Schriften des 16. Jahrhunderts', *Festschrift fur Dietrich Kralik*. Horn: Berger, 1954. pp. 218–239.

Sacken, Eduard Frh. von. 'Werke von Albrecht Dürer in der k.k. Ambraser-Sammlung', *Mitteilungen der Kaiserlich-Königlichen Central-Commission zur Erforschung und Erhaltung der Baudenkmale*, 8 (1863): pp. 123–131.

Salerno, Luigi. 'Seventeenth-Century English Literature on Painting', *Journal of the Warburg and Courtauld Institutes* 14 (1951): pp. 234–258.

Sarton, George. 'Art and Science', *Leonardo da Vinci, Aspects of the Renaissance Genius*. Edited by Morris H. Philipson. New York: G. Braziler, 1966.

Schedel, Hartmann. *The Nuremberg Chronicle: a Facsimile of Hartman Schedel's Buch der Chroniken printed by Anton Koberger in 1493*. New York: Landmark Press, 1979.

Scheicher, Elisabeth. *Die Kunst- und Wunderkammern der Habsburger*. Vienna: Molden Editions, 1979.

Scheicher, Elizabeth. 'The Collection of Archduke Ferdinand II at Schloss Ambras: its Purpose, Composition and Evolution', in *The Origins of Museums: The Cabinet of Curiosities in Sixteenth- and Seventeenth-century Europe*. Edited by Oliver Impey and Arthur MacGregor. Oxford: Clarendon Press, 1985. pp. 29–38.

Schlosser, Julius von. *Die Kunst- und Wunderkammern der Spätrenaissance. Ein Beitrag zur Geschichte des Sammelwesens*. 2nd edition. Braunschweig: Klinkhardt and Biermann, 1978.

Schlumberger, Exeline. 'La Nature d'après Dürer', *Connaissance des Arts* 399 (1985): pp. 76–85.

Schminke, Ilse. 'Der Dürerbuchmeister: Ein Buchbinder aus dem rudolfinischen Prag', *Archiv fur Buchbinderei* 42 (1982): pp. 75–80.

Schoch, Rainer. '"Die kostbare unter allen nürnbergischen Kunstkammern". Glanz und Ende des Praunschen Kabinetts', *Kunst des Sammelns. Das Praunsche Kabinett. Meisterwerke von Dürer bis Carracci*, edited by Katrin Achilles-Syndram. Nuremberg: Verlag des Germansichen Nationalmuseums, 1994. pp. 25–34.

Schreiber, Renate. *'Ein Galerie nach meinem Humor': Erzherzog Leopold Wilhelm*. Wien: Kunsthistorisches Museum, 2004.

Schulteiss, W. 'Ein Vertrag Albrecht Dürers über den Vertrieb seiner graphischen Kunstwerke', *Scripta Mercaturae* 1/2 (1969): pp. 77–81.

Schuster, Peter-Klaus. *Melencolia I – Dürers Denkbild*. Berlin: Gebr. Mann, 1991.

Schweikhart, Gunter. 'Novita e bellezza: zur frühen Dürer-Rezeption in Italien', in *Die Kunst der Renaissance*. Edited by E. Hubala and G. Schweikhart. Würzburg: F. Schöningh, 1978. pp. 137–154.

Schwemmer, Wilhelm. 'Aus der Geschichte der Kunstsammlungen der Stadt Nürnberg', *Mitteilung des Vereins für Geschichte der Stadt Nürnberg* 40 (1949); pp.97-206.

Scott, Izora. *Controversies over the Imitation of Cicero in the Renaissance: With a Translation of Letters between Pietro Bembo and Gianfrancesco Pico On Imitation, and a Translation of Desiderius Erasmus, The Ciceronian (Ciceronianus)*. Davis, California: Hermagoras Press, 1991.

Segal, Sam. 'Die Entstehung der Stilleben-Tradition im Hinblick auf Dürer, *Jahrbuch der Kunsthistorischen Sammlungen in Wien* 82/83 (1986): pp. 273–286.

Seneca, Annaeus. *Seneca's Moral Epistles*. Selected and edited with an Introduction by Anna Lydia Motto. Wauconda: Bolchazy-Carducci Publishers, 2001.

Shearman, John. *The Power of Images: Studies in the History and Theory of Response.* Chicago: University of Chicago Press, 1989.

Smith, Pamela H. and Paula Findlen. *Merchants and Marvels: Commerce, Science and Art in Early Modern Europe*. New York, London: Routledge, 2002.

Sohm, Philip L. *Style in the Art Theory of Early Modern Italy*. Cambridge: Cambridge University Press, 2001.

Soussloff, Catherine M. 'Imitatio Buonarroti', *Sixteenth Century Journal* 20/4 (1989): pp. 581–602.

Spicer, Joaneath A. '*Adam and Eve after the* Fall by Paulus van Viannen and the Interrelationship of the Arts', *Prague um 1600: Beiträge zur Kunst und Kultur am Hofe Rudolfs II*. Freren: Luca Verlag, 1988. pp. 273–283.

Springell, Francis C. *Connoisseur and Diplomat, The Earl of Arundel's Embassy to Germany in 1636 as Recounted in William Crowne's Diary, the Earl's Letters and other Contemporary Sources with a Catalogue of the Topographical Drawings made on the Journey by Wenceslaus Hollar*. London: Maggs, 1963.

Springer, A. 'Vorbilder zu zwei Dürerschen Hand zeichnungen in der Ambraser Sammlung', *Mitteilungen der Kaiserlich-Königlichen Central-Commission zur Erforschung und Erhaltung der Baudenkmale*, 7 (1862): p. 80.

Sřoněk, Michal. 'Sculpture and Painting in Prague, 1550–1650', *Rudolf II and Prague: The Court and the City*. Ed. Eliška Fučíková. London: Thames and Hudson, 1997. pp. 353–375.

Stackelberg, Jürgen von. 'Das Bienengleichnis: Ein Beitrag zur Geschichte der literarischen *Imitatio*', *Romanische Forschungen* 68 (1956): pp. 271–293.

Stauber, Richard. *Die Schedelsche Bibliothek*. Edited by Otto Hartig. Freiburg im Breisgau: Herder, 1908.

Steiner, Reinhard. '"Idea del Tempio della Pittura": Giovanni Paolo Lomazzo und die Entstehung des "Kanonschrift"', *Kunstforum International* 162 (2002): pp. 96–101.

Steinraths, Felix J.F. *Albrecht Dürers Memorialtafeln aus der Zeit um 1500: Holzschuher Epitaph-Glimm'sche Bewinung-Paumgartner-Altar; Rezeption, Forschungsstand und offene Fragen*. Doctoral dissertation, Universität München, 1998. Frankfurt am Main: Lang, 2000.

Strauss, Walter, ed. *Hendrik Goltzius (1558–1617): The Complete Engravings and Woodcuts*. New York: Abaris Books, 1977.

Strauss, Walter ed. *The Complete Engravings, Etchings and Drypoints of Albrecht Durer*. New York: Dover Publications, 1972.

Strieder, Peter. 'Albrecht Dürers *Vier Apostel* im Nürnberger Rathaus', *Festschrift Klaus Lankheit*. Edited by Wolfgang Hartmann. Cologne: M. DuMont Schauberg, 1973. pp. 151–157.

Stumpel, Jeroen and Joelein van Kregten. 'In the name of the thistle: Albrecht Dürer's self-portrait of 1493', *Burlington Magazine* 1186 (2002): pp. 14–18.

Taylor, Francis Henry. *The Taste of Angels. A History of Art Collecting from Rameses to Napoleon*. Boston: Little, Brown, 1948.

Térey, Gabriel von. 'Eine Kunstkammer des 17. Jahrhunderts', *Repertorium für Kunstwissenschaft* 19 (1896): pp. 31–35.

Thausing, Moritz. *Dürer: Geschichte seines Lebens und seiner Kunst*. Leipzig: E.E. Seemann, 1884.

Thompson, Martyn P. 'Reception Theory and the Interpretation of Historical Meaning', *History and Theory* 32/3 (1993): pp. 248–272.

Tietze, Hans and Erika Tietze-Conrat. *Der junge Dürer*. Augsburg: B. Filser, 1928.

Tomasi, Lucia Tongiorgi. 'Daniel Froeschl before Prague: his artistic activity in Tuscany at the Medici Court', *Prague um 1600: Beiträge zur Kunst und Kultur am Hofe Rudolfs II*. Freren: Luca Verlag, 1988. pp. 289–298.

Troutman, Philip. Albrecht *Dürer: Sketchbook of his Journey to the Netherlands, 1520–21.* London: Elek, 1971.

Trux, Elisabeth M. Untersuchung zu den Tierstudien Albrecht Dürers. Würzburg: Ergon, 1993.

Ulrichs, Ludwig. 'Beiträge zur Geschichte der Kunstbestrebungen und Sammlungen Kaiser

Rudolf's II. 3. Die Sammlung Granvella', *Zeitschrift für bildende Kunst* 5 (1870): pp. 136–141.

Urbánková, Emma. *Rukopisy a vzáčné tisky Pražské Universitní Knihovny*. Prague: Státní Pedagogické Nakladatelství, 1957.

Urzidil, Johannes. *Wenceslaus Hollar, der Kupferstecher des Barock*. Vienna: R. Passner, 1936.

Velde, A.J.J. 'Les Livres des sciences de la Natur de Conrad Gessner et Ulysse Aldrovandi', *Biologisch Jaarboek Dodonaea* 17 (1950): pp. 195–199.

Venturi, Lionello Venturi. *History of Art Criticism*. Translated from the Italian by Charles Marriott. New York: E.P. Dutton, 1964.

Vignau-Wilberg, Thea. 'Künstlerische Beziehungen zwischen Prag und München zur Zeit Rudolfs II', *Prague um 1600: Beiträge zur Kunst und Kultur am Hofe Rudolfs II.* Freren: Luca Verlag, 1988. pp. 299–308.

Vignau-Wilberg, Thea. *Durch die Blume: Natursymbolik um 1600*. Munich: Staatliche Graphische Sammlung, 1991.

Vincent, B. 'Une copie de la fête du Rosaire d'Albert Dürer', *Bulletin des Musées et Monuments Lyonais* 4 (1969/71): pp. 165–170.

Vlnas, Vit. 'Der Kampf um Dürers Rosenkranzfest im Jahr 1928', *Bulletin of the National Gallery in Prague* 2 (1992): pp. 111–120.

Walther, Sigrid. *Hans Süss von Kulmbach*. Dresden: Verlag der Kunst, 1981.

Warburg, Aby. *The Renewal of Pagan Antiquity: Contributions to the Cultural History of the European Renaissance*. Introduction by Kurt W. Forster; translation by David Britt. Los Angeles: Getty Research Institute for the History of Art and the Humanities, 1999.

Weiss, Josef. 'Kurfürst Maximilian von Bayern als Gemäldesammler. Neue archivalische Beiträge', *Historisch-politische Blätter für.das katholische Deutschland* 142 (1908): pp. 545–569.

Wessely, Joseph Eduard, 'Das Manuscript von Paul Beheim's Kupferstichkatalog im Berliner Museums', *Repertorium für Kunstwissenshcaft* 6 (1883): pp. 54–63.

Wettengl, Kurt, ed. *Georg Flegel (1566–1638): Stilleben*. Stuttgart: G.Hatje, 1993.

White, Harold Ogden. *Plagiarism and Imitation during the English Renaissance: A Study in Critical Distinctions*. Cambridge: Cambridge University Press, 1935.

Wickhoff, Franz. 'Beiträge zur Geschichte der Reproducierenden Künste: Marcantons Eintritt in den Kreis Römischer Kunstler', *Jahrbuch der kunsthistorischer Sammlungen der allerhöchsten Kaiserhauses* 20 (1899): pp. 181–194.

Wilson, Jean C. 'Enframing Aspirations: Albrecht Dürer's Self-Portrait of 1493 in the Musée du Louvre', *Gazette des Beaux Arts* 126 (1995): pp. 149–158.

Winkler, Friedrich. *Albrecht Durer: Leben und Werk*. Berlin: Gebr. Mann, 1957.

Wölfflin, Heinrich. *Drawings of Albrecht Durer*. New York: Dover Publications, 1970.

Woods-Marsden, Joanna. *Renaissance Self-Portraiture: The Visual Construction of Identity and the Social Status of the Artist*. New Haven, London: Yale University Press, 1998.

Wuttke, Dieter. Humanismus als Integrative Kraft: die Philosophia des deutschen 'Erzhumanisten' in *Conrad Celtis: eine ikonologische Studie zu programmatischer Graphik Dürers und Burgkmairs*. Nürnberg: H. Carl, 1985.

Winter, Zikmund. *Řemeslnictvo a živnosti XVI. věku v Čechách,1526–1620*. Prague: Ceské akademie císaře Františka Josefa, 1909. pp. 209–210.

Zander-Seidel, Jutta. Textiler *Hausrat – Kleidung und Haustextilien in Nürnberg von 1500–1650*. München: Deutscher Kunstverlag, 1990.

Zerner, Henri. *Ecole de Fontainebleau Gravures*. Paris: Arts et métiers graphiques, 1969.

Zimmerman, Max Georg. *Die Bildenden Kunst am Hof Herzog Albrechts V*. Strassburg, J.H.E. Heitz, 1895.

Zorach, Rebecca, ed. *Paper museums: the reproductive print in Europe, 1500–1800*. Chicago: David and Alfred Smart Museum of Art, University of Chicago, 2005.

Exhibition catalogues

Berlin 1971. Hinz, B. ed. *Dürers Gloria. Kunst, Kult, Konsum: Ausstellung der Kunstbibliothek Staatliche Museen Preussischer Kulturbesitz Berlin, 24. September bis 28. November 1971*. Edited by B. Hinz. Berlin: Mann Verlag, 1971.

Brussels 1977. Anzelewsky, Fedja ed. *Albrecht Dürer aux Pays-Bas, son voyage 1520–21, son influence*. Exhibition catalogue edited by Fedja Anzelewsky. Brussels: Palais des Beaux-Arts, 1977.

Coburg 1975. Gmelin, Hans Georg, ed. *Meisterwerke europäischer Grafik 15.–18. Jahrhundert aus dem Besitz des Kupferstichkabinettes Coburg: Kataloge der Kunstsammlungen der Veste Coburg*. Coburg: Kunstsammlungen der Veste Coburg, 1975.

Frankfurt 1981. Beck, Herbert and Berhard Decker. *Dürers Verwandlung in der Skulptur zwischen Renaissance und Barock: Ausstellung im Liebieghaus Museum Alter Plastik, Frankfurt Am Main, 1. November 1981 bis 17. Januar 1982*. Frankfurt am Main: Liebighaus Museum Alter Plastik, 1981.

Hannover 1979. Gmelin, Hans Georg, ed. *Dürerrenaissance um 1600: Im Blickpunkt*. Edited by Hans Georg Gmelin. Hannover: Niedersächsische Landesgalerie, 1979.

London 2002. Bartrum, Guilia, ed. *Albrecht Dürer and his Legacy: The Graphic Work of a Renaissance Artist*. London: The British Museum Press, 2002.

Munich 1971. *Dürer-Renaissance: München, 7. Mai–29. August 1971*. Edited by Gisela Goldberg and Barbara Heine. Munich: Alte Pinakothek, 1971.

Nuremberg 1994. Achilles-Syndram, Katrin, ed. *Kunst des Sammelns. Das Praunsche Kabinett. Meisterwerke von Dürer bis Carracci*. Nuremberg: Verlag des Germansichen Nationalmuseums, 1994.

Nürnberg, 1978. *Vorbild Dürer: Kupferstiche und Holzschnitte Albrecht Dürers im Speigel der europaischen Druckgraphik des 16. Jahrhunderts* (Ausstellung des Germanischen Nationalmuseums Nürnberg, 8. Juli bis 10. September 1978). Munich: Prestel Verlag, 1978.

Prague, 2006. Kotkova, Olga, ed. *Albrecht Durer: The Feast of the Rosegarlands 1506 2006*. Prague: Národní Galerie v Praze, 2006.

Vienna, 1994. Schütz, Karl and Bauer, Rotraud, eds. *Albrecht Dürer im Kunsthistorischen Museum*. Wien: Kunsthistorisches Museum, 1994.

Williamstown, 1975. *Dürer Through Other Eyes: His Graphic Work Mirrored in Copies and Forgeries of Three Centuries (An exhibition prepared by students in the Williams College-Clark Art Institute graduate program in art history, March 14–June 15, 1975*. Williamstown, Massachusetts: Sterling and Francine Clark Institute, 1975.

Appropriations of Dürer Portraits and Self-portraits

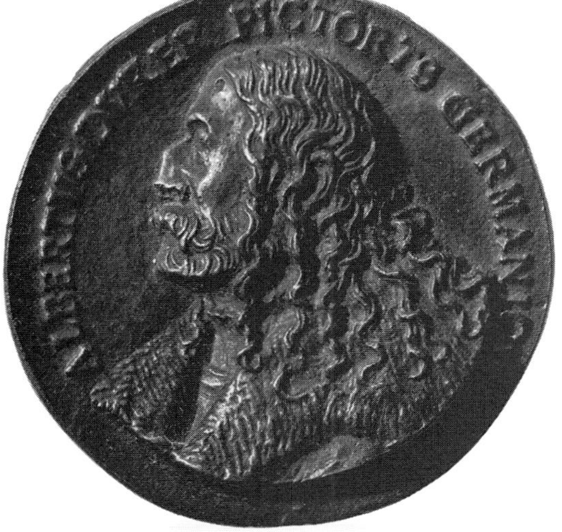

1 After Hans Schwarz, *Portrait of Albrecht Dürer*, late sixteenth century

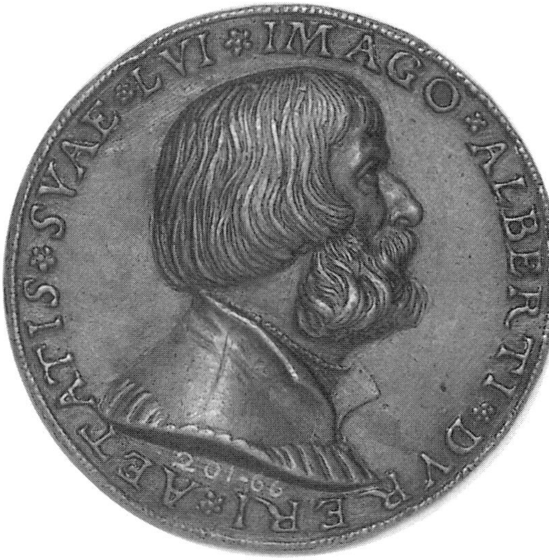

2 Mathis Gebel, *Portrait of Albrecht Dürer*, 1528

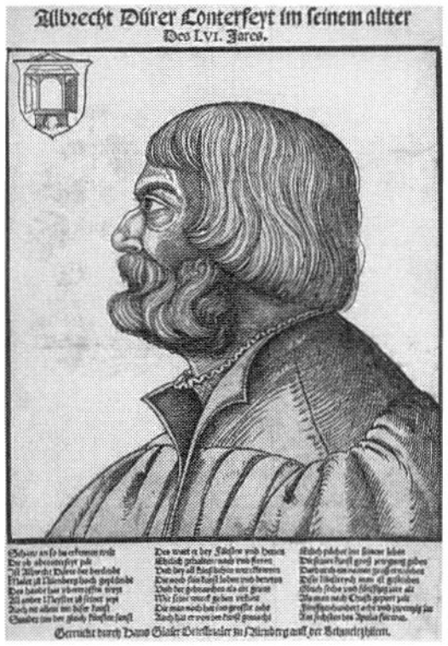

3 Erhard Schön, *Portrait of Albrecht Dürer*, *c.*1528–9

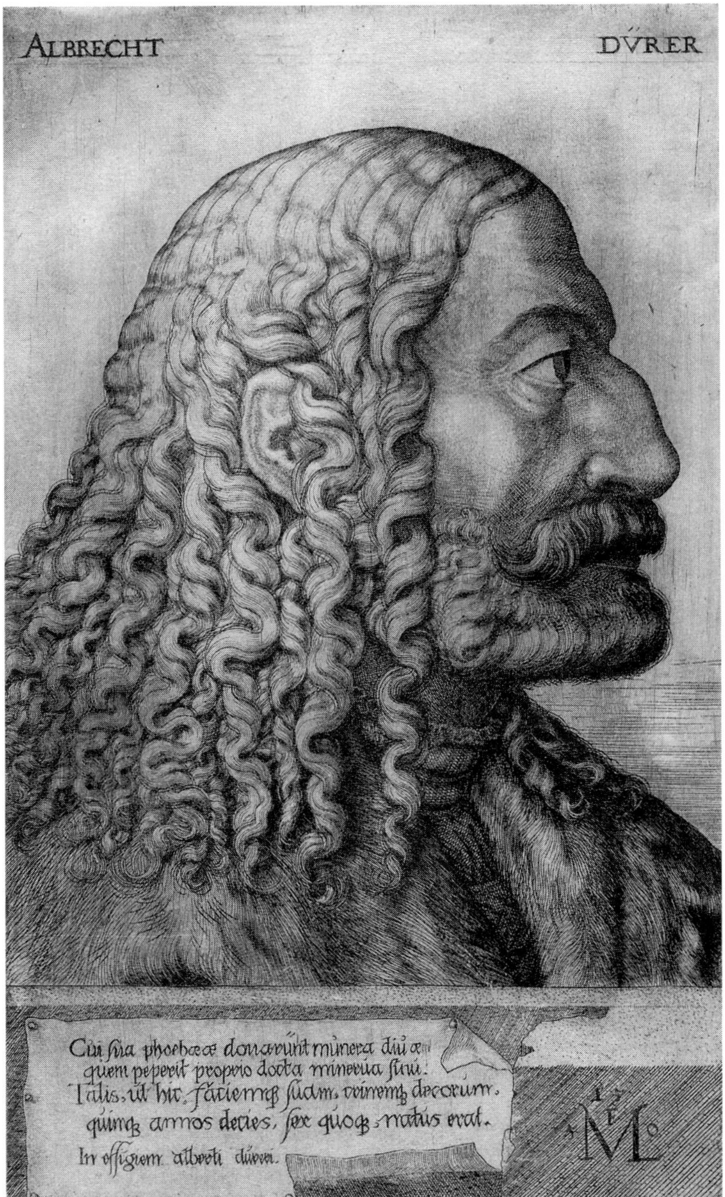

4 Melchior Lorck, *Portrait of Albrecht Dürer*, 1550

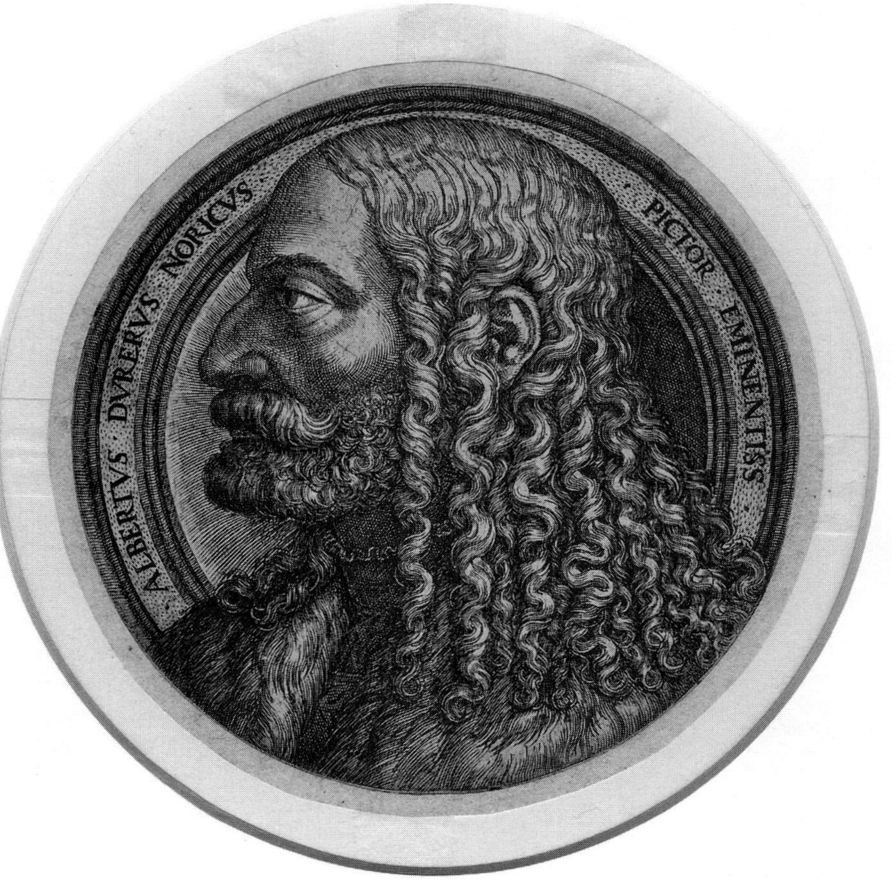

5 Anonymous, *Portrait of Albrecht Dürer*, *c.*1570

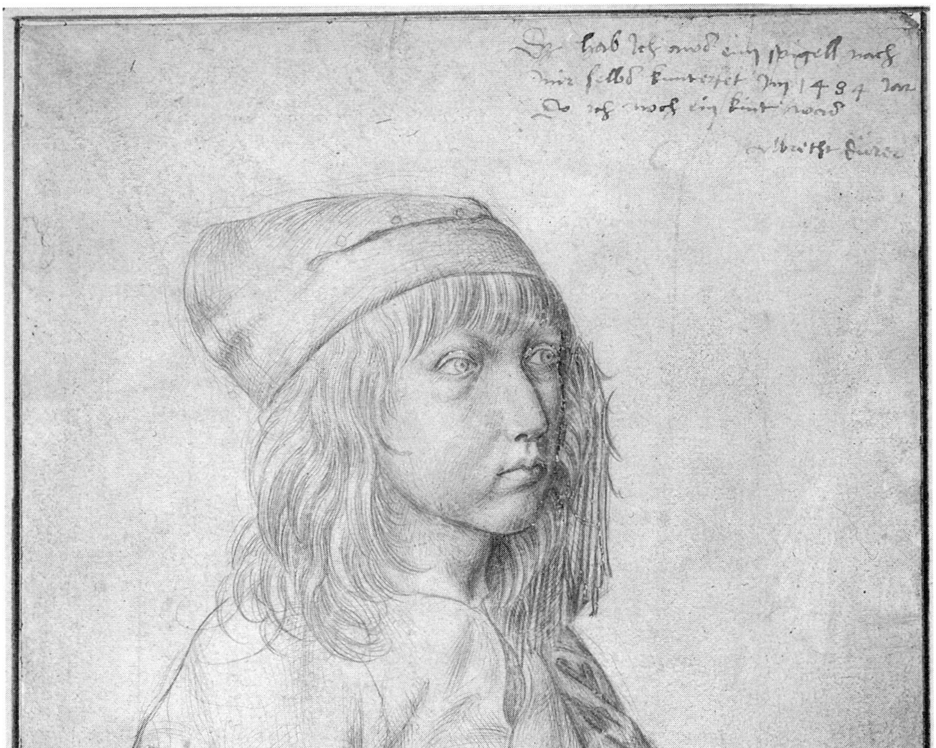

6 Albrecht Dürer, *Self-portrait at Thirteen*, 1484

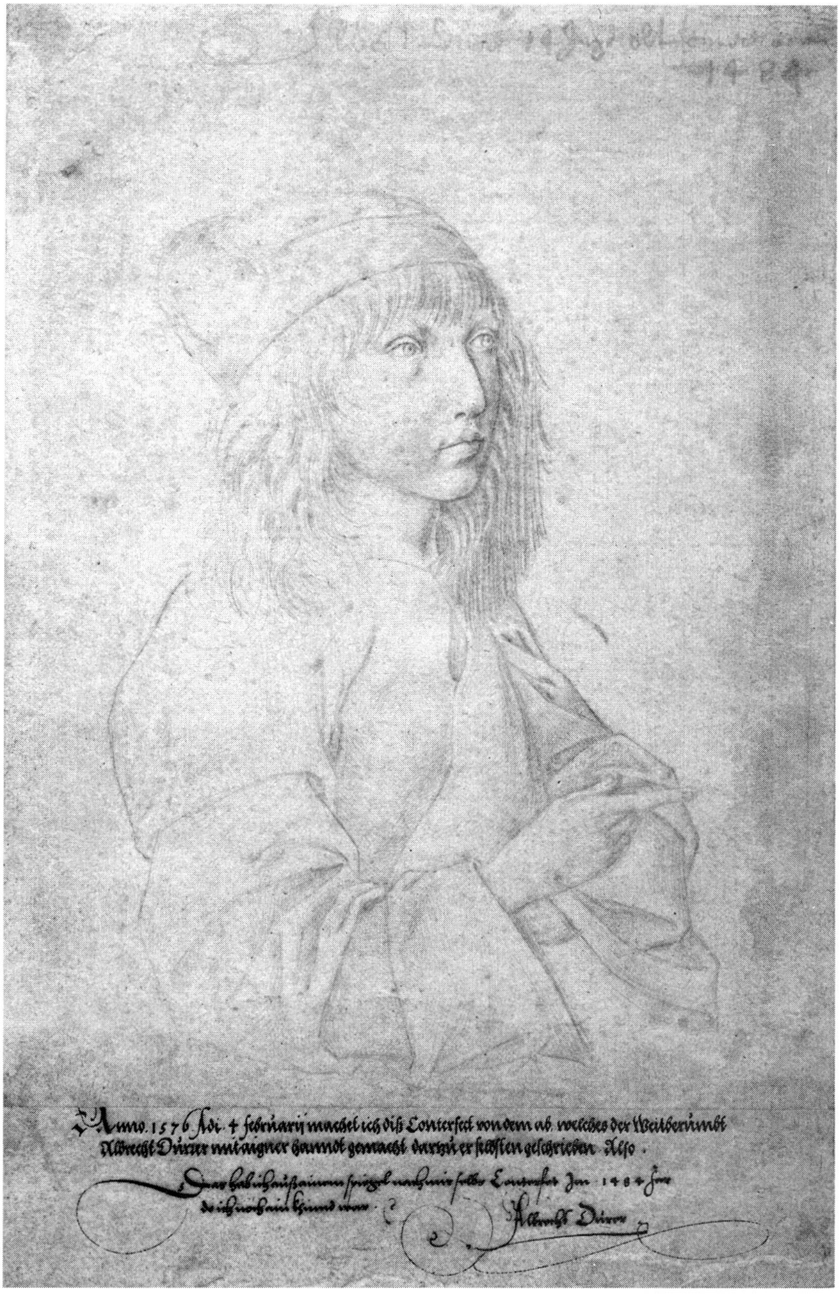

7 Hans Hoffmann after Albrecht Dürer, *Self-portrait at Thirteen*, 1576

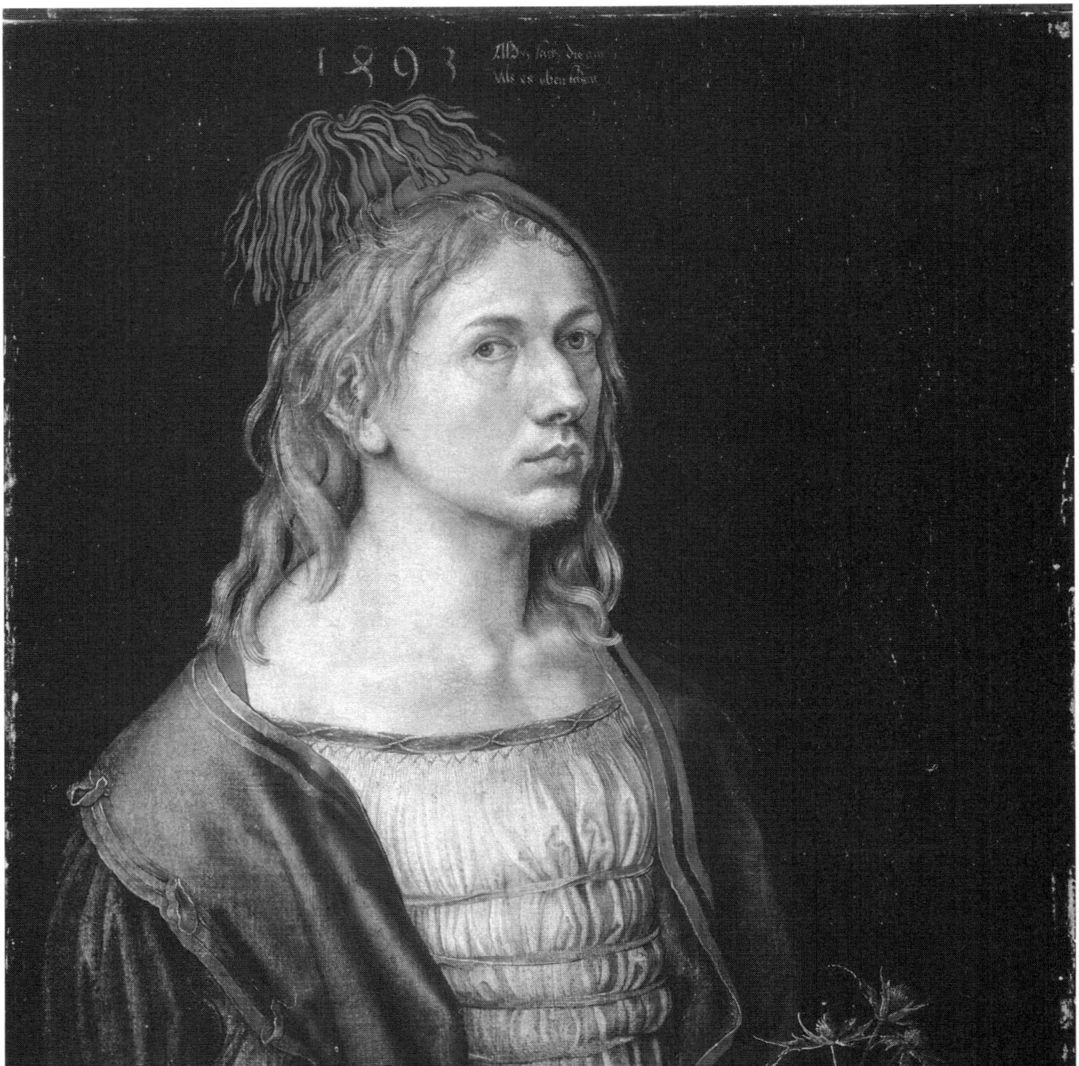

8 Albrecht Dürer, *Self-portrait at Twenty-two*, 1493

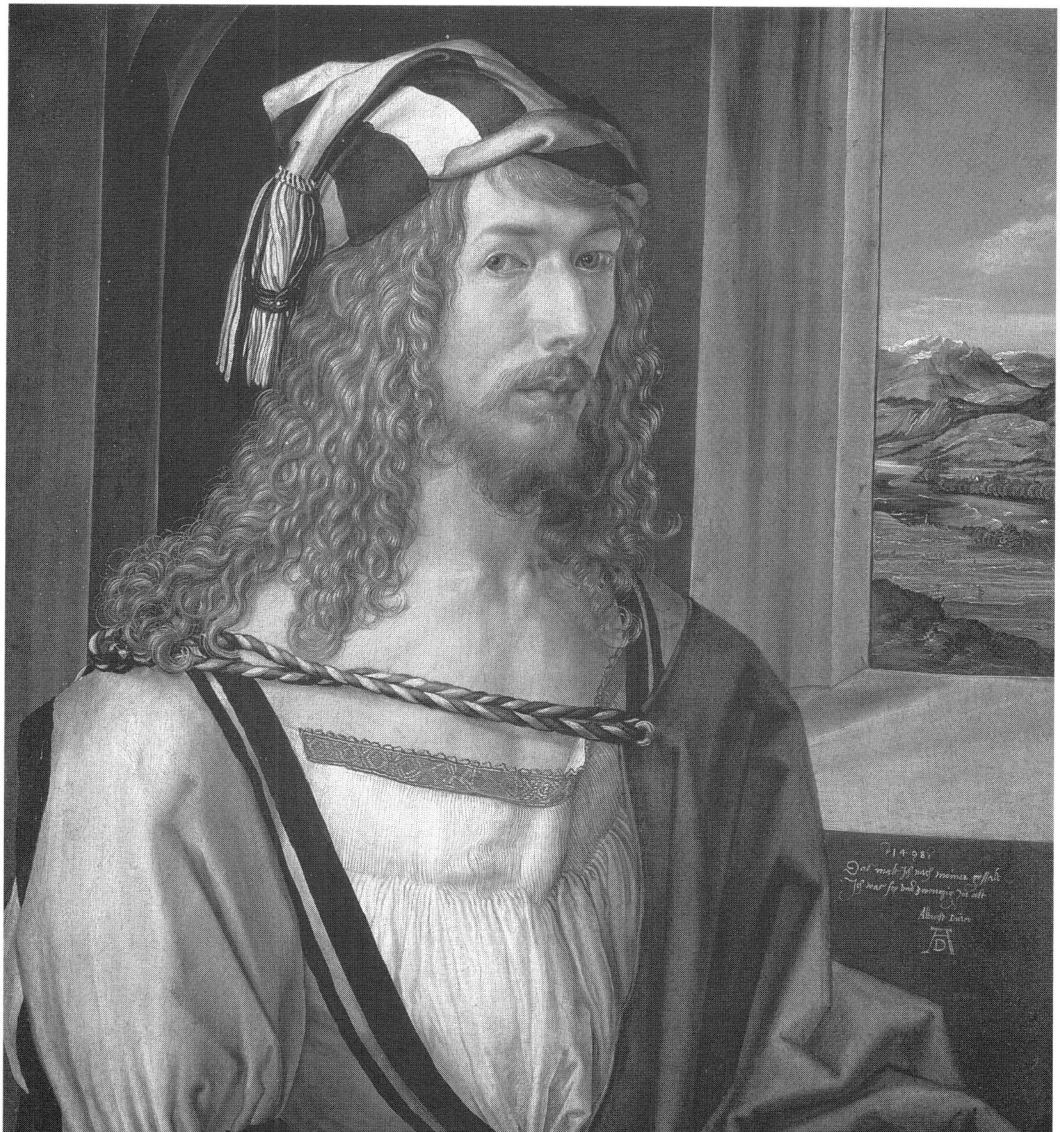

9 Albrecht Dürer, *Self-portrait at Twenty-six*, 1498

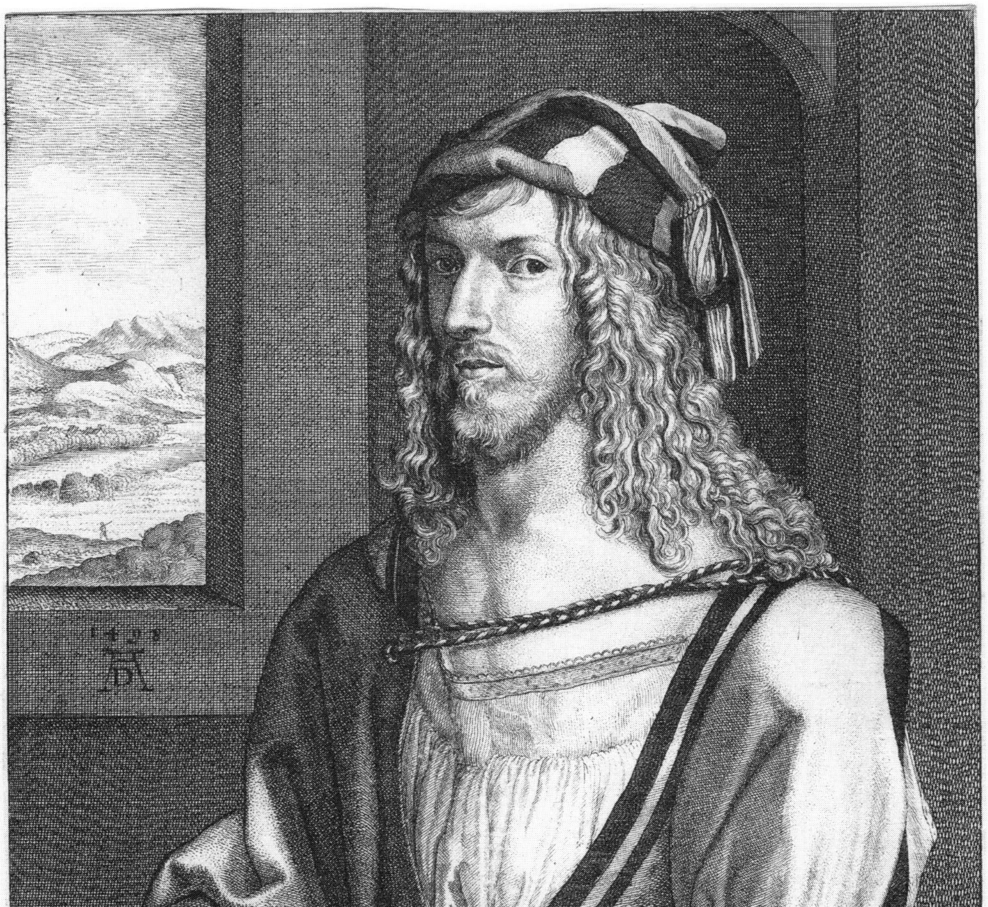

10 Wenceslaus Hollar after Albrecht Dürer, *Self-portrait at Twenty-six*, 1645

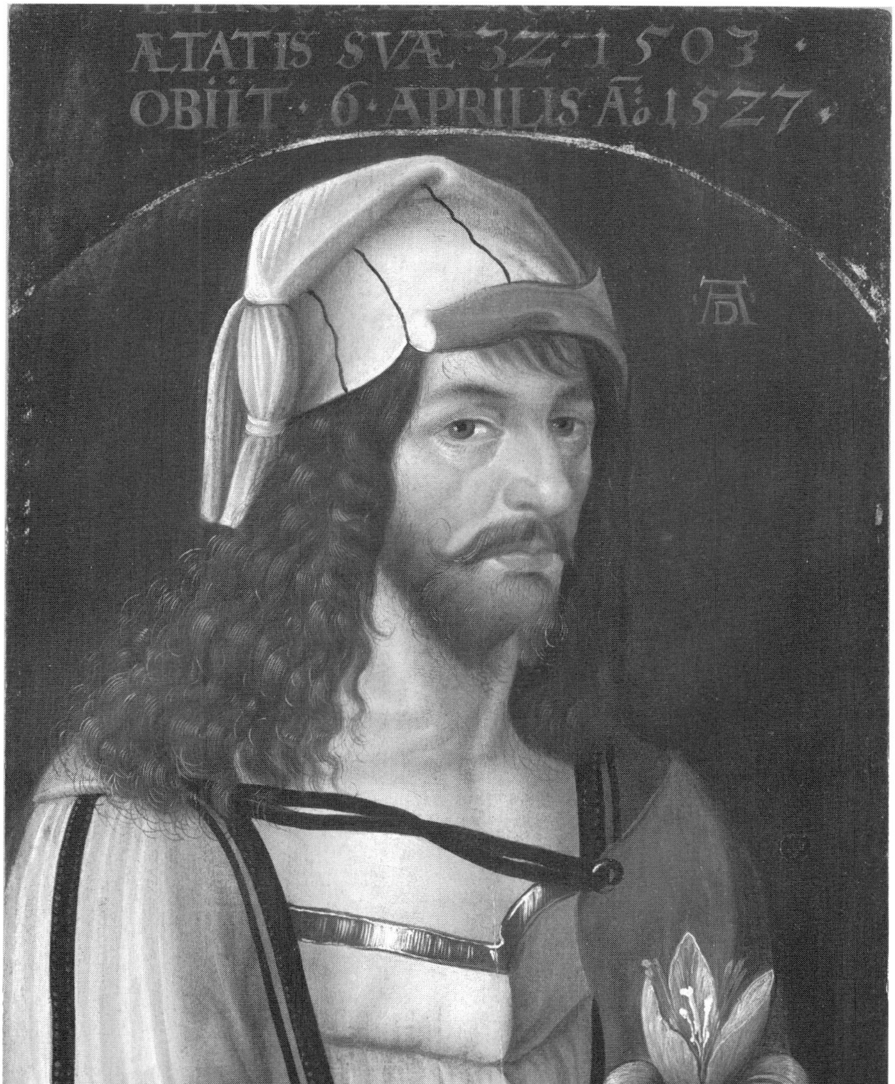

11 Anonymous after Albrecht Dürer, *Self-portrait at Twenty-six*, dated 1503 (?)

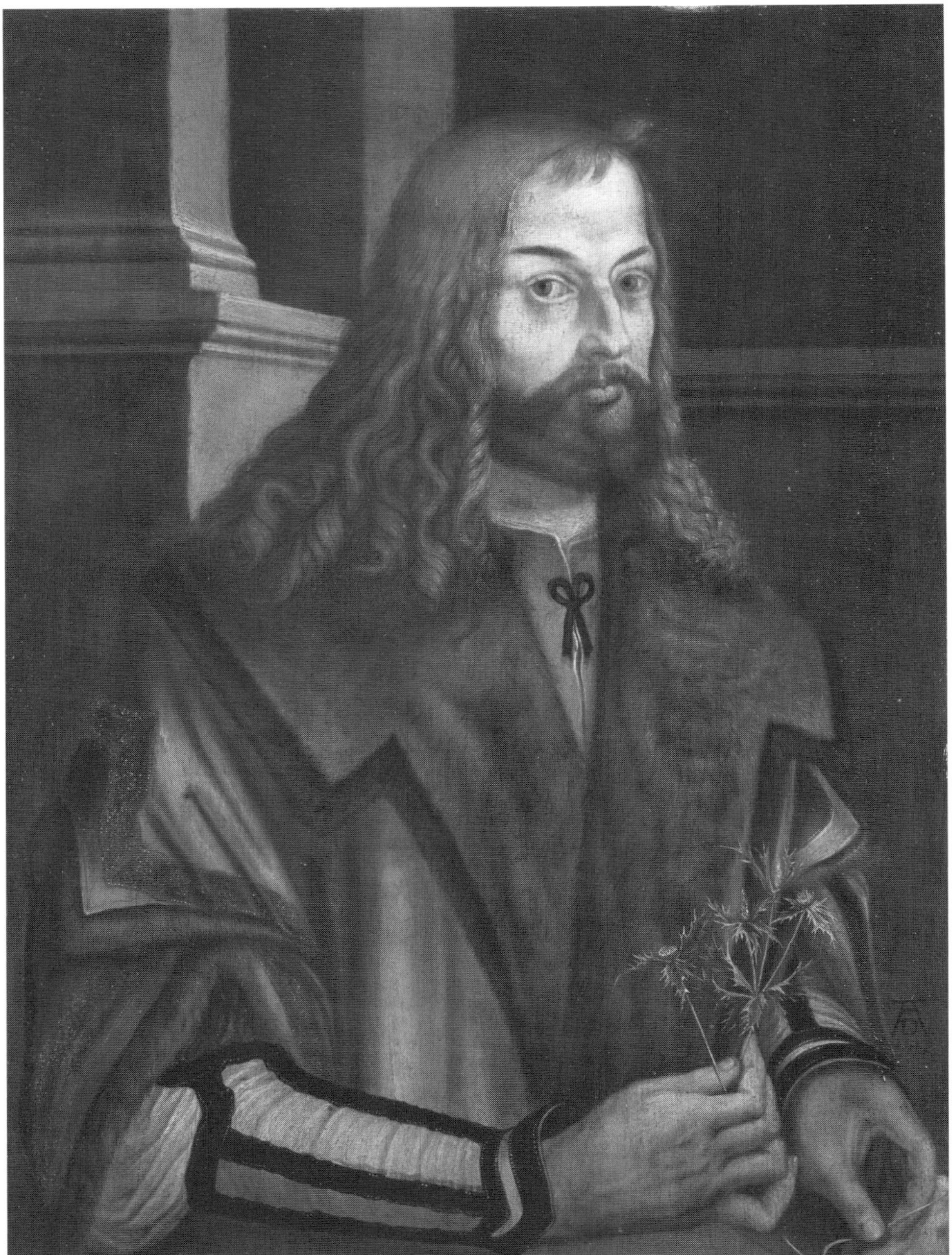

12 Anonymous, *Portrait of Albrecht Dürer*, late seventeenth century

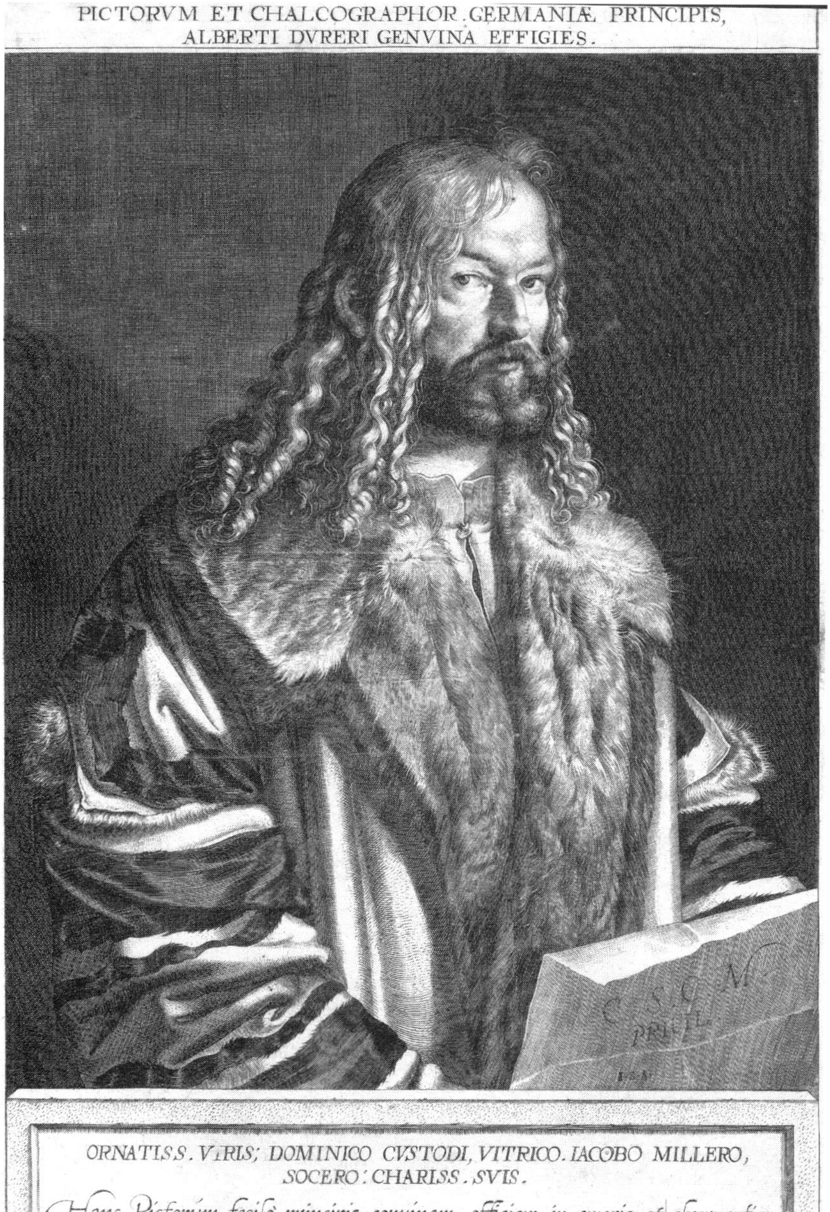

13 Lucas Kilian, *Portrait of Albrecht Dürer*, 1608

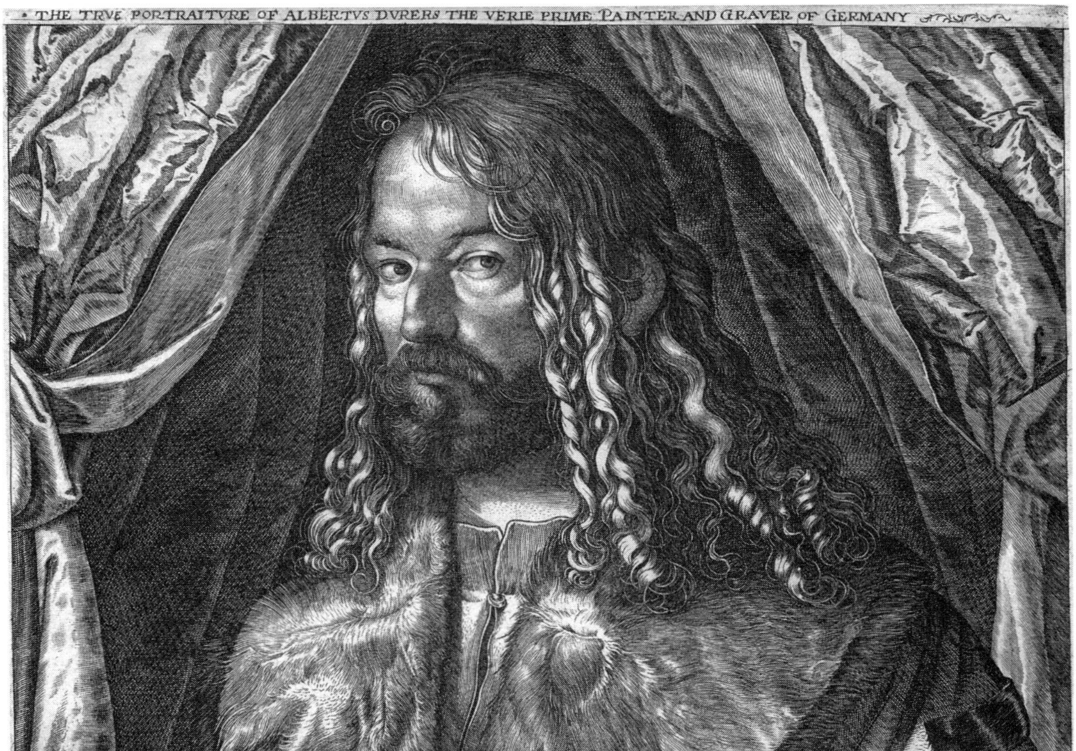

14 Francis Delaram, *Portrait of Albrecht Dürer*, *c.*1616–20

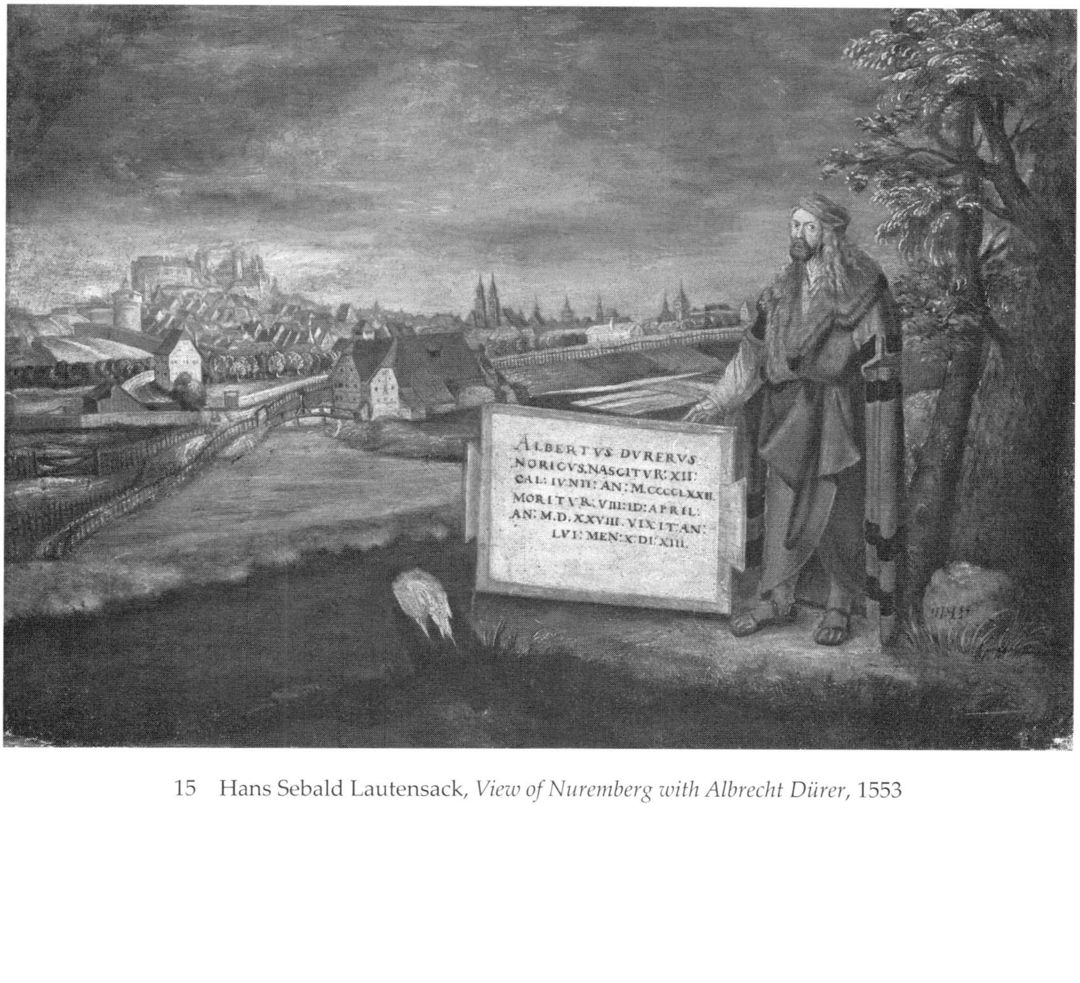

15 Hans Sebald Lautensack, *View of Nuremberg with Albrecht Dürer*, 1553

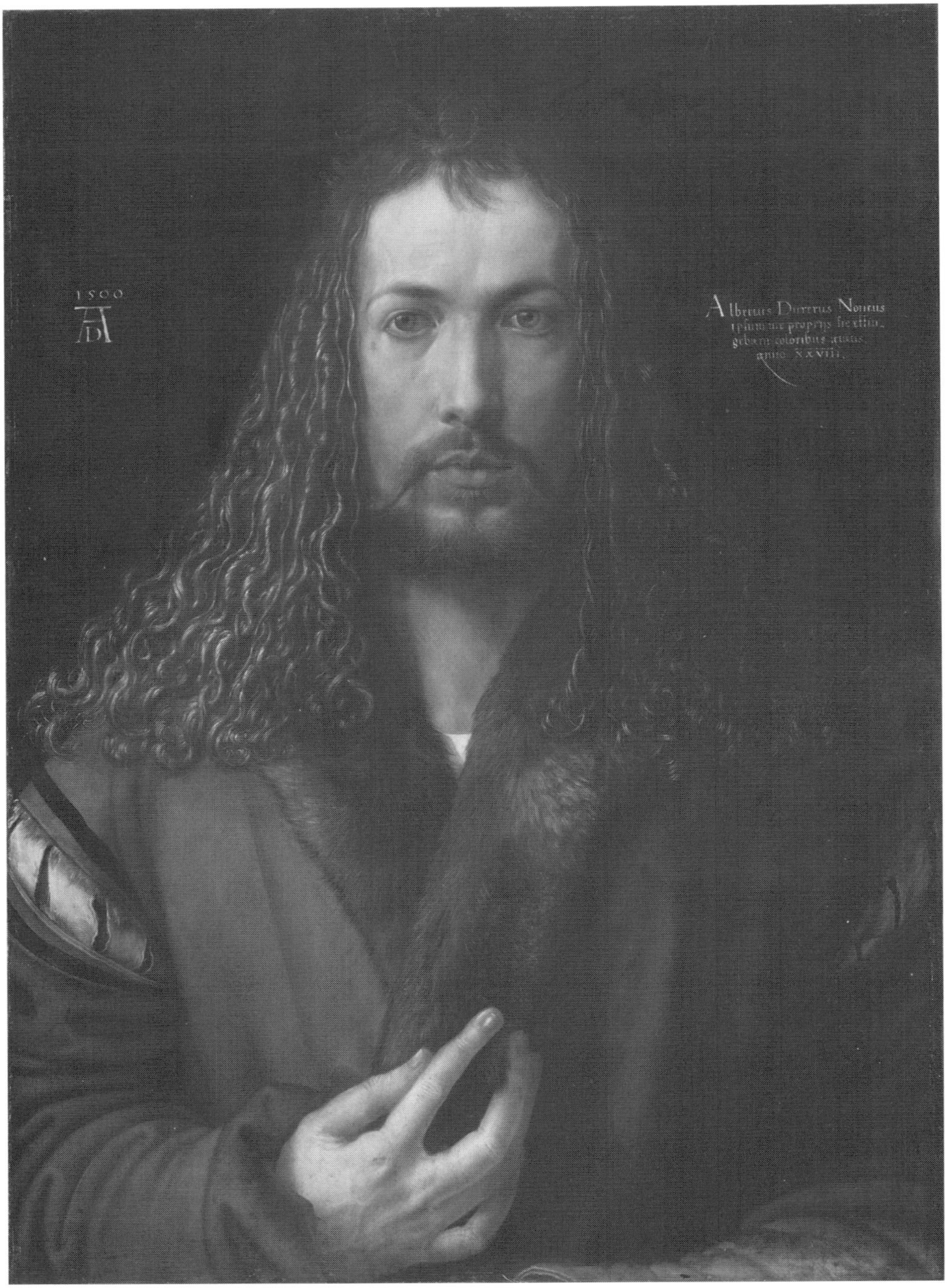

16 Albrecht Dürer, *Self-Portrait at the Age of Twenty-eight*, 1500

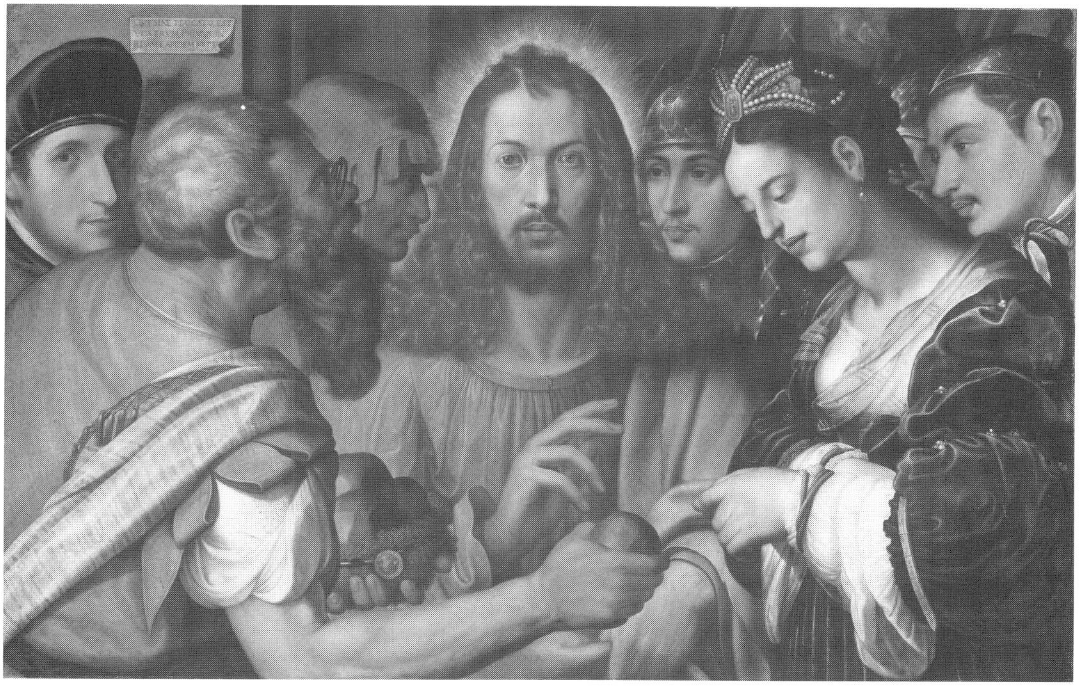

17 Georg Vischer, *Christ and the Adulterous Woman*, 1637

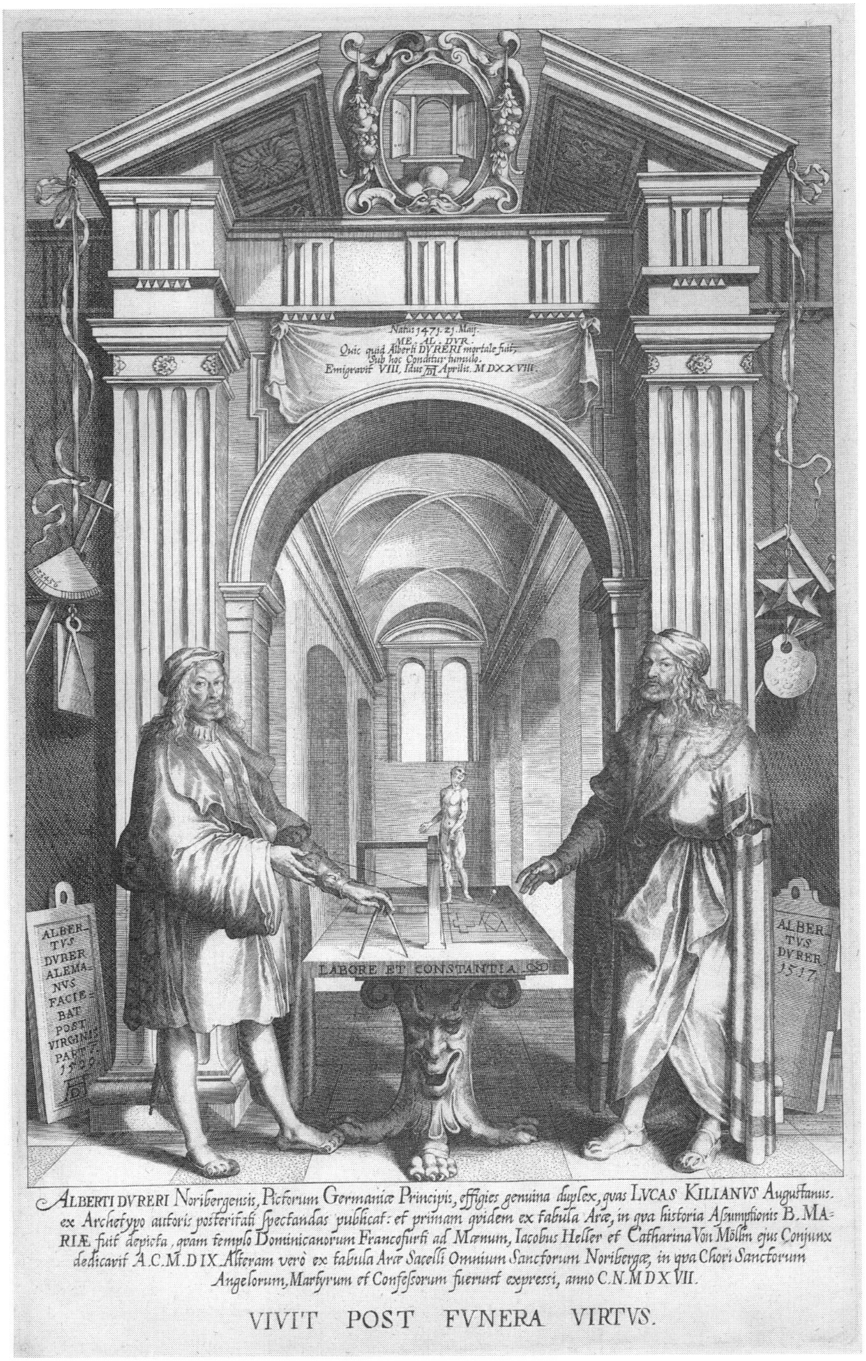

18 Lucas Kilian, *Double Portrait of Albrecht Dürer*, 1617

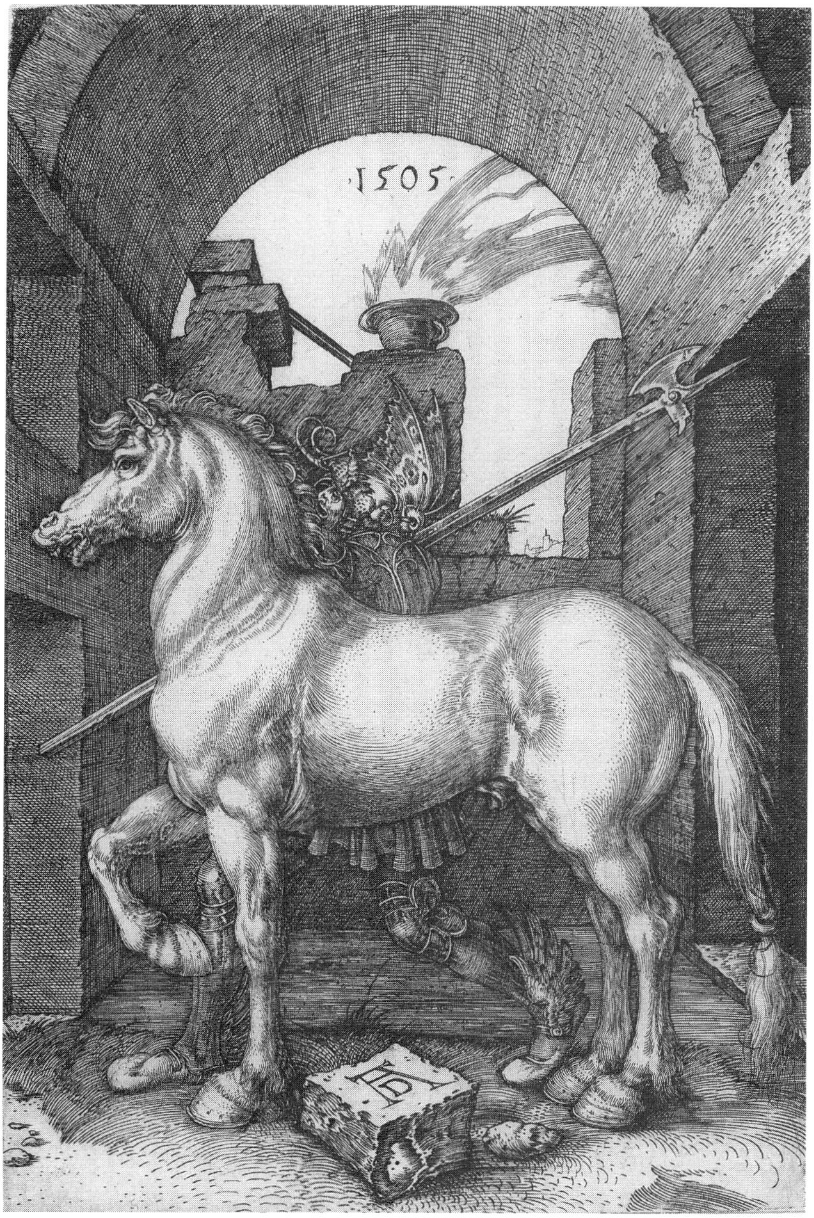

19 Albrecht Dürer, *Small Horse*, 1505

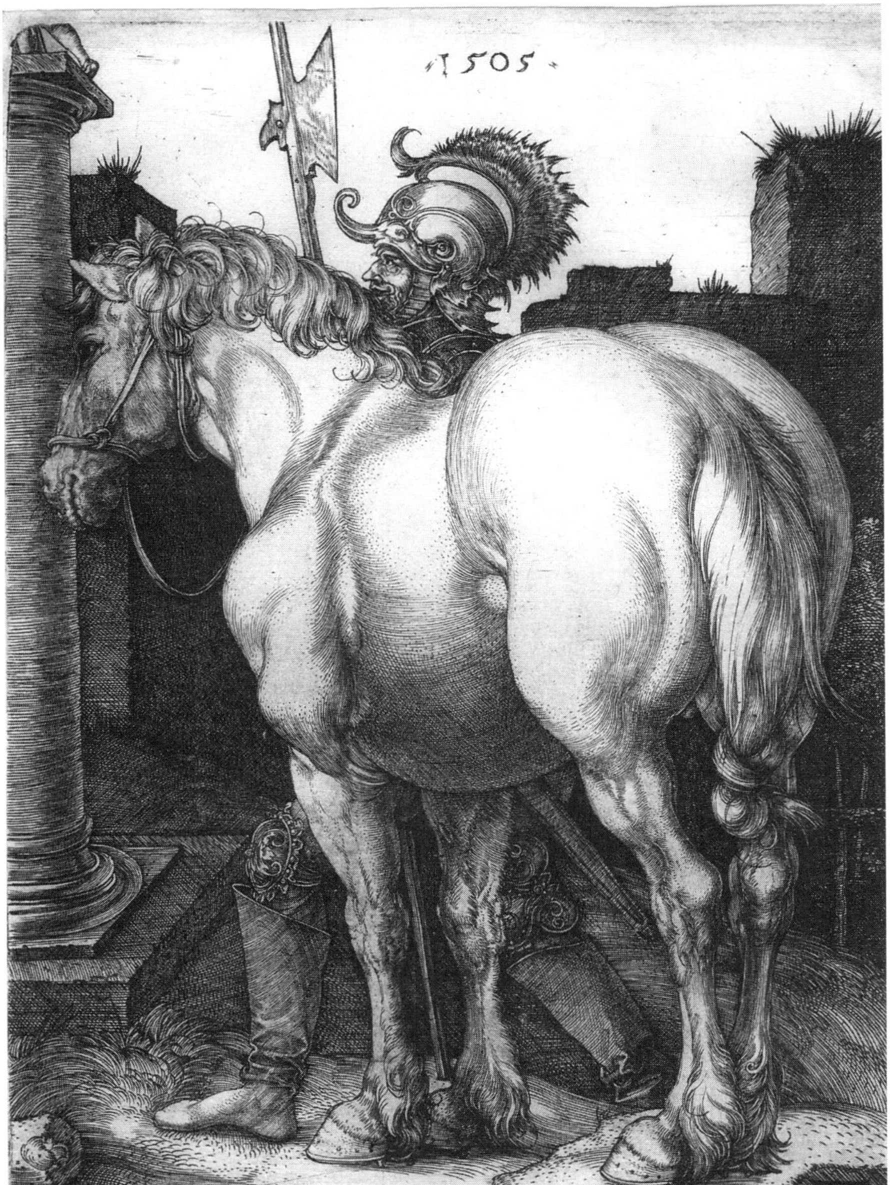

20 Albrecht Dürer, *Large Horse*, 1505

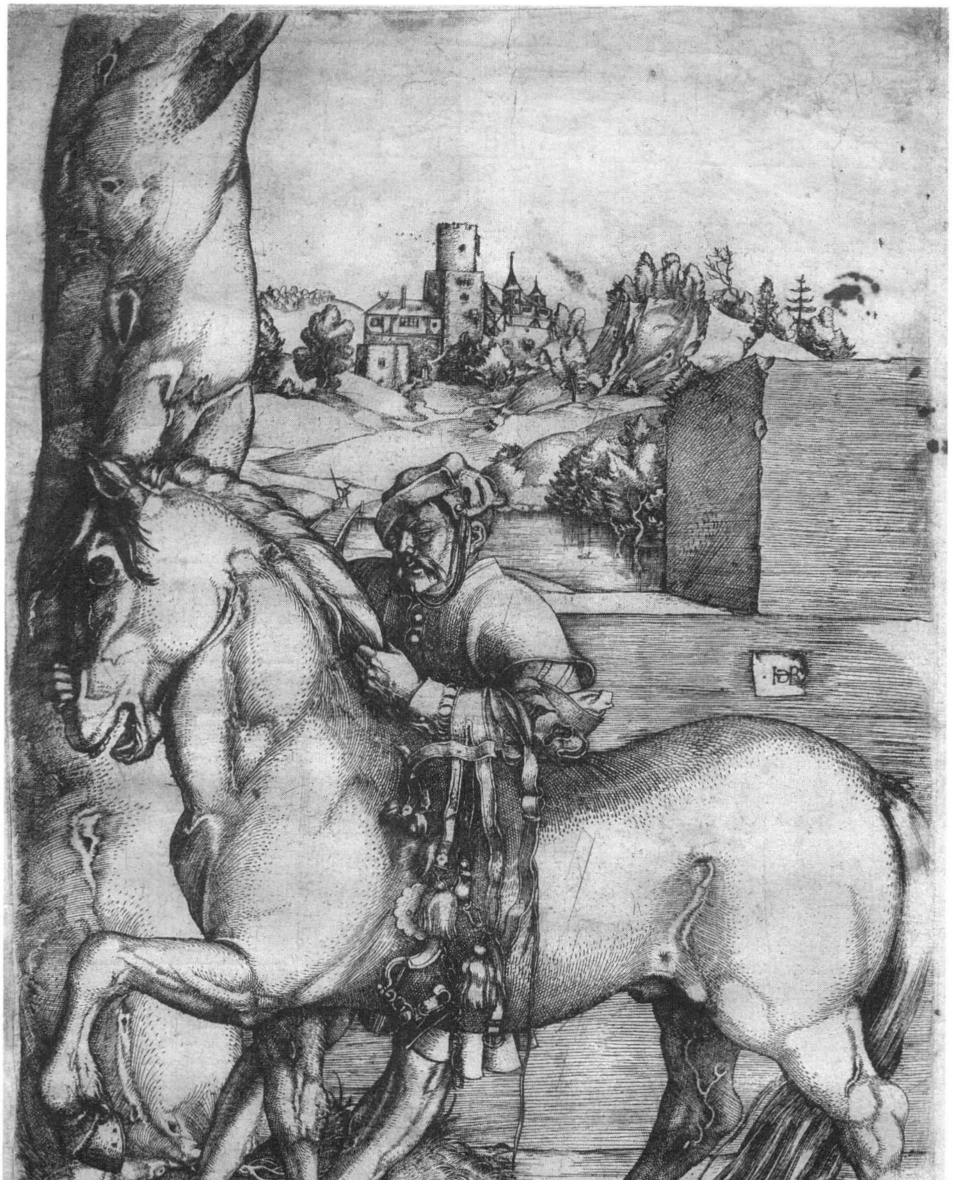

21 Hans Baldung, *Groom Bridling a Horse*, *c*.1510–12

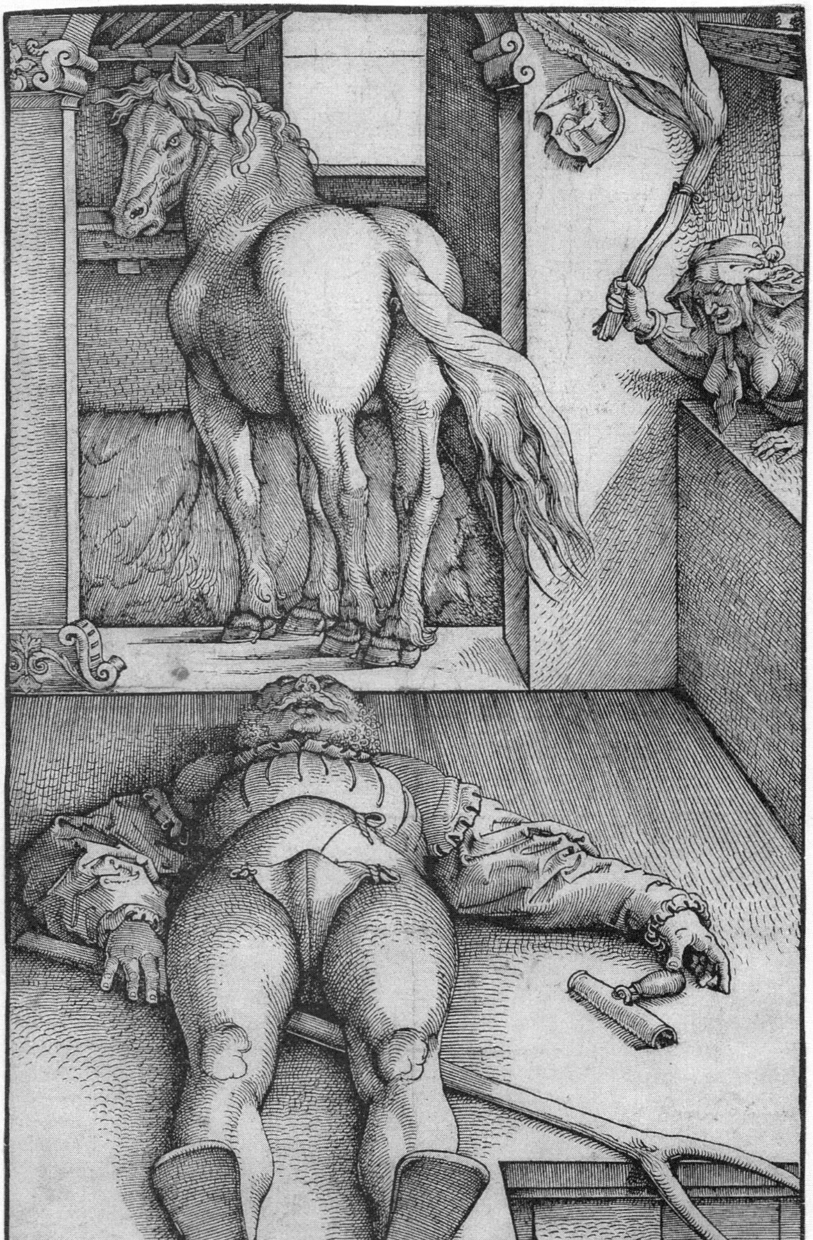

22 Hans Baldung, *Bewitched Groom*, 1544–45

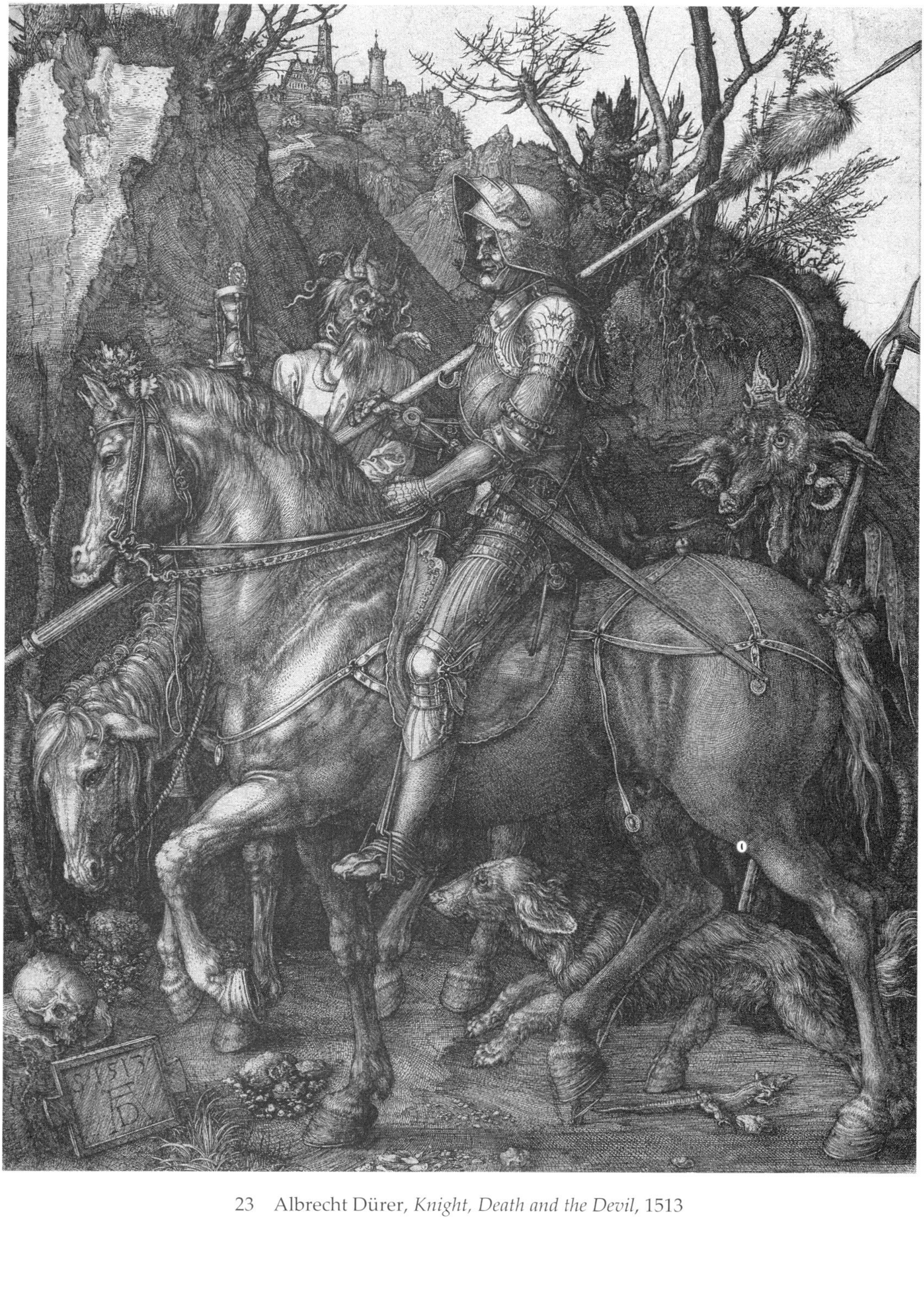

23 Albrecht Dürer, *Knight, Death and the Devil*, 1513

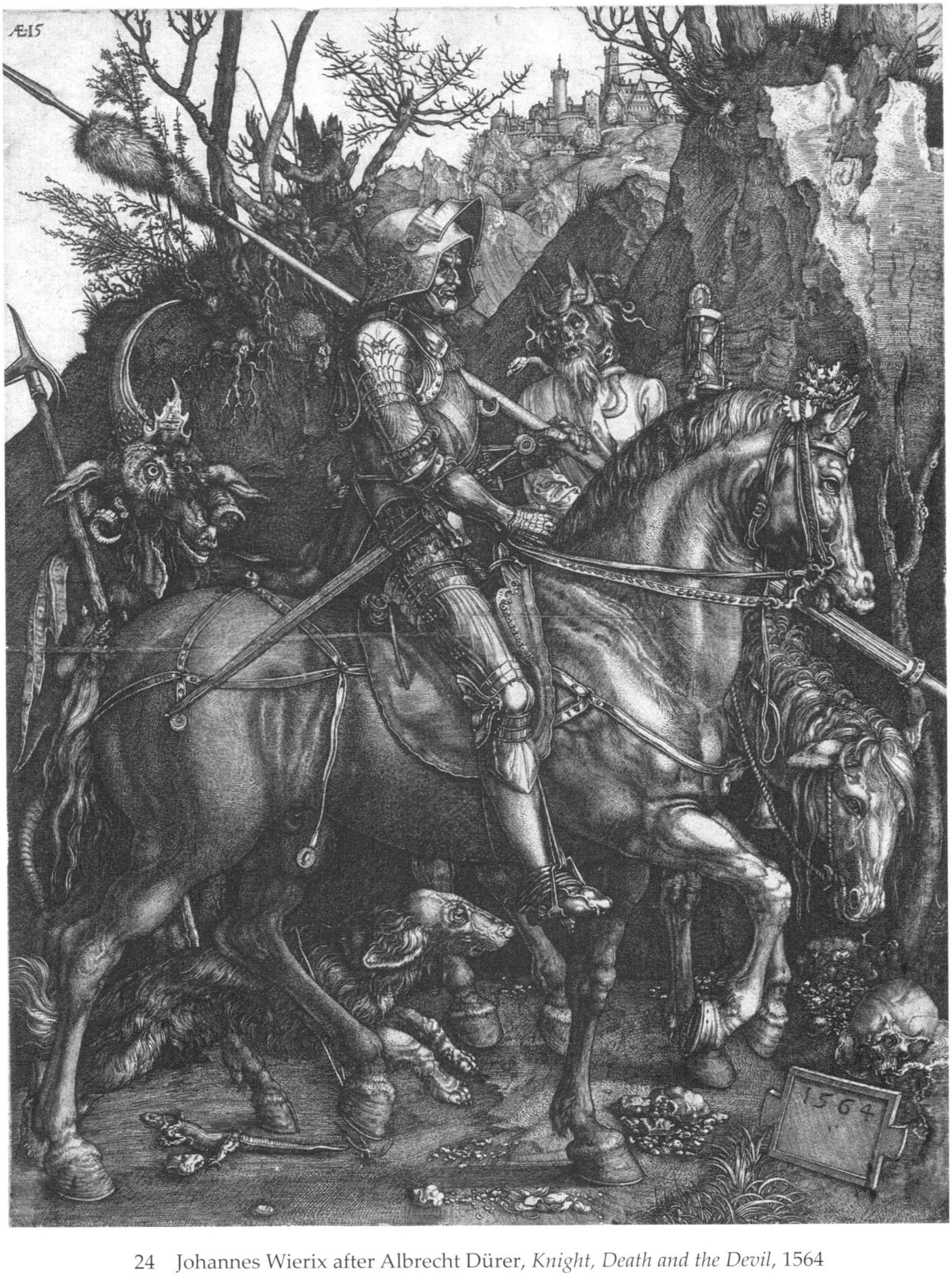

24 Johannes Wierix after Albrecht Dürer, *Knight, Death and the Devil*, 1564

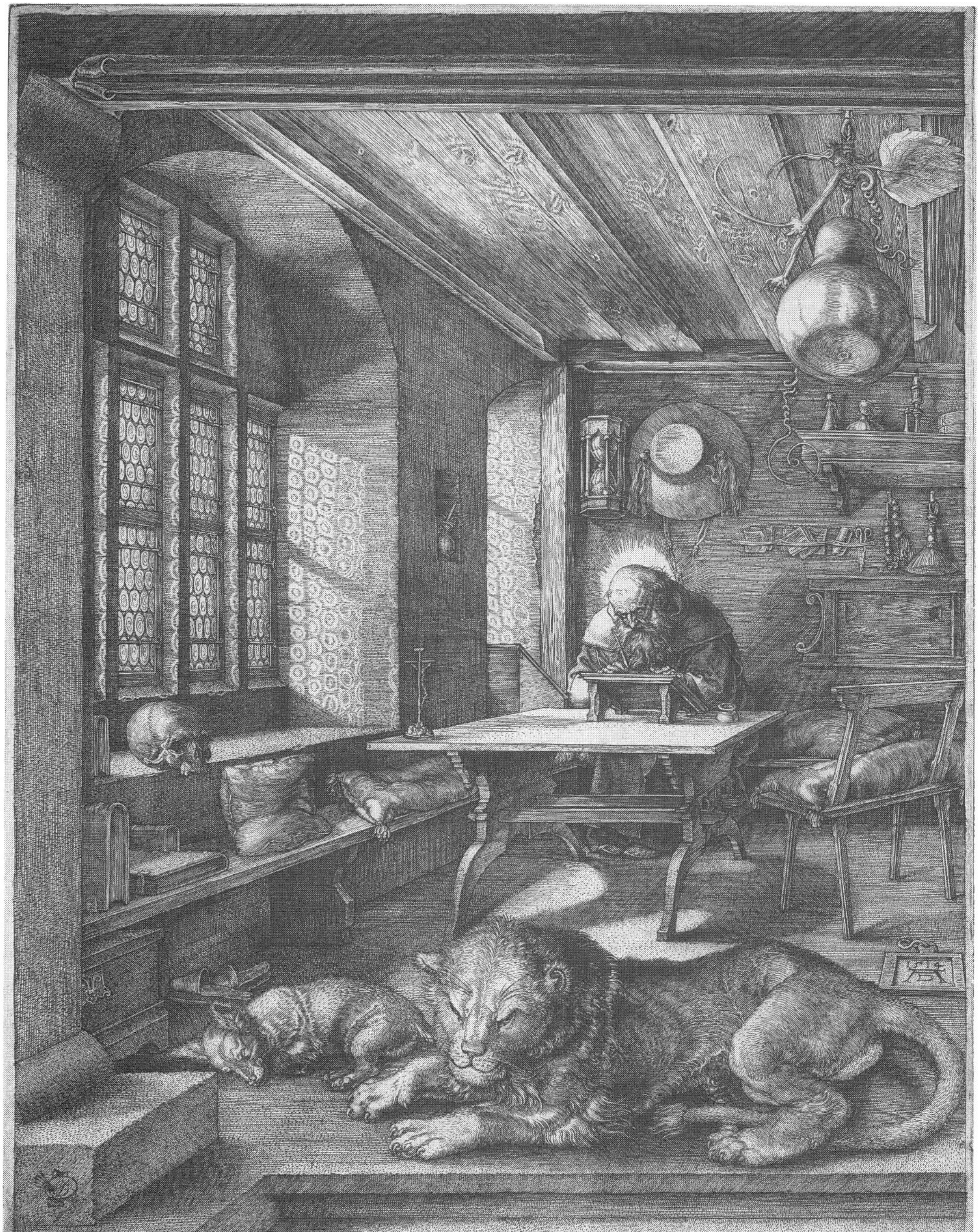

25 Albrecht Dürer, *St. Jerome in his Study*, 1514

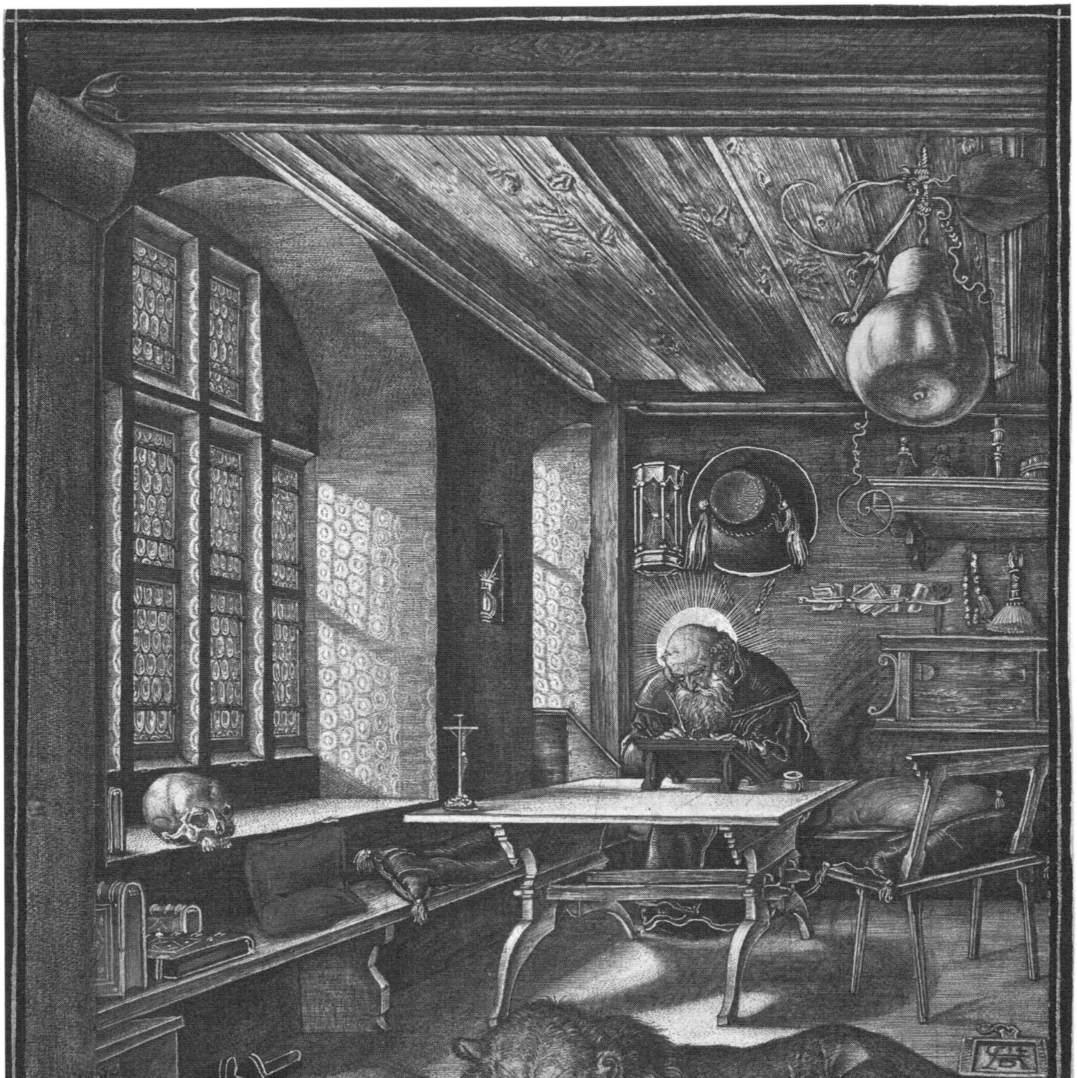

26 Domenicus Rottenhammer after Albrecht Dürer, *St. Jerome in his Study*, *c.*1600

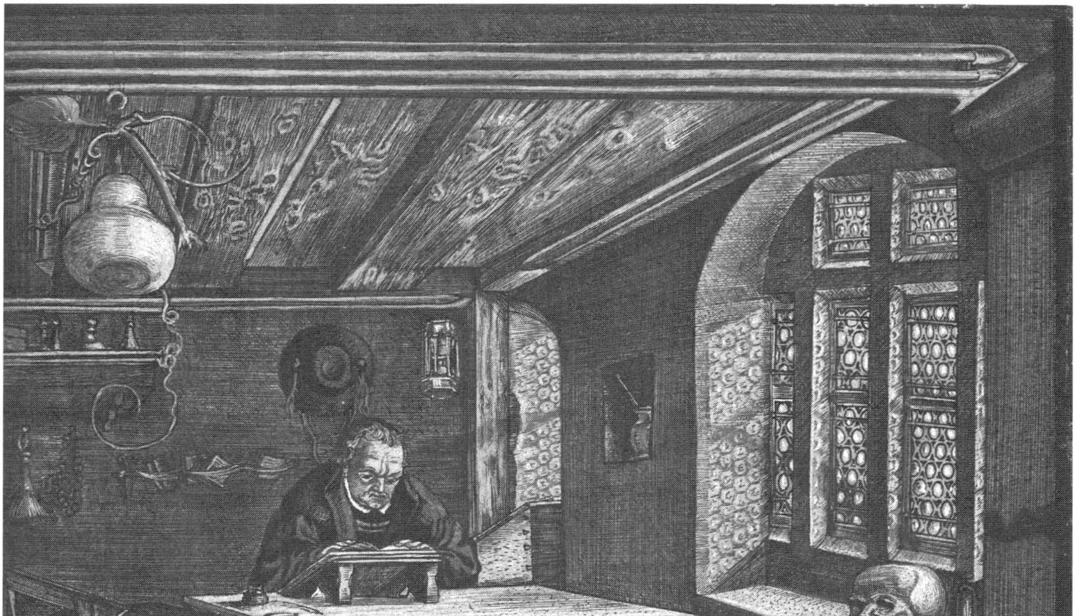

27 Wolfgang Stuber after Albrecht Dürer, *Luther as St. Jerome*, *c*.1587–88

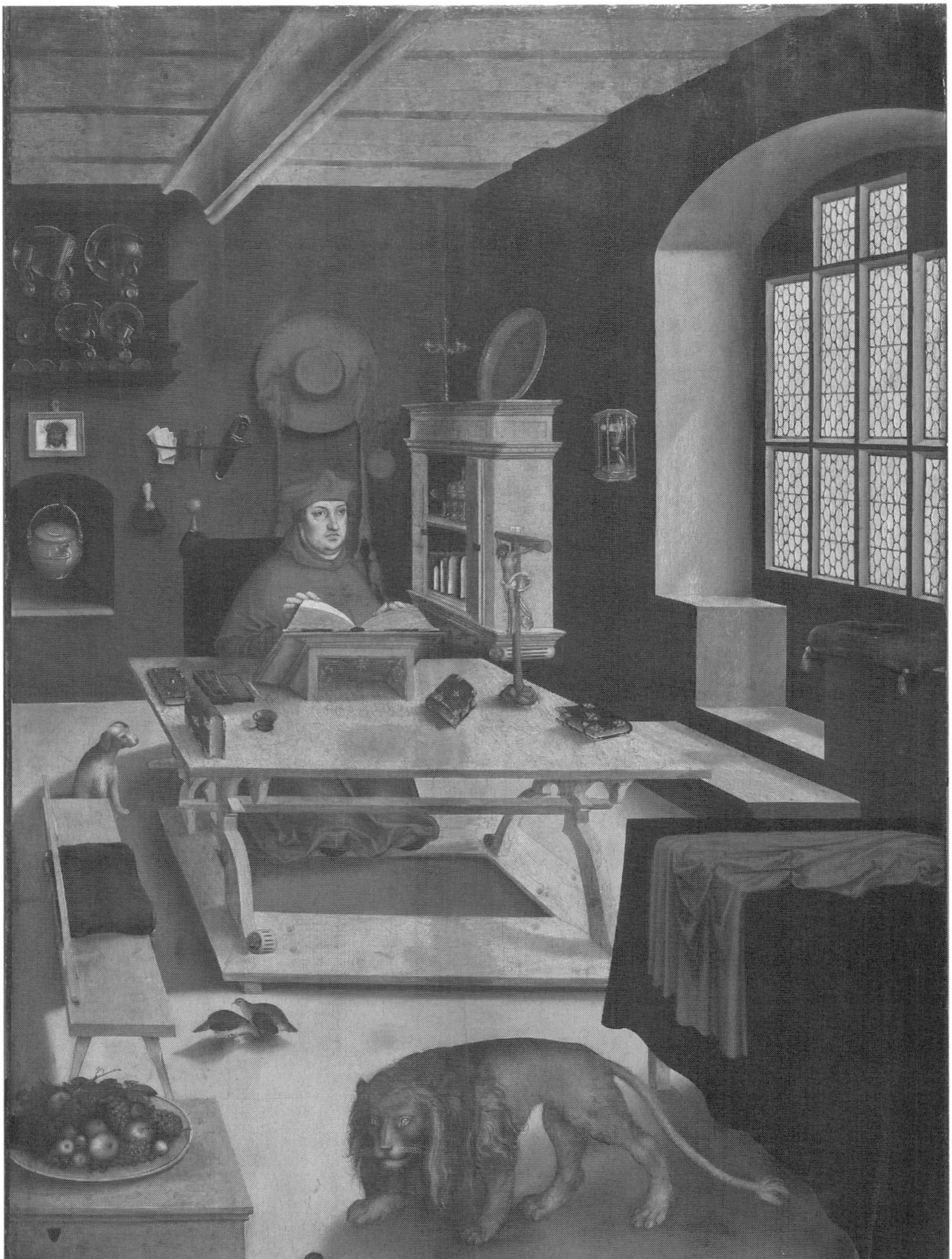

28 Lucas Cranach after Albrecht Dürer, *Cardinal Albrecht as St. Jerome*, mid 1500s

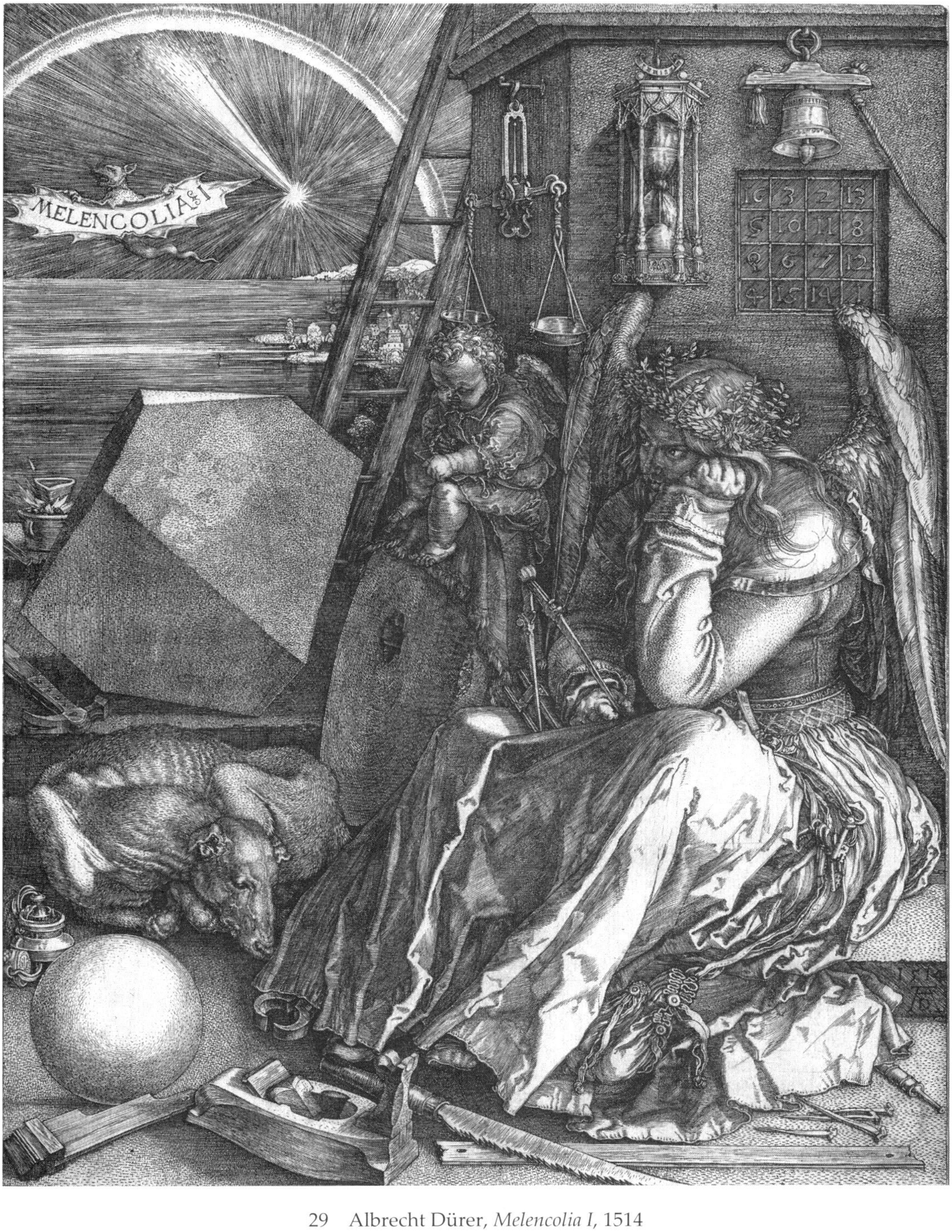

29 Albrecht Dürer, *Melencolia I*, 1514

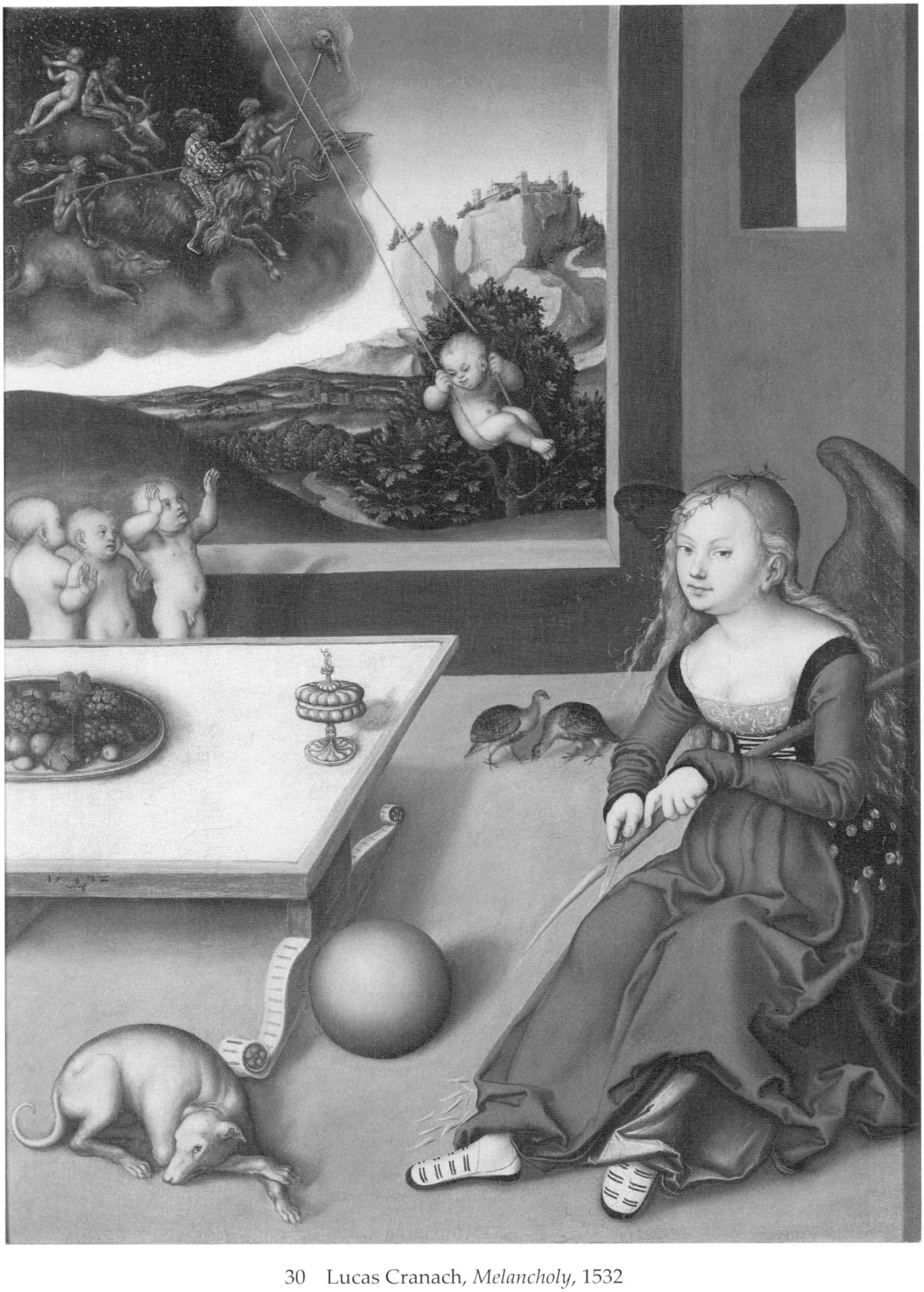

30 Lucas Cranach, *Melancholy*, 1532

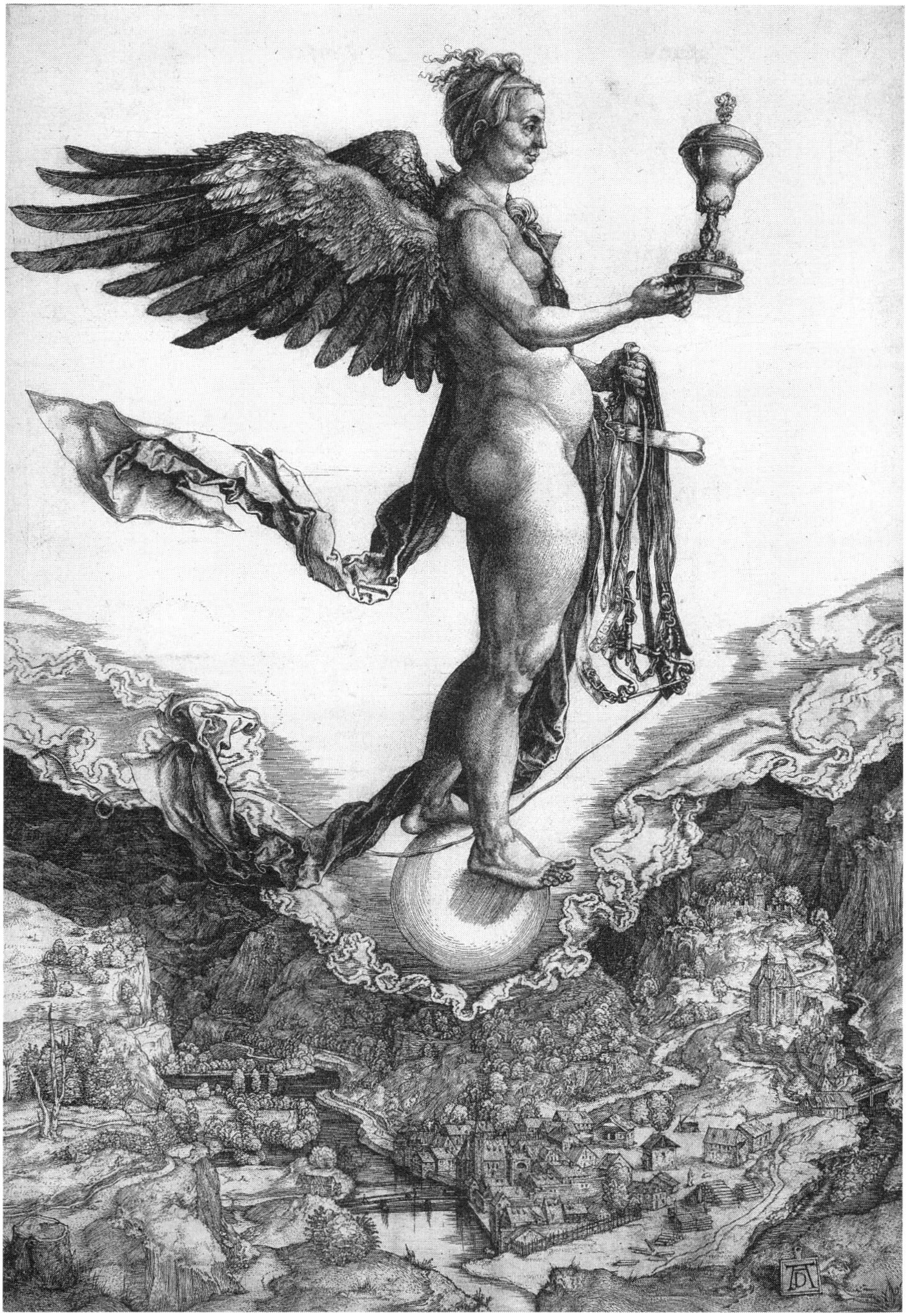

31 Albrecht Dürer, *Nemesis*, 1502

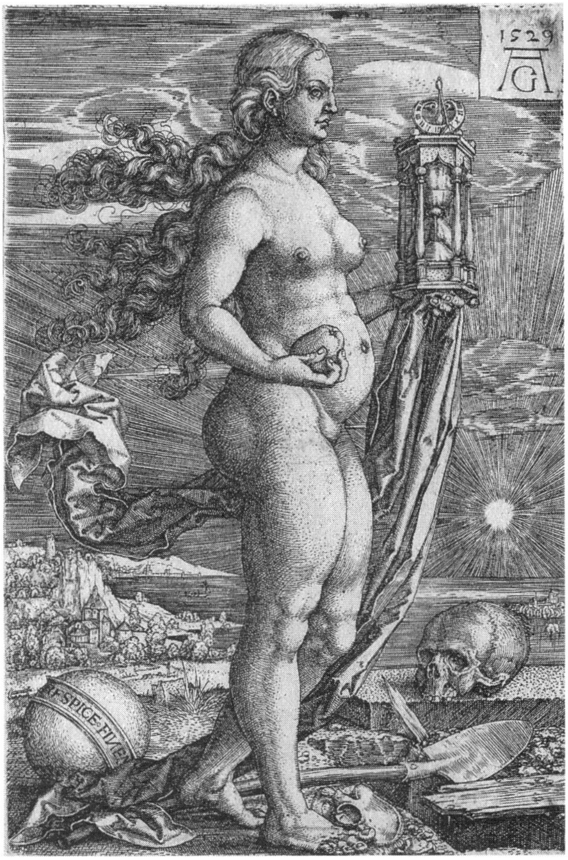

32 Heinrich Aldegrever, *Respice Finem*, 1529

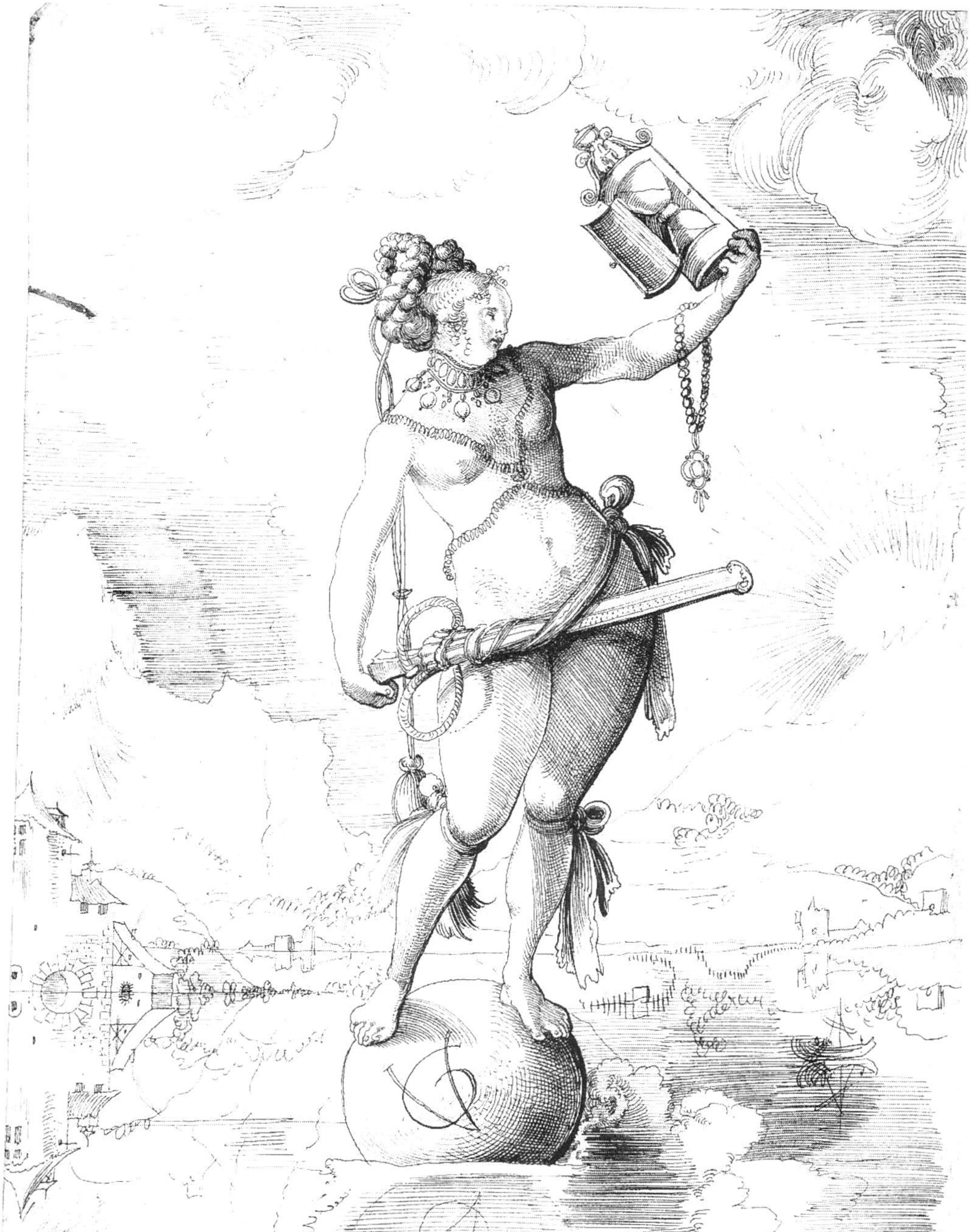

33 Urs Graf, *Allegory of Victory*, *c.*1518–20

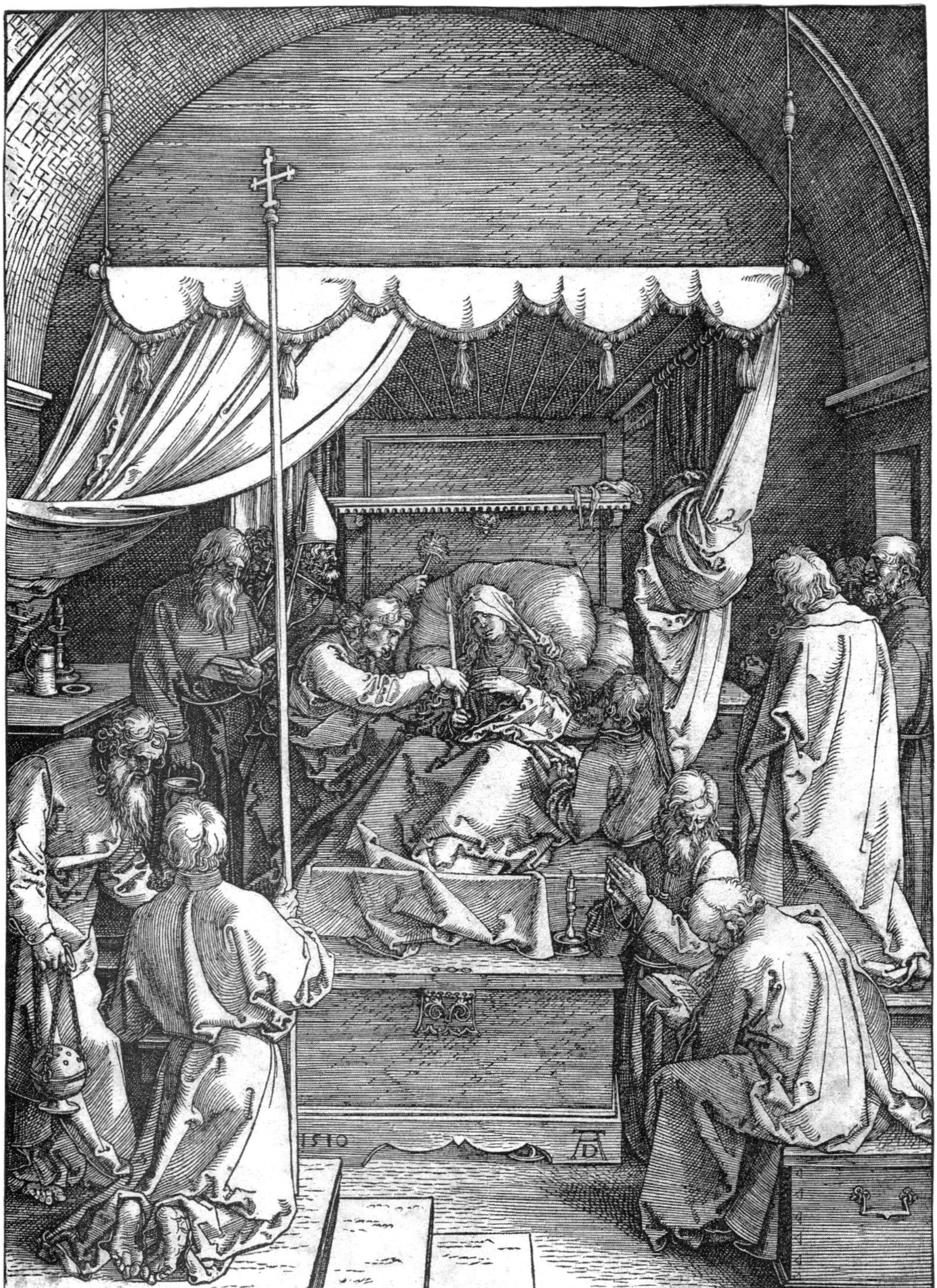

34 Albrecht Dürer, *Life of the Virgin: Death of the Virgin*, 1503–5

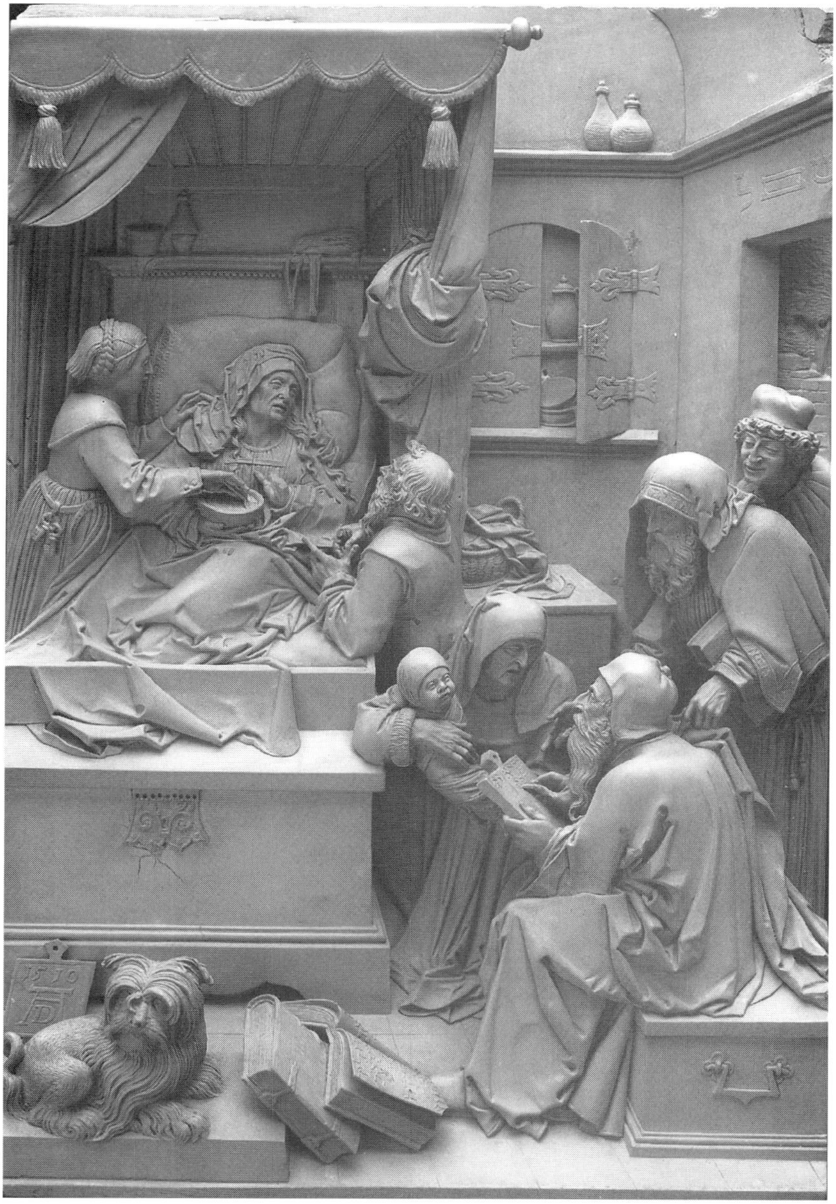

35 Georg Schweigger, *The Birth and Naming of John the Baptist*, 1642

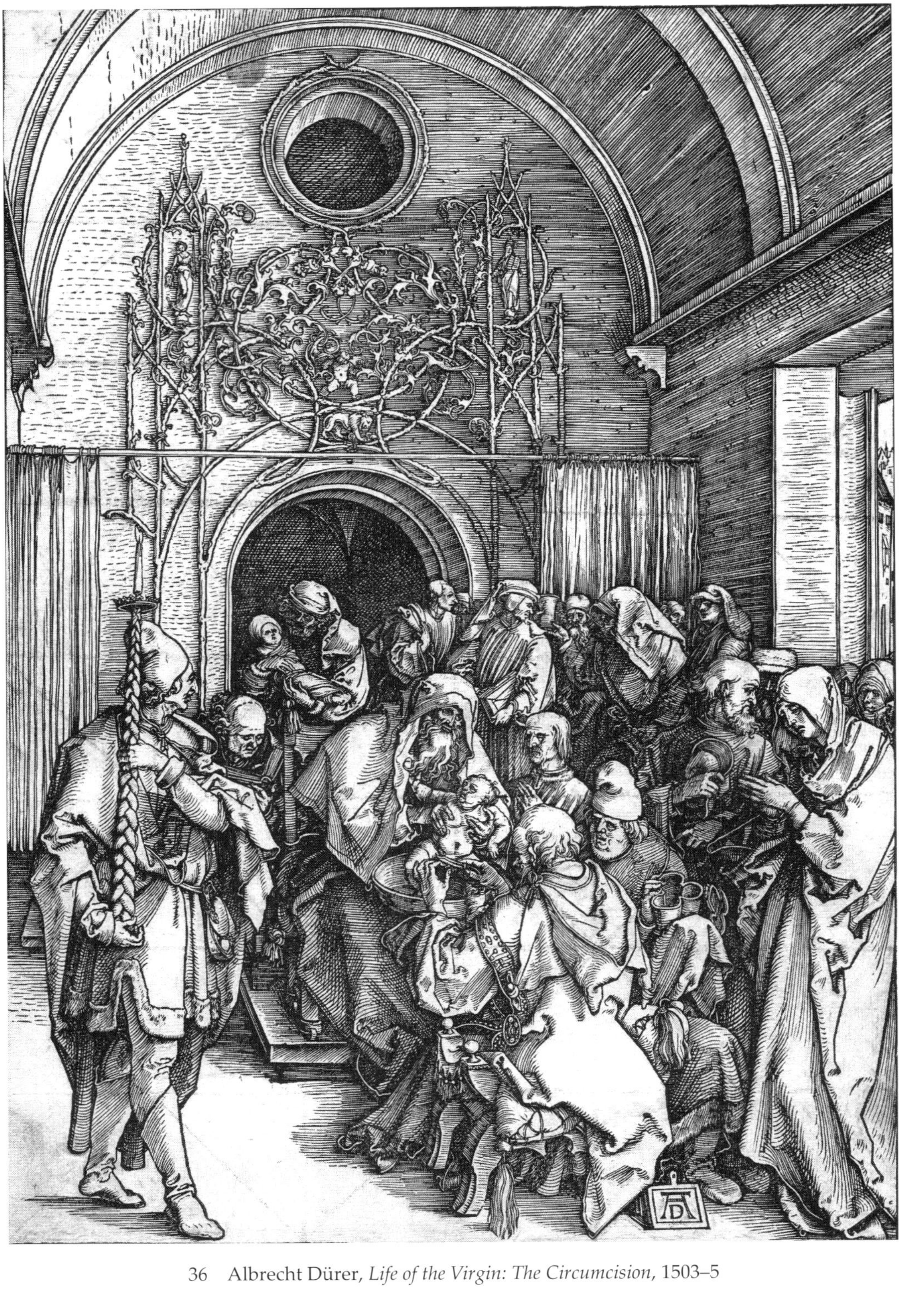

36 Albrecht Dürer, *Life of the Virgin: The Circumcision*, 1503–5

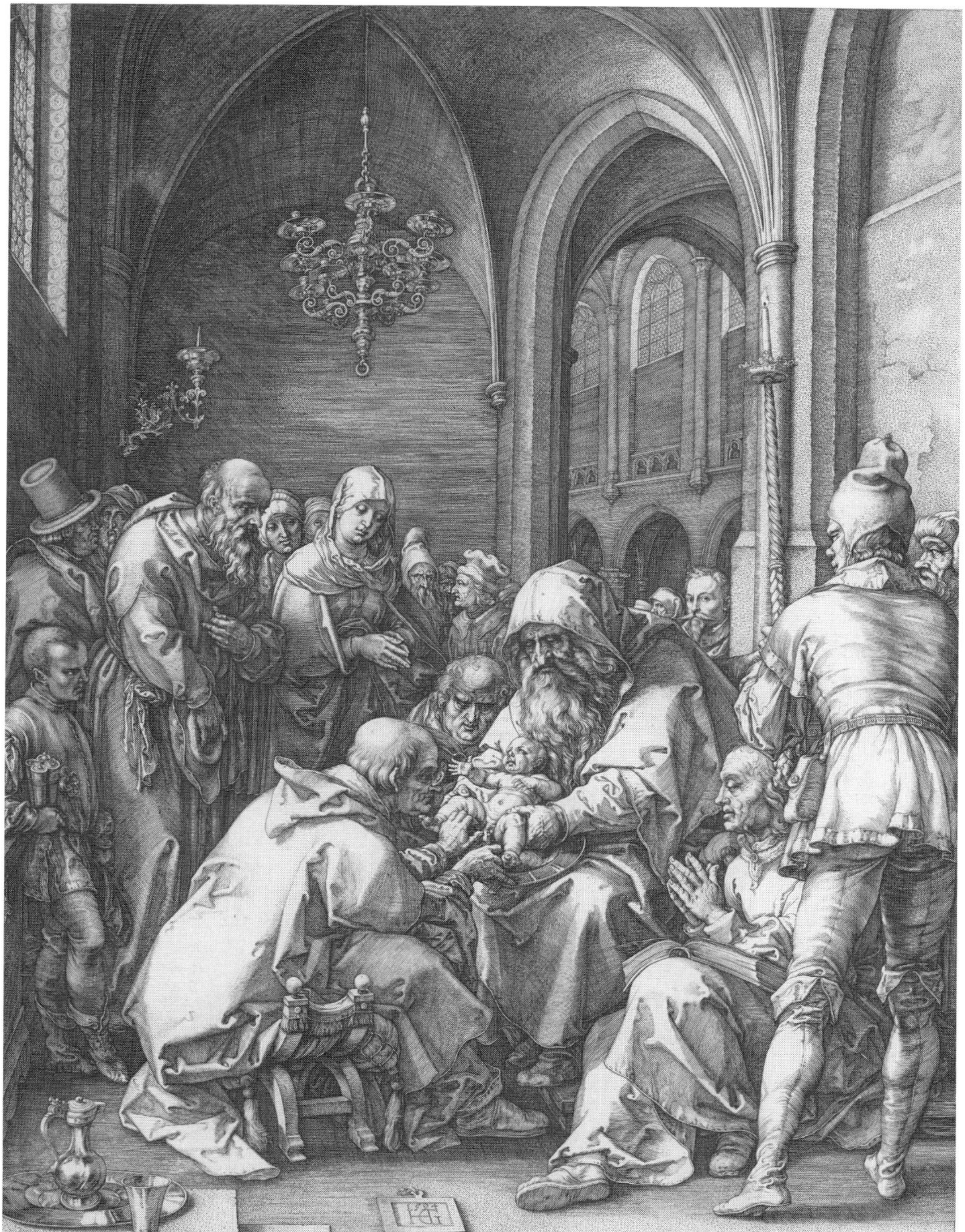

37 Hendrick Goltzius, *The Circumcision*, c.1593–94

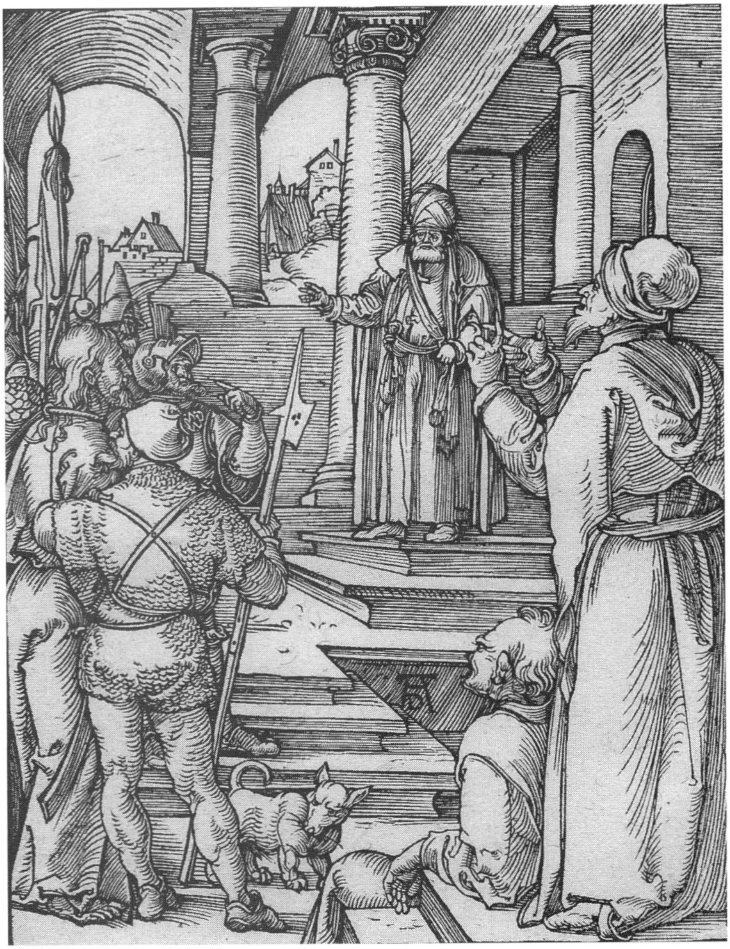

38 Albrecht Dürer, *Small Passion: Christ Before Pilate*, *c.*1509–11

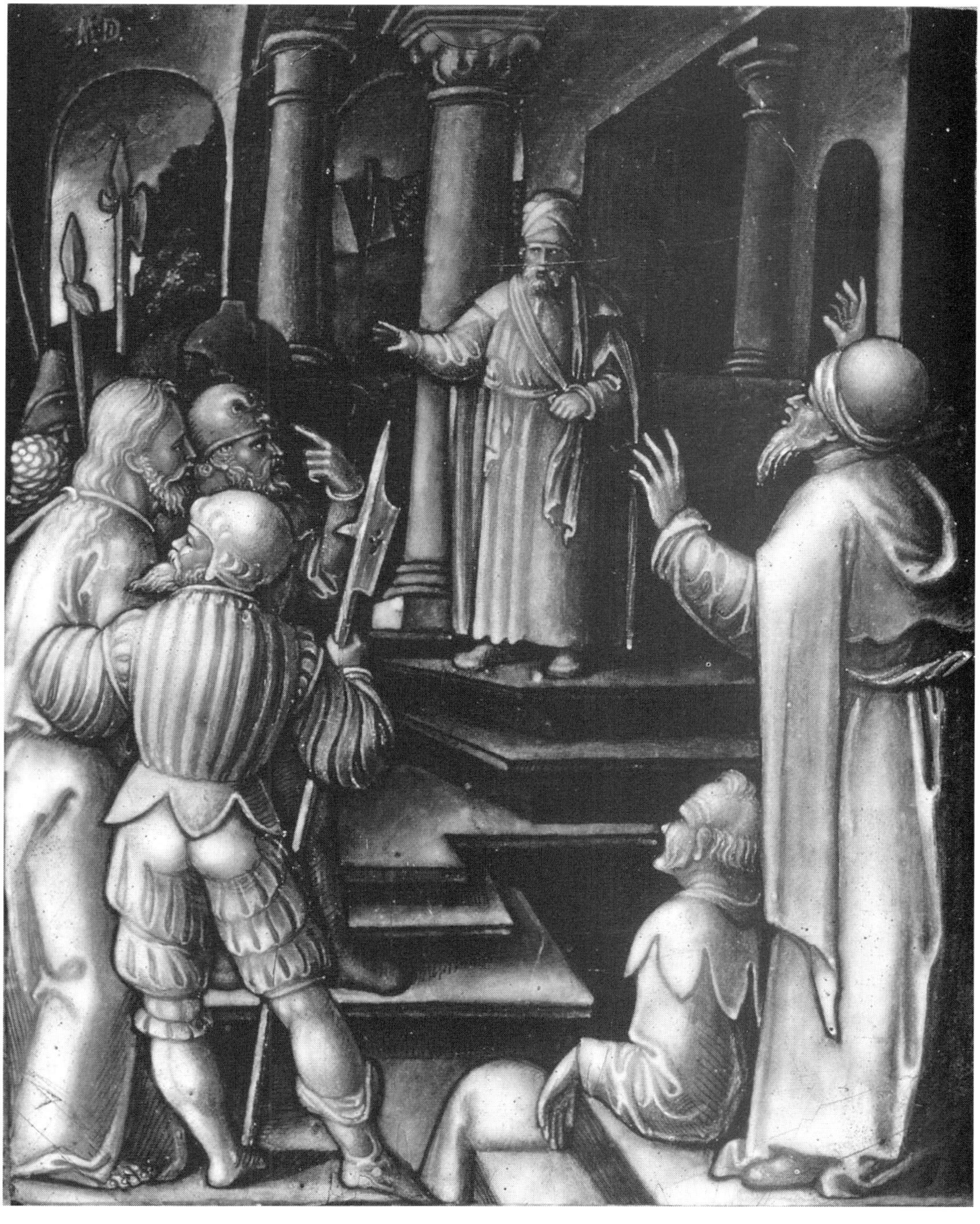

39 Martial Ydeux dit le Pape after Albrecht Dürer, *Christ Before Pilate*, *c*.1560

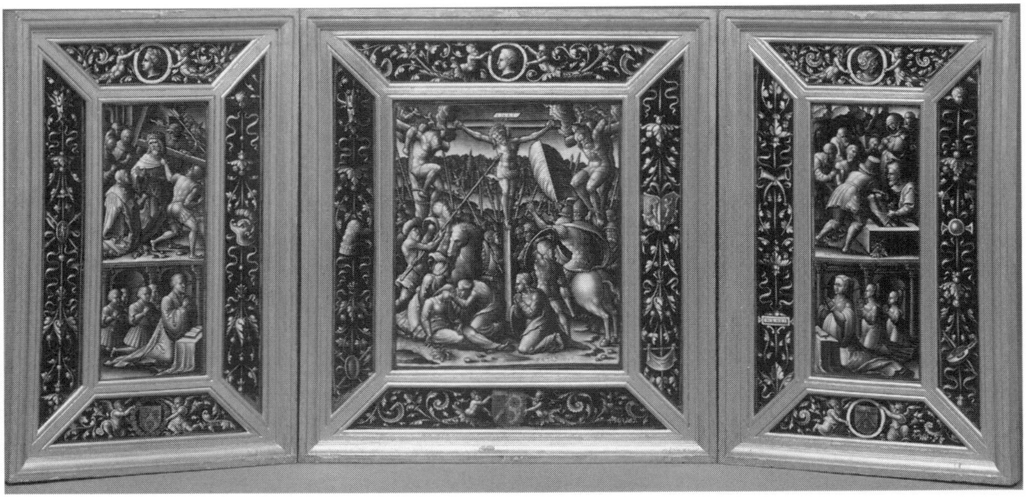

40 Pierre Reymond after Albrecht Dürer, *Scenes from the Passion*, 1543

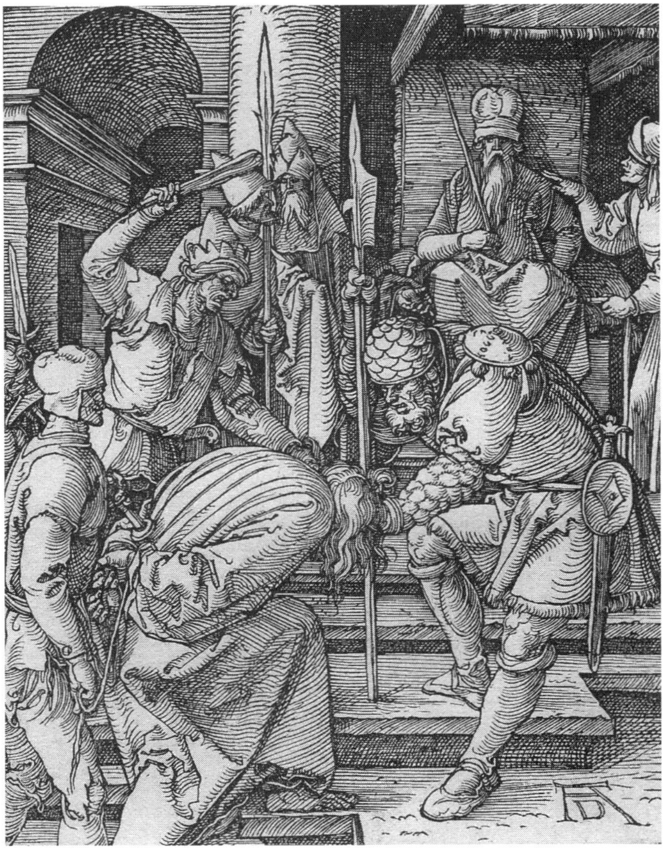

41 Albrecht Dürer, *Small Passion: Christ before Annas*, c.1509–11

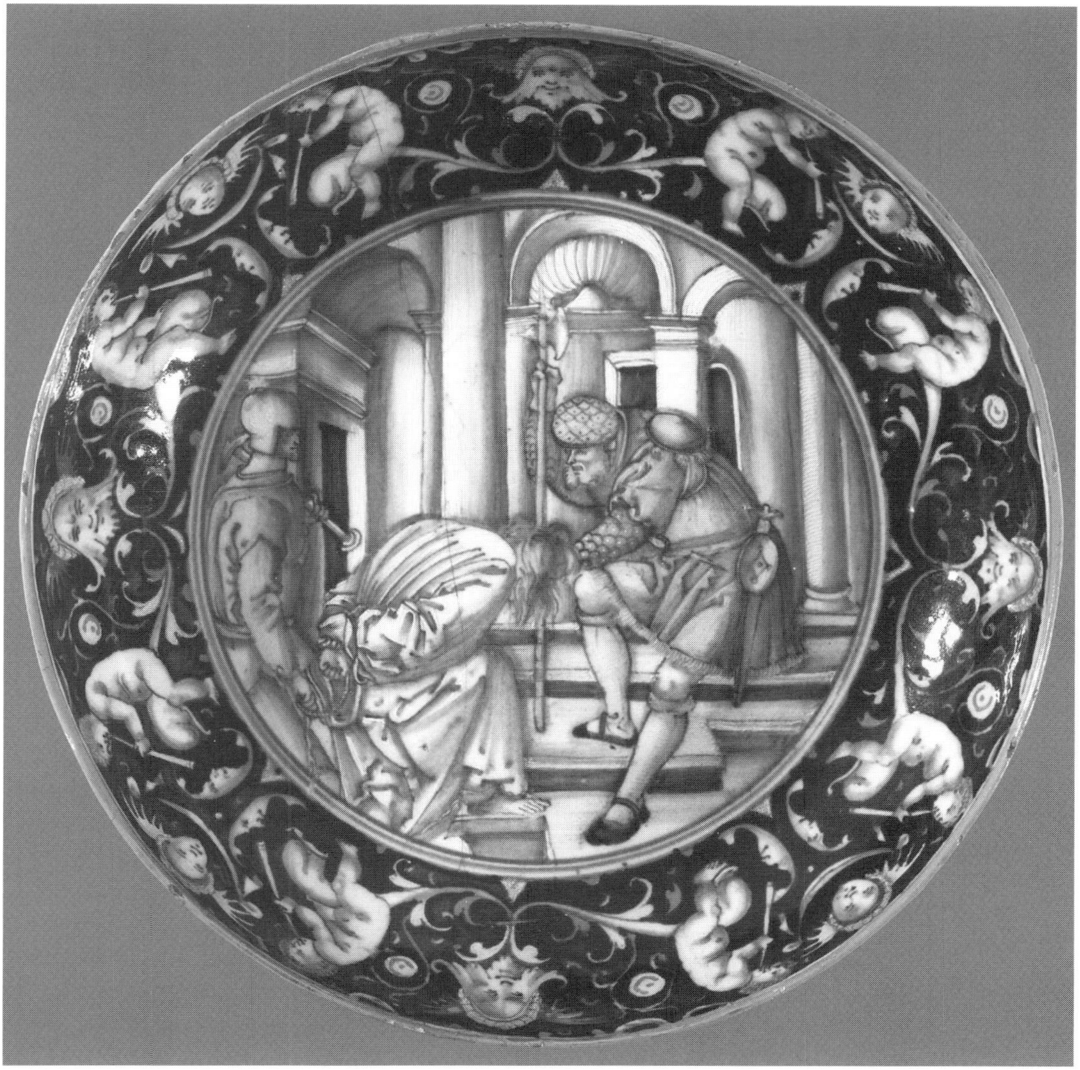

42 Anonymous after Albrecht Dürer, *Christ before Annas*, *c*.1515–25

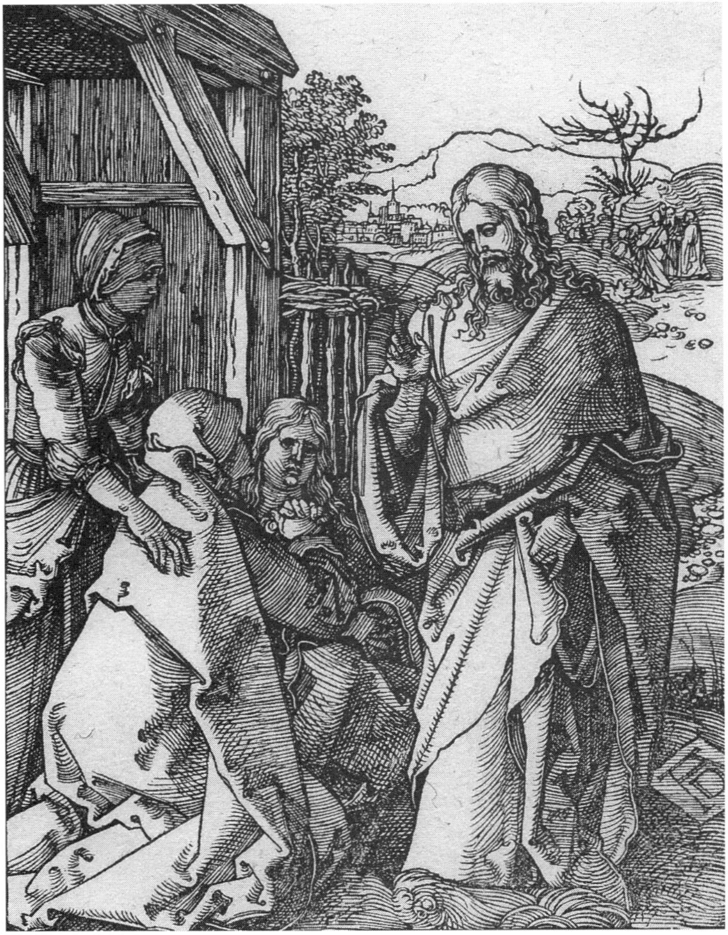

43 Albrecht Dürer, *Small Passion: Christ Taking Leave of His Mother*, 1508–1509

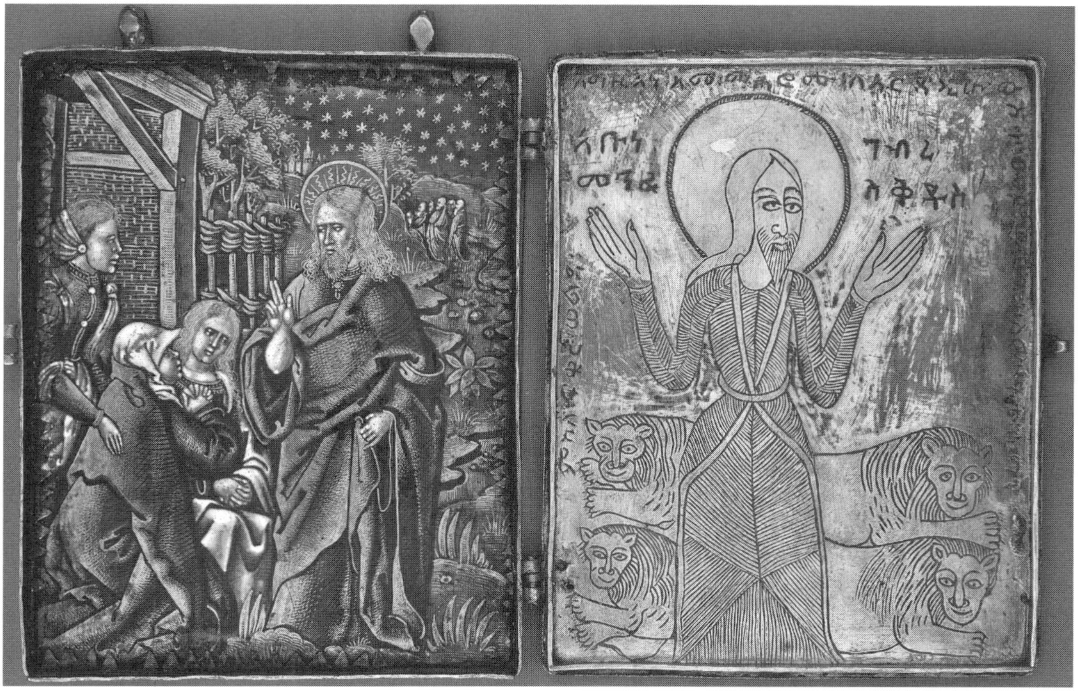

44 Anonymous after Albrecht Dürer, *Christ Taking Leave of His Mother*, seventeenth century

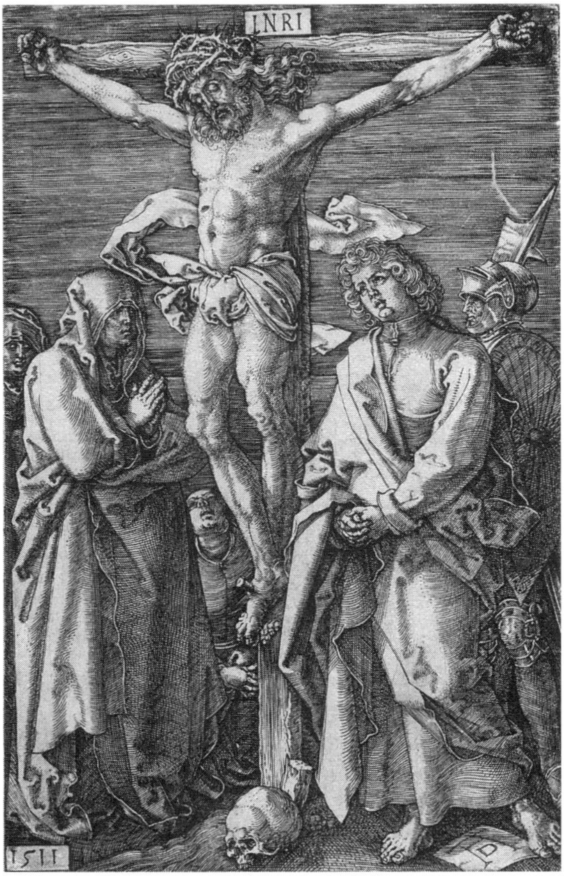

45 Albrecht Dürer, *Engraved Passion: Crucifixion*, 1511

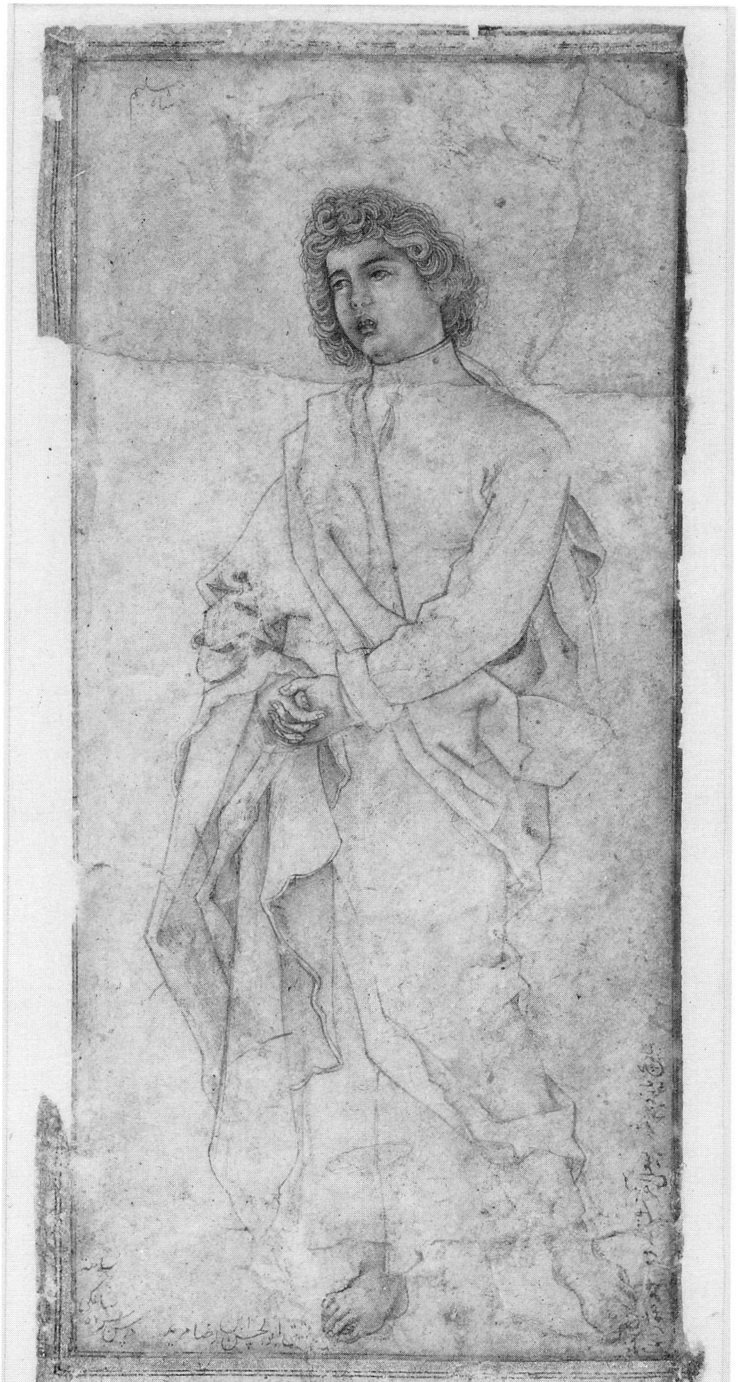

46 Abu'l Hasan after Albrecht Dürer, *St. John the Evangelist*, 1601

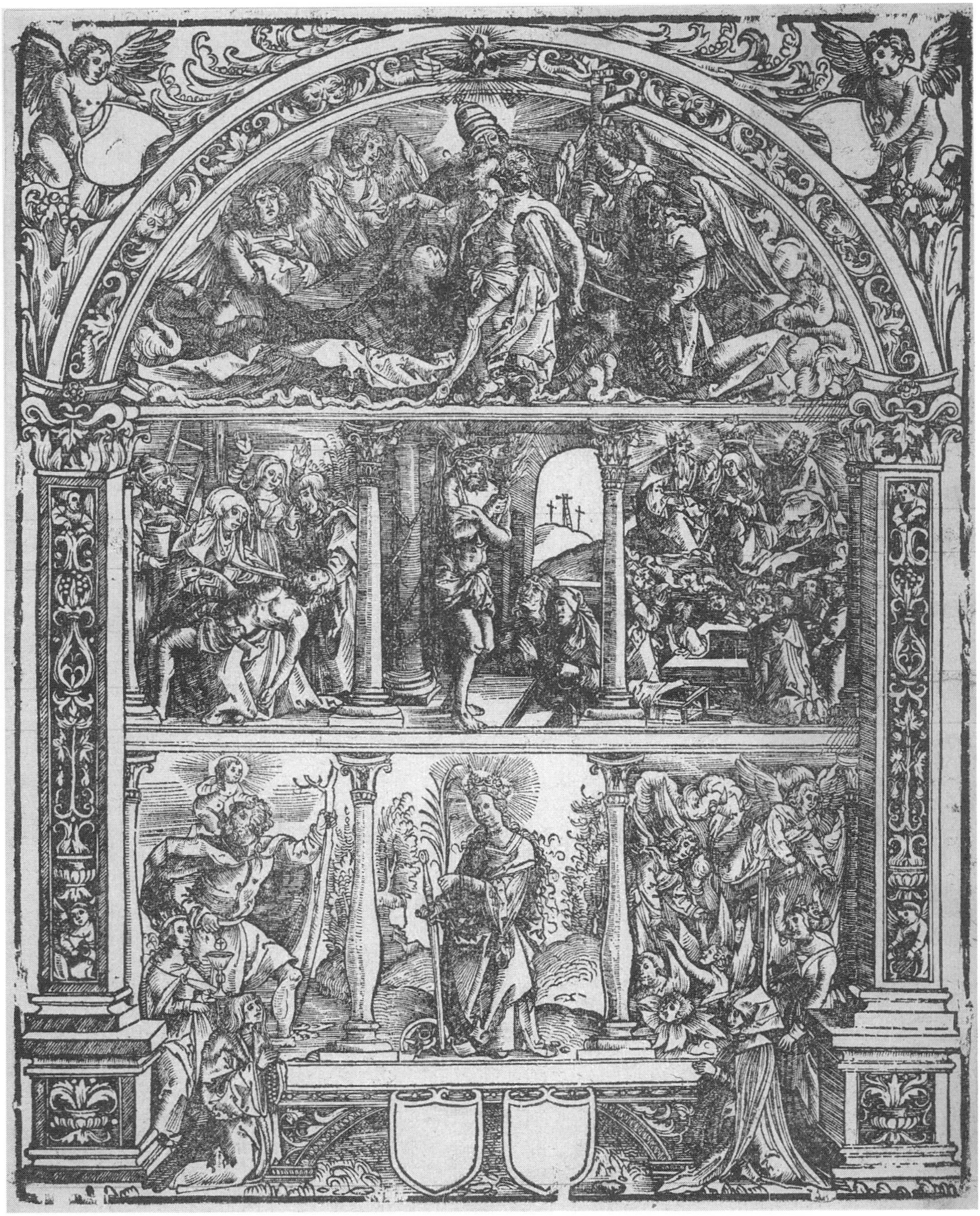

47 Erhard Schön, *Polyptych*, *c*.1511–1515

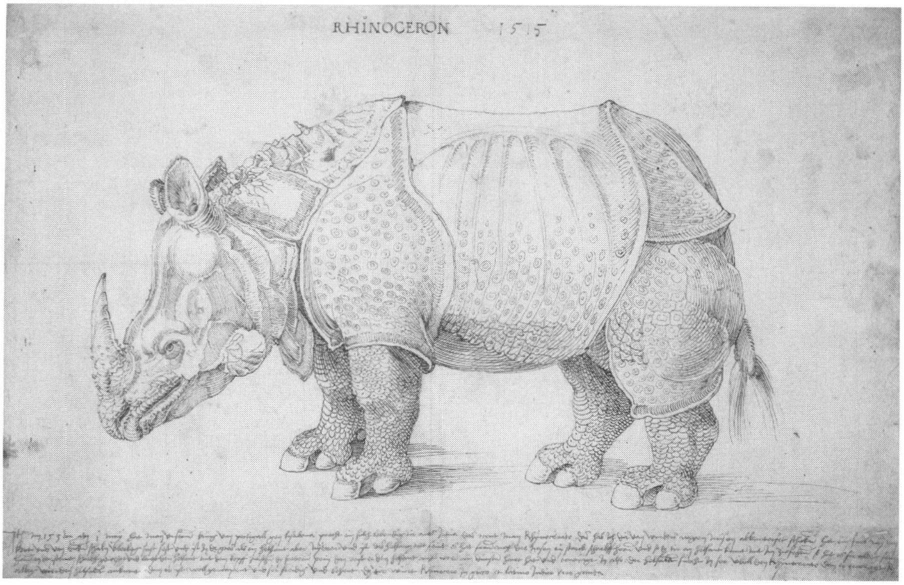

48 Albrecht Dürer, *Rhinoceros*, 1515

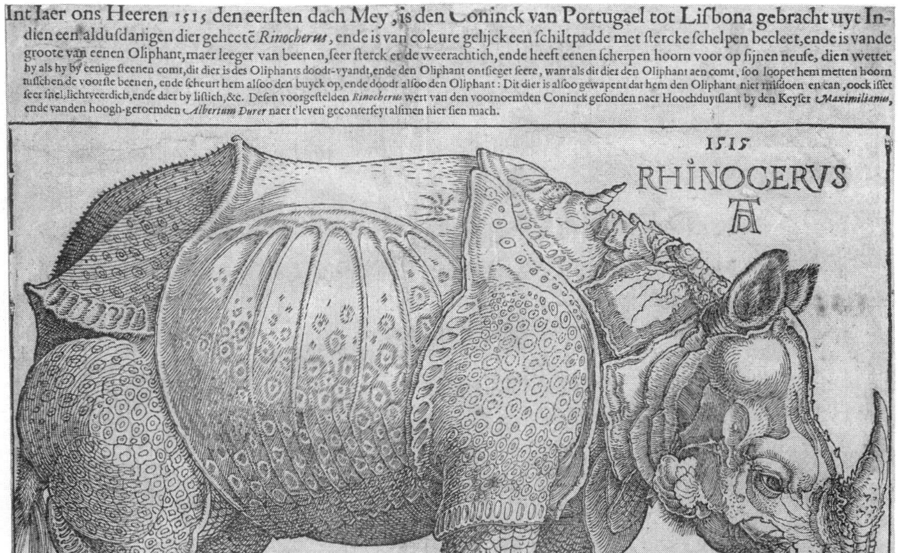

49 Albrecht Dürer, *Rhinoceros*, 1515

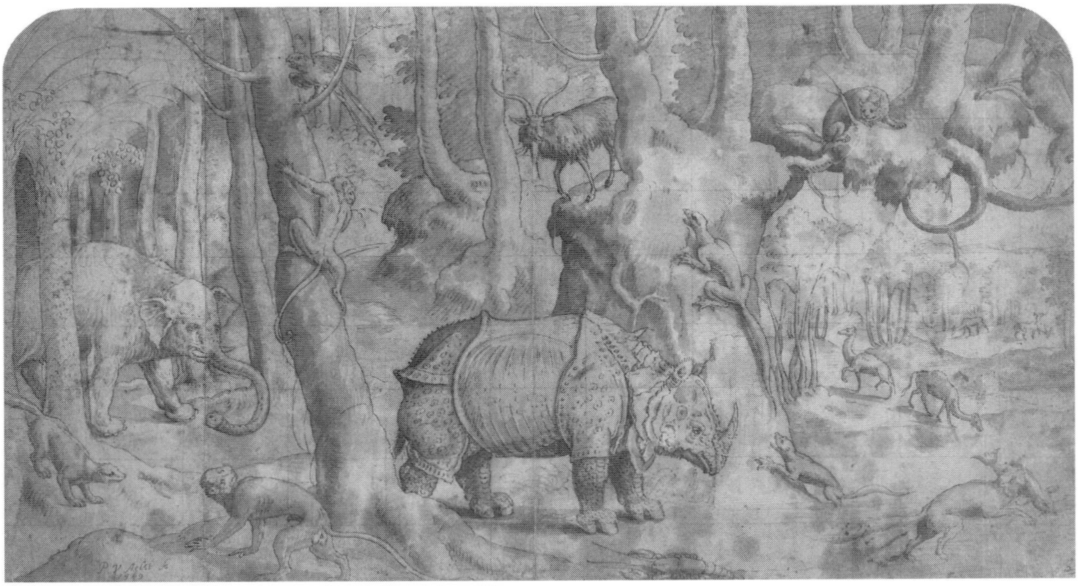

50 Attributed to Pieter Coecke van Aelst, *Woodland Scene with Animals*, *c*.1550

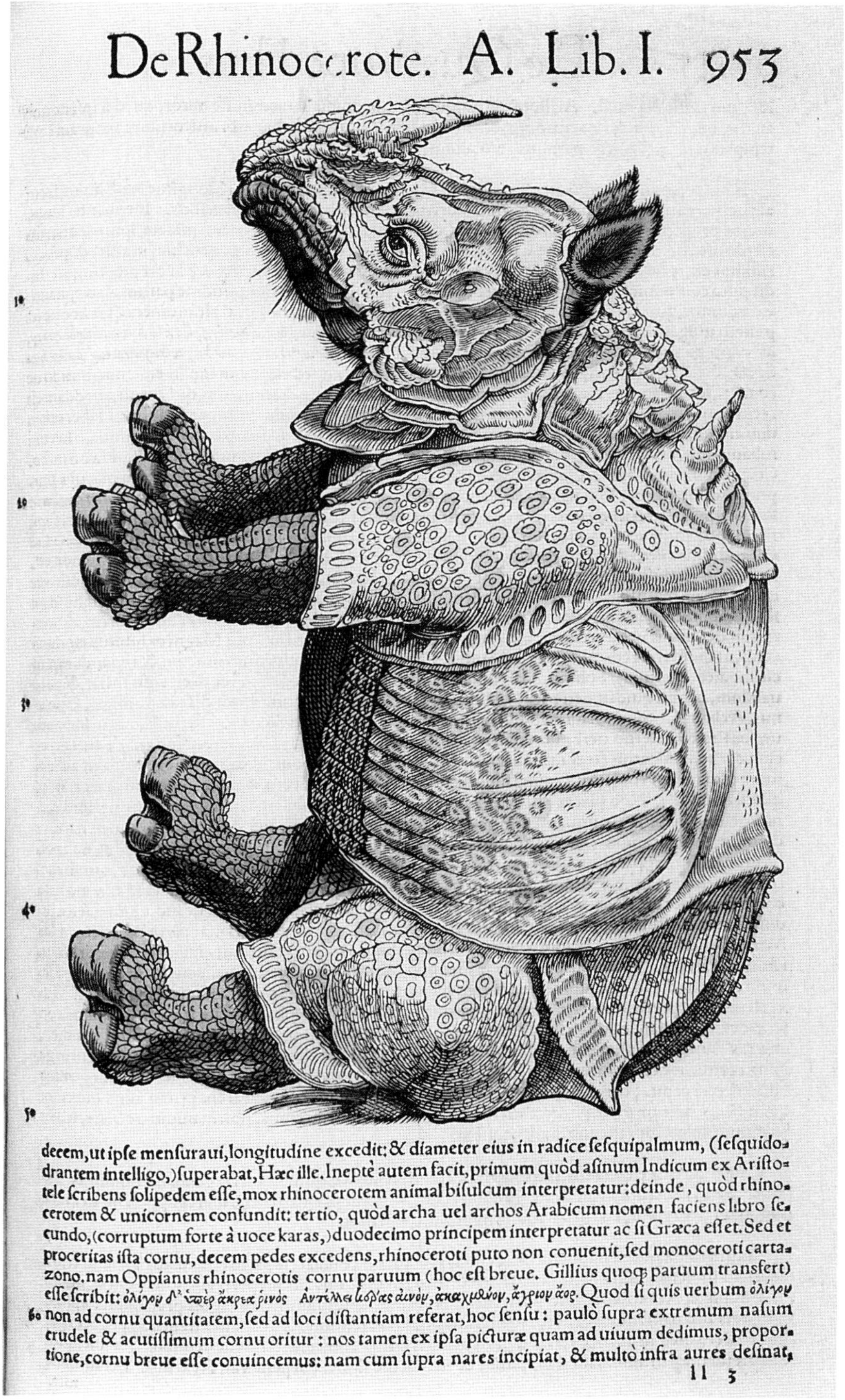
De Rhinocerote. A. Lib. I. 953

decem, ut ipſe menſuraui, longitudine excedit: & diameter eius in radice ſeſquipalmum, (ſeſquidodrantem intelligo,) ſuperabat, Hæc ille. Ineptè autem facit, primum quòd aſinum Indicum ex Ariſtotele ſcribens ſolipedem eſſe, mox rhinocerotem animal biſulcum interpretatur: deinde, quòd rhinocerotem & unicornem confundit: tertio, quòd archa uel archos Arabicum nomen faciens libro ſecundo, (corruptum forte à uoce karas,) duodecimo principem interpretatur ac ſi Græca eſſet. Sed et proceritas iſta cornu, decem pedes excedens, rhinoceroti puto non conuenit, ſed monoceroti cartazono. nam Oppianus rhinocerotis cornu paruum (hoc eſt breue. Gillius quoq; paruum transfert) eſſe ſcribit: ὀλίγον δ' ὑπὲρ ἄκρεα ῥινὸς Ἀντέλλει κέρας αἰνόν, ἀκαχμένον, ἄγριον ἆορ. Quod ſi quis uerbum ὀλίγον non ad cornu quantitatem, ſed ad loci diſtantiam referat, hoc ſenſu: paulò ſupra extremum naſum crudele & acutiſſimum cornu oritur: nos tamen ex ipſa picturæ quam ad uiuum dedimus, proportione, cornu breue eſſe conuincemus: nam cum ſupra nares incipiat, & multò infra aures deſinat,

11 3

51 Conrad Gessner, *De Rhinocerote (from Historiae Animalium, Liber I)*, 1551

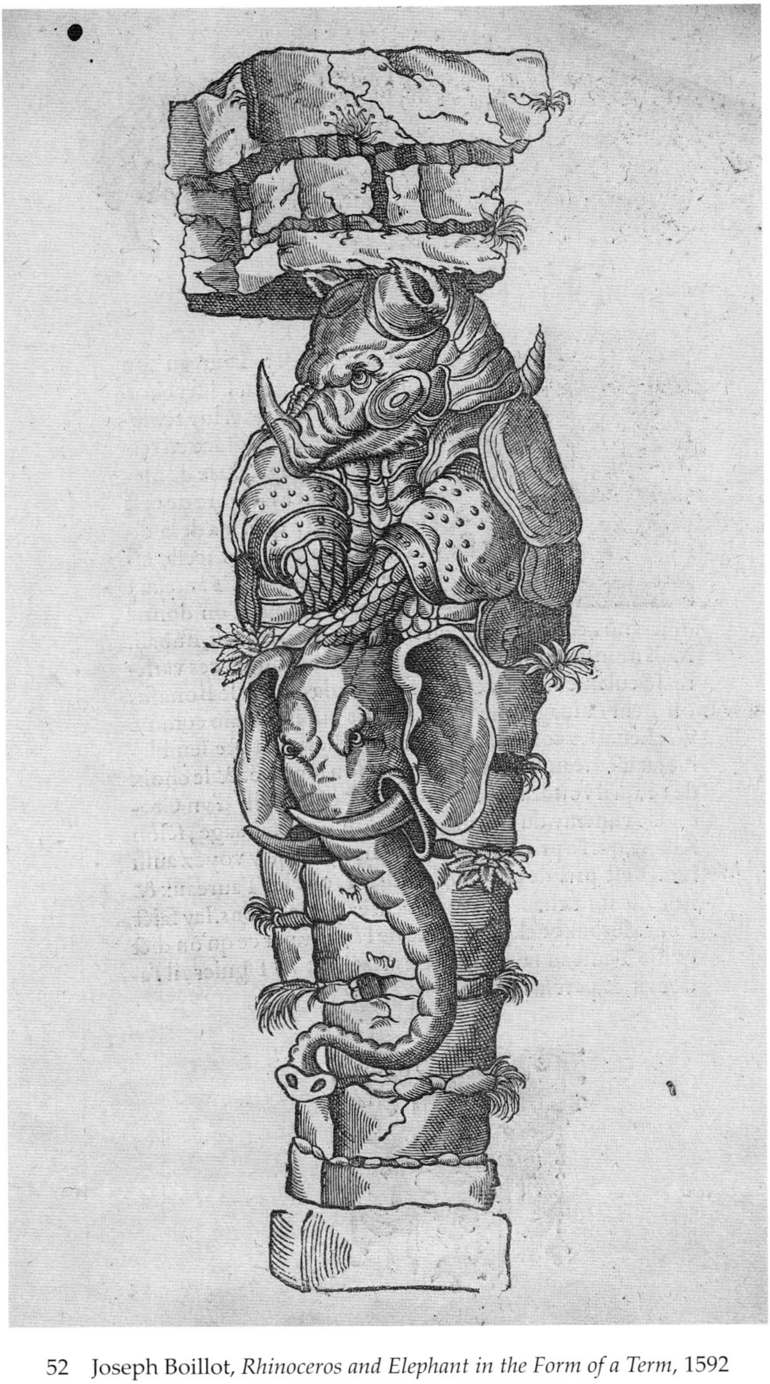

52 Joseph Boillot, *Rhinoceros and Elephant in the Form of a Term*, 1592

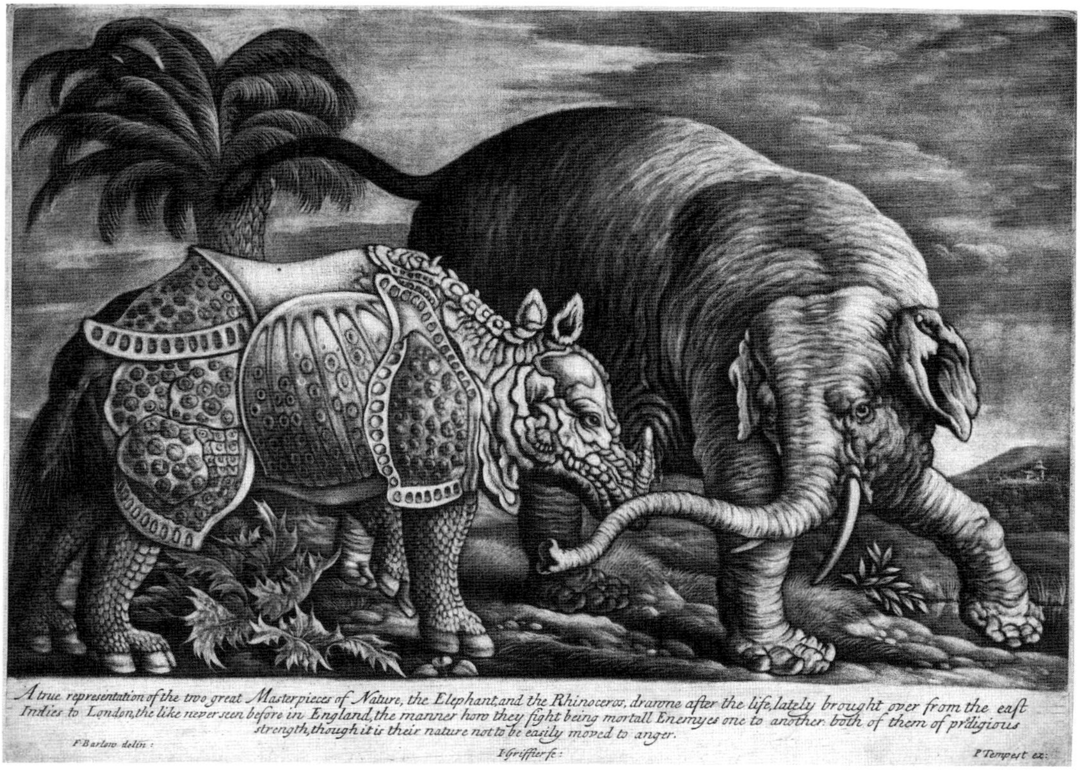

53 John Dunstall, *Rhinoceros and Elephant*, after 1675

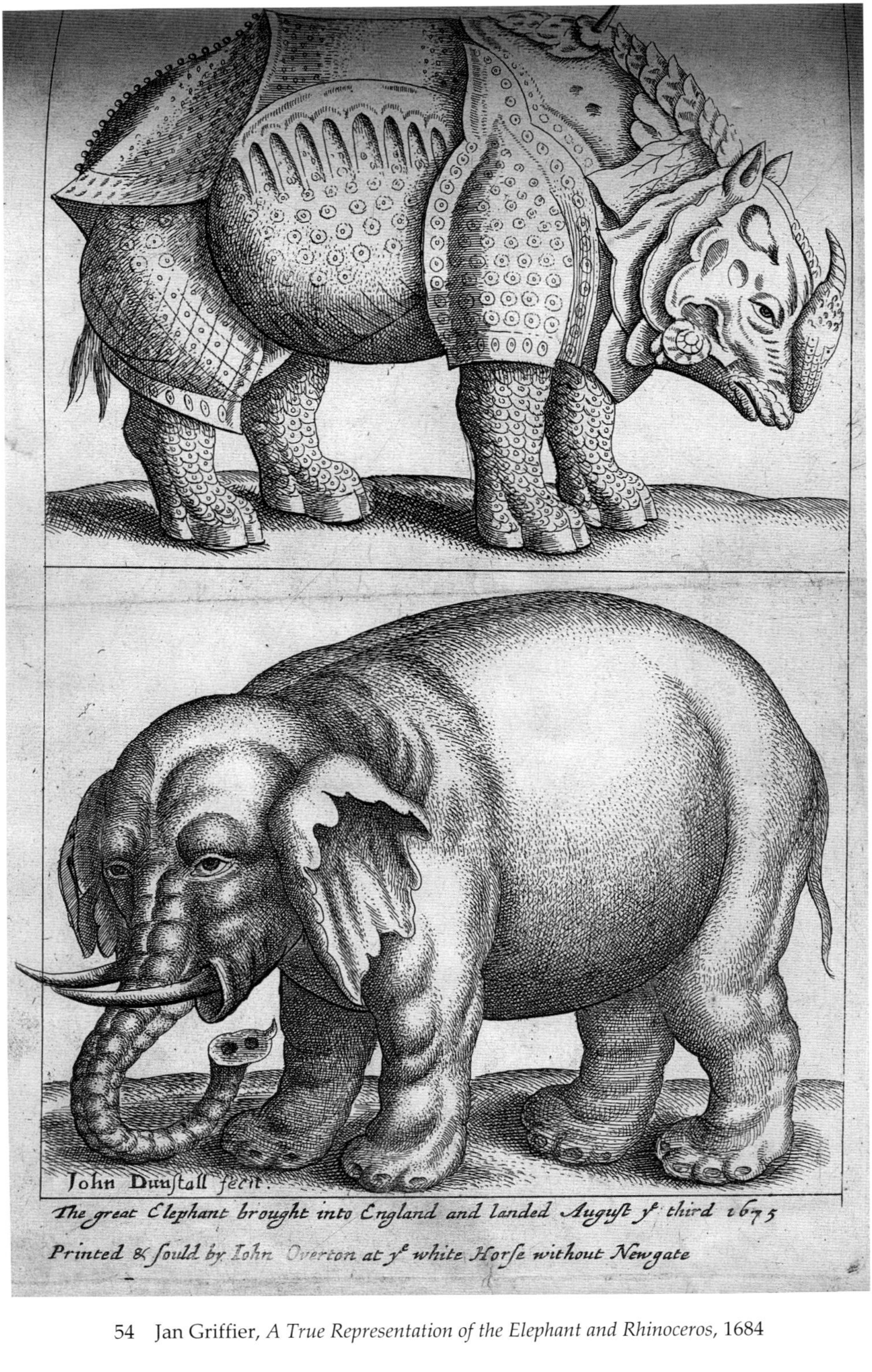

54 Jan Griffier, *A True Representation of the Elephant and Rhinoceros*, 1684

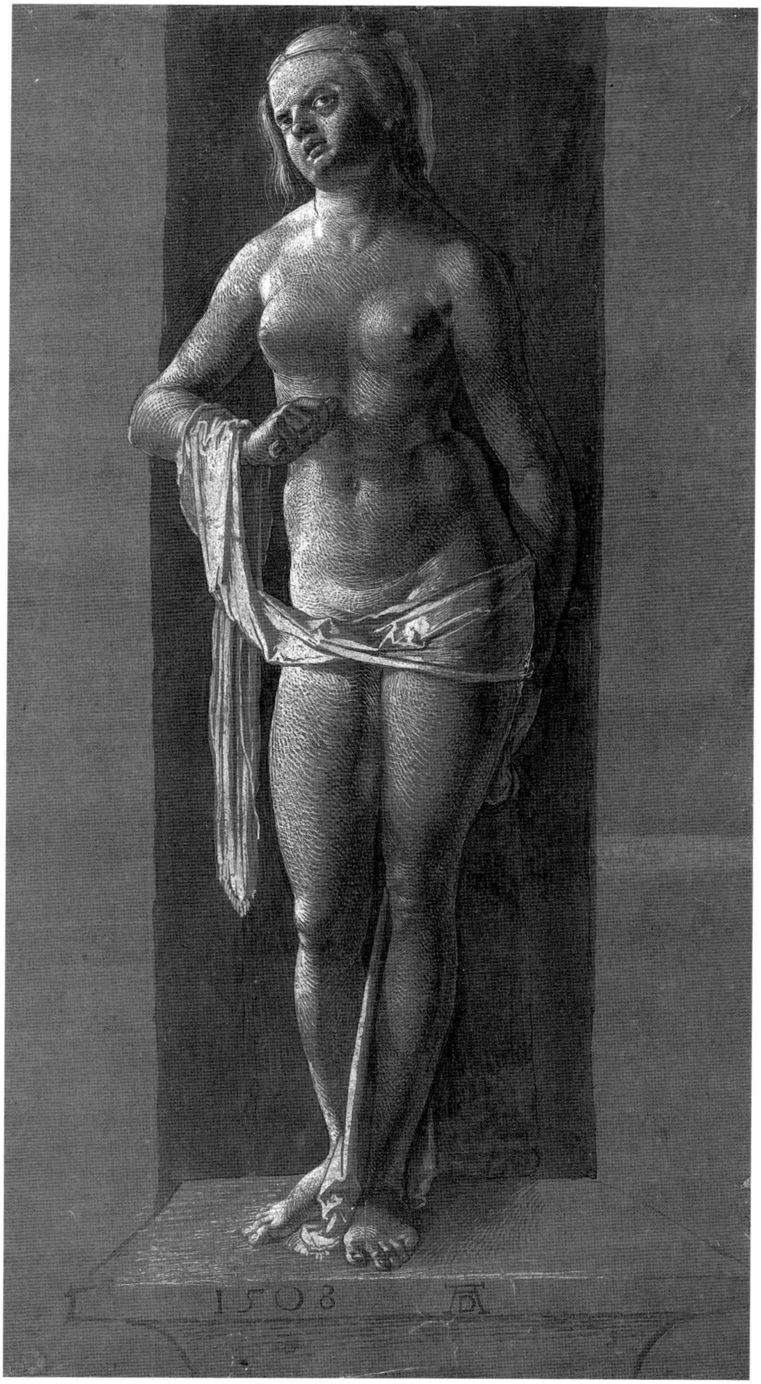

55 Albrecht Dürer, *Lucretia*, 1508

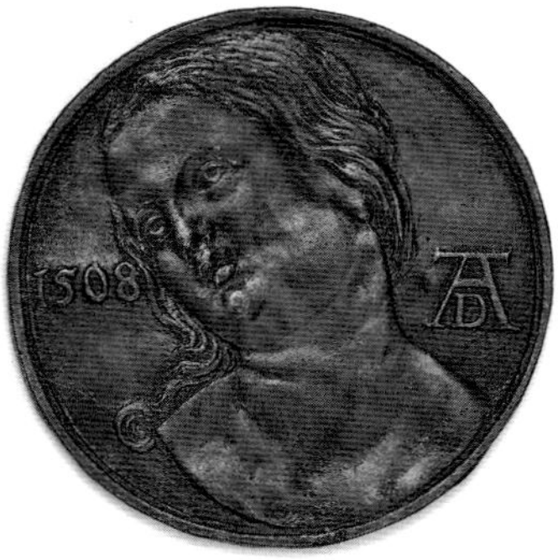

56 Anonymous after Albrecht Dürer, *Lucretia (bust)*, c.1580

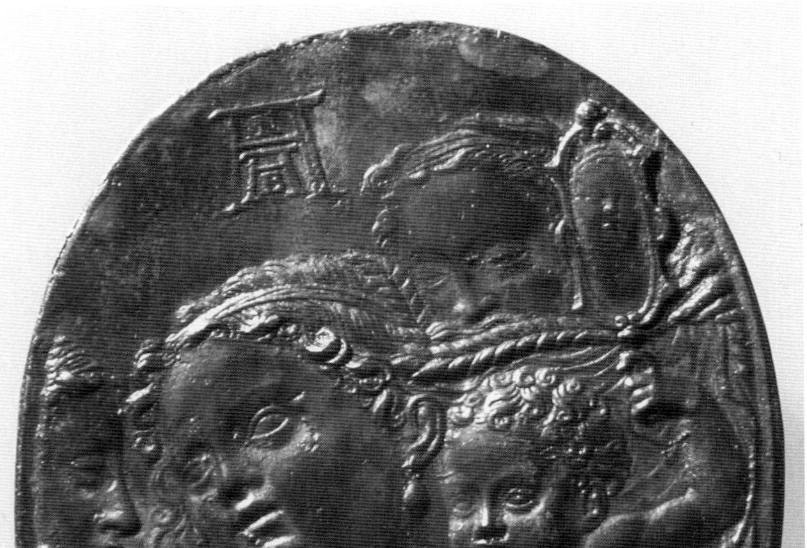

57 Antonio Abondio after Albrecht Dürer, *Lucretia (bust)*, 1587

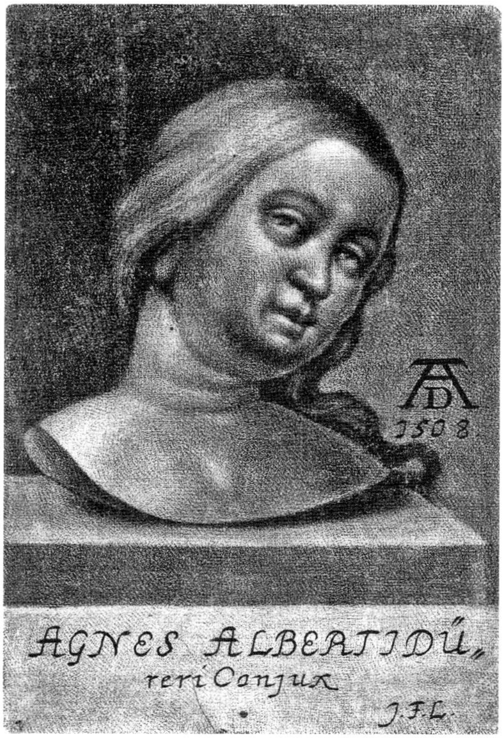

58 Johann Friedrich Leonart, *Head of a Woman (called Agnes Dürer)*, *c*.1670

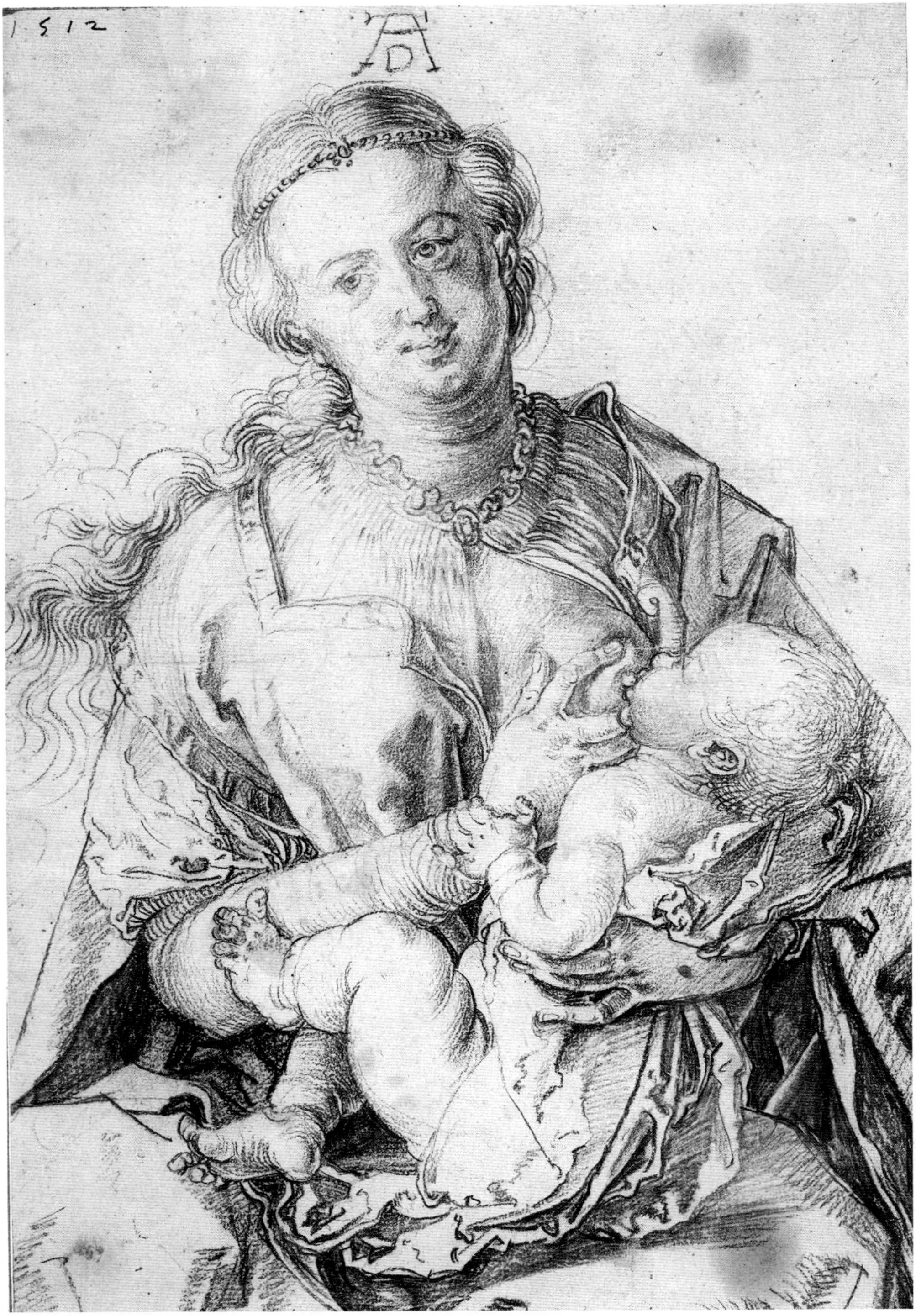

59 Albrecht Dürer, *Virgin with Child*, 1512

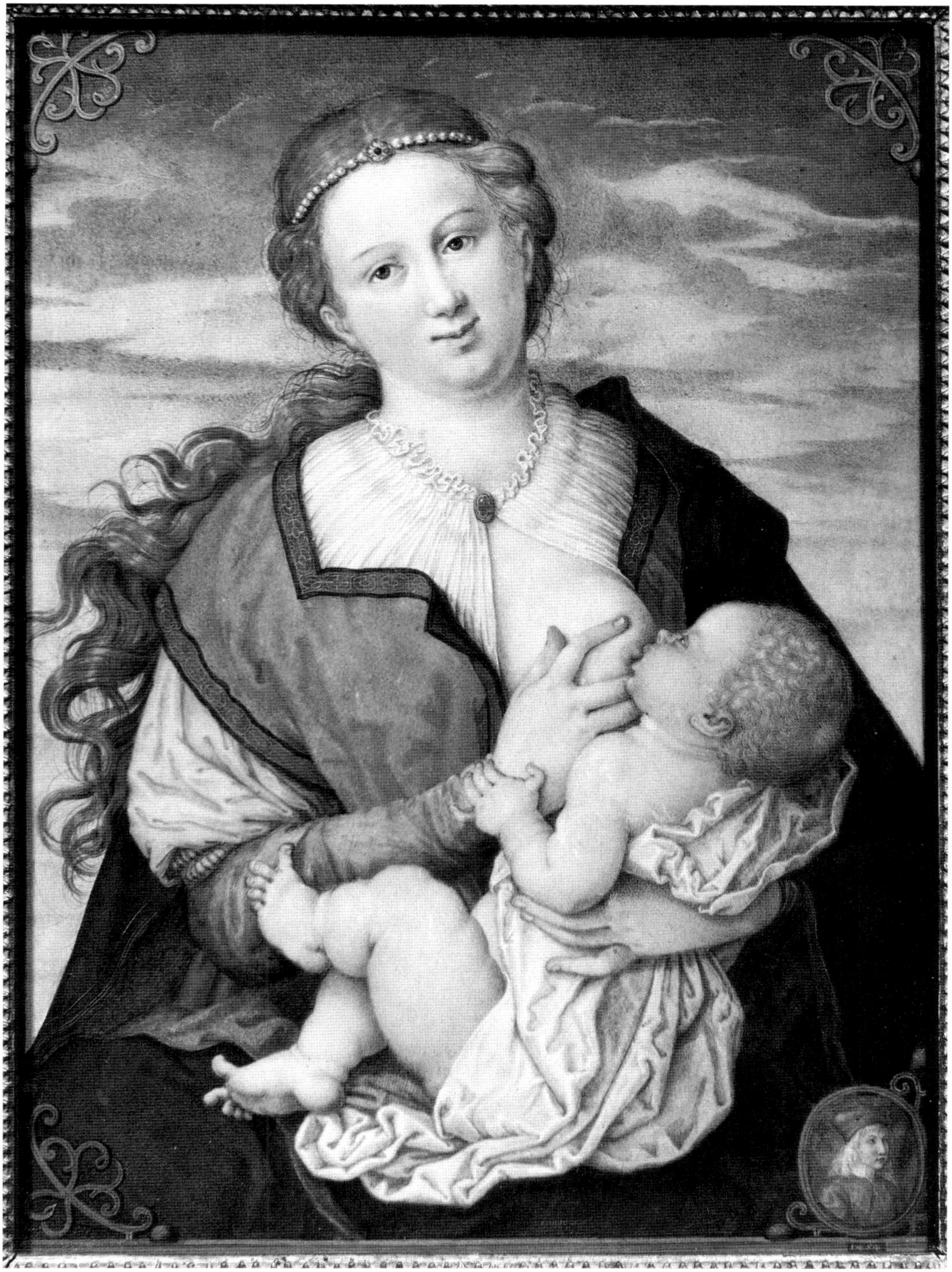

60 Daniel Fröschl after Albrecht Dürer, *Virgin with Child*, 1604–5

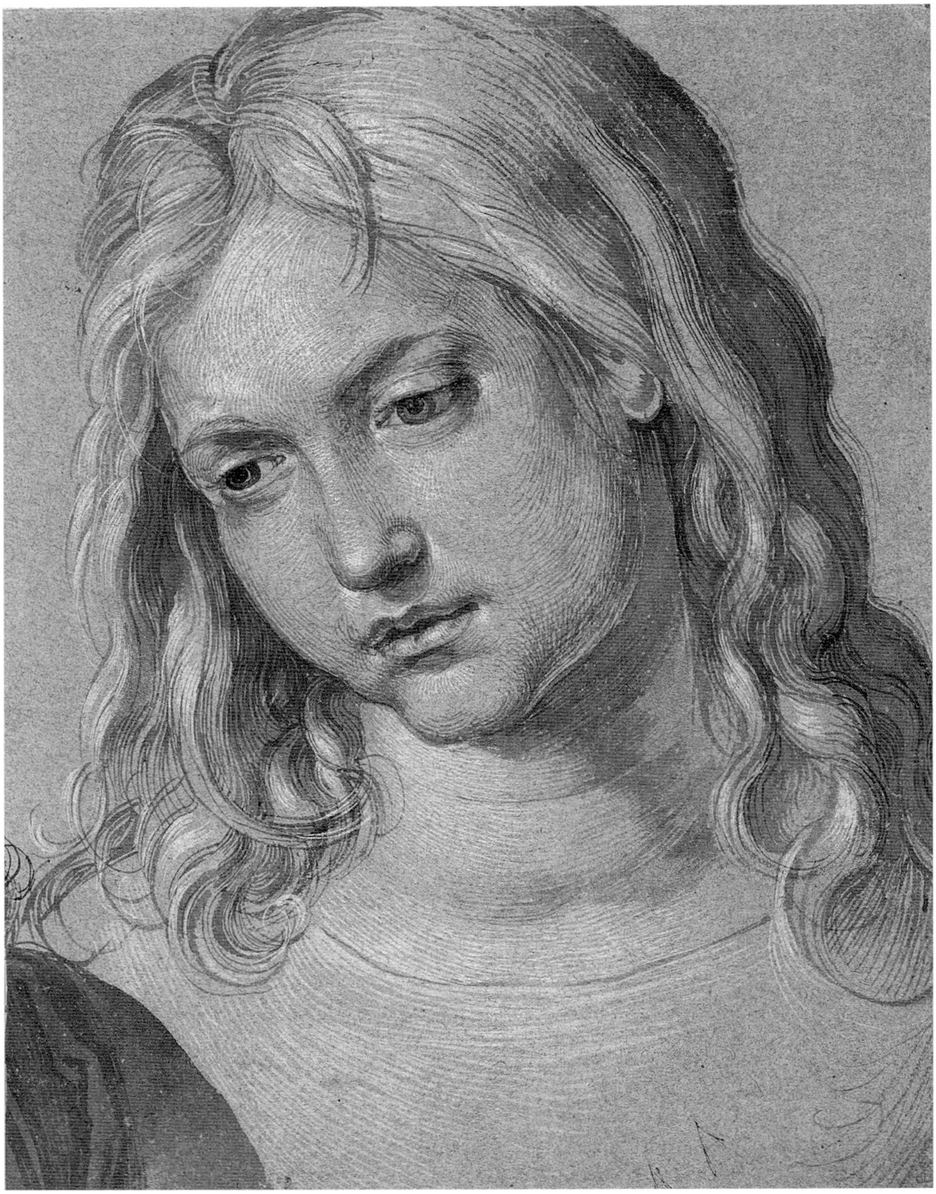

61 Albrecht Dürer, *Christ (Christ among the Doctors)*, c.1506

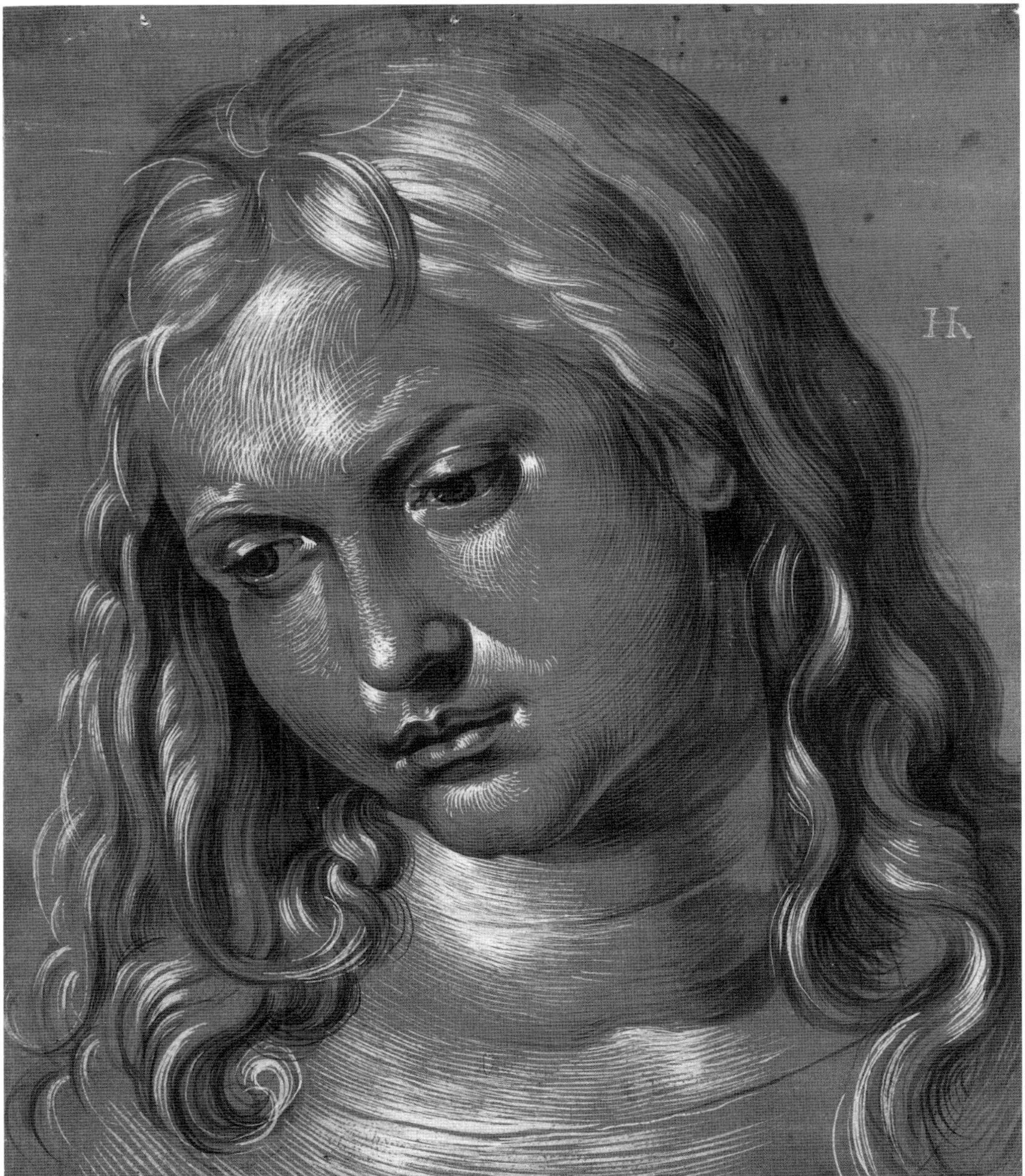

62 Hans Hoffmann after Albrecht Dürer, *Christ (Christ among the Doctors)*, *c*.1580

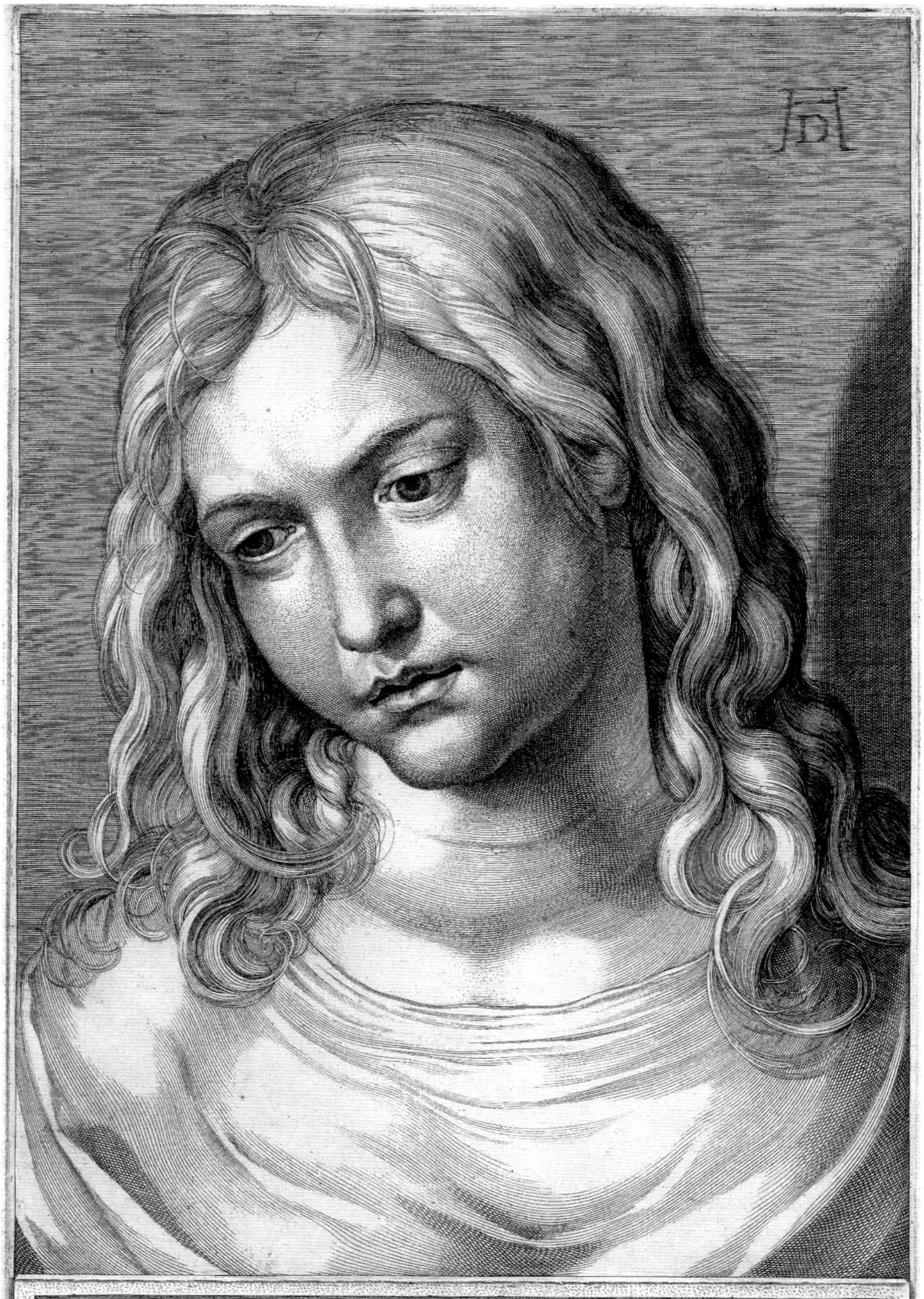

63 Aegedius Sadeler after Albrecht Dürer, *Christ (Christ among the Doctors)*, 1598

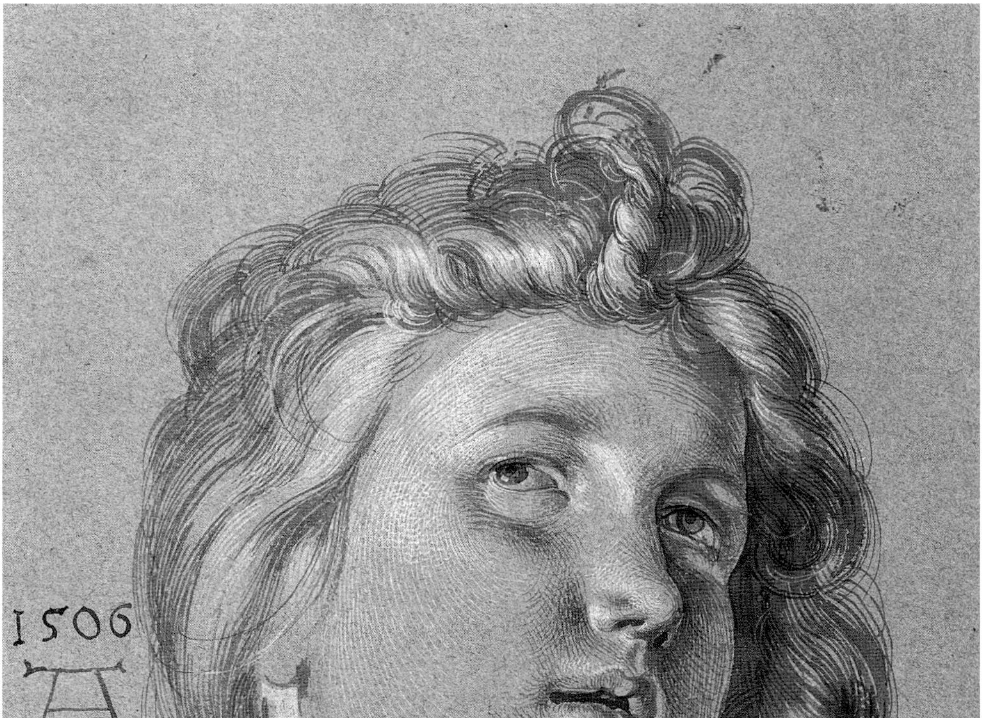

64 Albrecht Dürer, *Angel (Feast of the Rosegarlands)*, 1506

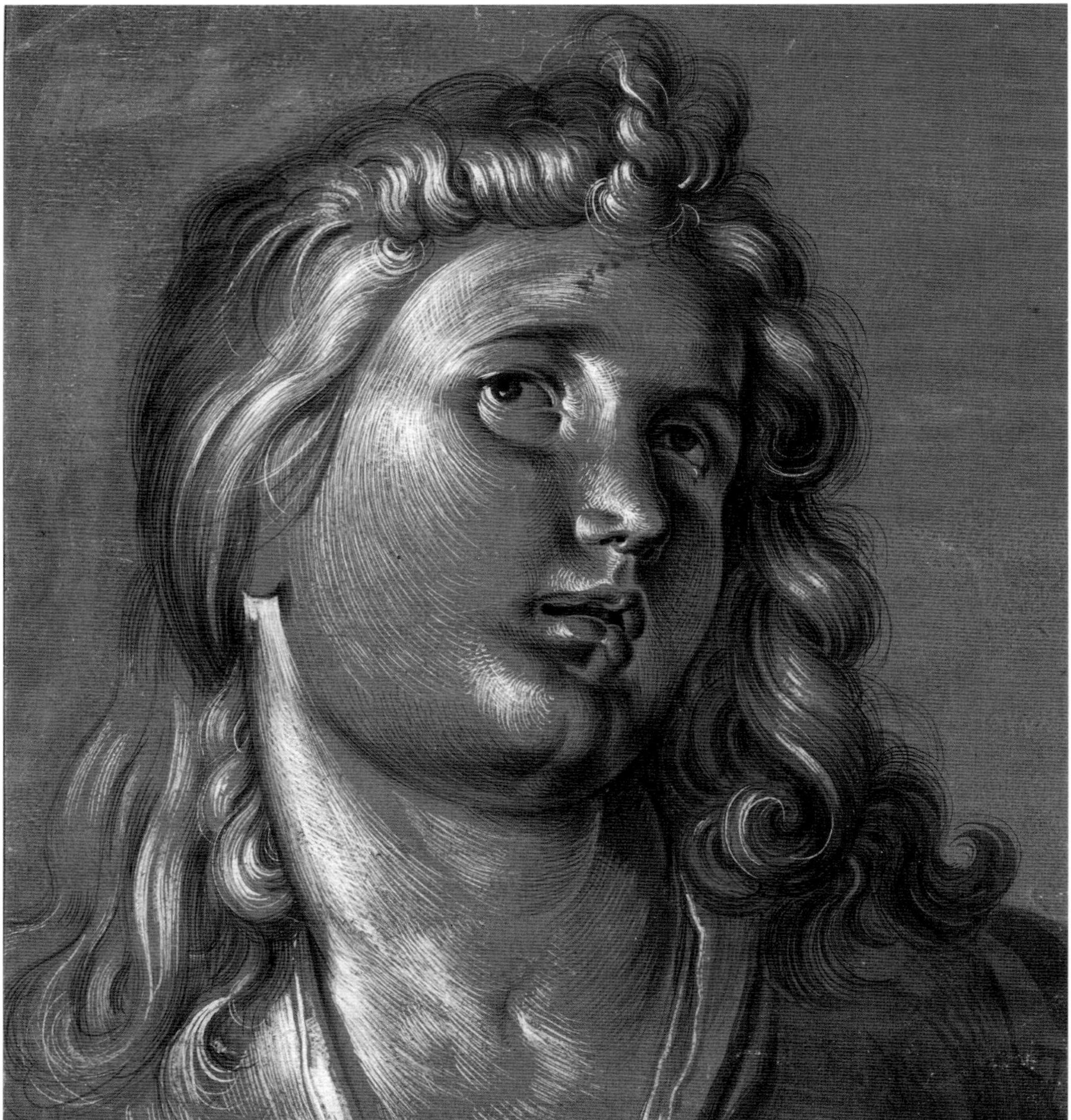

65 Hans Hoffmann after Albrecht Dürer, *Angel (Feast of the Rosegarlands)*, *c.*1580

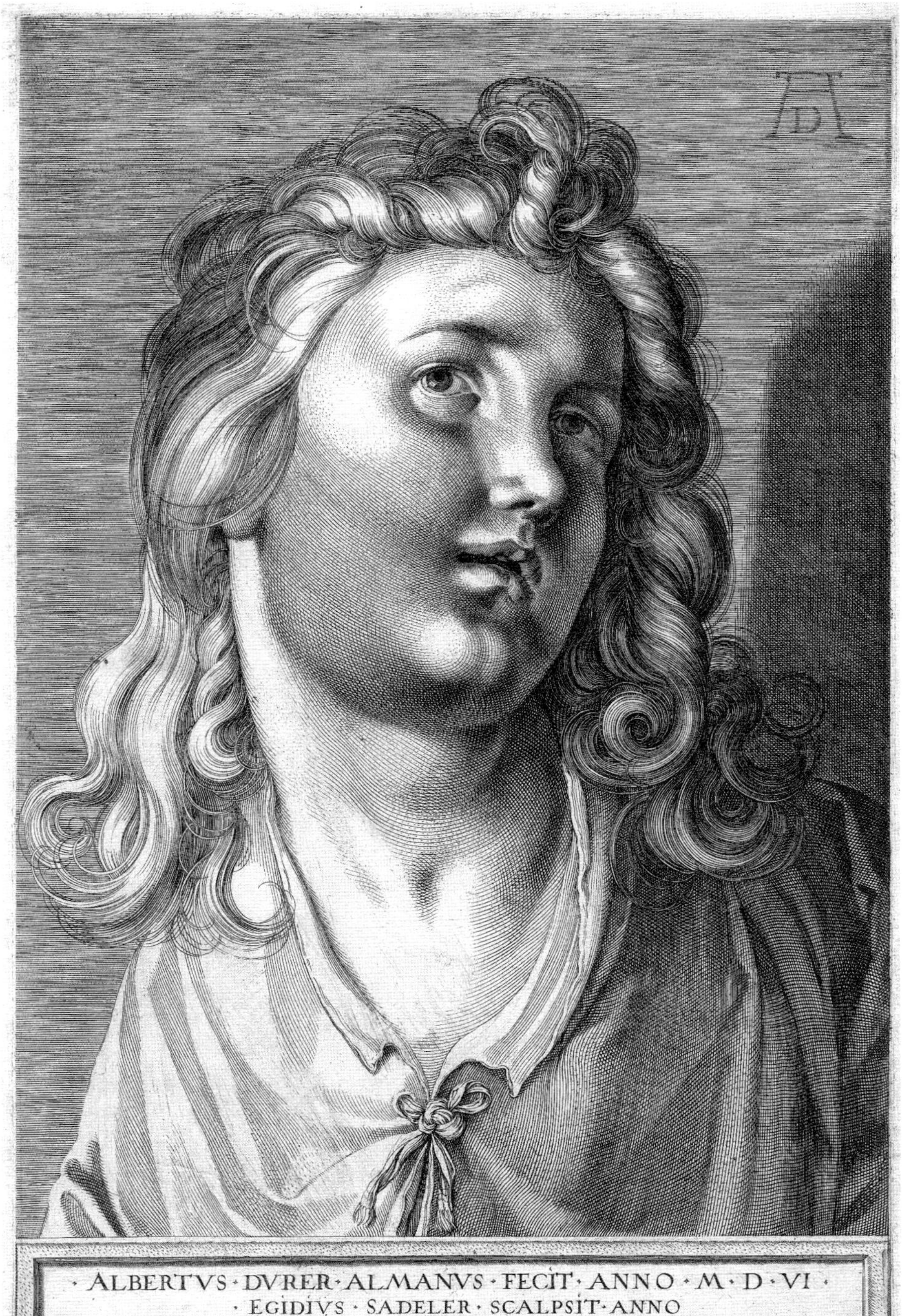

66 Aegedius Sadeler after Albrecht Dürer, *Angel (Feast of the Rosegarlands)*, 1598

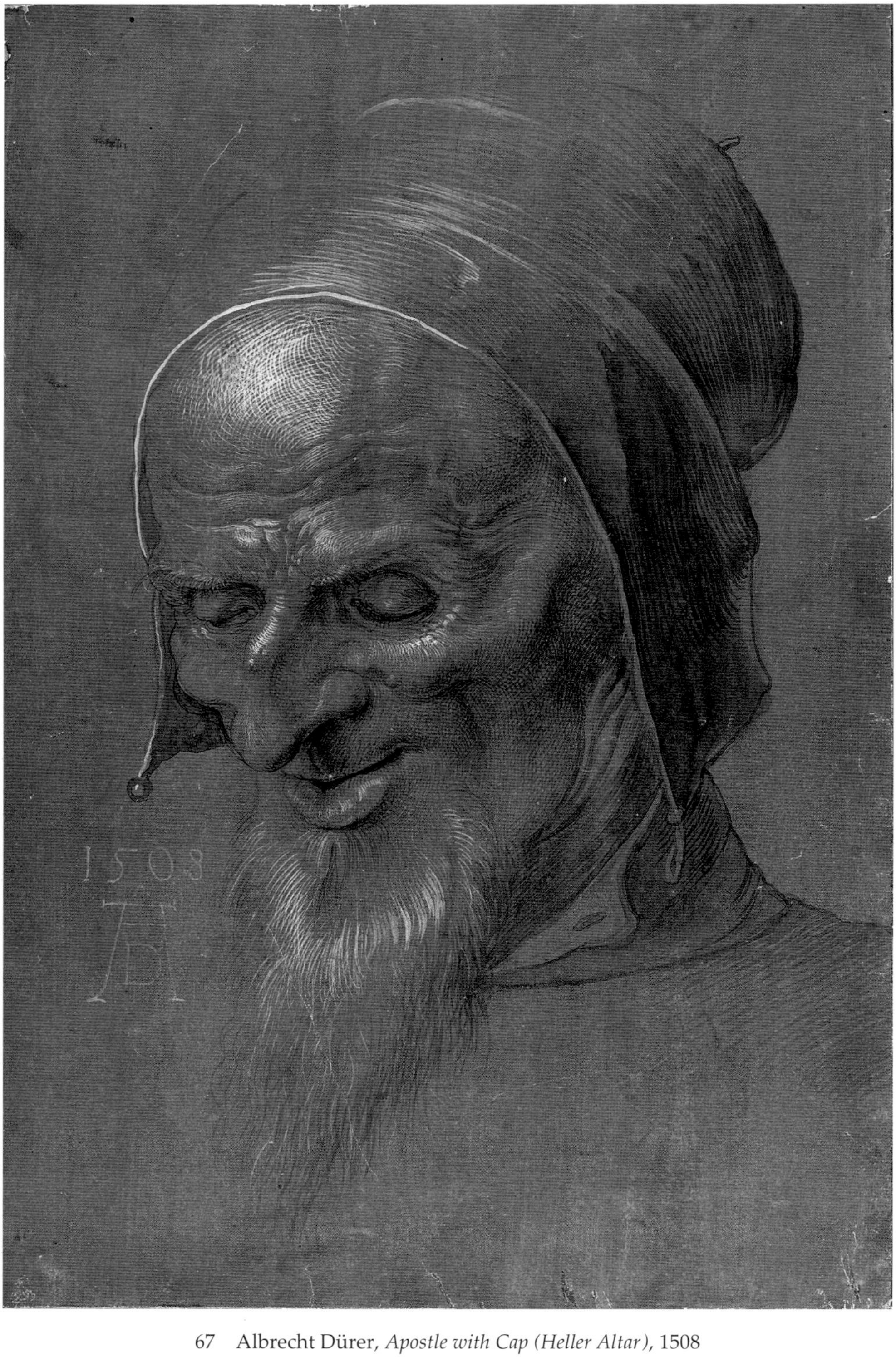

67 Albrecht Dürer, *Apostle with Cap (Heller Altar)*, 1508

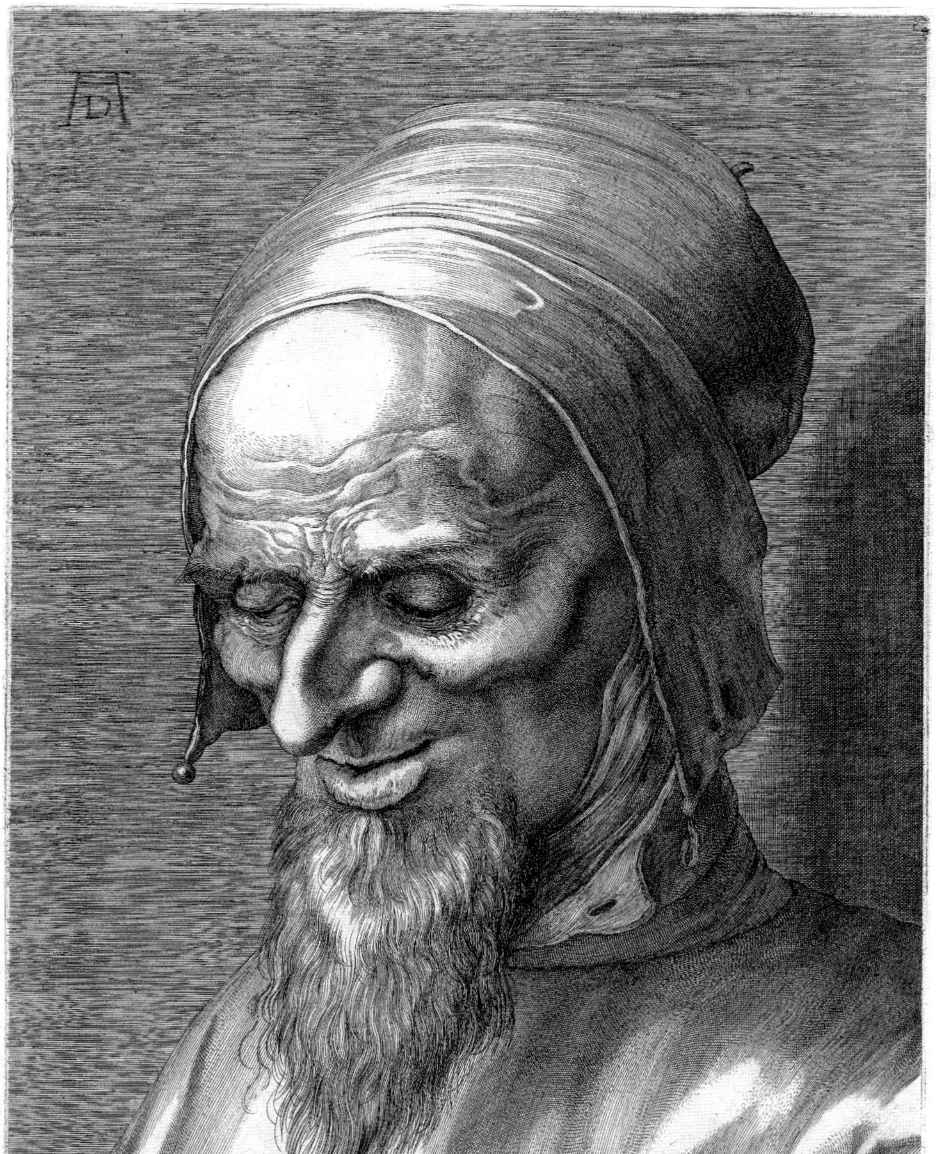

68 Aegedius Sadeler after Albrecht Dürer, *Apostle with Cap (Heller Altar)*, 1597

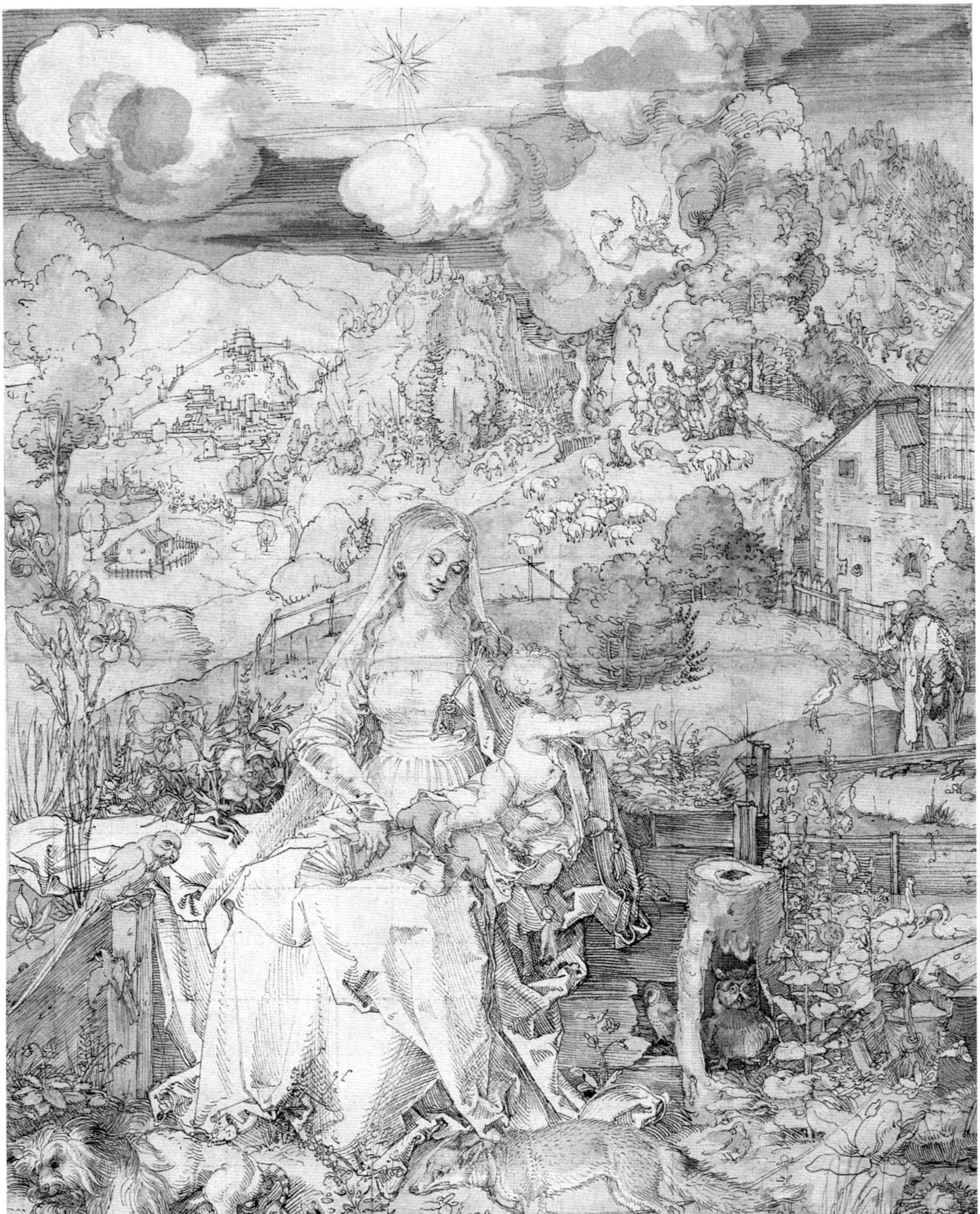

69 Albrecht Dürer, *Madonna with the Multitude of Animals*, c.1503

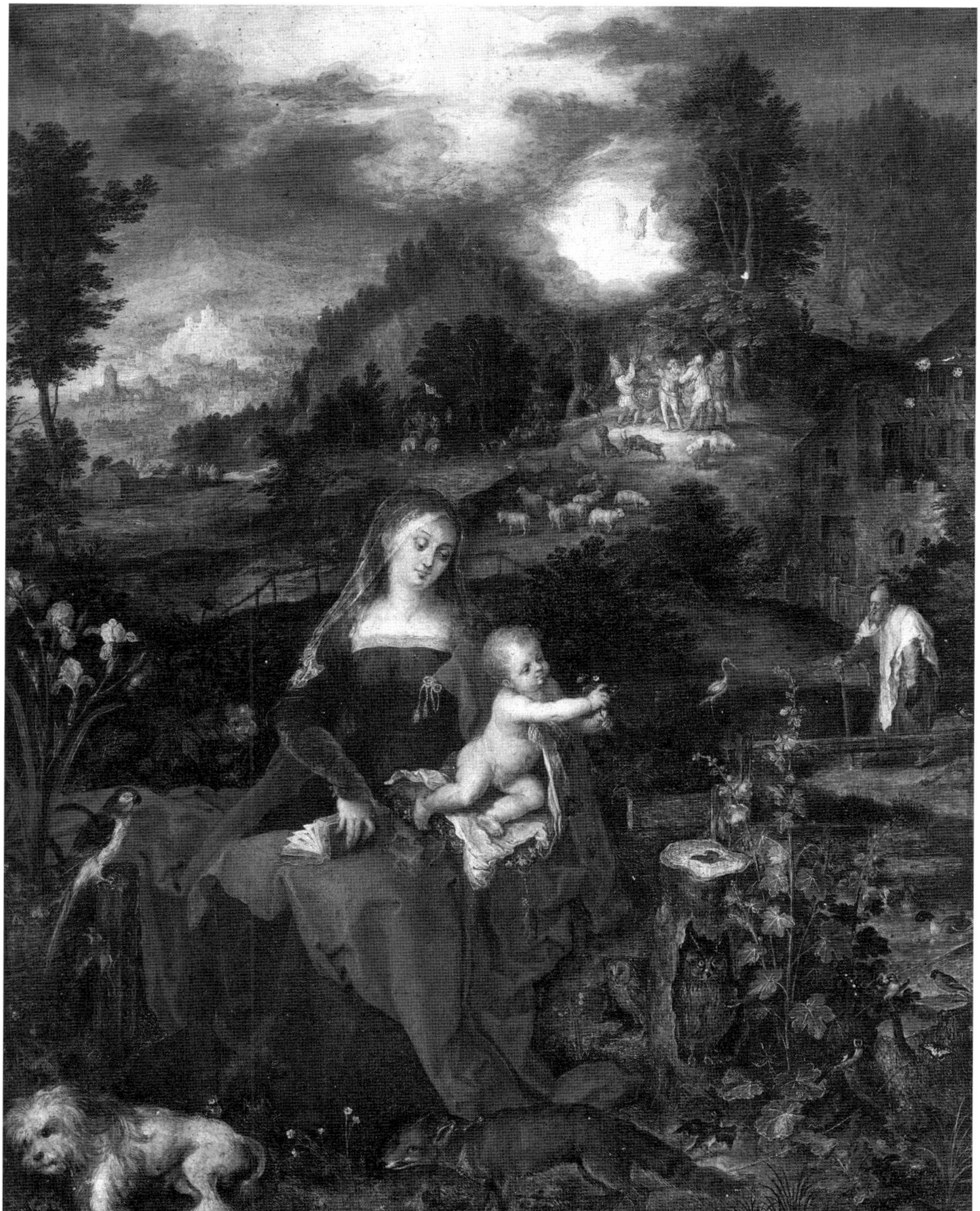

70 Jan Brueghel after Albrecht Dürer, *Madonna with the Multitude of Animals*, 1604

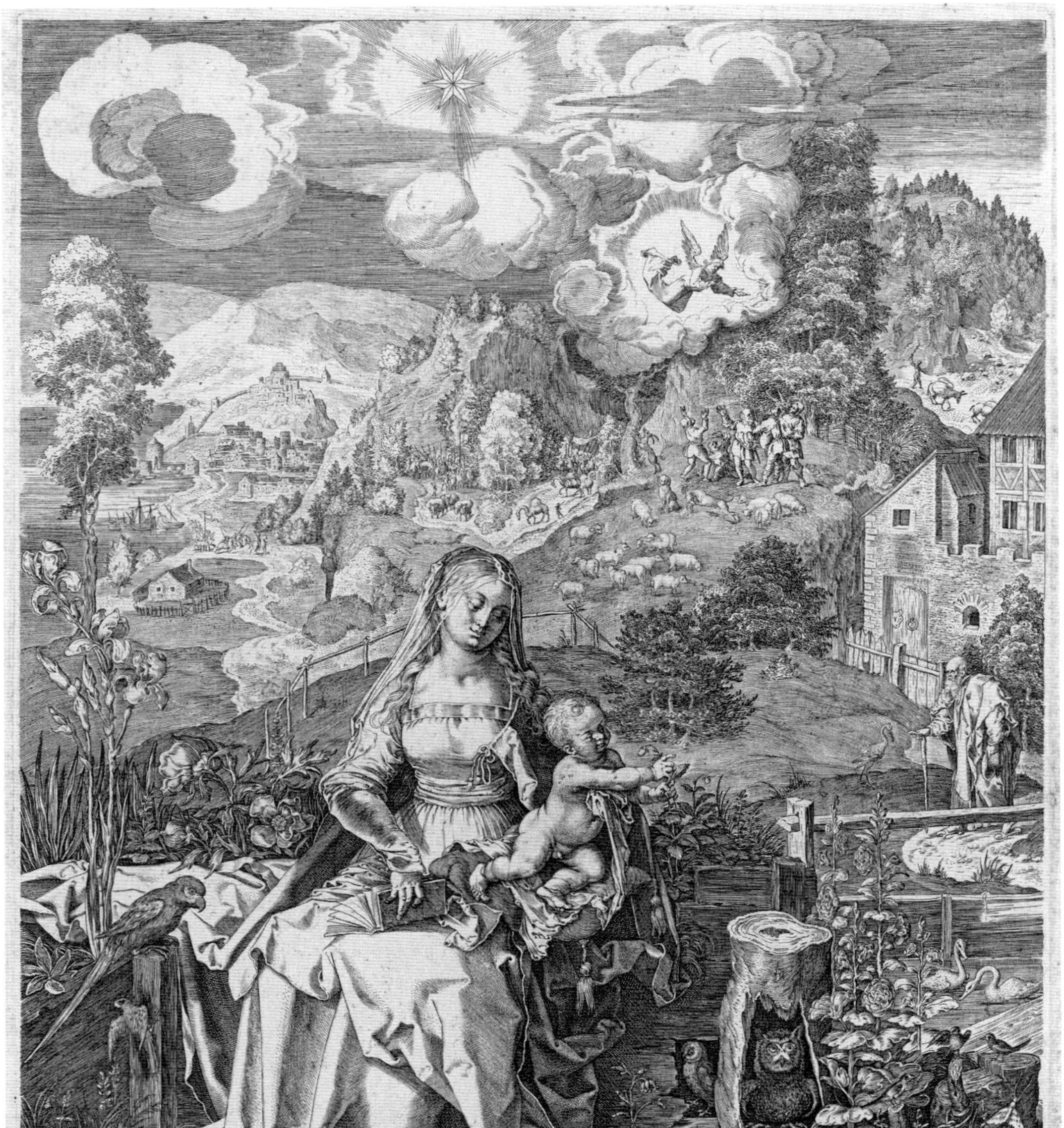

71 Aegedius Sadeler after Albrecht Dürer, *Madonna with the Multitude of Animals*, after 1597

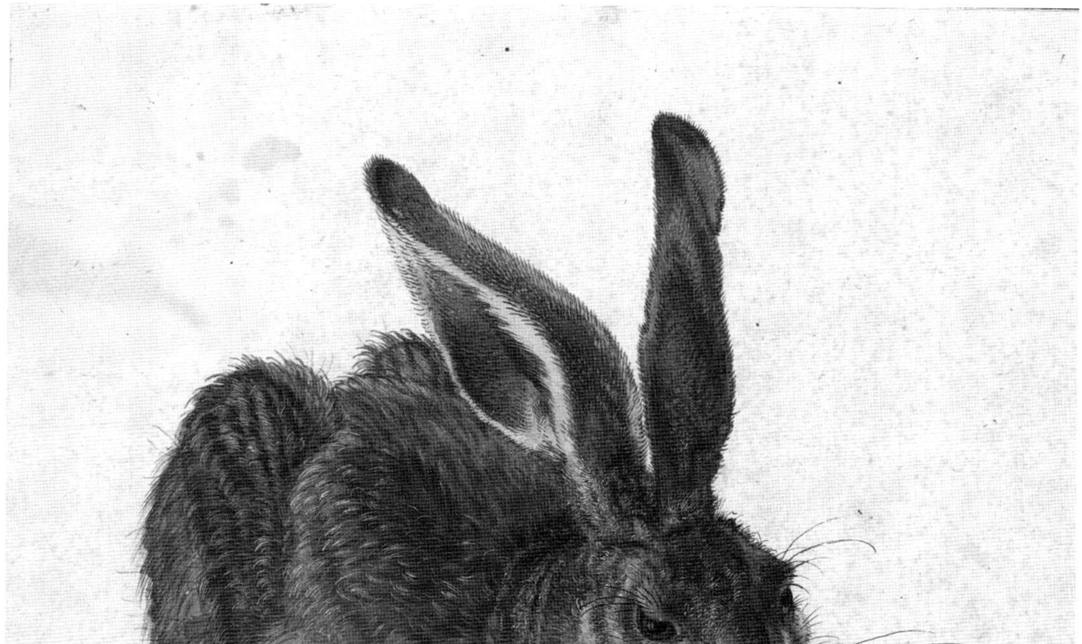

72 Albrecht Dürer, *Hare*, 1502

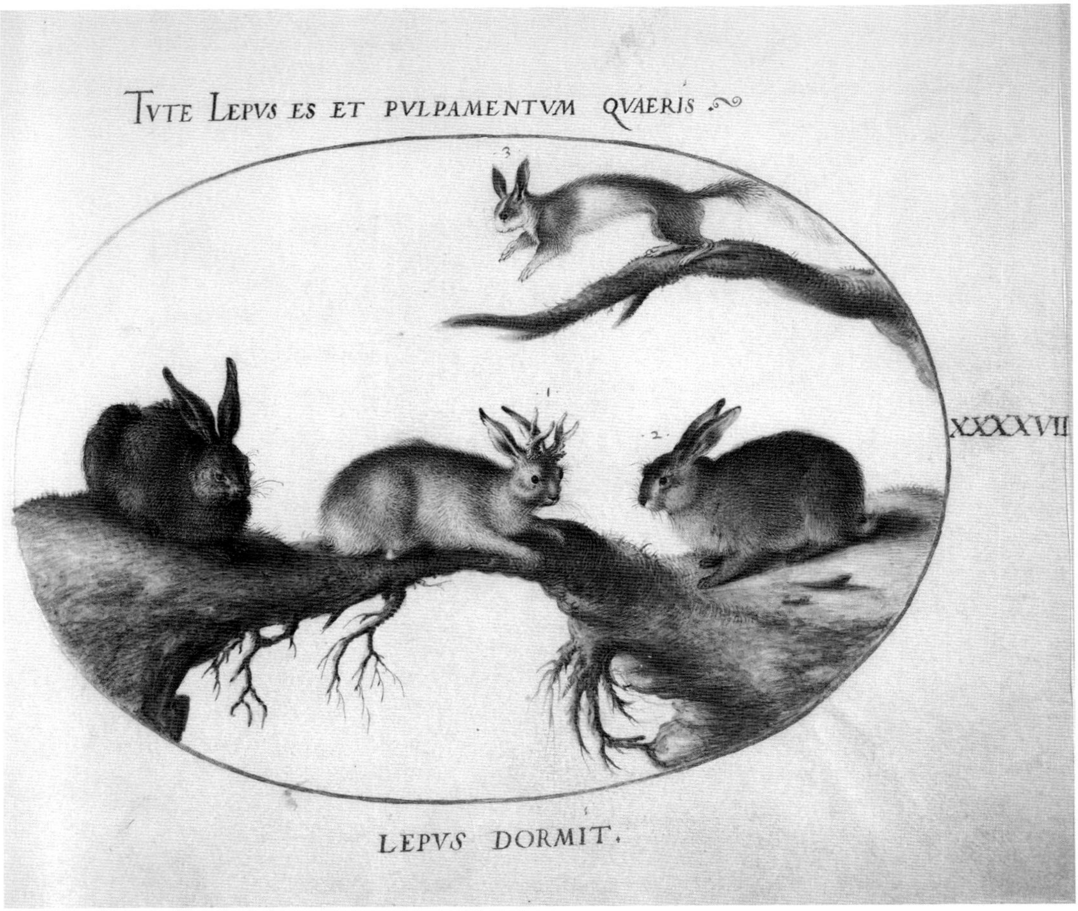

73 Georg Hoefnagel, *Hare, Rauracki, Squirrel*, c.1575–80

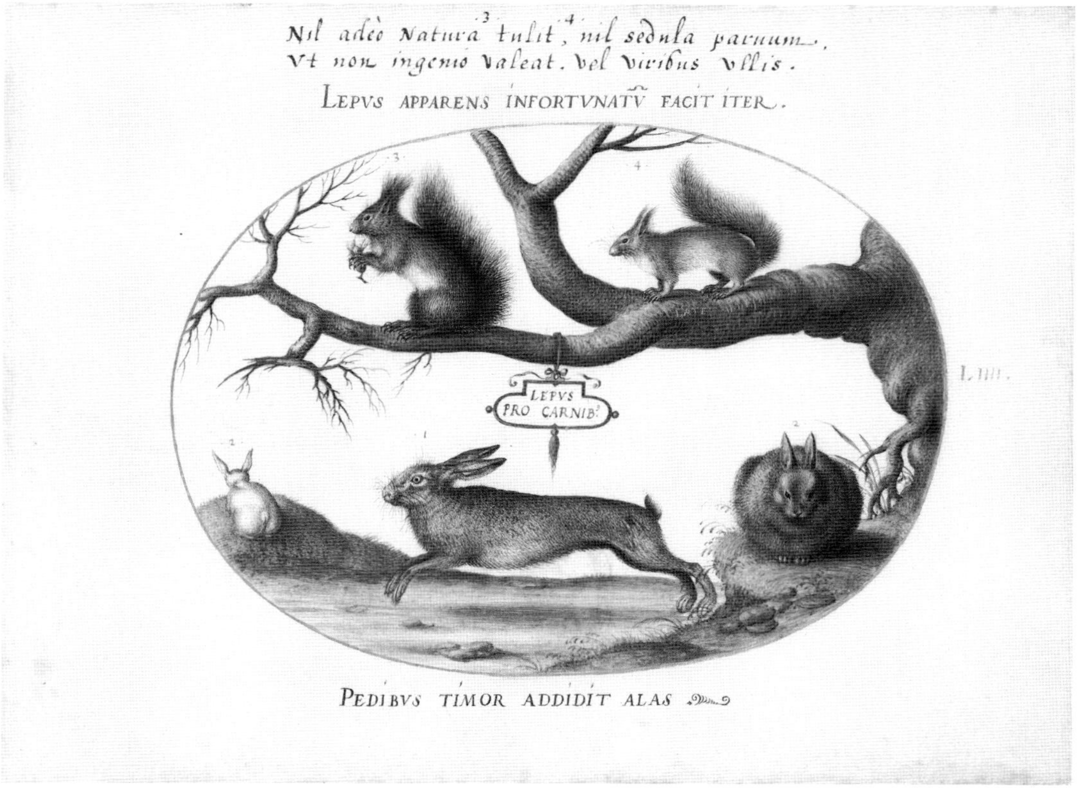

74 Georg Hoefnagel, *Hare and Squirrels*, *c.*1575–80

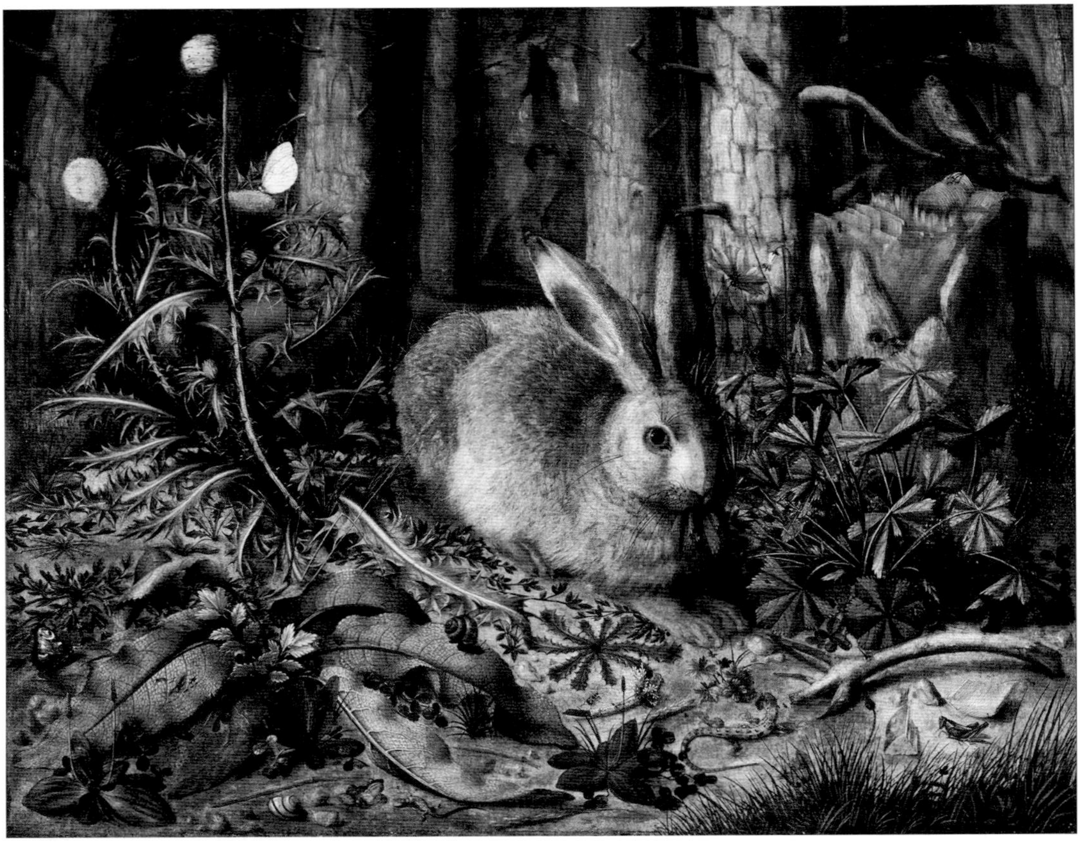

75 Hans Hoffmann, *Hare Among Grasses*, 1585

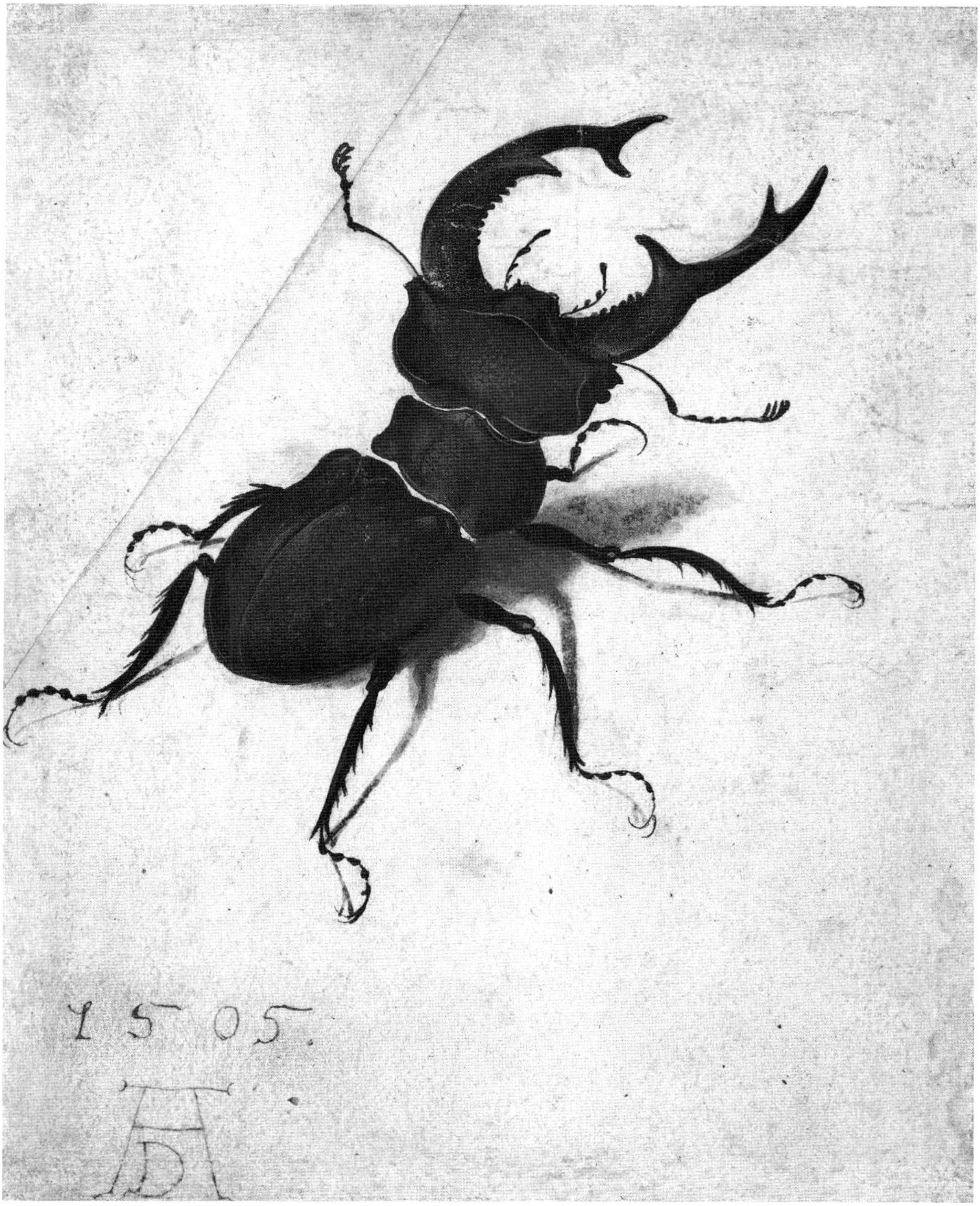

76 Albrecht Dürer, *Stag Beetle*, 1505

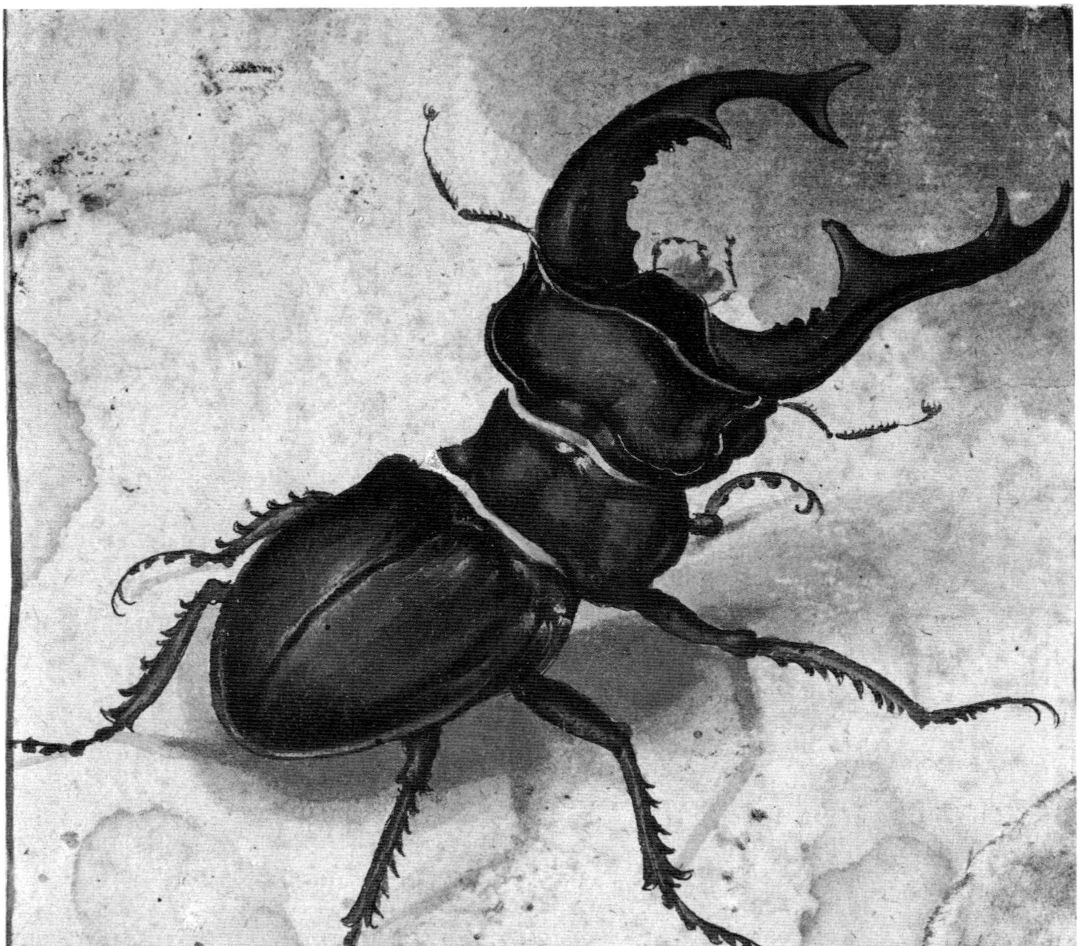

77 Hans Hoffmann after Albrecht Dürer, *Stag Beetle*, 1574

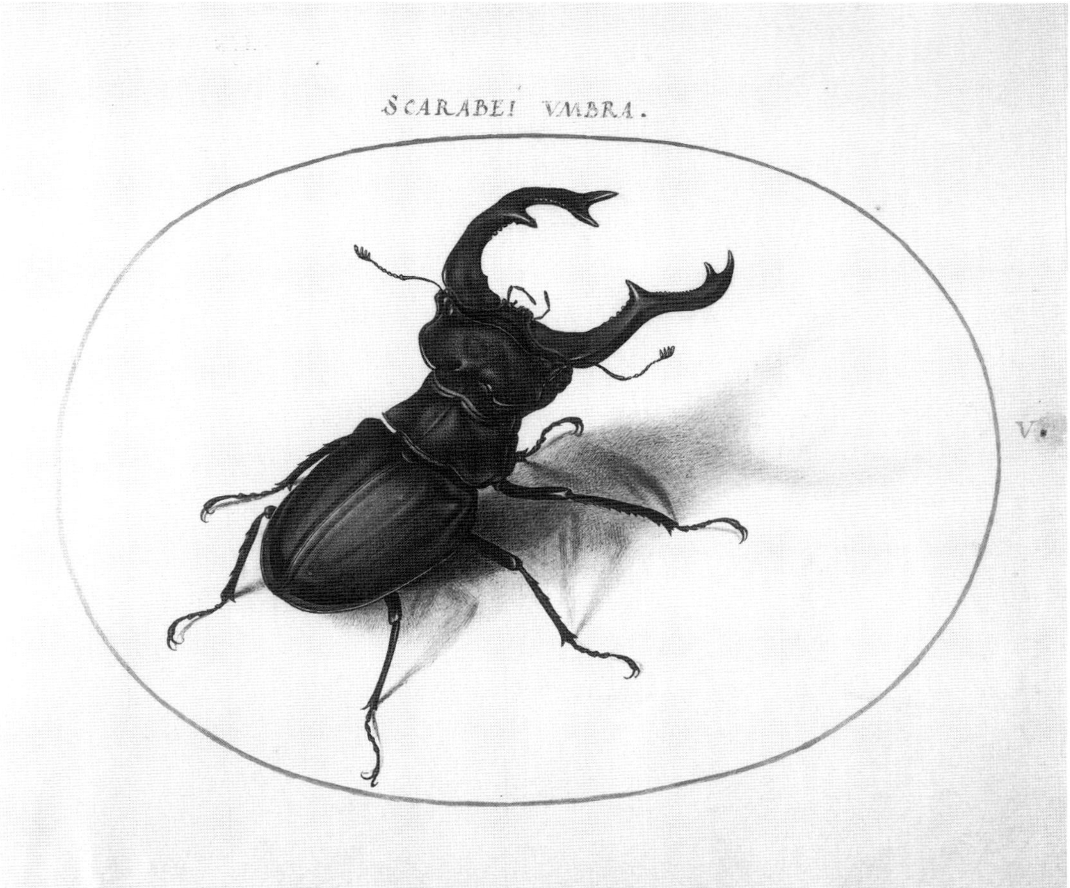

78 Georg Hoefnagel after Albrecht Dürer, *Stag Beetle*, *c*.1575–80

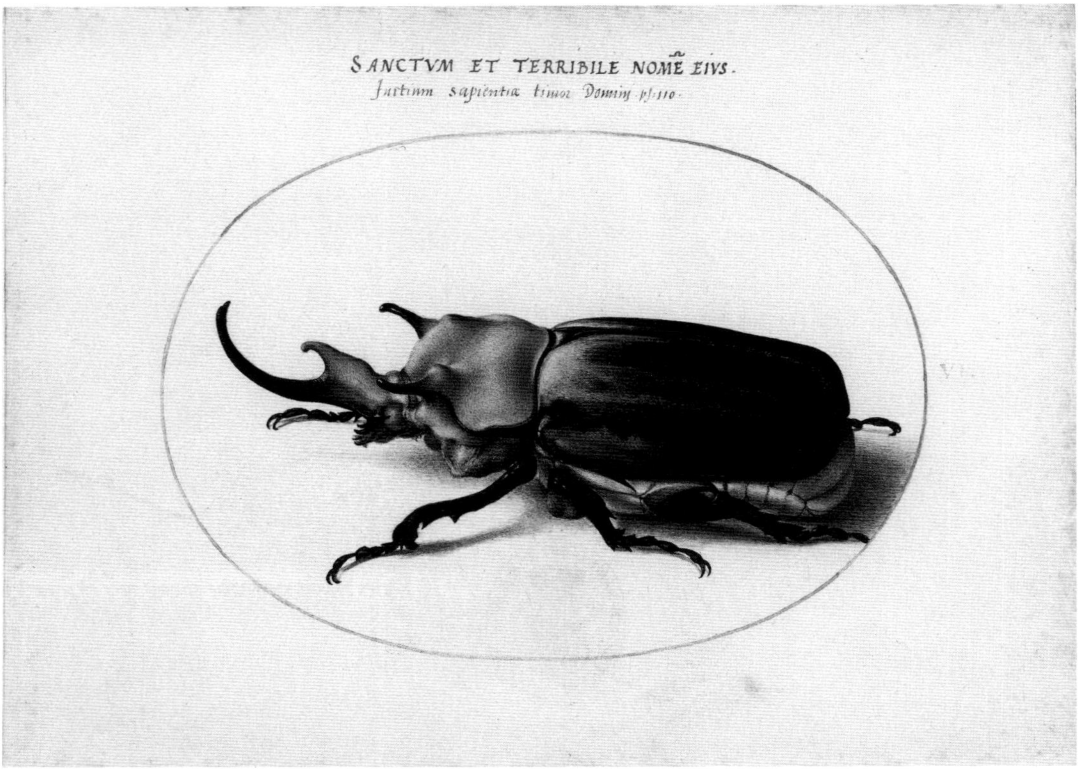

79 Georg Hoefnagel, *Stag Beetle*, *c.*1575–80

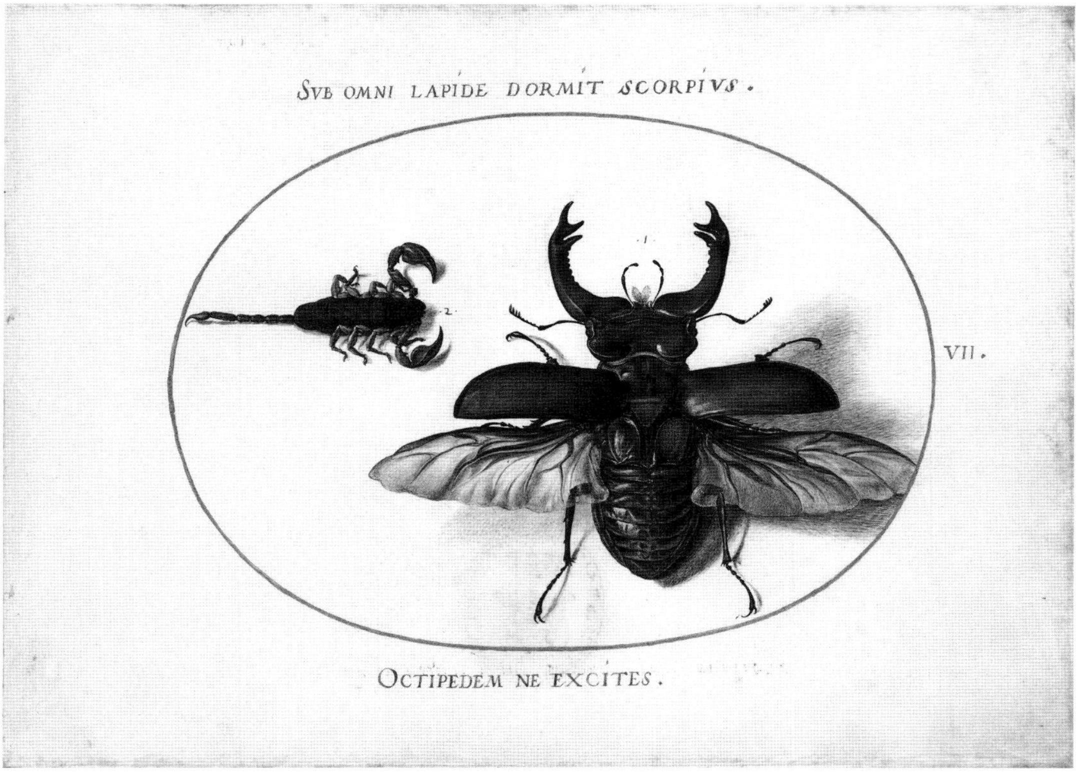

80 Georg Hoefnagel, *Stag Beetle and Scorpion*, *c*.1575–82

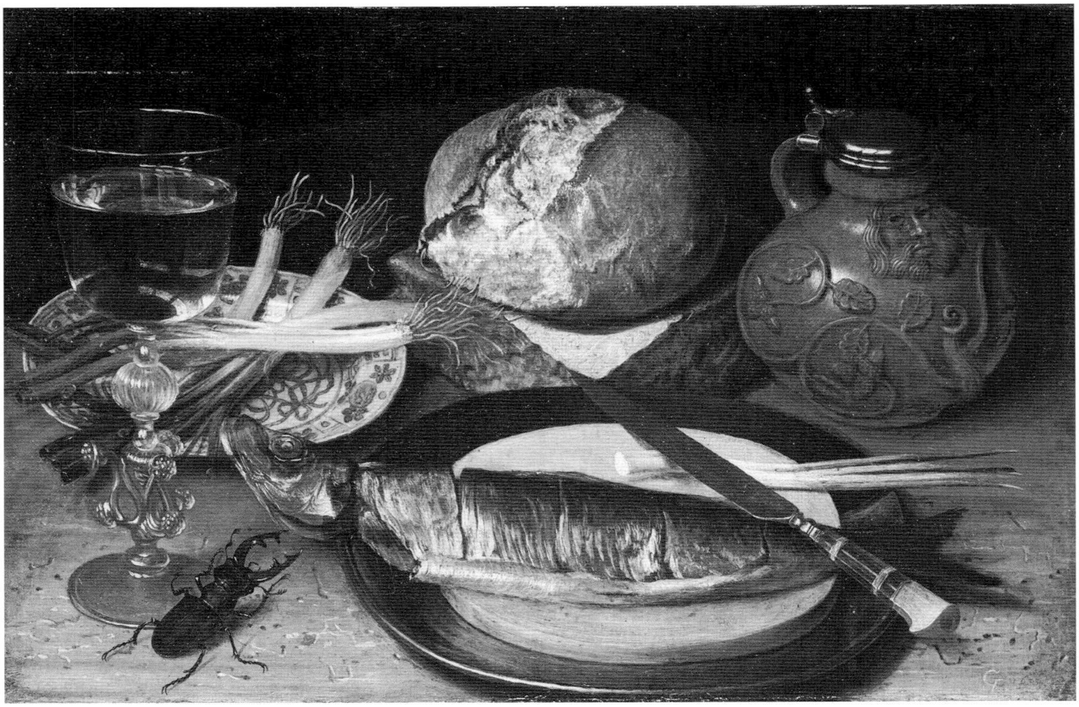

81 Georg Flegel, *Still Life with Stag Beetle*, 1635

Appropriations of Dürer Paintings

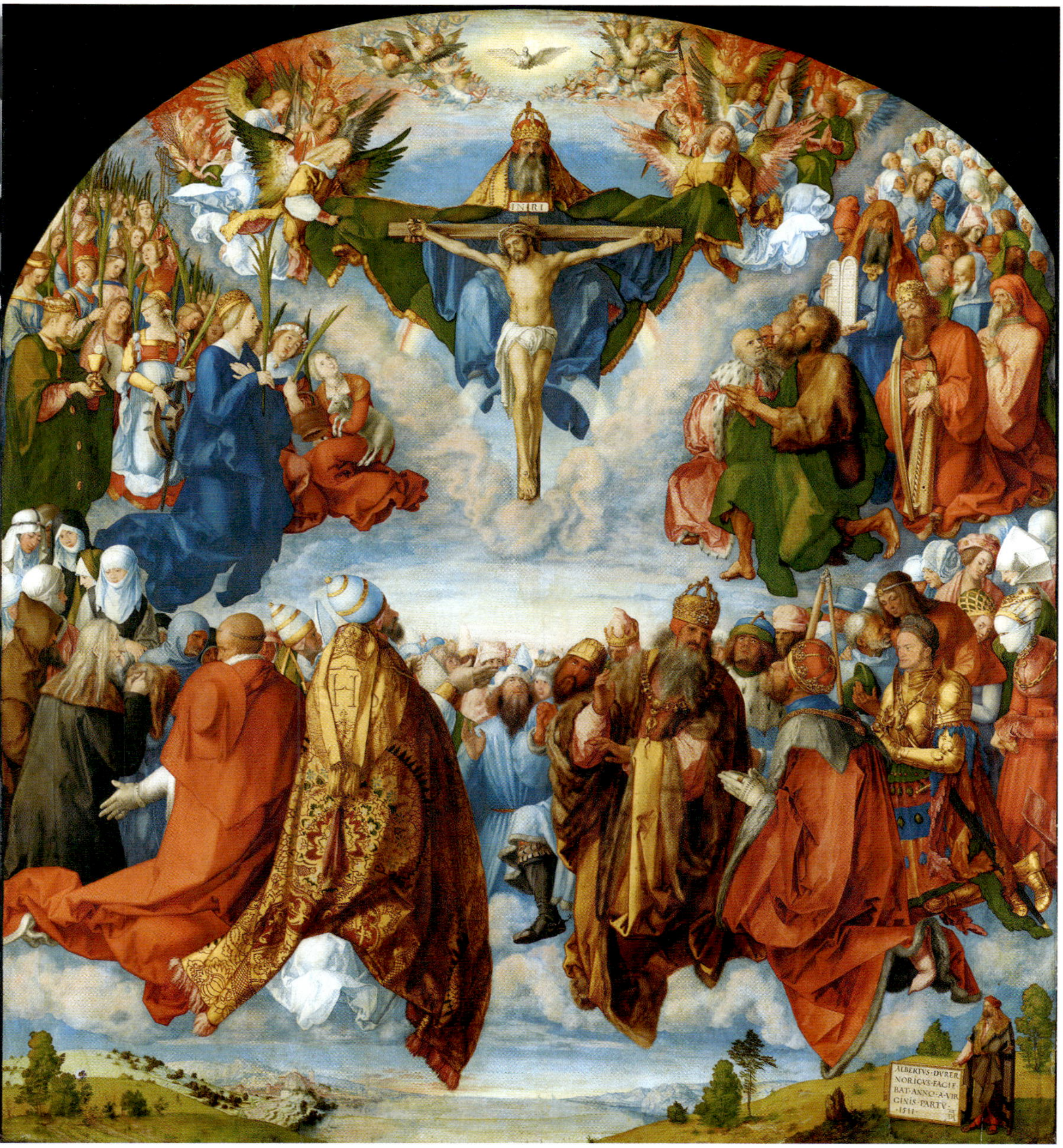

Plate 1 Albrecht Dürer, *Adoration of the Trinity*, 1511

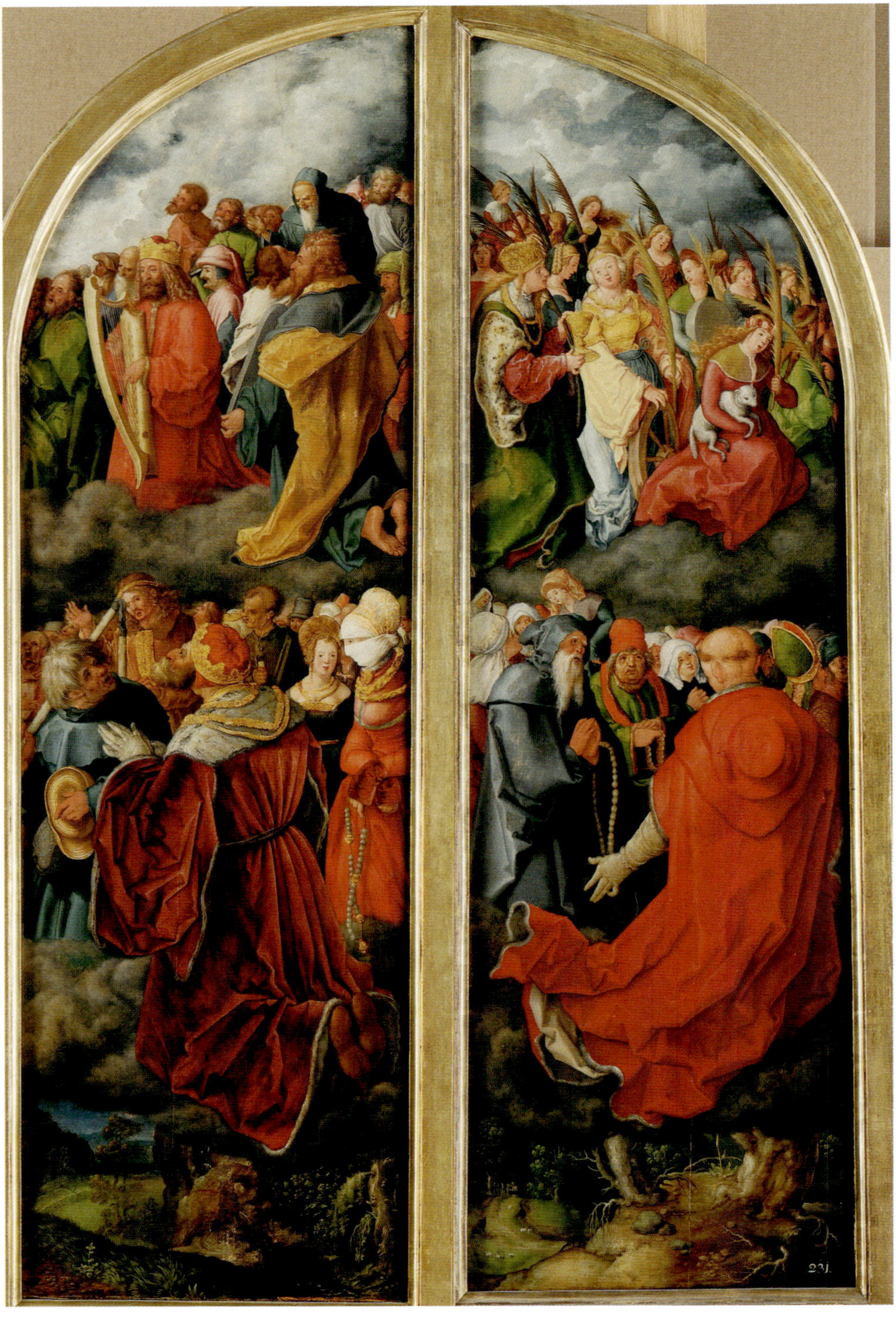

Plate 2 Anonymous after Albrecht Dürer, *Adoration of the Trinity*, seventeenth century

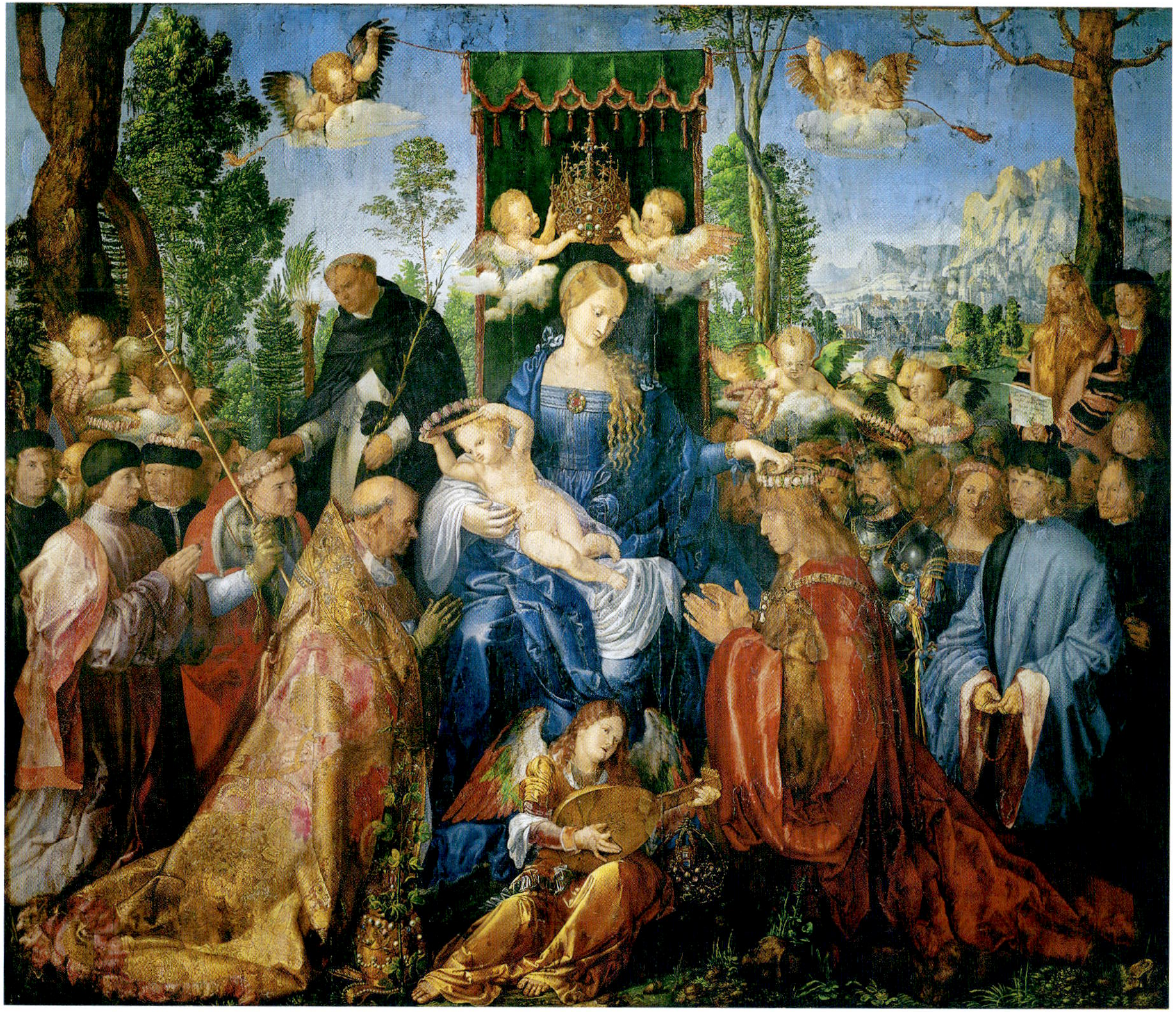

Plate 3 Albrecht Dürer, *Feast of the Rosegarlands*, 1506

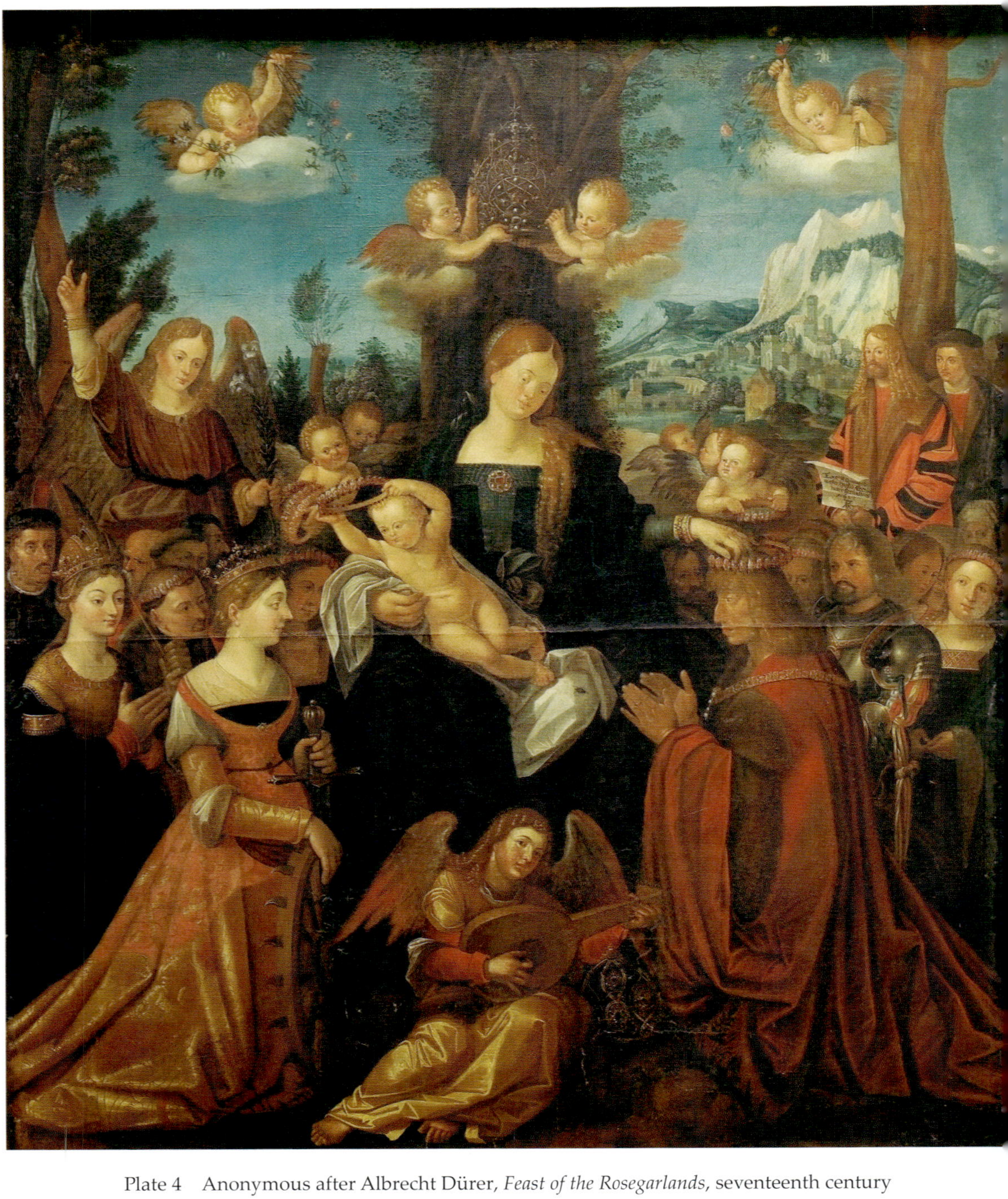

Plate 4 Anonymous after Albrecht Dürer, *Feast of the Rosegarlands*, seventeenth century

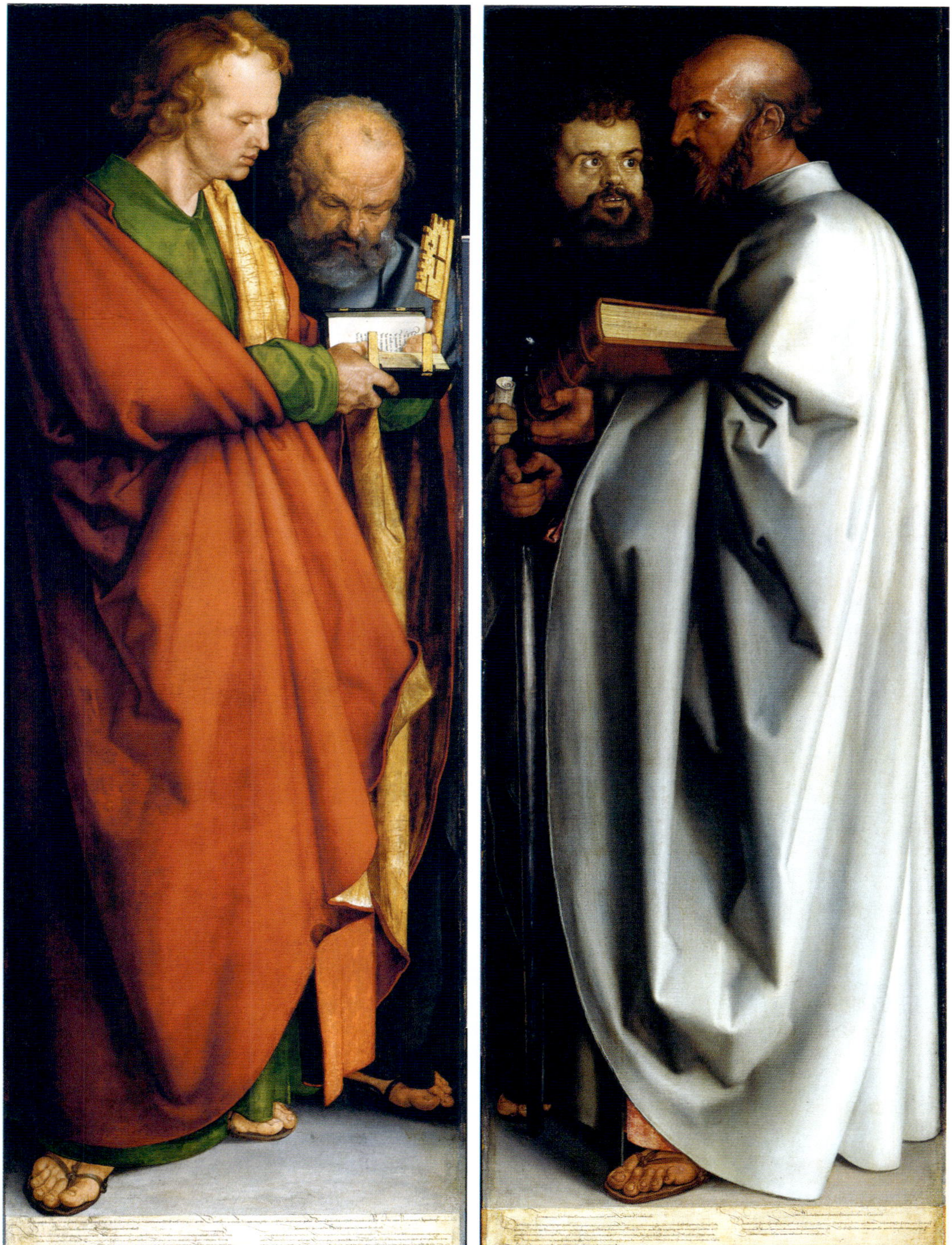

Plate 5 Albrecht Dürer, *Four Holy Men*, 1526

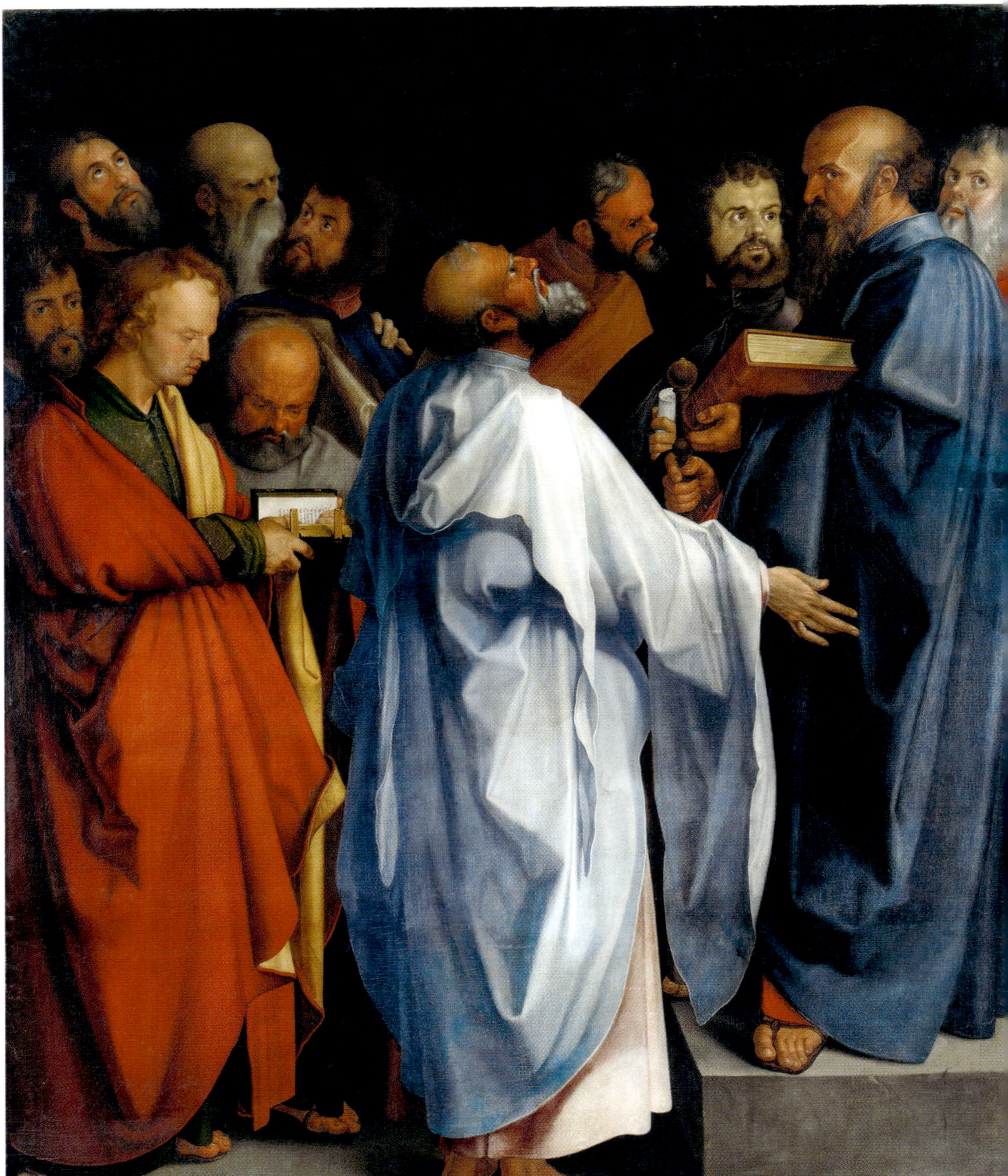

Plate 6 Anonymous after Albrecht Dürer, *Eleven Apostles*, seventeenth century

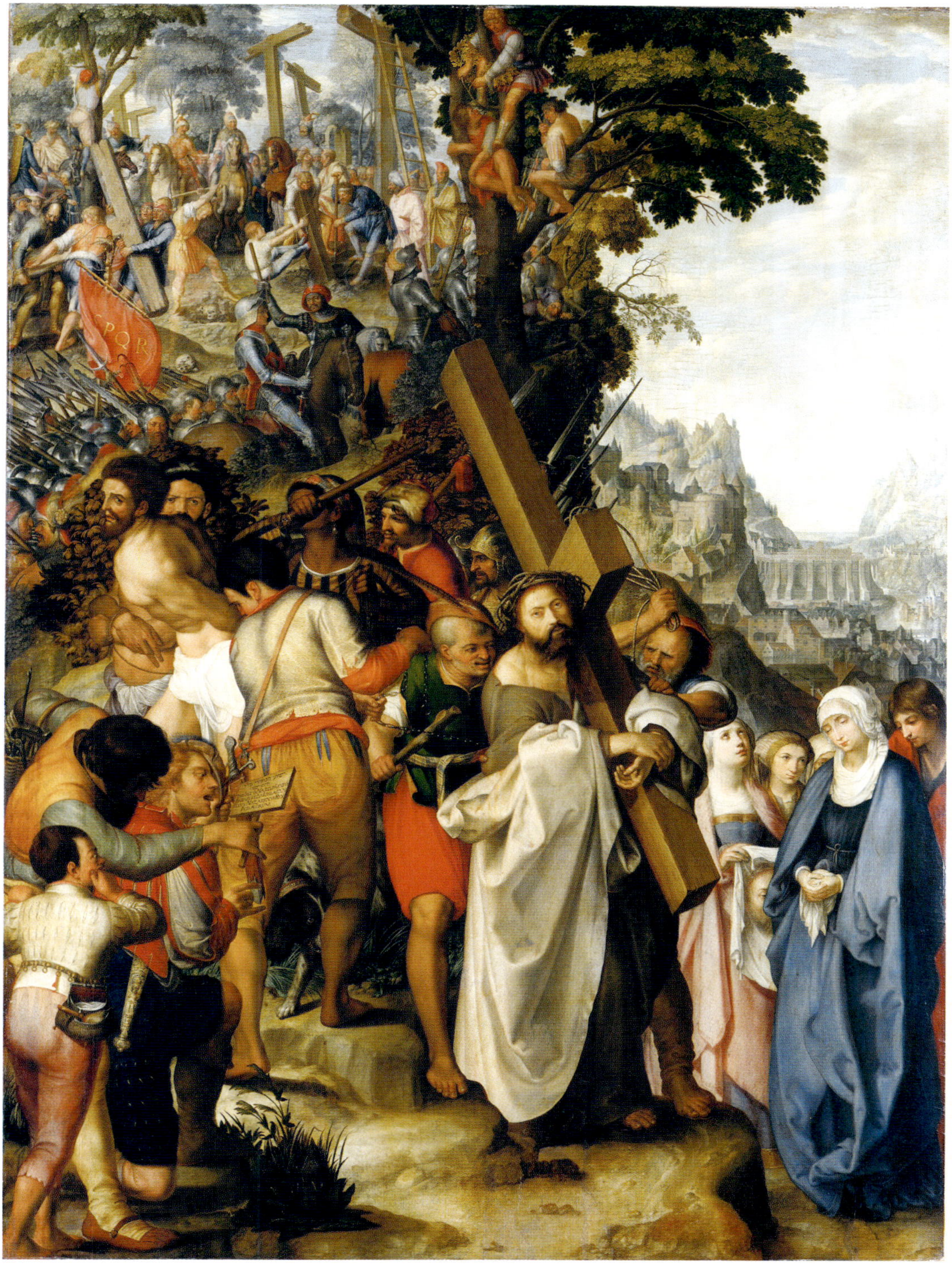

Plate 7 Georg Vischer after Albrecht Dürer, *Christ Carrying the Cross*, seventeenth century

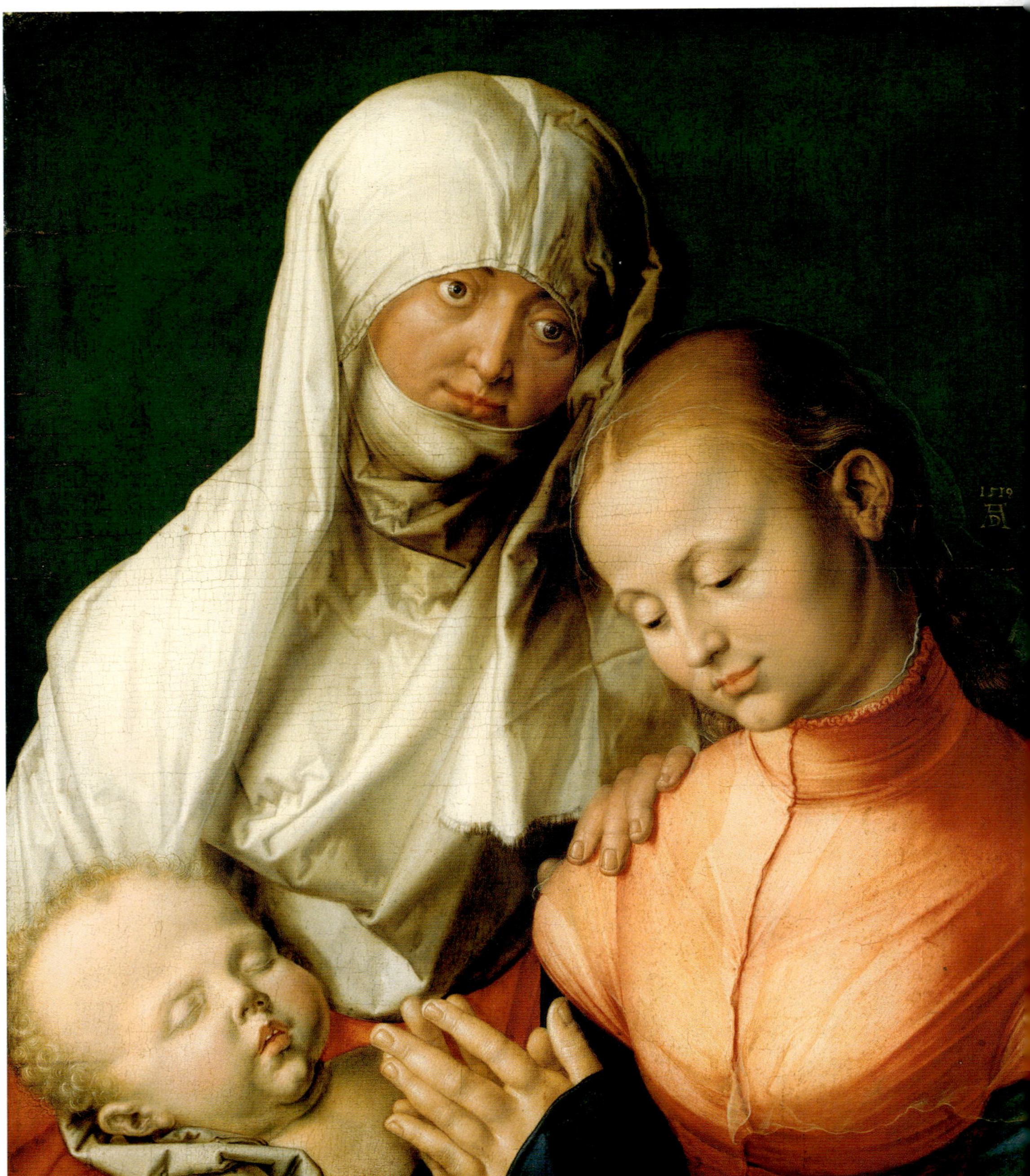

Plate 8   Albrecht Dürer, *St. Anne with Virgin and Child*, 1519

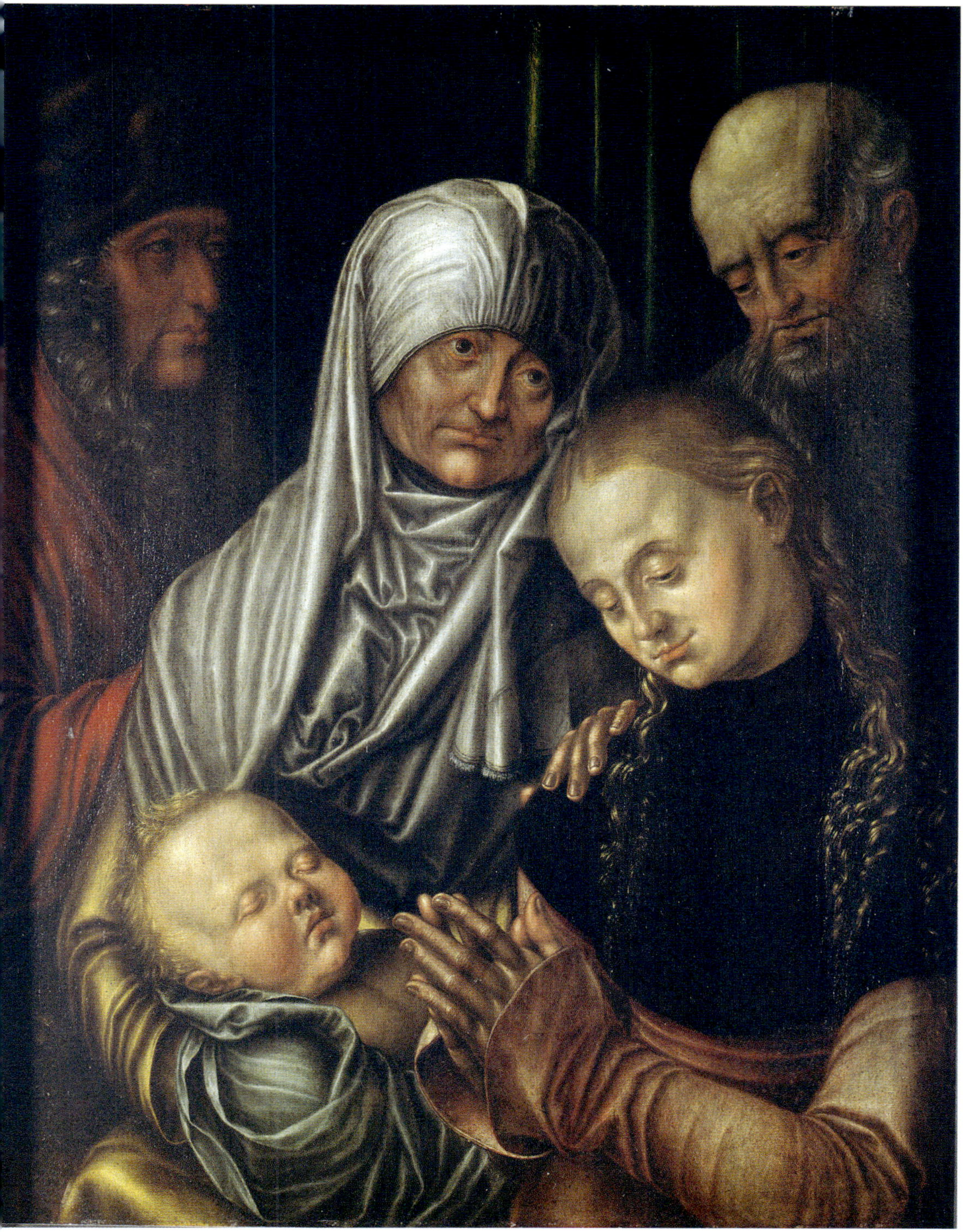

Plate 9 Anonymous after Albrecht Dürer, *St. Anne, Virgin, Child, Joseph, Joachim*, *c.*1600

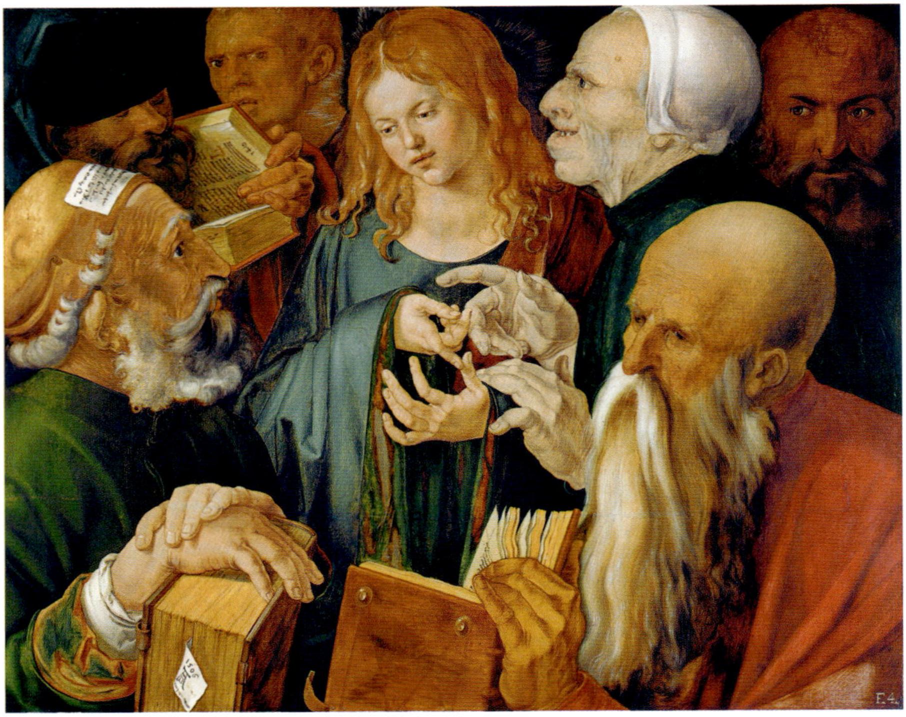

Plate 10 Albrecht Dürer, *Christ Among the Doctors*, 1505–6

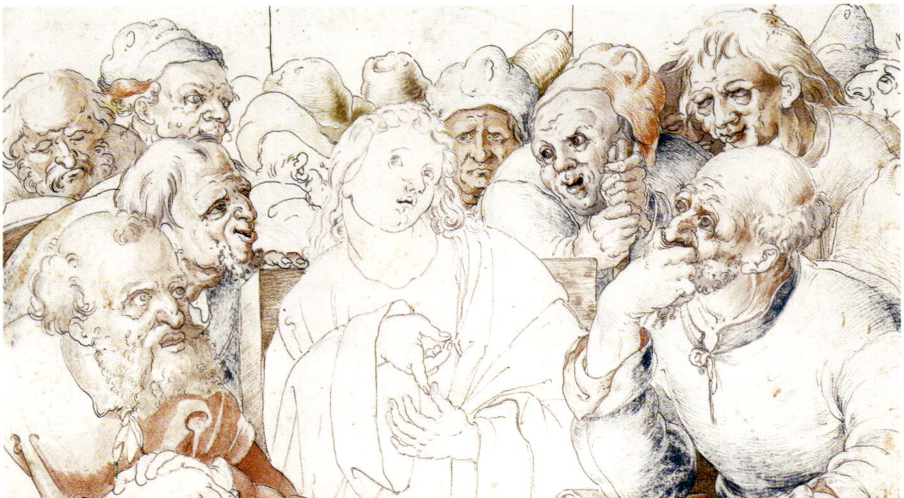

Plate 11 Hans Hoffmann, *Christ Among the Doctors*, c.1580–85

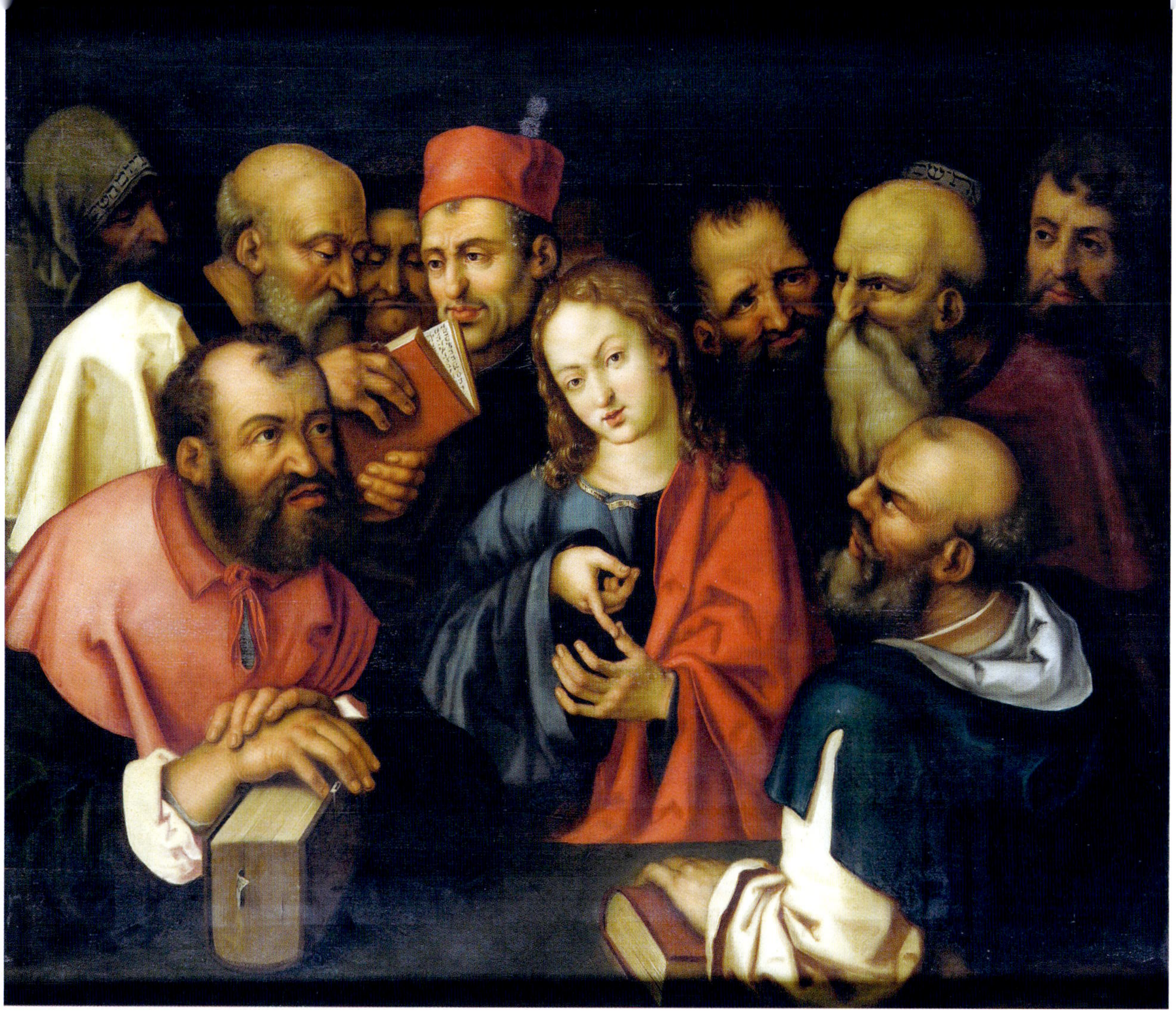

Plate 12 Anonymous, *Christ Among the Doctors*, seventeenth century

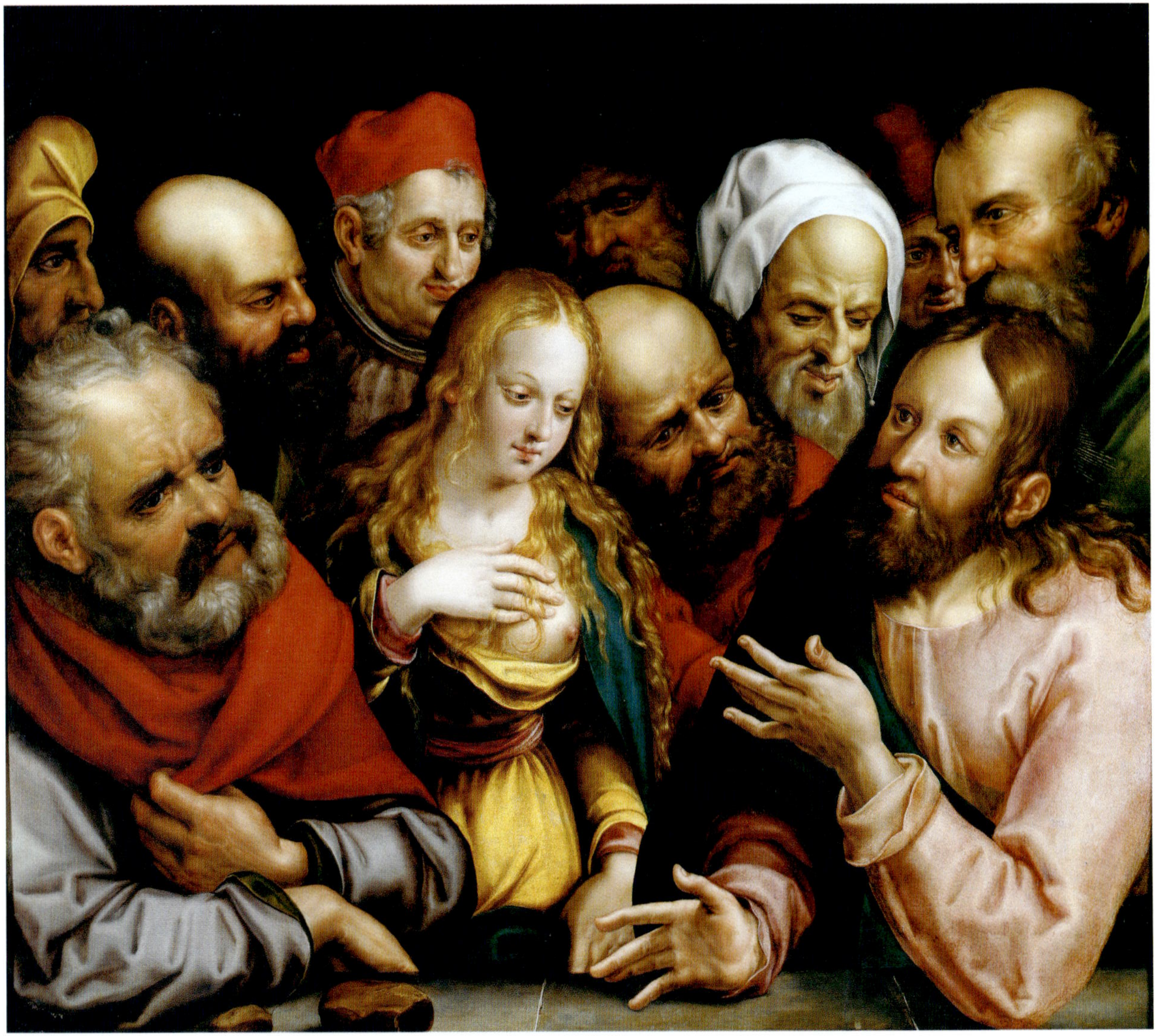

Plate 12 Jobst Harrich, *Woman Taken In Adultery*, sixteenth century

Index